GW00802383

DIRECTING PUBLIC COMPANIES

Cavendish
Publishing
Limited

London • Sydney

DIRECTING PUBLIC COMPANIES:

Company Law and the Stakeholder Society

Janice Dean, MA (Oxon), LLM (Manchester)
PhD (Brunel), Solicitor
Lecturer in Law, University of Warwick

Cavendish
Publishing
Limited

London • Sydney

First published in Great Britain 2001 by Cavendish Publishing Limited,
The Glass House, Wharton Street, London WC1X 9PX, United Kingdom
Telephone: +44 (0)20 7278 8000   Facsimile: +44 (0)20 7278 8080

E-mail: info@cavendishpublishing.com
Website: www.cavendishpublishing.com

British Library Cataloguing in Publication Data

Dean, Janice
Directing public companies: company law and the stakeholder society
1 Corporation law – England 2 Corporation law – Wales
3 Stakeholders – Legal status, laws, etc – England
4 Stakeholders – Legal status, laws, etc – Wales
I Title
346.4'2'0664

ISBN 1 85941 635 7

Printed and bound in Great Britain

PREFACE

Modern Company Law for a Competitive Economy – **the final result?**

After more than three years of lively deliberations and consultations, the influential Steering Group of the Company Law Review delivered its Final Report entitled *Modern Company Law for a Competitive Economy* to the new Secretary of State for Trade and Industry, Patricia Hewitt, as this book was about to go to press (July 2001). Having followed the progress of the Review from the outset, I am very grateful that Cavendish Publishing and my editor, Ruth Massey, have given me the opportunity to add a few comments here on its outcome.

In brief, the Company Law Review, established by the recently-elected Labour Government in 1998, was charged with updating the UK's company law so as to meet the needs of the modern world, thereby helping to make UK business and UK law successful in the international marketplace. It was organised under the auspices of, but with administrative independence from, the DTI. Chapters 1 and 9 below explain my view of how the once-in-a-generation task of overhauling UK company law was approached on this occasion. While the 'think small first' policy may have resulted in proposals for simpler rules to serve private companies, my view is that complex issues relating to economically and socially powerful public companies were not squarely addressed.

It is appropriate firstly to point out that there is much in the rhetoric of Chapter 1 of the Steering Group's Final Report that recognises and supports the position taken and expanded below. For example at para 1.23:

> Effective management and control of resources requires a decision-making process which takes proper account of all the factors relevant to the outcome ... Relevant factors include the need to manage relationships with employees, with suppliers of all kinds of resources – physical, intangible and intellectual – and with customers ... They include the need to manage wider impacts on consumers, the community and the environment. Reputational assets are also of critical importance in a world where external perceptions can transform business prospects, for better or worse.

I concur with those observations and much of this book explores arguments that seem to me to support them.

The Final Report continues (at para 1.24):

> All these constituencies can impact, positively or negatively, upon a company's success and this should be reflected not only in the operational rules but also in the basis of accountability for stewardship. Companies, whether consciously or not, are managing as part of their everyday operations a wide range of resources and assets beyond the traditional balance sheet fixed assets cash and investment, in the shape of accumulated human resource and know how, intellectual property, brands, ongoing relationships, plans and strategies and other wider reputational assets.

Again, readers of Chapter 8 below will find support for this assertion from discussions with officers of major public companies.

In terms of the role of company law in these modern circumstances, the Steering Group proposes (at para 1.56):

- [a codified statement of directors duties] embodying a modern, inclusive view of the range of decision-making and objective standards of professional care and skill
- [a disclosure regime for large companies] reflecting stewardship of assets and relationships which are of real importance in the modern economy, with public accountability for these ...

Thirdly, however, it adds:

- a sharper focus on the shareholder.

This is underlined by para 6.26 which expressly refers to:

- the Review's *reliance on shareholder-oriented directors duties and transparency* as the basis for stewardship discipline [emphasis added].

From a practical point of view, the Final Report itself identifies some difficulties with the 'shareholder-oriented' approach in public companies. Paragraph 6.24 notes the following concerns among others:

- that such [institutional] investors may be spontaneously influenced in the exercise of voice or entry/exit powers by conflicting interests of themselves or their associates
- 'slacking' by fiduciary investors – ie omitting actively to intervene in cases of management failure where clearly necessary.

Some suggestions are given for improving shareholder 'performance' as monitors. It is not acknowledged that those in other business companies, with an interest in its performance (employees, suppliers and customers in particular) might have a role to play in plugging the gap.

Even more fundamentally, however, it is submitted that to pay lip-service to the recognition of various stakeholders in public companies while putting in place a new legislative statement of directors' duties that, while being broadly 'inclusive', enshrines shareholder primacy above other considerations (as discussed in Chapter 5 below) goes less than halfway to dealing with the issue of the 'other' constituencies. Without some adequate means of enforcement in law, new duties are unlikely to have much of an impact in the very companies where they might change existing practice.

The Steering Group also places a great emphasis on transparency, recommending a new annual Operating and Financial Review for public companies, except the smallest (see Chapter 8 of the Final Report). It says:

para 3.29: Others [in addition to shareholders] – whether employees, trading partners, or the wider community – also have a legitimate interest in the company's activities, particularly in the case of companies which exercise significant economic power. Our proposals must satisfy these wider concerns for accountability and transparency.

para 3.30: We therefore make proposals which will:

- improve the quality, usefulness and relevance of information available to shareholders *and to others with an interest in the company* [emphasis added]
- provide more timely information ...

There are, however, no concrete proposals to give these newly-informed and interested non-shareholder groups any new legal means to challenge public company boards or have an input into corporate decisions. In the wake of 'anti-globalisation' and 'anti-capitalism' protests in Seattle and Genoa, could more knowledge without greater influence simply lead to more suspicion of 'big business' by employees, suppliers, customers and citizens? These points seem not to have been considered. Chapter 6 below discusses the issue of stakeholder rights and remedies in more detail. There are undoubtedly many possible ways of tackling the issue. To disregard it completely seems unwise in the current climate.

The Steering Group's conclusions are all said to proceed from 'the general principle that company law should be *primarily enabling or facilitative*' (para 1.10, emphasis in the report). While noting the arguments in favour of well-drafted regulation in some circumstances (for example to correct possible market failures or uphold the public interest), the Steering Group comments, 'nonetheless the net effect of our proposals is one of substantial simplification and deregulation' (para 1.16). If all effective corporate governance systems must 'balance' the ability of boards to drive businesses forward with ensuring effective control of management in extremely powerful corporations (see in particular Chapter 3 below), this approach appears to rank the first of those concerns rather more highly than the second. This is unlikely to satisfy many non-shareholder stakeholders, such as employees, customers and suppliers (as described in Chapter 4 below).

Constraints of time and space do not permit me here to go through all aspects of the Final Report (which contains many welcome proposals to update and simplify current law). In these brief remarks I have naturally focused on areas of relevance to the arguments in this book. The remit of the Review itself was narrow, as the Steering Group pointed out. It remains to be seen what the official response from the Secretary of State to the Final Report will be. In addition to the technical and restricted 'core company law' matters examined by the Steering Group, as a Cabinet Minister Ms Hewitt will doubtless wish to have regard to broader economic and social factors. If academic and analytical work (including this text) assists with that task in a small way, it will have proved its worth.

Janice Dean
August 2001

ACKNOWLEDGMENTS

Thanks first and foremost to my supervisor John Lowry for his advice and support, not only on my Thesis but on academic life generally. Also to the interviewees, who generously gave their valuable time and expressed their views with candour and clarity. Last but not least to Brunel and Kingston Universities for the financial support that made the study possible.

This work is dedicated with thanks to everyone whose inspiring visions and practical support helped towards it completion, especially friends from Manchester University (among many, thanks to Nick Molyneux, Colenzo Jarrett-Thorpe and Rupesh Chandrani), the Young Fabians (in particular Seema Malhotra) and colleagues at Brunel and Kingston Universities.

Shorter versions of some of the material in Chapters 1 and 9 appeared as articles in *Company Lawyer* in March 2001 (Vol 22(3)) and April 2001 (Vol 23(4)) respectively, under the titles 'Stakeholding and company law' and 'The future of UK company law'.

CONTENTS

Contents

TABLE OF CASES

TABLE OF LEGISLATION

TABLE OF STATUTORY INSTRUMENTS

CHAPTER 1

INTRODUCTION: STAKEHOLDING AND COMPANY LAW

1.1 INTRODUCTION TO THE ISSUES

This book considers the duties of directors of public companies in the light of the 'stakeholder' approach to the firm. It examines the theory that directors are not simply agents of corporate shareholders, but have a duty to consider and, where appropriate, to balance the interests of several constituencies, each of which has a legitimate 'stake' in the company, its activities and development. Examples of suggested stakeholders in corporate activity have included employees, customers, suppliers and creditors, as well as the local community and the natural environment. The categories of stakeholders and the debate around their claims will be discussed in Chapter 4. The essential point to make here is that, if this broader view of public company responsibility is warranted, the role of the law in securing a 'stakeholder' style of management in UK public companies needs to be examined with care. It will be argued that the implications for industry and commerce, and for Britain's national competitiveness and prosperity, could be very great.

This commentary is about public companies, rather than private companies. The main distinction in law between the two is that the latter are not permitted to offer their securities to the public. This gives them a greater role in the economy and community as a whole. In recognition of this, public companies must have at least two directors and a qualified company secretary must make greater disclosure of their financial affairs than small or medium-sized private companies. The likelihood is that the differences between regulations governing the two kinds of company will increase in a new UK Companies Act. Even companies that do not immediately make a public offer when converting to public company status accept a greater level of regulation.

It is not denied that in the world of 2001, regulation of the largest companies is a matter of concern to many countries and international organisations. However, in terms of the operation of the parent company, even large transnationals are ruled from one jurisdiction. The majority have headquarters in Western Europe or the United States, with rather fewer based in Japan. States continue to play an important regulatory role, either individually or at regional level (for example, in the European Union).[1] If there is to be access to a given national market for raising capital, rules on this can be set and enforced at a national level. Furthermore, the system in one

---

1   Nilsson, J-E, Dicken, P and Peck, J, *The Internationalization Process*, 1996, p 161.

particular country can set a standard of management and governance that can offer a competitive advantage to that national economy. 'Less' regulation, in short, is not always 'better', either socially or economically. History suggests that the appropriate form of capitalism for a particular country depends on its context and culture.[2]

All companies in a globalising economy have to deal with what Thomas Friedman in his book *The Lexus and the Olive Tree* called 'The Democratization of Technology', ''The Democratization of Finance' and 'The Democratization of Information'.[3] Quicker and cheaper access to information, financial products and new technology empowers investors, consumers and employees to be discerning and demanding. Nation states in drafting new regulations need to run with these trends – or else be prepared to pay a heavy economic price.[4] Change happens faster than ever before, yet individuals and organisations remain rooted in localities and cultures. 'Finding the appropriate social bargain to democratise globalisation'[5] and equipping individuals and organisations to respond to the new competition, remain key roles for the nation states.

In considering UK law, the writer, a legal academic, did not wish merely to discuss theory without reference to those who actually run public companies. Their views and attitudes are crucial to the success of any corporate governance model. Empirical research was therefore carried out in the form of interviews with public company officers, from a wide range of organisations operating in many business sectors, in order to investigate:

(a) the extent to which at present they view their role as requiring assessment and inclusion of the interests of stakeholders;

(b) the manner in which such assessment and inclusion is actually carried out;

(c) the impact a statutory formulation of directors' duties to incorporate stakeholder interests would or might have on decision making in practice;

(d) the effect of the unitary board structure on corporate decision making.

The consequences of the stakeholder orientation or otherwise of directors for the economic performance and social impact of public companies was assessed in the light of that evidence.

The DTI's Company Law Review Steering Group referred to the distinction between 'Enlightened Shareholder Value', which views the 'ultimate objective of companies' as being 'to generate maximum value for shareholders' and the 'Pluralist' approach (essentially stakeholding arguments by another name), which considers shareholders as one constituency among

---

2   Moore, K and Lewis, D, *Birth of the Multinational*, 1999, p 279.

3   Friedman, T, *The Lexus and the Olive Tree*, 1999, Chapter 4.

4   *Ibid*, Chapter 6.

5   *Ibid*, p 444.

many.[6] The Steering Group appeared to assume that the two approaches were the only relevant schools of thought and that they were necessarily in conflict. Considerable space in the Strategic Framework document was devoted to discussing 'counter arguments to such pluralist views'; moreover, some of the questions posed for discussion were somewhat loaded against those views.[7] This study further reviews the arguments and seeks to set them in their wider commercial and international context.

Company law in Britain has suffered from a regrettable period of neglect by legislators. It seems to be perceived by politicians as a 'difficult, technical' subject. In particular, proposals by the Law Commission on directors' duties and shareholder remedies have not found legislative time.[8] As progress is made by a DTI Company Law Review (driven by an independent Steering Group) towards a new, modern Companies Act, some practical ideas for legislation are set out in the following chapters. It has already become clear that the key areas for legislative attention as regards public companies are directors' duties, shareholder rights and reporting requirements.[9] All of these are very closely linked to the stakeholder agenda. Proposals in this book are supported by discussion of management theory and the literature on stakeholding, principally in Chapters 3 and 4. Examples from other jurisdictions and the thoughtful comments of interviewees, as discussed in Chapters 7 and 8 respectively, provided a valuable check on the feasibility of the ideas advanced below.

1.2 THEORETICAL BACKGROUND – WHAT IS A COMPANY?

Any consideration of directors' duties that is to be defensible and practicable must proceed from an examination of the nature of the company and the role of directors, drawing on the available law and management material. The work of public company boards has been said to include strategic planning, ethical leadership and overall monitoring of management. Chapter 3 considers these diverse, sometimes contradictory, roles. In the context of public companies, opinion as to their main responsibilities is divided along broadly political lines. This work will attempt to reconcile these distinct perspectives to produce a coherent set of priorities. The place of the board in

---

6   Company Law Review Steering Group, *Modern Company Law for a Competitive Economy: The Strategic Framework*, February 1999, para 5.1.

7   *Ibid*, Qus 4(a) and (b) and 5.

8   The Law Society: Company Law Committee, *The Reform of Company Law*, Law Society Memorandum No 394, February 2000, pp 3–6.

9   Company Law Review Steering Group, *Modern Company Law for a Competitive Economy – Final Report*, July 2001, Chapters 6–8.

the system is of central importance, and it is therefore essential to be clear about what directors should be aiming to achieve.

The Law Commission's report on directors' duties published in 1999 specifically excluded from consideration 'the identification of the interests which company law should serve.'[10] It is submitted that this is not a coherent approach to reform, particularly given that the 'guiding principles' for company law reform set out by the Law Commission included 'law as facilitator', 'inclusivity' (defined in a somewhat circular fashion as 'concern that the law should permit directors to take into account the interests of persons other than shareholders, to the extent the law allows this'), 'usability' (defined as meaning that 'the law should be accessible, comprehensible, clear and consistent with common sense'), and 'efficiency and cost-effectiveness'.[11] It is difficult to see how these matters can be judged without reference to the parties whom company law is designed to protect or assist. The intention was that the somewhat technical work on directors' duties should 'feed in' to the DTI's broader Company Law Review. The Company Law Review Steering Group has attempted to integrate both elements of reform. To what extent has it succeeded so far and is there a better approach?

1.2.1 The nature of the public company

It has long been argued by observers that the public company functions as a social institution with an independent existence, rather than as the private property of shareholders. According to this 'organic' theory of corporate life, shareholders cannot properly be regarded as the sole owners of public companies, given the practical separation of 'ownership' (of shares) from 'control' (which rests with management). This separation gives the management some latitude to pursue goals other than profit maximisation. If shareholders for practical reasons cannot undertake active stewardship of the resources owned and controlled by public companies, the board, which stands at the apex of internal corporate control systems, must perform that task. No single participating group, neither shareholders nor managers, employees nor consumers, has any natural claim to control of the company. Prosperity depends on the strategic marshalling of assets to the advantage of all concerned, rather than exclusive focus upon returns to shareholders.

In the view of management expert Professor John Kay, the 'organic' concept of the company as an independent entity has strong descriptive validity – that is, it makes sense of what one actually sees in practice:[12]

---

10 Law Commission, *Company Directors: Regulating Conflicts of Interests and Formulating a Statement of Duties*, Report No 261, September 1999, p 8.

11 *Ibid*, pp 25–26.

12 Kay, J, 'The Stakeholder Corporation' in Kelly, G, Kelly, D and Gamble, A, *Stakeholder Capitalism*, 1997, p 126.

Much of the concern with corporate governance – a concern which is largely Anglo-American – arises from the tension between that Anglo-American model and the practical reality of how large companies operate everywhere. The organic model of corporate behaviour – which gives to the corporation life independent from its shareholders and stakeholders – describes the actual behaviour of large companies and their managers far better than does the principal–agent perspective, and this is as true in Britain and the United States as it is in Japan.

In addition, company lawyer Professor John Parkinson advances a normative argument for what he calls social enterprises – he gives an ethical reason for the approach:[13]

> Since the public interest is the foundation of the legitimacy of companies, it follows that society is entitled to ensure that corporate power is exercised in a way which is consistent with that interest. To describe companies as social enterprises is thus to make a claim about the grounds of their legitimacy, and its practical significance is to hold that the state is entitled to prescribe the terms on which corporate power may be possessed and exercised.

Opposed to this 'organic' interpretation of the company has been the theory that describes the firm as a 'nexus of contracts'. This analysis holds that all those who deal with companies, including employees, customers, lenders and local and national government, can agree by bargaining at the outset what are to be the respective obligations of themselves and the companies. Shareholders, as ultimate risk-bearers for emerging new business who face practical difficulties in contracting for uncertain future events, are protected by being the subject of the fiduciary duties of directors. If public company boards had to consider other interests, it is argued, directorial activity would become less focused and vital equity investment would be lost. Only express contractual terms and laws restrict the decision making of company directors. Within these boundaries boards are charged with producing as much wealth as possible for shareholders by whatever means the directors may see fit, since that is the investment 'contract' with shareholders.

Macey and Miller put forward this contract-based view:[14]

> It is desirable to maintain a system of corporate governance in which fiduciary duties are owed exclusively to shareholders because no suitable alternative means of protecting shareholders' claims exist other than by way of a judicially enforced regime of fiduciary duties. By contrast, the obligations owed to other claimants can be enforced by contract because they are more precisely defined than the obligations to shareholders.

---

13 Parkinson, JE, *Corporate Power and Responsibility*, 1993, p 23.
14 Macey, JR and Miller, GP, 'Corporate Stakeholders: A Contractual Perspective' (1993) 43 University of Toronto Law Journal 423.

It is at least arguable that fiduciary duties have not, to date, proved a particularly effective protection for shareholders in widely held UK public companies.

The primacy of shareholder wealth maximisation as a corporate goal is staunchly defended by Van der Weide in these terms:[15]

> [N]onshareholder constituencies are in a better position to dictate corporate behavior to their advantage through explicit contracting than are shareholders. Other stakeholders who do not contract to prevent the firm from restructuring, relocating or downsizing to their detriment generally have chosen to take risks of restructuring, relocating or downsizing in exchange for higher returns on their investment.

The real ability of employees, customers and suppliers in a particular sector to 'shop around' as suggested here depends on the level of competition and general economic conditions.

It does not, in any event, follow from the contractarian interpretation of the firm that directors have no responsibility to consider the interests of non-equity stakeholders. In order to operate and to develop, major companies need continuing, high-quality inputs of all the factors of production, including skilled labour and natural resources, and they need to gain recognition from customers, employees and authorities as reliable, legitimate entities. In a free market, companies are always competing, not only for capital but also for sales and customer 'brand loyalty', for the services of the most able employees and the most favourable supply terms. The excellent company performs well in all of these competitions. If such excellence is to be achieved, co-ordination is required to set goals and deal with the expectations of all key constituencies. The board, as the ultimate supervisor of management, is in a position to provide this co-ordination.

Wright observes:[16]

> Nexus of contracts theory views the firm not as an entity, but as an aggregate of various inputs acting together to produce goods and services. Employees provide labour and creditors provide debt capital. The role of shareholders is viewed initially as providing equity capital and subsequently as bearing the risk of losses and monitoring the performance of management. Management monitors the performance of employees and co-ordinates the activities of all the firm's inputs.

Without constraints of ownership by any one participant, the activities of the public company can be orchestrated for the benefit of all its stakeholders. Even in terms of 'bottom line' profitability, reliance on the strict terms of

---

15 Van der Weide, ME, 'Against Fiduciary Duties to Corporate Stakeholders' (1996) 21 Delaware Journal of Corporate Law 55.

16 Wright, MJ, 'Corporate Governance and Directors' Social Responsibilities: Responsible Inefficiency or Irresponsible Efficiency?' (1996) 17 Business Law Review 178.

written contracts will often not be sufficient to produce outstanding results. Mutual advantages can flow from extended commitment rather than 'one shot' contracting. There is scope within contractual theory for the recognition of implicit as well as explicit contractual terms between the company and other parties, particularly those employees and suppliers who have had or anticipate lengthy relationships with the company. Over time, such stability of connections leads to shared expectations of quality and value. Successful and lasting companies appear to develop an identity that comes from, and becomes greater than, the sum of its contractual relationships (the reader need only walk down any High Street in Britain to be reminded of the ubiquity and power of corporate brands).

There is, moreover, a recognition that the images of companies and of business generally depend in large part on the degree of social responsiveness they demonstrate. To that extent it is simply unrealistic to describe public limited companies as private contractual organisations. Social expectations of public companies have grown beyond the delivery of profits to shareholders. In an era when many citizens are investors and employees, environmentalists and consumers, similar standards are expected from companies encountered in all of these roles and consistent messages are important.

Carroll sets out four levels of responsibility for business – the economic ('be profitable'), the legal ('obey the law'), the ethical ('do what is right, just and fair; avoid harm') and the philanthropic ('contribute resources to the community, improve quality of life'). They are briefly and helpfully defined as follows:[17]

Economic responsibilities

First and foremost, the American social system calls for business to be an economic institution. That is, it should be one whose orientation is to produce goods and services that society wants and sell them at a fair price – a price that society thinks represents the value of goods and services delivered and that provides the business with an adequate profit for its perpetuation, growth and reward to investors.

In the UK too, the economic responsibility of companies is concerned with more than simply making the largest possible profit and starts from the fair satisfaction of genuine consumer demands.

Legal responsibilities

Legal responsibilities reflect a view of 'codified ethics' in the sense that they embody basic notions of fairness as established by our law makers.

There is no room here for disregarding or flouting the law on the grounds that it might be profitable to take the risk of doing so.

---

17 Carroll, AB, *Business and Society: Ethics and Stakeholder Management*, 2nd edn 1993, pp 32–33.

Ethical responsibilities

Ethical responsibilities embody the range of norms, standards or expectations that reflect a concern for what consumers, employees, shareholders and the community regard as fair, just and in keeping with the respect for or protection of stakeholders' moral rights.

Stakeholders are likely to exert pressure on a corporate board that does not strive to meet appropriate standards. It is for directors to keep themselves informed of the current ethical expectations of their stakeholders and to act accordingly.

Finally, there are the voluntary efforts, which result from business's own desire to engage in socially useful activities, but are neither required by the law nor generally expected of business (though many large, and some small, companies do engage in such efforts). Charitable giving is one example of this category of actions, as is direct community involvement via employee placements. These may have commercial benefits if they enhance the company's reputation in the community. However, such 'spin-offs' are practically difficult to quantify.

The way seems to be open for a reconciliation of 'organic' and 'nexus of contract' theories of the company in terms of corporate identity constructed through key relationships. This possible synthesis will be the subject of Chapter 2. One can argue from either perspective that management is at the hub of a set of spokes that make up a company's activities. Directors have the task of providing economic and ethical structures for, and overall monitoring of, organisational decisions. Where there is failure to meet the standard an important constituent expects, it is directors who must ultimately shoulder responsibility. Corporate power comes about because of the financial and political strength of the organisation, but the concomitant responsibility needs to be vested in an identifiable group of individuals, which in law is the board of directors.

1.2.2 The role of directors

In corporate management theory, the idea has been mooted that the board of directors should not simply be a senior executive committee, but ought to take a broad-ranging, long-term view of the company's activities and objectives. Public company directors in reality do not attend exclusively to maximising shareholder returns. The long-term enhancement and prosperity of the corporation for the benefit of all its stakeholders is the board's primary goal. Accountability to all those who directly contribute to the company's activities, and for the company's reputation and status, rests with the directors. Several key objectives for the corporate board, not all of which sit easily with the duties and structures required by UK company law, have been canvassed by management theorists. Some observations on key directorial tasks follow below and interviews with public company officers provided further insights.

Any corporate governance system needs to enable businesses to be driven forward. If the board does not make sufficient time to construct an effective overall strategy and keep it under regular review, all the efforts of management and employees will not produce optimal results. Directors do not always ensure that they concentrate sufficiently on strategic planning as opposed to operational review. Board agendas and efforts have to be structured so as to strike an appropriate balance between audit and organisation. Individuals who lack the capacity to contribute to a strategic vision for a company are not needed on its board. Technical experts and specialist executives can be asked to advise directors as and when required. Directors as such have an altogether broader remit.

The board has also been said to function as the 'corporate conscience', setting the overall standards and reviewing major plans from legal and ethical standpoints. Company managers take their lead from, and expect to be accountable to, directors in this respect. Preparation of codes of ethics, for example, is normally initiated by directors whose commitment or otherwise to the whole concept sets the tone for such exercises. In daily decision making throughout the company, the attitudes of directors and the consequences of breaches of corporate codes are a constant influence and communication channels to disseminate this knowledge are extremely important.

Mills expounds his view of this directorial task and its wider effects:[18]

It [the board] is the keeper of the company's conscience and the measure of corporate morality. By setting the standards of corporate courage it delimits the management's morale. From the boardroom to the shopfloor, both productivity and performance are most closely affected by morale, which is itself most visibly affected by visible morality. The effective company meets its creditors on time, especially the small ones; does not abuse its suppliers or maltreat its physical environment; is clinically correct with its customers, employees, auditors, analysts, shareholders, lenders and taxmen.

The monitoring role of directors vis à vis managers is highlighted by Goldschmid as follows:[19]

The first function of the board ... should be to provide a meaningful, independent check. The focus would be on the corporation's structure, process of management, and decision making techniques. Second, the board should choose, evaluate, and, if necessary, discharge all senior corporate officers. Third, it should review and approve major corporate policies and long-range objectives.

---

18 Mills, G, *Controlling Companies*, 1988, p 21.
19 Goldschmid, HJ, 'The Governance of the Public Corporation: Internal Relationships' in Schwartz, DE, *Commentaries on Corporate Structure and Governance: the ALI-ABA Symposiums 1977–78*, 1979, p 174.

Effective accountability is the other important factor in corporate governance. Indeed, giving substance to the monitoring task of the board might be the most valuable contribution the law could make. Increased use of outside directors and board committees (for example, to deal with audit and remuneration) is intended to make board scrutiny of management more effective. Regular communication and reporting requirements in themselves act as a discipline for managers. This appraisal demands more time and attention than non-executive directors have traditionally allotted to their role. In advance of full monthly meetings, one day's formal preparation and fact-finding and discussion by non-executives is the minimum to ensure that board members can contribute with confidence. Such requirements impose a natural limit on the number of non-executive directorships an individual can handle. A full-time executive would normally be unable to attend to more than one non-executive post, while four public company directorships would provide an ample portfolio for a professional independent non-executive.

In addition to the time factor, other practical matters can affect board performance. A board that is too large is likely to prove ineffectual. The consensus in practical management literature seems to be that, when larger than 12 or so members, the group tends to operate less cohesively and swiftly than a smaller board. The provision of full and frank (not overwhelming or obscure) information to board members for proper consideration in advance of meetings is obviously important. Arrangements for non-executive directors to have access to company sites and records, to meet with employees and perhaps key customers and suppliers, need to be made. More generally, a culture that encourages sharp questioning, rather than deferential politeness, is certainly required in every boardroom. All of these issues have had to be considered in relation to non-executives working on the boards of NHS Trusts. The lessons to be learned by the private sector from 'new model' public sector experiences, including the privatised utilities and the role of the law in spreading good governance practice will be briefly considered.

Cannon[20] regards directors as being responsible for trusteeship of corporate assets as a whole, primarily for the shareholders:

> The responsibilities of the trustee centre on the disinterested care of assets belonging to another party. The executor is an agent entrusted with the deployment of resources on behalf of another. A manager is expected to marshall assets to get the best return for his employer. Each of these components are included in the notion of effective governance.

Sappideen's view is different in emphasis:[21]

---

20 Cannon, T, *Corporate Responsibility*, 1994, p 135.
21 Sappideen, R, 'Ownership of the Large Corporation: Why Clothe the Emperor?' (1996) 7 King's College Law Journal 53.

[T]he symbiotic nature of the relationship between all stakeholders must be highlighted. Managers are not mere agents of shareholders. They are fiduciaries of the corporation and play the role of intermediary to the various claimants against the corporation. Shareholders and employees are claimants against the corporation to whom management is accountable, and for whom management is responsible via the corporate structure.

Some theorists have explicitly discussed the board as a forum for the balancing of interests of constituencies concerned with or affected by the company. This is the essence of the board's role in a corporate governance system that takes stakeholder interests seriously. Any credible effort at such balancing requires the directors to demonstrate far wider vision than is implied by the shareholder primacy model and will require teamwork and advice. A keen awareness of the parties affected by or who affect the company's operations, their needs and expectations, is essential to successful decision making.

It is not asserted that public company boards succeed in meeting, or even attempt to reach, all of these targets at present, but that in principle they emerge as the key tasks of directors. All of this work, which will be further examined in Chapter 3, presupposes a certain detachment of the directors as a body from day to day organisation. Long-term priority-setting, ethical monitoring, performance appraisal of executives and overall balance of interests of competing parties in the operation of the company require an adequate measure of independence from management. Possible ways of ensuring this objectivity will be considered below.

1.2.3 Stakeholding theory

As far as companies are concerned, stakeholder theory proposes that all parties affected by the activities of a company should be given a place in corporate decision making. This may be by direct participation, by representation or other appropriate consideration of their interests.[22] As a matter of general principle, stakeholding seeks to achieve a balance of risks and rewards, of rights and responsibilities that is properly inclusive and fair in a way that the present order has not been. In practice, to give one example, the primacy of shareholders within the UK system has often resulted in employees bearing the brunt of economic difficulties. The advocates of a stakeholding approach often contend that it enhances both social justice and economic prosperity. Trusting relationships are said to foster investment and development which, in turn, produce rewards for all stakeholders.

---

22 Smith, NC, *Morality and the Market*, 1990, pp 55 *et seq* and 84, points out that board-level participation is not the only option for stakeholders and may be impractical because of conflicts of interest.

From a stakeholding perspective, the substantive questions are whether employee and customer interests could be more effectively protected and whether other stakeholder groups are entitled to recognition. Examples often quoted include sub-contractors, lenders, environmental monitors and the community in which the company is situated.[23] There are practical issues around involvement of all such bodies, quite apart from arguments of principle. Direct participation in decision making at board level is one possibility. Another is the creation of enforceable duties on the part of directors to have full regard to stakeholder interests and to consider appropriate representations when making their decisions. Greater shareholder involvement should itself be part of the stakeholding agenda for public companies in Britain.

The (essentially political) argument, moving from the economic and social impact of large companies to the assertion that company law is inadequate, is put by Janet Williamson of the TUC:[24]

> Employees are affected by the wide range of decisions that impact upon their employment with the company; customers are affected by decisions on the price, specifications and standards of products; suppliers are affected by purchasing decisions; creditors are affected by financial procedures; and the local community is affected by recruitment policy and environmental impact ... The groups directly affected by the operation and decisions of a company can be said to have a stake in that firm; they are its stakeholders.

> The law as it stands, while it reflects the need for companies to take some note of the interests of stakeholder groups, in no way reflects the true weight and complexity of company–stakeholder relationships. What is required is a new approach to corporate governance, one in which it is recognised that companies are not just vehicles for the maximisation of shareholder value but institutions with a life of their own in which the interests of several disparate stakeholder groups are vested.

Just as, in a democratic state, parties affected by decisions are involved in the making of those decisions, so in a company, relevant groups should enjoy appropriate input. The democratic model can have a powerful influence on corporate governance thinking. Stakeholder theory goes beyond both the simple attempt to describe the realities of substantial corporations and the assertion that stakeholder satisfaction produces better results in the long term. At its core is the moral imperative of balancing varied property rights, none of them absolute but all of them valid.

Donaldson and Preston express this normative case for stakeholding as follows:[25]

---

23   See eg, Parkinson, n 13 above, Chapter 9 and Cannon, n 20 above, Chapter 3.

24   Williamson, J, 'The Road to Stakeholding' (1996) 67 Political Quarterly 209, 212.

25   Donaldson, T and Preston, LE, 'The Stakeholder Theory of the Firm: Concepts, Evidence and Implications' (1995) 20 Academy of Management Review 65, 67.

(1) Stakeholders are persons or groups with legitimate interests in procedural and/or substantive aspects of corporate activity. Stakeholders are identified by their interests in the corporation, whether the corporation has any corresponding functional interest in them.

(2) The interests of all stakeholders are of intrinsic value. That is, each group of stakeholders merits consideration for its own sake and not merely because of its ability to further the interests of some other group, such as the shareowners.

There is, of course, no conflict between the moral assertion that all stakeholders have intrinsic value and the empirical claim that a balanced stakeholder approach will produce better long-term results for the benefit of all parties. A cursory examination of public company Annual Reports reveals that some seem to focus particularly on customer relationships, some on employee development, others on technological advances, as well as on delivering returns to shareholders. The challenge for advocates of a stakeholding approach is to foster a proper regard for key relationships in all major companies. The benefit will be that the company's network of relationships as a whole will become stronger.

Where the British system appears to fall short, there may be lessons from other competing jurisdictions that place more emphasis on the stakeholding concept. If they are producing better results over time, the implications of that have to be assessed. As Michael Porter of Harvard Business School writes:

> The Japanese and German systems ... appear to come closer to optimising long-term private and social returns. The greater focus on long-term corporate position – encouraged by an ownership structure and governance process that incorporate the interests of employees, suppliers, customers and the local community – allow the Japanese and German economies to better capture the social benefits of private investment.[26]

Porter's comparison was with the US, but the UK is open to similar criticisms.

Philosophical and political dissatisfaction with the Anglo-American system has been widely expressed in recent years. As Lord (Ralf) Dahrendorf succinctly put it:

> [C]ompanies are more than profit machines. As employers, as purchasers and suppliers, and as centres of community life, they are the nub of a network of stakeholders. Shareholders can dispose of their assets; stakeholders are at risk of being disposed of themselves. Are we right to concentrate on shareholders to the exclusion of all others?[27]

---

26 Porter, M, 'Capital Choices: Changing the Way America Invests in Industry' in Chew, D, *Studies in International Corporate Finance and Governance Systems*, 1997, p 13.

27 Dahrendorf, R, 'On the Dahrendorf Report' (text of a speech delivered to the House of Lords on 21 February 1996) (1996) 67 Political Quarterly 195.

The message is that it is neither just nor reasonable to expose other contributors to the risks of corporate activity, while shielding investors who can and do protect themselves by holding diversified, fast moving portfolios of shares.

Corporate activity is not an end in itself (though some executives might suggest otherwise). Its purpose is to contribute to the satisfaction of needs and wants – not only the desire of shareholders for income but also the aspirations of employees, the requirements of customers, the work of suppliers and value added for the community. The appropriate balance of interests will vary between different companies, as, for instance, some are highly labour-intensive while some have a particular environmental impact. Exclusive or excessive concentration upon only one element of the whole network will mean, on the stakeholding view, unacceptable neglect of others who are also entitled to due consideration and fair treatment. There will inevitably be conflicts between the interests of the various groups, which must be carefully handled so as to retain their trust and confidence for the future. Managers must strive to make decisions and deploy resources in a manner consistent with the claims of relevant stakeholder groups.

Chapter 4 will consider the justifications for the stakeholder approach and the task of identifying and classifying stakeholders. The essence of the stakeholding vision is not artificial equality but inclusion for all, in the corporate setting as in the wider political sphere. Those who directly contribute to the company's performance (for example, employees, customers, suppliers, investors) can be dealt with differently from those who are affected by the company's outputs (such as community and environmental groups). For directors, it is argued that the priority should be to assess the network of stakeholders in their company and the requirements and relative claims of each of them.

1.3 LEGAL IMPLICATIONS

If stakeholder principles are to be put into effect in the daily operations of public companies, the law as it now stands may well be inadequate. Many proposals have been put forward for changes to the fiduciary duties of directors, mechanisms for the enforcement of directorial duties and alterations to the structure of the board itself. The law should reflect the reality that boards need to pay proper attention to all stakeholders. In the absence of effective sanctions to back them up, however, new legal responsibilities are likely to prove ineffectual. Without sound work by, and the commitment of, board members who set the agenda for companies, advances towards inclusive behaviour will be blocked. Legislation can be something of a blunt instrument, but its use is sometimes essential to bring about change where cultural shifts by themselves are unacceptably slow.

Since relationships are two-way, stakeholders themselves need to demonstrate the ability and the willingness to interact with public company leaderships. Other jurisdictions have much to teach the United Kingdom in this respect. Voluminous legislation governing relations with stakeholders, including specific employment and environmental measures, is already in place, but typically takes the form of restraints on the most egregiously harmful or socially unacceptable practices, rather than positive measures to improve engagement and dialogue. Nor does a plethora of detailed prohibitions necessarily contribute to a holistic view of corporate responsibility on the part of business leaders. Details of annual and more frequent reporting requirements are also practically important to all those who interact with public companies. What, then, is the proper role of 'core' company law?

1.3.1 Changes to company law to broaden responsibilities of directors

Arguments have been advanced for a change in UK companies legislation to reflect a stakeholder approach towards directors' responsibilities. This would supersede the duty to take decisions 'in the interests of the company', which has been practically interpreted as meaning the interests of shareholders. The enactment of such a provision could be said to have two potential benefits:

(a) it would legitimise the actions of directors in considering factors other than the maximisation of shareholder returns;

(b) it would foster a change in boardroom culture to accommodate recognition of the importance of a company's relationships with its employees, customers and suppliers and the community and environment in and through which it operates, as well as those with providers of capital.

One conclusion of the RSA's Tomorrow's Company Inquiry[28] was that directors were being led by a misunderstanding of current law to believe that they were obliged to take a more short-termist and shareholder-centric view of planning than was actually required. It was pointed out that the current law did not prevent directors from having regard to the interests of non-member stakeholders if they judged that to be in the best interests of 'the corporation' – not only present members, but also future investors. Without the stimulus of changes to the law, it is, however, difficult to foresee a change of culture such that balanced long-term planning would become the norm for UK public companies. The existing law limits any accountability to stakeholders within a framework of, and to the overall purpose of, profit maximisation for

---

28 RSA Inquiry, *Tomorrow's Company*, 1995.

shareholders. A more fundamental change in legislation is appropriate if it is accepted that all stakeholders have value in their own right, as ends in themselves. Shareholder concerns will not invariably be aligned with the demands of customers, employees and suppliers, let alone legitimate environmental and community concerns, and the law should explicitly permit directors to address these issues as part of their work.

Professor John Kay proposed the following wording:[29]

- A director of a PLC shall at all times act in the manner he considers in the exercise of his business judgement best fitted to advance the interests of the company. The interests of the company include:
- the payment of returns to shareholders and investors sufficient to remunerate past investment and encourage future investment in the company;
- the development of the skills and capabilities of employees and suppliers of the company;
- the achievement of stability and security in the company's employment and trading relationships;
- the provision of goods and services of good quality to the company's customers at fair prices; and
- the enhancement of the company's reputation for high standards of business conduct.

Such provision would not demand major change in the way effective public companies are already run but would legitimate their actions and help to bring others to the same standard.

The late George Goyder suggested a general objects clause to be incorporated into the memorandum of association of a public company:[30]

To make the company economically and financially strong in order to ensure its continued growth and future development as a means of providing good service, secure employment and a fair return to its investors and shareholders.

To provide goods and services of the best quality and the most reasonable prices consistent with its other objectives.

To give its employees every reasonable opportunity for their interests to be heard within the company and for their promotion and development in skill and to allow reasonable time off for attention to public duties.

To act towards the community of which it is a member in as responsible a manner as would be expected from a responsible citizen in like circumstances.

Such a formula would be a public declaration of intent against which subsequent performance could be publicly judged.

---

29 Kay, n 12 above, p 137.
30 Goyder, G, *The Just Enterprise*, 1993, p 56.

Since the board is the body that has the task within the current system of setting the corporate agenda and monitoring managerial performance, it seems appropriate to give responsibility for balancing stakeholder interests to directors in the manner Kay suggests. This makes board members clearly accountable for delivering stakeholders' objectives. It is not clear from Goyder's work whether the suggested objects clause would be mandatory or if a narrower approach could be adopted in a particular company much as an individual corporate constitution may vary the model Table A at present. The enforcement of objects clauses is currently limited to a right of shareholders to restrain *ultra vires* conduct before a legal commitment has been entered into, which would not be an effective mechanism to secure performance of a wider set of obligations.

Criticisms of such proposals include the argument that the range of issues for consideration would reduce efficiency when compared with the shareholders' wealth maximisation standard. Clarity is required to guide the everyday discussions of boards. The fair expectations of customers as to prices, employees as to earnings and the community as to involvement by corporations would, however, all be linked to company performance and market conditions, just as dividend expectations of shareholders are now. Too broad a requirement to examine the public interest in the round, on the other hand, would be uncertain and demand of directors that they attempt tasks to which politicians would be better suited. A specific, focused formula that reflects popular expectations of public companies is required in order to command the adherence of directors. Chapter 5 sets out a possible definition of directors' duties composed in the light of the above matters.

Codification of existing duties that in the UK have been set out in case law is one objective of company law's modernisation. It will be a missed opportunity, however, if consideration is not given to a more fundamental re-appraisal of the role of directors and of companies themselves. Non-Governmental Organisations such as Traidcraft Exchange, Oxfam, Amnesty International and War on Want in their submissions to the DTI during the Company Law Review process have certainly recognised that fact. The implications of this for boards are further discussed in Chapter 5.

1.3.2 Enforcement of stakeholder remedies

Any law that is not enforced or enforceable is likely to become a mere dead letter. Whatever the precise wording of any new set of directors' duties, two practical questions must therefore be answered:

(a) How are board decisions to be judged in the light of more expansive stakeholder duties?

(b) How can such standards effectively be enforced?

A legislative change to this end would arguably promote the type of decision making that is already common among successful public companies. Without a facility for relevant constituencies to seek review of board decisions in court, there would be little impetus for directors currently operating otherwise to change their working methods and ethos. To this end one must consider the standing of affected groups to enforce consideration by directors of their interests. Neither the shareholders nor any other single group can claim to be entitled to priority in all decisions. They can complain only if they have been improperly ignored or disadvantaged. There is a balance to be struck between proper managerial discretion and the rights of legitimate stakeholders.[31]

Mitchell proposed:[32]

[A] remedial cause of action structured around the least common denominator of the new board's duties: the duty not to harm. Each constituent identified by legislation as entitled to the board's consideration would be permitted to bring an action against the board asserting that the board had breached its duty not to harm; that is, in making a corporate distribution or distributions, or by failing to do so, it allocated excessive corporate costs or insufficient corporate wealth to the complaining constituent. The court would be required to evaluate the terms of the constituent's initial contract with the corporation, to study the course of the constituent's relationship with the corporation to determine the overall fairness of its treatment by the board, and then to determine whether the board had harmed the constituent in the light of the contract and relationship.

Stakeholders would have a direct incentive to act if the board fell short of its responsibilities, rather as shareholders can now claim 'unfair prejudice' and, if successful, gain one of a range of remedies.

Du Plessis and Dine suggested what was described as an 'associative model' of the company.[33] The holders of associative rights would be those, such as some employees and lenders, who had 'very close' relations with a company. Such parties would be able to petition the courts if their associative rights were being disregarded. The procedure in the event of any dispute would be:

[A] derivative action reflecting similar features to a shareholder derivative action. Thus, such an action could only be brought to defend the interest of the company and the eventual 'winner' of any successful action would be the company itself. The action would only succeed where the court was able to determine that the interests of the company had been contravened. Where

---

31 See Keasey, K and Wright, MJ, 'Corporate Governance, Accountability and Enterprise' in Keasey and Wright, *Corporate Governance: Responsibilities, Risk and Remuneration*, 1997, for general discussion.

32 Mitchell, LE, 'A Critical Look at Corporate Governance' (1992) 45 Vanderbilt Law Review 1313.

33 Du Plessis, JJ and Dine, J, 'The Fate of the Draft Fifth Directive on Company Law' [1997] JBL 45–46

associative rights had been totally disregarded the action would succeed, but where associative rights had been considered and other interests had prevailed a successful action would be rare indeed.

This type of action is premised on the assumption that the survival and prosperity of the company will be advanced if it maintains and develops its key relationships.

If stakeholder inclusion is thought of as being valuable for its own sake, a direct right of petition to the courts for stakeholders whose rights have been violated would be deemed appropriate. This may mean that returns to shareholders would be reduced while other parties would benefit. If satisfaction of stakeholders is regarded as a means to the end of profitability for investors, an arrangement more closely comparable to a derivative action would be preferred. The objective would be to protect the profitability of the firm. The view advanced below is that, in the context of a proven associative relationship, recovery should be allowed to a stakeholder who had suffered unfair prejudice. Without the eventual threat of such a sanction, it is difficult to foresee real changes in corporate decision making.

It is suggested that employees, customers and suppliers who could show that the business of a company had been conducted in a manner that was unfairly prejudicial to their interests (having regard to the investment of time and/or funds they had made in the relationship with the company and their reasonable expectations of proper consideration) would have a right of redress. The remedy provided would be flexible but might include compensation or enforcement of agreements or understandings. The claimant would need to bring evidence of their expectations and how the company had violated that trust. The balance to be struck between the interests of all relevant constituencies would be explicitly acknowledged and no one constituency would be able to claim automatic priority.

Chapter 6 will examine the arguments for and against such a new species of stakeholder action, its possible boundaries and the standards the courts might use in adjudicating such claims. Procedural complexities such as those which inhibit current shareholder challenges to board decisions would need to be avoided by legislation if new rights were to be effective. Among the points to be considered are these: How far would this legal change move matters from where we now stand in the UK? Would it, as some commentators argue, allow courts to intrude too far into business decision making? The law needs to keep corporate decision making in line with modern social expectations without unduly hampering board creativity.

1.3.3 The structure of the board and European models

If the board is to achieve the objectivity discussed above, its composition must be critically examined in two important respects:

(a) the proportion of executives to non-executives and backgrounds of potential non-management directors;

(b) the unitary board structure as compared with the separate management board and supervisory tier.

The European Union Draft Fifth Company Law Directive on public company structures provides for the unitary board to be retained if preferred by a Member State, and enables employee representation to take place other than at board level. Nevertheless the functioning of two-tier board systems in Europe, with the duty to establish Works Councils in enterprises of significant size, will have a substantial impact on UK practice. Some pan-European convergence of corporate governance systems is already discernible, with continental jurisdictions tightening up their rules on financial reporting and accountability to shareholders while the UK examines possible mechanisms for non-equity stakeholder input at or near board level.

Extension of the non-executive role should indeed improve shareholder protection if a genuinely independent stance can be maintained in the monitoring task. In continental Europe, this formal separation of functions has also been associated with a more participative, community orientated view of the company as an institution. The issues of effective monitoring and stakeholder representation are not logically linked. Nevertheless, British suspicion of worker participation in management has led to rejection of supervisory boards.

Within the UK context and looking from a practical angle, Mills concludes:[34]

> At times even the non-executive, if alone, can stray from objectivity, and 'desperate courage makes one a majority' can become quite exhausting. So one-third of the board is a workable minimum. If two-thirds of the board is non-executive there may not be room for the good executives, so this proportion represents a workable maximum for the largest boards. Between one-third and two-thirds thus constitutes a working range, with fewer non-executives on the smaller company boards, and more on the larger company holding boards.

Similarly, the Hampel Committee noted that:[35]

---

34 Mills, n 18 above, pp 95–96.
35 Committee on Corporate Governance (Chair: Sir Ronald Hampel), *Final Report*, January 1998, para 3.14.

> Non-executive directors have an important part to play in corporate governance. We believe that it is difficult for them to be effective if they make up less than one third of the board.

Board decision making in British public companies remains dominated by management, despite the efforts of the Cadbury Committee[36] and PRO NED[37] to give non-executive directors higher profiles and clearer roles. A minimum requirement of one-third non-executive representation would seem to meet with an emerging consensus. How much would a strengthening of the non-management element improve the quality of decisions from the stakeholding viewpoint? As far as direct stakeholder 'voice' is concerned, continental European experience shows that it would be practicable to institute a legislative system of employee representation in public companies, if the political will existed to do so. Other participants, such as subcontractors and community representatives, are more diverse in their characteristics. Any board member will, of course, only be effective if he or she has the skills and personality to be sufficiently persuasive.

As for the various stakeholding groups, the first question is whether they should have representation in a supervisory board separate from core managerial decision making or whether a unified board structure is preferable. The danger of separate supervisory bodies is that they can become isolated from daily decision making and depend for their information on reports from management.[38] If they are to play a full part in influencing the direction of management, it may be better, given the British context, to grant representatives seats on unitary boards. The consensus has grown up within the present system that the chairman should be someone other than the chief executive and should be an individual sufficiently experienced and skilful to act as a check on the chief executive. The board has the task of setting the company's direction for the benefit of all who are involved with or affected by its activity. The quality of the members and their capacity to work together will be of prime importance, as will the reliability of the information they receive from the management.

Chapter 7 discusses the lessons to be learned by the UK from continental Europe. In the global market, responsiveness to customers, the skills and adaptability of employees and reliable supply chains are increasingly important, particularly for businesses that are seeking to compete not on price alone, but on added value. For this reason a brief discussion is included of

---

36 Committee on the Financial Aspects of Corporate Governance (Chair: Sir Adrian Cadbury), *Final Report*, December 1992.

37 The organisation established in 1982 'to promote the use of non-executive directors and to provide a register of suitable candidates for non-executive directorships' (PRO NED Code Clause 4).

38 This is a difficulty for non-executive directors generally – see Stratton, IC, 'Non-Executive Directors – Are They Superfluous?' (1996) 17 Co Law 162.

how France and Germany, as the major continental European economies, deal with these issues. It is at least useful to note that there are other methods of stimulating and disciplining executive directors than the Anglo-Saxon takeover market, with its often over-inflated bid prices for companies.

The German and Dutch systems feature employee representation, but there is no reason why, for example, environmental experts could not also have an input into public company supervision. It would be logical for the number of employee directors to be proportional to the number of the company's employees, starting at, say, one board member for 500 employees. Environmental factors obviously vary with the nature of the business but as a baseline, each division or department of operations needs proper 'green' assessment that carries weight at board level. The importance of subcontractor links and community ties will vary from industry to industry and company to company and it is therefore less practical to prescribe specific methods and levels of representation, though consultation on key decisions could certainly be encouraged far more than it now is. The possibilities for diversification of the board have barely been explored in the UK to date. Wider stakeholder representation would be more practicable if the board were to concentrate on its monitoring and supervisory role than if it were also attempting to manage operational detail.

Will Hutton states the position strongly, but in practical terms does not exaggerate, when he writes: 'The chairman of the board, who may also be the chief executive ... can appoint whoever he likes to the board as a non-executive director to bolster his own position; can set the level of his own salary; need not consult nor communicate with his workforce; and can manipulate the firm's constitution to get his way.'[39] The Cadbury Committee Code of Best Practice recommended that public company boards should have non-executive directors 'in sufficient numbers and of suitable status to provide a genuinely independent voice in decision making'.[40] Where genuine independence is particularly crucial, as in setting executive salaries and contract termination, non-executives of proven calibre, trusted by shareholders and other stakeholders, should have their say.[41] Given the importance of their task, appointments of public company non-executive directors need to be approved by shareholders, or perhaps in time by another key constituency (for example, employees, creditors) and to be for a fixed term of, say, three years with perhaps the possibility of one re-election.

Chapter 7 will discuss the arguments for and against provisions in law, for example to require a set proportion of non-executives on public company boards, and who such directors might be, across the European Union.

---

39   Hutton, W, *The State We're in*, 1995, p 294.

40   Cadbury, n 36 above, Code of Best Practice Section 2.

41   Study Group on Directors' Remuneration (Chair: Sir Richard Greenbury), *Final Report*, July 1995, Code of Best Practice Section A and *passim*.

Pragmatically it could be said that the task for legislators (or regulators) is to make universal those standards that have been shown to succeed. Going further, if boards are to be effective as standard-setters and monitors, a separate supervisory level completely distinct from management may be logically desirable. This also opens up the prospect of direct participation by particular stakeholders – not necessarily only employees, but also major creditors and, where a company's impact is great, appropriate community and environmental experts. Whether in a separate tier or not, however, the crucial point is that the distinct task of direction be recognised and done well. If this can be achieved within a unitary structure, the need is satisfied.

1.4 PUBLIC COMPANY OFFICERS' VIEWS

Perhaps surprisingly, public company officers' views have seldom been investigated by academics. Despite the difficulties of gaining access to such busy (and often guarded – in both senses) people, empirical work was required to ascertain whether directors of public limited companies already viewed their role in the manner envisaged by advocates of stakeholding and whether boards would approach matters differently if a stakeholder formulation of directors' duties were to be enacted. The issues of the breadth of board responsibility in terms of stakeholders and the impact of potential enforceability of duties to stakeholders were raised to gauge their reaction. Most, if not all, public company directors are aware of stakeholding and corporate social responsibility arguments and the debate as to possible new legislation.

Issues for discussion at interview included the primary responsibility of directors, the groups taken into consideration in decision making and the 'ranking', if any, of these groups. As far as possible changes to the law are concerned, the participants were asked how they reacted to the prospect of an inclusive stakeholder centred statement of directors' duties and quasi-derivative enforcement actions. Twenty-one individuals from 20 public companies (not counting their numerous non-executive appointments) took part in meetings over the Summer and Autumn of 1999 and 2000. Their roles included chief executives, with one former chairman/chief executive and one recently retired chairman/chief executive, finance directors, directors of business development, company secretaries and legal directors, a personnel director with a board seat and four very experienced non-executive directors. Within the small group of interviewees, representation from a broad spread of industry sectors (primary, secondary and tertiary) was obtained. There were also representatives from a cross-section of public companies in terms of size within the sample.

It is worth considering the personal impact upon directors (and managers) of freedom to address social and environmental issues when acting on behalf of their company as they might in personal dealings. Pressure to disregard the consequences of corporate activities for non-equity stakeholders has perhaps caused discomfort that was offset by the effects of collective responsibility and 'groupthink' in boards. Errors have resulted from inflexible cultures, which denied individual values and fostered collective overconfidence and arrogance.[42] An examination of the concerns of those connected with the company – customers, employees, suppliers, neighbours – is a healthy corrective to such narrow visions.[43]

Mitchell writes persuasively on the psychological issues involved:[44]

> [A] single-minded focus on efficiency, on the corporation as a narrowly defined economic institution, sacrifices the human values of those who play a part in its functioning. The efficiency model does this by legally cabining the actions of corporate actors within confining, distinctly nonhuman roles. It is this denial of humanity, which ultimately denies reality, that is at the heart of the current debate over stakeholder status.

When people are not expected to divorce their working behaviour from the rest of their lives or to use different value systems at work from those that operate at home, it seems plausible that they are likely to experience less stress and far greater job satisfaction.

Davis, Schoorman and Donaldson note that, conversely, when managers are motivated by vision other than profit, they are more likely to act for the benefit of the company and use its resources in a way which will benefit stakeholders as a whole over the long-term:[45]

> Managers whose needs are based on growth, achievement and self-actualization and who are intrinsically motivated may gain greater utility by accomplishing organizational rather than personal agendas. Likewise, managers who identify with their organizations and are highly committed to organizational values are also more likely to serve organizational ends. Finally, situations in which the managerial philosophy is based on involvement and trust and the culture is based on collectivism and low power distance generally result in principal – steward relationships.

---

42   Schwartz, HS, *Narcissistic Process and Corporate Decay*, 1990, discusses various examples including General Motors and NASA.

43   Kotter, JP and Heskett, JL, *Corporate Culture and Performance*, 1992, p 46 and *passim*.

44   Mitchell, LE, 'Groundwork of the Metaphysics of Corporate Law' (1993) 50 Washington & Lee Law Review 1479.

45   Davis, JH, Schoorman, FD and Donaldson, L, 'Towards a Stewardship Theory of Management' (1997) 22 Academy of Management Review 47.

This observation is consistent with the findings of classic organisational 'success studies' such as Peters and Waterman's *In Search of Excellence*[46] and Porras and Collins' *Built to Last*.[47]

A significant minority of those interviewed clearly understood their role as being agents of the shareholders, with all other responsibilities subordinate to that relationship. Others spoke of balancing the concerns of investors, employees and suppliers and the community and environment where applicable. It was found that to some extent the emphases placed on different constituencies varied with the activities in which the interviewee's company was engaged – for example, primary production or services. The Company Law Review Steering Group is seeking a compromise and, while supporting the 'Enlightened Shareholder Value' approach as opposed to 'Pluralism', aims to emphasise the importance of companies' relationships.[48]

Major changes in public company structure, for example two-tier boards, were almost universally unpopular as a legislative proposal. Some commentators felt that corporate governance requirements were already too onerous. The key point made was that valuable executive time spent, for example on reporting, must be seen to have an output. Improved relationships with contributors and increased 'brand value' would confer such a benefit.

Many of the directors believed that the dichotomy posited in the Company Law Review Steering Group's Strategic Framework document between shareholder value and pluralism was false. They endeavoured to pay due attention to all key stakeholders, particularly customers, employees and suppliers but also the natural and social environment, as part of their daily work, being conscious of the economic impact of good or poor stakeholder management.[49] Several interviewees, however, spoke of the demands of the market, and particularly institutional shareholders, constraining freedom of action. New rules to give other stakeholders more attention would have to be accompanied by a cultural change on the part of major shareholders. Public company directors and secretaries, on the evidence collected in these meetings, well understand that the board's responsibility is to develop and maintain the business for the long term. The extent to which they feel able, in practice, to do this depends at present on the demands of finance providers.

---

46 Peters, TJ and Waterman, RH, *In Search of Excellence*, 1982.
47 Collins, JC and Porras, JI, *Built to Last*, 1994.
48 Company Law Review Steering Group, n 9 above, paras 3.8–3.9.
49 See Whysall, P, 'Stakeholder Mismanagement in Retailing: A British Perspective' (2000) 23 Journal of Business Ethics 19; LaBerge, M and Svendsen, A, 'New Growth: Fostering Collaborative Business Relationships' (2000) 23 Journal for Quality and Participation 48.

1.5 CONCLUSION: TRUST AND UK PUBLIC COMPANIES

The likely impact on company performance of board adherence to a stakeholder management style (in the sense of continued efforts to balance the interests of all stakeholders in the company) will be addressed in Chapter 9. The literature on the benefits of trust within a company's network of relationships is important in this context.[50] Even without active acceptance of the case for stakeholder management on philosophical or political grounds, the prospect of strong economic advantages could lead to widespread adoption of its main precepts. The basic instrumental argument for stakeholding highlights the fact that explicit and detailed contracting is costly. Trusting relationships and reputations for trustworthiness can reduce the need to incur that expense. This is in addition to the fact that shareholders themselves may hold (and increasingly will demonstrate, for example, via ethical investment funds) a preference for companies that deliver quality to their customers, treat their employees well, respect their environment and play a constructive role in the communities where they operate.

The history of management thinking in the 20th century, in very broad terms, has been a contest between scientific and humanistic management, with the two schools vying for the ascendancy. Andrea Gabor, after surveying the pre-eminent business gurus in her work *The Capitalist Philosophers*, concludes that electorates and managers share: 'a growing acceptance of the notion that for capitalism to succeed globally, it must be made bearable for society at large.'[51] The operations of public companies are central to solutions to these key political problems. The UK, taking influences and inspiration both from North America and continental Europe, needs to find its own approach.

It has become something of a truism that British politicians, whatever their party affiliation, have not 'understood business' (usually meaning large corporations). The present administration has appeared to listen closely to high profile businesspeople but also faces other political pressures, for example from the environmental movement and the trade unions. In *Jihad v McWorld*, an essay on the conflict between global capital and local culture, Benjamin Barber writes: 'Democracies prefer markets but markets do not prefer democracies.'[52] Just as democracy and the rule of law help free markets to operate effectively, it is for the democratic process to control the operation of markets, in Britain as elsewhere. In turn, regulation provides a stable

---

50 See eg Fukuyama, F, *Trust: The Social Virtues and the Creation of Prosperity*, 1995; Bidault, F, Gomez P-Y and Marion, G, *Trust: Firm and Society*, 1997.
51 Gabor, A, *The Capitalist Philosophers*, 2000, p 330.
52 Barber, B, *Jihad v McWorld*, 1997, p 243.

framework for the operation of business. This is the significance of new company law for the whole UK.

Will Hutton's view is that:[53]

> If a firm could trust its shareholders to refuse a takeover offer while its profits were temporarily depressed during a period of investment or restructuring, then it would be more likely to go ahead with the action. If workers knew that in a recession they could trust the firm not to lay them off (as long, say, as they offered some temporary wage cut in return), then it would be worth their while to retrain and upgrade their skills. Trust is the key ingredient to stop contract capitalism dissolving into a hire and fire, slash and burn market jungle.

In a similar vein, Professor Tom Cannon writes:[54]

> When executive management does not trust its investor groups to back its judgement and let it manage, it will lose confidence in its ability to succeed. Often this will prompt conspicuous consumption, overhead – to cover every option – and risk avoidance. When shareholders do not trust executive managers to act with proper diligence they will lose confidence in their ability to prosper. This produces increasing demands for more information, power and action. Together they create a vicious circle of decline.

If all parties can be confident that the board is taking proper account of all relevant interests in its leadership of a public company, a virtuous circle with mutually beneficial interchange of ideas and efforts becomes more likely to develop. When difficult choices have to be made by the board, they will enjoy the confidence of those affected and can work with these groups to find constructive solutions. The perceived need for yet more specific legislation and regulations to protect employee, consumer, environmental and community interests may also be reduced. With greater board openness and accountability, all-round satisfaction with business performance can be increased. Existing public companies in the UK, as well as models from other jurisdictions, have shown this process at work over long periods. What is now required, as the DTI's Company Law Green Paper acknowledged,[55] is to bring others up to the standard of the best companies for the benefit of all their stakeholders.

---

53 Hutton, W, *The State to Come*, 1997, p 31.
54 Cannon, n 20 above, p 139.
55 DTI Consultation Paper, *Modern Company Law for a Competitive Economy*, March 1998.

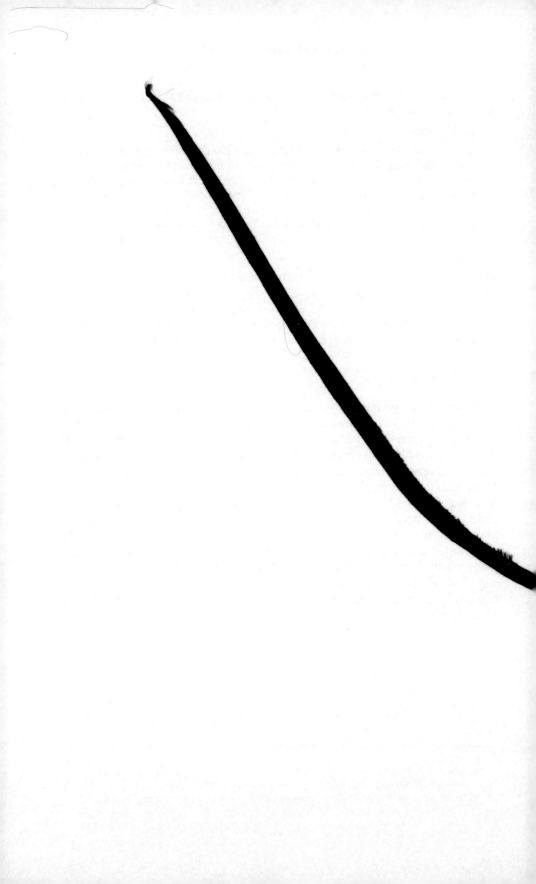

CHAPTER 2

THE NATURE OF THE COMPANY

2.1 THE ORGANIC THEORY OF THE COMPANY

The separate legal personality of the company is at the very heart of modern company law.[1] If a venture fails, it is this device that enables entrepreneurs and investors to enjoy limited liability; if the business succeeds, it permits a company to outlive its first leaders and develop in ways the founders could hardly have imagined.[2] It is, therefore, perhaps surprising that economic and legal theorists should have questioned the concept that a company has a genuine independent existence, distinct from that of its members, directors, employees or lenders.[3] Yet the notion of the company as a real entity has long been a matter of academic dispute.

The conduct of public companies themselves, not only in targeting customers but also in training employees and dealing with suppliers and neighbours, fosters the idea of a consistent, identifiable unit with dependable, enduring values. The desirability of setting clear goals for the company is expressed in many popular management texts.[4] There has been considerable academic research on the cultures of business organisations and their impact on economic performance.[5] It is the employees 'in the front line' who must act out corporate codes and policies that are usually formulated by directors. In relation to public companies specifically, two initial observations may be made:

(a) companies have, and seek to have, social identities and appear to believe that these images will have an impact on their performance;[6]

---

1 'The company is at law a different person altogether from its subscribers' *Saloman v Saloman & Co* [1897] AC 22, *per* Lord Macnaughton; 'The undertaking is something different from the totality of the shareholdings' *Short v Treasury Commissioners* [1948] AC 534, *per* Evershed LJ.

2 See Collins, JC and Porras, JI, *Built to Last*, 1994, for selected examples and discussions of 'clockbuilding' and core values.

3 *Lee v Lees Air Farming* [1961] AC 12 (a sole director and major shareholder may also be an employee of a company); *Macaura v Northern Insurance Company* [1925] AC 619 (property owned by a company does not legally belong to its members).

4 Eg Peters, TJ and Waterman, RH, *In Search of Excellence*, 1992.

5 Eg Kotter, JP and Heskett, JL, *Corporate Culture and Performance*, 1992; Casson, M, *The Economics of Business Culture*, 1991; Denison, DR, *Corporate Culture and Organisational Effectiveness*, 1990; Brown, AD, *Organisational Culture*, 1995.

6 At the time of writing, for example, environmental pressure group Greenpeace had launched a campaign against Exxon Mobil and other US oil companies highlighting their apparent opposition to the intergovernmental Kyoto Protocol on climate change, a campaign expected to hit Exxon's non-US sales.

(b) it is the board of directors that sets the tone and the targets in a major public company, just as the partners (or perhaps more accurately, equity partners) do in professional firms.[7]

In the name of the company, premises will be leased, staff employed and contracts made to purchase supplies and sell products. The company can protect its own legal interests (for example, by suing overdue creditors) and is subject to liabilities (for example, to pay Corporation Tax) in its own right. Griffiths notes:

> Public companies have evolved into organisations which are far more powerful and autonomous than would have been possible without the governance structure provided by the standard legal model, and their size and longevity has enabled them to exploit other facilities provided by the law, such as property rights, contracts and subsidiaries, to a much greater extent. The contribution of law to the development of public companies is a basis for arguing that there is a legitimate public interest in their affairs which justifies some form of public accountability beyond mere accountability to shareholder 'owners'.[8]

The organisation's purposes are independent of those of individual participants. Sheikh and Rees comment:[9] 'The modern corporation is perceived as a 'caring corporation' which discharges social as well as economic obligations' so that, for instance, plant closures may cause protests in affected communities, even if they appear to be commercially justifiable,[10] while charitable activity is widely supported, even if unconnected with the main business goal. Furthermore, these companies function as public institutions, in that their impact on the economic and social environment is inevitably substantial (as are decisions on the location of production).[11] Whether as extractors of primary materials, users of technology in manufacturing industry or retailers who define Britain's townscapes, they have a great impact on national life (and some have attempted to expand across Europe).[12] White makes the point as follows:

> The language of making money is wholly inadequate, even in the most conservative view – especially in the most conservative view – as to what goes on and should go on in the business world. In my view, the proper way to talk about this is to subordinate economic language to a formula such as the

---

7   See for example 'Can Sir Christopher [Bland, the new Chairman] rescue BT?', ft.com discussion, May 2001.

8   Griffiths, A, *Corporate Governance and the Uses of the Company*, 1993, p 5.

9   Sheikh, S and Rees, W, *Corporate Governance and Corporate Control*, 1995, p 2.

10 The recent controversy (April 2000) over BMW's disposal of Rover's operations at Longbridge in the West Midlands are a prominent case in point.

11 Bowe, C, Heckel, M, Peel, M and Shrimsley, R, 'Motorola Faces the Prospect of Repaying £17m: Government to Seek Aid Clawback after US Telecoms Giant Sacks 3100 Workers', 25 April 2001, front page.

12 Dombey, D and Voyle, S, 'Marks & Spencer Claims Clearance on Belgian Jobs', *Financial Times*, 25 April 2001.

following: 'The business corporation should always endeavour to act as a responsible citizen in its economic and other activities.'[13]

The question of possible changes to the law to reflect a socialised view of corporations will be discussed in Chapter 5. If directors themselves take the view that they have both private and public obligations, any new legislation would do well to acknowledge both sets of concerns.[14] The organic theory of the company provides a firmer basis than the alternative models for separate legal personality and the powers of the directors. It is to their considerable autonomy that attention now turns.

2.1.1 Separation of ownership and control

Senior executives gained *de facto* control of most widely held industrial companies from the First World War onwards, as dispersed, passive shareholders lost the ability and inclination to exercise any real hegemony. Recognising this phenomenon as long ago as the beginning of the 1930s, Berle and Means in their text *The Modern Corporation and Private Property*[15] famously suggested that top managers might use their considerable freedom of action to address social concerns in running major corporations. Herman points out that there may nevertheless be variations in and constraints on managerial activity:

> There is ... an ambiguity in the managerialist premise, which tells us that management controls, but leaves open the question of the determinants of and the limits to managerial authority. The premise is thus sufficiently elastic to accommodate a range of possibilities, extending from unrestricted managerial discretion to levels of constraint that raise questions about the extent and even the reality of management control.[16]

Not only markets for capital (financial and technological), labour (managerial and operative) and products but also governmental and public regulation, are capable of constraining management's discretion. Since the 1970s in the UK, there has, for example, been far greater employment and consumer protection by law than Berle and Means would have contemplated when writing in the pre-Second World War US. More recently, Bauman argues that transnational corporations have an interest in the weakening of the nation state. 'Weak, quasi-states can be easily reduced to the (useful) role of local police precincts,

---

13 White, JB, 'How Should We Talk About Corporations? The Languages of Economics and of Citizenship' (1983) 94 Yale Law Journal 1416, 1424.

14 As Wolfe, A, 'The Modern Corporation: Private Agent or Public Actor?' (1993) 50 Washington and Lee Law Review 1673, 1693 asserts.

15 Berle, AA and Means, GC, *The Modern Corporation and Private Property*, 1932, revised edn 1968.

16 Herman, ES, *Corporate Control, Corporate Power*, 1981, p 14.

securing a modicum of order required for the conduct of business, but need not be feared as effective brakes on the global companies' business.'[17]

In law, subject to these limits, the public company board is invariably given the power to make all day to day decisions.[18] Directors are subject to no instructions from the shareholders or anyone else in their daily work.[19] Almost universal among the larger public companies is the practice, expressly permitted by the 'standard form' of corporate constitution,[20] of delegating routine matters to an executive committee, which runs the organisation between full board meetings – and this despite political opposition from major companies to formal two-tier boards in the UK. Shareholders place their funds in the hands of the executive, in principle under the regular scrutiny of the full board, while employees, suppliers and customers must accept directorial decisions (within the limits of the law) or avoid dealing with the company.

The retention of capital to finance corporate growth has been a cornerstone of the modern industrial system, facilitating technological progress and social change. Major US corporations from the 1890s through to the 1950s, and Japanese and German industrial groups since then, appear to have had more freedom to reinvest their earnings than their British counterparts, which are far more obviously subject to the disciplines and constraints of an active stock market.[21] Nevertheless, in the UK as elsewhere, it is the directors who declare company dividends, and in reality they have discretion to withhold considerable sums of profit for investment. This capital accumulated from retained profits 'belongs' to the shareholders in law only once a dividend has been declared.[22]

With over 70% of shares in UK quoted companies now held by financial institutions (such as insurance companies, pension funds, unit and investment trusts), there has been some reconcentration of corporate membership in recent years. Even so, a study in the early 1990s found that the four largest institutional shareholders could not have carried a resolution on their own in any of the large listed companies examined and they would have succeeded alone in only a limited number of medium-sized companies,[23] while there are severe practical obstacles in the way of building a coalition of five or more members. Moreover, so long as others can be found to purchase their shares, investing institutions are usually disinclined to involve themselves in

17 Bauman, Z, *Globalization*, 1998, p 68.

18 Companies (Tables A to F) Regulations 1985 (SI 1985 No 805), Table A Art 70.

19 Eg *John Shaw & Sons (Salford) Ltd v Shaw* [1935] 2 KB 111 CA; *Scott v Scott* [1943] 1 All ER 582.

20 Companies (Tables A to F) Regulations 1985 (SI 1985 No 805), Table A Art 72.

21 Lazonick, W and O'Sullivan, M, 'Big Business and Corporate Control' in Warner, M, *International Encyclopedia of Business and Management*, 1996, p 365.

22 Marris, R, 'The Economic Theory of "Managerial" Capitalism' in Archibald GC, *The Theory of the Firm*, 1971, p 301.

23 Stapledon, GP, *Institutional Shareholders and Corporate Governance*, 1996, pp 111–16.

company management. While the dividend expectations of major investors are usually understood by management, it can be argued that such requirements are not different in kind from other factors, such as pay demands and customer requirements, which executives and the board must address when planning corporate strategy. The author's discussions with corporate officers demonstrated an awareness among the majority of the need to maintain an appropriate balance.

2.1.2 Power relationships

The organic model of the public company envisages it as a truly public sphere where the choices of contracting parties are not always sovereign. One cannot ignore externalities occasioned by corporate activity for which none of the beneficiaries pays (for example, environmental pollution, health risks). Those who may be affected by the company's present activities well into the future or in an unpredictable fashion cannot easily contract with its management to deal with those risks. Without regulation, those who manage corporate business, except to the extent that specific legislation applies, could therefore disregard the social and environmental consequences of its activity.

If obedience to the law is to be treated as having value above and beyond profit and loss calculations, the purely private element is already being supplemented by rules that do not arise from contract. The state's right to set bounds to activity carried out in the name of private profit is also being acknowledged. The optimum level of violations of the law is itself not zero in the 'profit maximisation as the agents of the shareholders' version of directors' duties. If compliance would increase costs or reduce sales, thereby damaging corporate profits, and there is no legal penalty that would cost as much (taking into account the likelihood of being caught), from an economic perspective the directors should break the law. This is clearly not a view to which any of the pubic company officers to whom the author has spoken would subscribe!

Very large companies are not always subject to market pressures in their product pricing, nor sometimes in salary rates and materials prices. As controversy over bank charges and petrol prices in the UK during 2000 showed, such companies are 'price-makers' rather than 'price-takers'. Competition policy (in the EU and also under the Competition Act 1999 in Britain) aims to deal with cartels and abuses of monopoly or oligopoly positions, but it acts slowly and will not in itself prevent employee and supplier dependence. The executives of public companies are taking the decisions that shape the futures of customers, employees and suppliers as well as neighbours. A narrow view of corporate responsibility without acknowledgment of these political factors is surely unrealistic in modern circumstances. Dr Noreena Hertz, among many others, points out that business entrepreneurs are increasingly using their money and influence to solve social problems, with many of which the elected politicians seem increasingly unable to cope. She asks: 'While the business of government seems more than ever to be business, is the business of business by contrast increasingly becoming that of government?'[24]

Power imbalances are inherent in the organisation of production itself. Potential employees in areas of job shortages and small supply firms needing orders in competitive markets will not be able to propose, let alone to dictate, terms to public companies. In other circumstances, from consumer protection to judicial review, UK law intervenes to prevent or curtail potential abuse of power. Governmental action is subject to scrutiny in court and it is submitted that that of public companies is no less a matter of genuine and legitimate public concern.

2.1.3 Managerial theory

The corporate form is a legal vehicle for business which, together with employment contracts and trade connections, produces a combination of continuity and flexibility. Historically, this contributed to the rise of incorporated business over the partnership form in the UK. In their writing on behavioural studies for business and management, Fincham and Rhodes link work culture explicitly to an 'organic' concept of organisational reality and suggest that this fosters employee commitment.[25] Internalised goals, which employees have 'made their own', and a sense of common purpose between them are said to produce an adaptive organisation, which, in turn, enables work habits and authority structures to be modified according to changing demands.

Buchanan and Huczynski, when commenting on organisational behaviour, point out that for common values, beliefs and forms of behaviour to evolve, a reasonably stable group of people needs to 'share a history' at work, including dealing with problems. A company provides the setting for such collective history and learning, which in turn produces a culture and pattern of work that can endure.[26] New employees are socialised into the culture, customers and suppliers develop a clear idea of what to expect and, importantly, potential investors can choose whether to 'buy in' to the approach chosen by management. Companies that survive and thrive tend to have strong traditions and leaders.

---

24 Hertz, N, *The Silent Takeover*, 2001, p 169.
25 Fincham, R and Rhodes, PS, *The Individual, Work and Organisation*, 2nd edn 1992, p 412.
26 Buchanan, D and Huczynski, A, *Organizational Behaviour*, 3rd edn 1997, p 519.

2.1.4 Implications for social activism

A recognition of the power already wielded by major companies leads to caution by way of the 'specific competence' argument, which runs to the effect that business should stick to its economic task and avoid seeking social influence which it is not qualified to handle.[27] Since this applies to charitable giving and community projects outside the company's normal sphere of activity, it does not preclude attention to constituencies that participate in, or are affected by, those usual business activities. Charitable giving often purports to serve some strategic business purpose, but the outcome of donations is often not specifically measured as the results of other expenditure would be. Since management appears to have a relatively free hand in choices of donations and sponsorship, restraint by law may seem to be reasonable.[28] The rationales for corporate charitable donations are usually that the company, as a major force in the community, has a responsibility to 'put something back' and that the image of the company is improved by such deeds. Shareholders have not so far objected to the (admittedly modest) sums of UK public companies' charitable giving,[29] despite the lack of proof that such donations do bring financial benefits to the company.

Those who view public companies as autonomous and powerful institutions are more likely to favour allotting to them a wide range of social responsibilities, from fair treatment of employees, consumers and suppliers, to showing respect for their neighbours and the local and global environment. Individuals conducting business in a community are held accountable for their actions and made to pay (in loss of business) for any breach of communal rules. Public companies, wielding greater social and economic influence, stand in need of no less exacting treatment in law. Allen writes:

> The social model (of the corporation), in one of its weaker forms, is highly consistent with the managerialist concept of the firm that has, in fact, dominated the real world of business and politics since the great depression. That view sees senior management as empowered to give fair consideration to workers, communities and suppliers as well as to suppliers of capital.[30]

If the political element in the independent life of corporations is lost, the will for adopting any regulatory initiative can be lost with it. In the case of the privatised utilities, for example, it was found that the original model of 'light

---

27 Cannon, T, *Corporate Responsibility*, 1994, pp 37–44.

28 Clarke, J, 'Shareholders and Corporate Community Involvement in Britain' (1997) 6 Business Ethics: A European Review 201; G Moore, 'Corporate Community Involvement in the UK – Investment or Atonement?' (1995) 4 Business Ethics: A European Review 171.

29 Fogarty, M and Christie, I, *Companies and Communities: Promoting Business Involvement in the Community*, 1990.

30 Allen, WT, 'Contracts and Communities in Corporation Law' (1993) 50 Washington and Lee Law Review 1395.

touch' regulation did not satisfy public demands and more needed to be done to acknowledge and protect the needs of consumers and satisfy community expectations.[31] The corporation exists through the survival of political and social accommodations with business. It needs to be recognised that the current regime is one policy choice; there could be others.[32]

2.2 THE NEXUS OF CONTRACTS THEORY OF THE COMPANY

There is a group of theorists in law and economics who see the company purely in terms of contracts made between the various participants, each for their own assumed benefit. The legal fiction of the company merely provides a vehicle to enable activities to be arranged at lower cost than in a 'spot market' for labour and supplies. Market sourcing of factors of production can be very costly. Having employees and equipment ready each working day to perform the tasks the management deems necessary represents a significant advance in efficiency.[33]

The notion of companies as voluntary associations of self-seeking individuals has strong intuitive appeal. Within the firm itself, contracts are generally set to run for a longer timescale than is the case with outsiders, but this is because both parties to each exchange rationally value certainty above flexibility. If they are to perform their task efficiently (that is, to compete in the open market on strictly economic terms) it is argued that they should be free of any non-essential constraints in their initial bargaining. A system of free contracting is said to move resources (including labour and materials) to their most highly valued use. There may be a place for legal intervention where imperfect information limits the rationality of decision making by a party or where there is some potential for dishonest or self-serving conduct, but very seldom otherwise.

The fact that shareholder approval is required for major transactions and for changes to the company's constitution seems to support the proposition that members contract with the management for the company to be run as the shareholders choose. In the public company setting, however, there are great

---

31   Eg Hain, P, 'Regulating for the Common Good' (1994) Utilities Law Review 88; see now the Government's Consultation Paper, tellingly entitled *A Fair Deal For Consumers*, on regulation of utilities.

32   Albert, M and Gonenc, R, 'The Future of Rheinish Capitalism' (1996) 67 Political Quarterly 184 gives an overview of a different system.

33   RH Coase's classic paper 'The Nature of the Firm' (1937) 4 Economica 386 discusses market costs and co-ordination costs in detail; OE Williamson's later contribution 'The Logic of Economic Organisation' (1988) 4 Journal of Law Economics and Organisation 65 extends and refines the basic approach.

practical difficulties in the way of effective instruction or monitoring by the shareholders. Griffiths notes: 'There is a significant co-ordination problem to overcome before the shareholders can act collectively and a large body of shareholders is in any event only suited to the crudest kind of decision making.'[34]

As Brudney puts it: 'Scattered stockholders cannot, and do not, negotiate with owners who go public (or with management – either executives or directors) over hiring managers, over the terms of their employment, or over their retention.'[35] One should note that similar arguments could be put forward in relation to employees and suppliers, except for example, trade unions, trade associations). As there is no single contracting party that negotiates to protect the interests of the local community or the natural environment, those interests are not represented in public company boardrooms. The notion that all affected parties are present at the bargaining table, let alone that they all have real opportunities to contribute, is illusory. All direct participants have a choice of whether to involve themselves in the company or not, but economic circumstances may limit their realistic options; other affected constituencies are currently absent, both from the establishment of the company and from its structures thereafter.

Managers contract personally with the company (for their own pay and conditions) and also deal with contractual arrangements made on its behalf. In a public company, the terms on which shareholders invest are set by managers for acceptance by those who decide to purchase its securities, just as individual employees and suppliers may not, realistically, be able to negotiate changes to the standard form contracts of large corporations. The board must oversee the use of resources *in toto* and the terms and conditions on which the company does its business. This co-ordination needs to reflect a long-term view, even if individual arrangements are made primarily for immediate advantage.

2.2.1 Transaction costs

If all the contracts needed to sustain production were precise and specific as to future requirements – what workers were to do, how managers were to act, the terms of provision of capital and what suppliers were to deliver – there would be no cost benefits to creating a company as compared with negotiating each contract separately. Since it is to reduce production costs that the corporate vehicle is used, there must be a zone of discretion for management as the business progresses. The principal advantage of the

---

34 Griffiths, n 8 above, p 4.
35 Brudney, V, 'Corporate Governance, Agency Costs and the Rhetoric of Contract' (1985) 85 Columbia Law Review 1403, 1412.

employment contract is that an employee can be required to perform any one of a whole range of functions, depending on current needs. Similarly, the benefit of the delegation of decision making by shareholders to executives is precisely that the shareholders do not have to spend time considering corporate decisions.

Given the existence of such presumptively efficient discretion, someone must decide how it should be exercised and in public companies the management, and ultimately board members, take on the task. They can choose to pursue any of a whole range of policies – for example, they may aim for high sales volume at modest prices or high profit margins on more expensive goods, focus the business on a core set of activities or pursue a range of diverse opportunities, expand production in new areas or close down existing sites of operation.[36] As the law stands, employees, suppliers and the community will have little influence on such choices, despite being directly affected by them. Investors will enter membership of the company if they approve of an existing policy and exit if things change to their distaste.

2.2.2 The contract with shareholders

Law and economics experts Fama and Jensen note that 'open corporations' (quoted public companies in UK terms) are characterised by use of unrestricted common stock[37] – that is, ordinary shares, which do not carry any obligation to become involved in company management and are freely alienable. Such stock is said to be attractive to finance the start of complex, relatively risky activities and to facilitate capital investment by its capacity to supply 'large amounts of wealth from residual claimants on a permanent basis'. The authors hypothesise that such separation of residual risk-bearing from decision management leads to the separation of decision management (by executives) from decision control (by directors), in order to control the discretion of managers.[38] The arrangement whereby investors provide funds to be utilised by managers is assumed to be advantageous for both sides despite (or perhaps because of) the indeterminate nature of the agreement. Relationships between executives and major investors show concern with strategy, particularly when mergers and acquisitions require members' consent.[39] The level of remuneration for executives remains a concern of

---

36 The Annual Reports of Dixon Group and Argos, John Waddington and Beresford plcs show examples of different approaches.

37 Fama, EF and Jensen, MC, 'Separation of Ownership and Control' (1983) XXVI Journal of Law and Economics 312.

38 *Ibid*, 322.

39 Eg O'Connor, A, 'ON Digital's Give-away suffers poor Reception', *Financial Times*, 14 April 2001; Benoit, B, Dombey, D, O'Connor, A and Targett, S, 'EMI set for Clash on Virgin's Future', *Financial Times*, 1 May 2001, front page.

shareholders despite the involvement of non-executives in setting management pay.[40]

The contract with shareholders is said to mandate the directors to set objectives, oversee management and return profits to shareholders. In practice, where a public company is concerned, shareholders will know the business strategy and main activities of the companies in which they invest – institutional investors are well qualified to obtain and evaluate this information and professional advice is available to individuals. A choice is made between different industrial sectors and different managerial approaches (and indeed different countries). The investors do not expect to dictate terms of business – it is a matter of 'standard form' contract. It may not be in the long-term financial interest of the shareholders that employees and equipment be mistreated or neglected, suppliers and customers antagonised or that the standing of the company in the community should suffer. Furthermore, investors may be content knowingly to put their money into a company that sets out to do more than the legally prescribed minimum in terms of social and environmental standards.[41]

2.2.3   Firm-specific investments

The notion that shareholders, as residual risk-bearers for the company, should enjoy special privileges is widespread. In fact, it is not only shareholders who make firm-specific investments, for example, employees may devote time to training which is of use only in the firm[42] and suppliers may invest in machinery to meet customer requirements. It is more practicable for shareholders to spread their risks by diversification than it is for employees, and often for suppliers, to deal with several firms. The potential for exit is very much greater in developed stock markets than in tight job markets or highly competitive supply situations.

Even Milton Friedman, so well known for his restrictive definition of corporate social responsibility as profit maximisation within the 'rules of the game' (as set by law and custom),[43] notes the unique quality of the collection of factors in a firm:

---

40   Eg Targett, S, 'Boards get the Message on Bonus Culture', *Financial Times*, 21 April 2001; Dowling, A, 'Revolt over Reuters Chief's Pay Deal', *Financial Times*, 25 April 2001, front page.

41   Websites such as those of the UK Social Investment Forum (www.uksif.org) and Shareholder Action Action Service (www.thesasuk.com), www.corporate-register.com and www.ethicsforuss.org.uk provide information for investors.

42   For a discussion of the employment contract in relational terms, see Van Wesel Stone, K, 'Labour Markets, Employment Contracts, and Corporate Change' in McCahery, J, Picciotto, S and Scott, C, *Corporate Control and Accountability*, 1993, p 61.

43   Friedman, M, 'The Social Responsibility of Business is to Increase its Profits' in White, TI, *Business Ethics: A Philosophical Reader*, 1993, p 162.

If these (profitable) firms could be reproduced by assembling similar collections of hired factors, there would be an incentive to do so. The fact that (in long-run equilibrium) there is no tendency for new firms to enter means that they cannot be reproduced, implying that the firms own some specialized factors.[44]

Some firms fend off new competition because they have developed particular combinations of factors, which are extremely difficult to emulate. If it were possible to contract in the market to secure the same labour and materials, as Friedman points out, others would do so. They cannot, because not all the relevant information can be encapsulated in the language of formal contract – continuing relationships add value.

Where, for the reasons discussed above, all the details of a contract are not set out *ab initio*, there may be profits to be gained for shareholders from action going against the spirit of previous arrangements with employees, suppliers and even customers. Takeovers produce premiums for target shareholders, it has been argued, because others associated with the company lose out on the long-term arrangements they had made with the ousted management team.[45] If breaches become commonplace, it seems likely that other parties will start to insist on more closely defined terms and greater short-term rewards (for example, employees who do not believe promises of job security will demand higher salaries, while suppliers will want higher prices for quick returns) The whole corporate structure, which facilitates and largely depends on retention of profits for future growth, then comes under threat.

Managers themselves invest their time and personal reputation in their chosen company. This in itself gives them an incentive to plan for the future of the business. After a prolonged incumbency, their value in the labour market is linked with the performance of the company, for better or for worse. Since they presumably will not wish to be forced to move job, their contract implicitly contains a bias towards long-termism.

2.2.4 Implications for social activism

With the acceptance of contractualism very often comes what is sometimes called the 'Shareholders' Money' argument[46] – the assertion that it is an improper deprivation of investors to allocate resources to employees, suppliers, community involvement or environmental protection, beyond what market forces absolutely demand. Nor may those who are entrusted with investors' money exercise personal preferences to the detriment of profit

---

44 Friedman, M, 'Theory and Measurement of Long-Run Costs' in Archibald, n 22 above.

45 Coffee, JC, 'Shareholders versus Managers: The Strain in the Corporate Web' (1986) 85 Michigan Law Review 1 assesses the winners and losers in this situation.

46 Parkinson, JE, *Corporate Power and Responsibility*, 1993, pp 333–35 *et seq*.

maximisation. This presupposes that the contract between the shareholders and managers acting on their behalf requires that profit be extracted by any means (or perhaps, more correctly, by any legal means), as otherwise the executives would not be meeting their obligations to shareholders. Non-executive directors, in particular, are said to be responsible for monitoring management on behalf of members. Quite apart from the fact that many shareholders (including the millions of small investors represented by financial institutions) may choose to see social and environmental standards upheld even at the expense of maximising their monetary returns, it seems far from clear that they should have the right to profit from actions that go against other interests in the economy and society. Contracts with key parties also contain implicit understandings as well as explicit terms, all of which can be said to require respect if the integrity of commerce itself is ultimately to be upheld.[47]

The proponents of the 'nexus of contracts' theory at times deploy it to deny that the corporation can partake of any responsibility in society. All the participants on this view are sheltered from moral responsibility by the contracting process itself. Fischel argues:

> A corporation ... is nothing more than a legal fiction that serves as a nexus for a mass of contracts which various individuals have entered into for their mutual benefit. Since it is a legal fiction, a corporation is incapable of having social or moral obligations much in the same way that inanimate objects are incapable of having these obligations.[48]

None of the human persons responsible for making the decisions about activities, which produce corporate profits, on this reasoning, is required to take account of these other considerations, so long as those directly involved (employees, customers, suppliers) have voluntarily agreed prices. A business upon incorporation is said to undergo a qualitative change that takes it from a realm of individual or joint and several liability to one where there is no effective locus of accountability.[49] The directors are relieved of the financial responsibilities of ownership although they are making the decisions. Shareholders enjoy limited liability and do not involve themselves in management.

In no sense are conscious contracts made with all the participants in a company – for the most part they do not know they have made contracts and

---

47 In Jacobs, J, *Systems of Survival: A Dialogue on the Moral Foundations of Commerce and Politics*, 1993, pp 37–40, 'Respect Contracts' is discussed as a precept of the 'Commercial Syndrome' on which it is said trading is based.

48 Fischel, DR, 'The Corporate Governance Movement' (1985) 35 Vanderbilt Law Review 1259, 1273.

49 Stone, CD, *Where the Law Ends: The Social Control of Corporate Behaviour*, 1975, spells out the difficulties of maintaining ethical sensibility and legal accountability in large corporations; see also Goodpaster, KE and Matthews, JB, 'Can a Corporation Have a Conscience?' [1982] Harvard Business Review 132.

would not recognise the idea if it were suggested to them.[50] Economic issues remain important for regulators, but they can take a far broader view than is implied by talk of trying to fill in contractual 'gaps'. The board is the co-ordinator at the centre of the whole web of contracts. In a public company, then, there is no *a priori* reason why the directors should seek to favour one party with whom they deal over others.

2.3 THE AMERICAN LAW INSTITUTE AND THE UK EXPERIENCE

In extremely protracted and controversial deliberations, the American Law Institute (ALI) grappled with these fundamental issues of corporate law and their implications for 'model' regulation. When the ALI's Principles of Corporate Governance were finally published in 1992, it was probably inevitable that they would advance a compromise solution. The Principles' governing section on The Objective and Conduct of the Corporation contained two distinct subsections. The first, 2.01(a), reads as follows:

> Subject to the provisions of subsection (b) and Section 6.02 (Action of Directors That Has the Foreseeable Effect of Blocking Unsolicited Tender Offers), a corporation should have as its objective the conduct of business activities with a view to enhancing corporate profit and shareholder gain.[51]

This appears to set the Principles squarely on a contractarian, stockholder-centred footing.

> However, the second part, 2.01(b), states:

> Even if corporate profit and shareholder gain are not thereby enhanced, the corporation, in the conduct of its business:
>
> (1) Is obliged, to the same extent as a natural person, to act within the boundaries set by law;
>
> (2) May take into account ethical considerations that are reasonably regarded as appropriate to the conduct of business;
>
> (3) May devote a reasonable amount of resources to public welfare, humanitarian, educational and philanthropic purposes.[52]

Examples of ethical considerations that may be permissible are said to include responsibilities towards employees, customers, suppliers and members of the local community.

---

50 A point addressed by David Campbell in a seminar on the Theory of the Firm, Leeds University, 30 April 1998.

51 American Law Institute, 'Principles of Corporate Governance: Analysis and Recommendations', 1992, 55.

52 *Ibid.*

2.3.1   Evaluation of the Principles

In his review of the Principles, Eisenberg regards the two part approach as basically satisfactory, since each part reflects an important truth of corporate life:

> The business corporation as an instrument through which capital is assembled for the activities of producing and distributing goods and services and making investments. Accordingly, a basic premise of corporation law is that a business corporation should have as its objective the conduct of such activities with a view to enhancing the corporation's profit and the gains of the corporation's owners, that is, the shareholders [the premise underlying subsection 2.01(a)] ...[53]

> A second premise of corporation law is that in pursuing the profit objective, the corporation should conduct itself with regard to the fact that it is a social as well as an economic institution. Accordingly, the pursuit of corporate profit and shareholder gain must be constrained by social imperatives and may be qualified by social needs [the premise underlying subsection 2.01(b)].[54]

On this view, it is accepted that shareholders are the owners of the company and directors are their agents. In appropriate cases, the company may temper profit-seeking zeal with evidence of a social conscience. While the reference to 'social imperatives' suggests obedience to law and is assumed to be mandatory, the suggestion of voluntary restraint where 'social needs' are in issue is a little more problematic. It is far from clear in this model when the economic duty can be overridden for ethical reasons.

In contrast, Mitchell criticises the ALI on the grounds that, by trying to pacify both sides of the debate, it ended up not satisfying anyone and producing an incoherent result:

> If the values (to be served by corporate regulation) were enhanced efficiency in the interests of stockholder owners, then it would be difficult to quibble with the convincing arguments put forward by the contractarian school. If, on the other hand, corporate regulation is to serve a more explicitly public-directed purpose, market efficiency is not determinative ...[55]

> Instead of asking the fundamental question of what corporate law should achieve, the ALI seems to have proceeded on the fallacious assumption that this question is best left unanswered. The ALI has thus produced a set of statements that combine all aspects of the current debate in unhappy discord.[56]

---

53   Eisenberg, MA, 'Symposium on Corporate Governance: An Overview' (1992) 48 The Business Lawyer 1271, 1275.

54   *Ibid*, 1276.

55   Mitchell, LE, 'Private Law, Public Interest? The ALI Principles of Corporate Governance' (1992) 61 George Washington Law Review 871, 879.

56   *Ibid*, 880.

The Illustrations to section 2.01 clearly show that the combination of its two subsections in fact gives the top decision makers in companies complete discretion with very little guidance. For instance, it is said that a corporation may choose to honour a contract that is technically unenforceable, on the ethical ground that seriously made business promises should be kept and therefore 2.01(b)(2) applies.[57] On the other hand, if the corporation decides not to honour the contract, it will be acting in accordance with 2.01(a).[58] There is no breach of the Principles either way. To quote another example, a corporation may purchase an annuity for a long-time worker who is incapacitated by an accident, because ethical considerations suggest making provision for an employee in such circumstances and therefore the expenditure can be justified under 2.01(b)(2).[59] If the corporation does not make such provision, 2.01(a) will apply.[60] Neither course of action would depart from the Principles. This indicates that trying to embrace both points of view is not helpful in practice.

2.3.2 UK company law reform

The UK government's Consultation Paper on Company Law Reform contained only brief reference to the responsibilities of directors and the 'stakeholder' debate, without any significant commitment or evaluation:

> A wider issue for the review is whether directors' duty to act in the interests of their company should be interpreted as meaning simply that they should act in the interests of the shareholders, or whether they should also take account of other interests, such as those of employees, creditors, customers, the environment and the wider community.[61]

The Company Law Review Steering Group's subsequent Strategic Framework Document gave fuller consideration to these issues, in a manner which placed great weight on the practical difficulties seen to stand in the way of what it called the more 'pluralist' options.[62] The Law Commission, in reporting on directors' duties, took a technical approach which attempted to avoid the whole controversy.[63] In a reference to s 309 of the Companies Act 1985, the

---

57 Principles of Corporate Governance, n 51 above, Illustration 11 at 64 (even disregarding possible economic gains from enhanced reputation).

58 Principles of Corporate Governance, n 51 above, Illustration 12 at 64.

59 Principles of Corporate Governance, n 51 above, Illustration 13 at 66 (setting aside the possibility of improved employee morale adding to profits).

60 Principles of Corporate Governance, n 51 above, Illustration 14 at 66.

61 DTI Consultation Paper, *Modern Company Law for a Competitive Economy*, March 1998, para 3.7.

62 Company Law Review Steering Group, *Modern Company Law for a Competitive Economy – The Strategic Framework*, February 1999, para 5.1.

63 Law Commission, *Company Directors: Regulating Conflicts of Interest and Formulating a Statement of Duties*, September 1999, p 8.

Draft Statement of Directors' Duties contains a bland statement that: 'A director must have regard to the interests of the company's employees in general and its members.'[64]

The Hampel Committee Report, in contrast, was much more definite in its conclusion that shareholder returns must be the priority for boards:

> The single overriding objective shared by all listed companies, whatever their size and type of business, is the preservation and the greatest practicable enhancement over time of their shareholders' investment.[65]

Business organisations, particularly City institutions and major corporations, would use this function as a defence against regulation of all kinds.

The Company Law Review Steering Group's first major Consultation Paper in 1999 placed considerable emphasis on the efficiency of the system and its favourable ranking by business in an international marketplace.[66] The Review sought to produce an outcome attractive to company directors themselves.[67] The emphasis was therefore on deregulation.

The Final Report published by the Steering Group in 2001 contains a statement of directors' duties, which states that:

> The 'material factors' (which a director is to take into account where a person of skill and care would consider them relevant) are –
>
> (a) the company's need to foster its business relationships, including those with its employees and suppliers and the customers for its products and services;
>
> (b) the need to have regard to the impact of its operations on the communities affected and on the environment; and
>
> (c) its need to maintain a reputation for high standards of business conduct.
>
> (d) its need to achieve outcomes that are fair as between its members.[68]

This is, however, all subject to the overriding requirement that:

> A director must in any given case – (a) act in the way he decides, in good faith, would be most likely to promote the success of the company for the benefit of its members as a whole.[69]

---

64 *Ibid*, 184.

65 Committee on Corporate Governance (Chair: Sir Ronald Hampel), *Final Report* (January 1998), para 1.16.

66 DTI, n 62 above, para 4.7.

67 Company Law Review Steering Group, *Modern Company Law for a Competitive Economy – Final Report*, July 2001, para 1.13.

68 *Ibid*, Annex C, Sched 2, para 2, note (2).

69 *Ibid*, Annex C, Sched 2, para 2(a).

While attempting 'to spell out the "inclusive" nature' of directors' overriding duties[70] and even emphasising that well-managed companies already adopt this approach,[71] the Steering Group rejected the idea of omitting the reference to members (which in effect maintains shareholder primacy).[72] This contrasts with the inclusion of the importance of long-term business planning.[73] It is submitted that, certainly for public companies, this approach is inadequate. These matters and details of drafting will be pursued in Chapters 5 and 6.

It should be noted at this point that UK company law has already recognised that two non-shareholder constituencies may be taken into consideration in the running of companies. As briefly noted above, under s 309(1) of the Companies Act 1985, it is the duty of directors to have regard to the interests of the company's employees in general, who nevertheless do not have *locus standi* to challenge board decisions in the courts. The duty to employees is not enforceable by employees themselves, but by members taking derivative actions, making it unlikely to have much practical impact.[74] When a company is no longer solvent, or arguably when it is approaching insolvency, the residual risk falls on creditors who are ahead of the shareholders in the distribution queue for the remaining assets. The directors at that point owe their fiduciary duties to the creditors.[75] Exclusive directorial accountability has thus not been reserved to shareholders for quite some time (if it ever was). This is, of course, aside from the voluminous environmental and planning and health and safety legislation and regulation to which all boards must pay close attention.

In its report at the end of 2000, the Steering Group attempted to clarify its intentions as regards directors' duties and stated:

that the hierarchy of obligations is:

1   to obey the constitution and decisions of the company which bind the director;

2   to promote what he calculates in good faith to be likely to promote success for members' benefit; and

---

70 Company Law Review Steering Group, *Modern Company Law for a Competitive Economy – Developing the Framework*, March 2000, para 3.55.

71 *Ibid*, para 3.58.

72 *Ibid*, para 3.52.

73 *Ibid*, para 3.54.

74 But see for example *Re Welfab Engineers* [1990] BCLC 833 in which directors accepted an offer for purchase of their ailing business from a buyer who was prepared to continue the business and preserve employment, rather than a higher cash offer for the premises. Hoffmann J (as he then was) held that the directors were not liable to contribute to the insolvency because they acted properly in taking employment into account.

75 See *West Mercia Safetywear Ltd v Dodd* (1988) BCLC 250 where it was said (at 252) that creditors in insolvency 'become prospectively entitled, through the mechanism of liquidation, to displace the power of the directors and the shareholders to deal with the company's assets' (*per* Dillon LJ).

3   as part of that process, to take account of the factors (after identifying and assessing them in accordance with his duty of skill and care) which he believes in good faith to be relevant including (where he believes them relevant) the matters listed in paragraph 1c [emphases added].[76]

References to the whole supply chain and to issues of community and environmental impact were all confirmed as being worthy of note even in a general statement of duties.

The Steering Group stated in 2001: 'Effective management and control of resources requires a decision making process which takes into account of all the factors relevant to the outcome'.[77] To a limited extent, the proposed statement of duties is 'inclusive' in its scope. However, the framework is one of overall shareholder primacy. Chapter 6 will discuss the 'ranking' of director's various obligations in public companies and particularly the place of shareholders.

On the general question of whether any particular set of corporate governance arrangements should be mandatory, Easterbrook and Fischel argue that the corporate regime ought to provide a set of default rules – 'off-the-rack' terms which can be used by parties to avoid the cost of negotiating 'from scratch'.[78] In small private companies where there is discussion between all the participants, this may be plausible. Where a public company is involved, both the practical difficulties of realistic contracting and the wider importance of the organisation lead to the conclusion that arrangements should reflect social and political requirements.[79] This points to the need for a mandatory governance system with effective enforcement mechanisms.

In order to meet the demands of the national economy and of wider society, the purpose to be served by company law needs to be defined. Property rights, contractual expectations and political authority all have parts to play. If the shareholders of public companies are indeed regarded as their owners and directors as agents to pursue their interests, any legal restraint on the pursuit of profit becomes difficult to justify. If the whole notion of ownership is treated as problematic, there is space to explore the totality of power relations that define the company.

---

76 Company Law Review Steering Group, *Modern Company Law for a Competitive Economy – Completing the Structure*, November 2000, para 3.20.

77 Company Law Review Steering Group, n 67 above, para 1.23.

78 Easterbrook, FH and Fischel, DR, 'The Corporate Contract' (1989) 89 Columbia Law Review 1416.

79 See eg Eisenberg, MA, 'The Structure of Corporation Law' (1989) 89 Columbia Law Review 1461.

2.4 OWNERSHIP OF THE PUBLIC COMPANY

The concept of the company as the property of the shareholders has underpinned the argument that directors have a duty to maximise profits and coloured the perceptions of many directors as to their responsibilities. The idea does not sit easily with the observation that shareholders are no more committed to the public company than other parties, including employees. Nor does it square with the underlying assumptions of the nexus of contracts model or the organic model. If public companies can be said to be 'owned' at all, it is submitted that that shared 'ownership' rights must extend beyond shareholders.

In relation to quoted public companies, the shareholders have voluntarily ceded part of their surplus capital to be used in the business, in the hope and expectation that the rewards from so doing will surpass those from safer investments such as savings accounts and government stock. Public company shares with diffuse ownership became in reality a source of steady income carrying little risk of loss and not attached to any participation in company management. It is anomalous and unwarranted to leave rights of control in the hands of shareholders alone when their interest is increasingly difficult to distinguish from that of other lenders.[80] Annual returns on equity are, of course, more variable than those on loan capital, but the increased possibility of periods without returns is balanced by the expectation of higher rewards when times are good. The level of risk preferred, and hence the type of investment chosen, is a matter for the investor. With a balanced portfolio, furthermore, a predictable stream of income can be assured from equity investment alone, since reductions in one company's dividend will generally be offset by increases in another.

Partners in professional firms (such as UK lawyers and accountants) can successfully retain ownership because they can co-operate on an equal footing and all are capable of sharing management control. Other firms, such as complex manufacturing and volume retailing, require far greater volumes of capital than one entrepreneur or group could normally provide and need specialist managers – this was the genesis of the public company. Public company equity investors are likened by management expert Charles Handy to punters at the races, who choose a likely prospect and bet cash on it. They know the 'form' and something of the prospects of the company they choose and the potential returns are connected, if imperfectly, to the risks undertaken.[81] If targets are not met, they are free to 'back another runner'. There is no expectation of direct involvement from day to day, just as stabling

---

80 A point addressed by Paddy Ireland in a seminar on the Theory of the Firm, Leeds University, 30 April 1998.

81 Handy, C, 'What is a Company for?' in *Beyond Certainty*, 1996, pp 63–66 (text of lecture delivered at the RSA in 1990).

and training of horses is left to others by gamblers on racing. Punters are not owners. The pressures for returns and shareholders' automatic right to sell out can impede business success in the long term.

In law, each member has a set of rights and the shares are the holder's property, but the company is not. The only way of securing a return of capital to members is by the break-up of the company. An experienced observer of corporate governance, Jonathan Charkham, also resorts to a gambling metaphor:[82] '[S]hares in a company are not a special form of gambling chip, but part ownership of a living organisation', usually intended to endure for generations. Even when controlled by experienced fund managers, however, shares have not been deployed in a way that reflects this view.

2.4.1 Institutional investors

With the concentration of public company holdings in the hands of the large institutional investors, the potential for active and knowledgeable shareholder involvement appears to have grown, challenging the Berle and Means thesis, which was based on a more dispersed and ill-informed membership. In fact, UK institutional investors have so far shown little appetite for close involvement in the management of the public companies in which they invest.[83] Dialogue between management and large shareholders in private keeps executives appraised of the requirements of institutions, but without any consideration of the impact of decisions on other parties, including the other shareholders. Shareholder intervention has been by action late in the day to change a completely discredited management.[84] Furthermore, most institutions sell out of problem companies far more frequently than they intervene.[85] The position at present does seem to be one of institutional investor power with little acknowledgment of responsibility.

The volume of institutional holdings in UK quoted companies gives fund managers the potential to exert direct influence. If those managers are pressing for distribution of short-term profits, the increasing weight of their votes adds to the uncertainties faced by other constituencies. It remains

---

82 Charkham, J, *Corporate Governance and the Market for Companies: Aspects of the Shareholder's Role*, 1989, p 4.

83 Parkinson, JE, 'Company Law and Stakeholder Governance' in Kelly, G, Kelly, D and Gamble, A, *Stakeholder Capitalism*, 1997, p 144; Stapledon in his study of the issue, n 23 above, p 281 states that: '99.24% of quoted UK companies were (each year) untouched by serious institutional intervention during the early 1990s. While it is undoubtedly true that the great majority of quoted UK companies are managed well, it is hard to believe that only seven-tenths of one per cent suffer from very poor management.'

84 Stapledon, n 23 above, pp 122–29.

85 Black, BS and Coffee, JC, 'Hail Britannia? Institutional Investor Behavior Under Limited Regulation' (1994) 92 Michigan Law Review 1997, 2053 quote a 10:1 ratio of sale over action estimated by a fund manager.

practically difficult for them to co-ordinate their efforts to engineer changes in top management, but an individual holder with a notifiable interest[86] can affect the price of shares, and therefore board prospects and often directors' remuneration, by selling. While inadequacies in the present system of information and consultation to and from shareholders may need to be rectified if they are to play their proper role in the life of public companies, nothing can make them act as true owners if they do not want to do so.[87] Measures designed to increase the accountability of directors to such powerful capitalists will in effect decrease the responsiveness of public companies to society. Fund managers who are subject to competitive quarterly performance measurement make unlikely committed investors, as Charkham has commented:

> [I]f fund managers do see themselves as being under such short-term pressures it must preclude their taking a long-term view of most companies in their portfolios and of establishing relationships with them. The more they are inclined to view the shares they hold as trading counters the less they will be sympathetic to the longer term view which is concerned with the underlying quality of a business and its management.[88]

The Hampel Committee Report, like Cadbury, counsels consideration of an 'active voting policy' and endorses the idea of 'dialogue' between companies and institutions about objectives,[89] without proposing to place any obligations on shareholders. Short and Keasey perceive a contradiction at the heart of expectations of greater institutional shareholder involvement and commitment:

> In their role as major shareholders, the Cadbury Report expects institutions to take the role of the large shareholder, who will monitor company management on behalf of smaller shareholders. Hence, in this context, institutions are expected to take a long-term view of their shareholding positions, and, where necessary, incur expenditure in intervening to correct mismanagement. However, in their role as investors, institutions need to be free to move funds around in order to find the best returns for the beneficiaries of those funds. In this respect, it is difficult, certainly in the current ideological free-market climate, to argue that institutions should continue to hold equity positions in problem companies and incur additional expense intervening in management ...[90]

---

86 Three per cent or more of the nominal value of the share capital (Companies Act 1985 s 199).

87 Davies, PL, 'Institutional Investors in the United Kingdom' in Prentice, DD and Holland, PRJ, *Contemporary Issues in Corporate Governance*, 1993, pp 88–93, points out that intervention is only one of a range of possibilities, including sale, in cases of concern, and fund managers select the most cost-effective option.

88 Charkham, n 82 above, p 12.

89 Hampel, n 65 above, para 5.

90 Short, H and Keasey, K, 'Institutional Shareholders and Corporate Governance' in Keasey, K and Wright, MJ, *Corporate Governance: Responsibilities, Risks and Remuneration*, 1997, p 26.

An institution may, however, come to own a holding that is too large to be disposed of without affecting the share price. Such 'lock-in' to a mature blue-chip company is not an entrepreneurial business risk but an investment decision. The presence of established shareholders can assist the stability of the enterprise and its investment and planning. If those members are primarily interested in a predictable rate of return, it does not mean that they will be inclined to intervene in the running of the company. Fund managers have their own businesses to run and targets to meet. The level of returns demanded by UK institutions has for decades been far higher than that of any other major industrialised country[91] and this has led to considerable misgivings about their influence. Other stakeholders, it is said, are treated unfairly because of dividend pressures from institutions. The focus of attention now broadens to take in those other participants.

2.4.2 Other 'owners'?

In order for business to continue and develop, a company needs to be assured of an appropriate quality and quantity of all the factors of production – labour, supplies, financial capital and organisation. No one input provider is properly entitled to claim ownership (where this is defined as 'possession' and 'proprietorship') when every input is necessary to the continuation and success of the business. Ownership itself is not a readily applicable concept where the functioning of the organisation depends on the assemblage of the appropriate parts. Universities and hospitals carry out their complex functions without an owner at all; surely public companies could get along equally well likewise, argue Kay and Silberston.[92]

Professor Michael Porter (of Harvard Business School) argues that the concept of ownership should be expanded to embrace not only shareholders, but also directors, managers, employees and customers and suppliers. He asserts that expanded ownership will foster commonality of interest and help to make investors aware of 'spillovers', such as more highly-skilled workers, that strengthen firms and also benefit related industries and the economy as a whole.[93] It is suggested by Porter that significant 'owners' (that is, of stock), customers, suppliers and community representatives be nominated to the board so as to broaden its perspective. Such proposals for direct inclusion of stakeholders will be further discussed in Chapter 7.

---

91 Hutton, W, *The State We're In*, 1996, pp 160–62.

92 Kay, J and Silberston, A, 'Corporate Governance' (1995) National Institute Economic Review 84, 87–88.

93 Porter, M, 'Capital Choices: Changing the Way America Invests in Industry' in Chew, D, *Studies in International Corporate Finance and Governance Systems*, 1997, p 14.

It is important to recognise the claims of these groups and their entitlement to proper consideration by directors. When all have different and sometimes conflicting interests, it is perhaps less than helpful to label these entitlements as amounting to 'ownership'. The law often permits ownership rights to be divided between several claimants, for example by creation of leases of land and life interests in funds. At the end of the period of devolution, however, there is a freeholder or remainderman with the right to dispose of the property, rather as the Takeover Code is designed to ensure that the majority of shareholders determine the outcome of a hostile bid for a public company.[94]

In the 'nexus of contracts' explanation of companies, while participants own and choose to sell a company their individual contributions, nobody can actually own the totality, since the company itself is treated as an 'efficient fiction'. In the 'organic' explanation, the preservation and welfare of the corporate enterprise come before the claims of any individual stakeholder. Both major theories of the corporation thus refute the argument that the shareholders are the owners of a public company with some claim to automatic priority in decision making. Freed from the constraints of ownership, those who are running and supervising public companies can plan for corporate life well beyond their individual tenures.

2.5 RELATIONSHIPS AND THE COMPANY

The reasons for choices made by customers, suppliers, employees and investors deciding between dealings with rival companies are difficult to identify with certainty. In the real world, there is not time to perform detailed analysis and investigation of records before each contracting decision, even if the individual has the knowledge required to make such assessments.[95] Parties therefore rely heavily on anecdotal and experiential evidence in choosing with whom to deal. Those companies known to have produced good results for the individual or group concerned in the past are taken to be likely to do so again. Failing these, corporate reputation comes into sharp focus.

The well known 'prisoners' dilemma' situation occurs when two parties to a given deal would both make themselves better off by co-operating. However, the co-operative act will entail some initial risk and neither party is willing to take the first gamble, since he or she is unsure that the other party will co-operate in turn. Both, therefore, are lead by their self-interest to settle

---

94 Paul, A, 'Corporate Governance and Takeovers' in Prentice and Holland, n 87 above, pp 139–43.

95 Cyert, J and March, J, *A Behavioral Theory of the Firm*, 1992, discuss the role of rules and routine in decision making within firms and also the problems posed by bounded rationality and individual opportunism.

for a result where both have get less than they could have gained by co-operation.[96] A repeated (or 'iterated') prisoners' dilemma game increases the prospects for and benefits of such co-operation between players.[97] In the corporate setting, Jacobs describes 'a great web of trust in the honesty of business' on which gossamer thread 'much that we take for granted in business' hangs.[98] The fostering of relationships of mutual confidence is the way to ensure that co-operation grows in the face of the 'prisoner's dilemma'.

A supplier's investment in new technology to meet the requirements of a particular customer and an employee's investment in training in company processes are examples of investments that are unlikely to be made in the absence of such trust. The company that wishes to succeed by building supplier partnerships and maintaining a well-trained workforce has an incentive not to renege on deals with its workforce and partners, just as it has good reason to keep delivering reliable returns which enable it to gain access to capital.[99] The development of relationships of confidence is, in fact, the way to avoid losing out from insecurity in the free-market environment. If the company is known for aggressive exploitation of all possible opportunities to cut costs and pursue profit, it is likely that that development will not take place. Adding value to materials and labour is the essential point of business. The alternative, cutting costs in order to 'beef up' profits for investors, is problematic for the UK in a tough international environment.[100]

The assets of public companies include their reputations, customer loyalty and supplier connections and the skills and commitment of employees. These advantages are not susceptible to ownership in the sense of possession or proprietorship and as matters stand they are not valued on the balance sheets.[101] Yet they do affect the profitability of the enterprise's operations and its equity value (since the share price of a functioning company will exceed the value of its physical property). The corporate image consists of more than logos and colourschemes – it covers the impression generated by a company's products, premises, people and publicity.[102] It is important for the board to

---

96 A lucid outline is Hofstadter, D, 'The Prisoner's Dilemma and the Evolution of Cooperation' in Castro, B, *Business and Society*, 1996, pp 183–90; see also Jones, TM, 'Instrumental Stakeholder Theory: A Synthesis of Ethics and Economics' in (1995) 20 Academy of Management Review 404, 412–15.

97 One of the most accessible and entertaining descriptions of Prisoners' Dilemma games I have yet read is in Richard Dawkins' *The Selfish Gene*, new edn 1989, Chapter 12.

98 Jacobs, n 47 above, p 5.

99 Hosmer, LT, 'Trust: the Connecting Link Between Organizational Theory and Philosophial Ethics' (1995) 20 Academy of Management Review 379, 386.

100 Cf Porter, M, Takeuchi, H and Sakakibara, M, *Can Japan Compete?*, 2000.

101 Sheikh, S, *Corporate Social Responsibility and Practice*, 1996, Chapter 9, discusses corporate social reporting and social audit provisions to broaden management's perspective.

102 Eg Smyth, J, Dorward, C and Reback, J, *Corporate Reputation: Managing the New Strategic Asset*, 1992; Dowling, GR, *Corporate Reputation: Strategies for Developing the Corporate Brand*, 1994.

ensure that the desired corporate personality is being projected to all parties who deal with the public company.

2.5.1 Customers

There has been increasing attention in many sectors to customer-base analysis and building up customer loyalty, by means that range from supermarket discount cards to bank product cross-selling. Marketing is expected to enhance existing relationships as well as to seek new ones.[103] Honest dealing, fair treatment and attention to the needs and wants of each client are vital if repeat orders and customer recommendations are to be secured. In the service industries in particular, a well known and highly respected name is a valuable asset. As far as suppliers to industry and commerce are concerned, there is a desire to be associated with long-established and well-regarded major customers, not only for security but also for prestige. Technical specifications and delivery requirements are naturally a matter for both parties working co-operatively.

Customer demand has induced new developments including 'just in time' delivery and comprehensive 'zero defects' systems. Constant attention to customers is proclaimed as a key feature of most business strategies. Relational strategies develop this the next logical step further from traditional market research approaches. Supply of a product, traditionally seen as a 'one shot' transaction, is now quite often regarded as the start of a continuing relationship, for example in computing. Supply of materials in relational contracts demands quality and reliability. Companies that offer the reassurance of a substantial history and time spent getting to know individual customers can go on to reap rewards in increased sales from repeat business and client recommendations.

2.5.2 Employees

So far as employees are concerned, if they do not feel part of a trustworthy network of internal relationships, or if they do not understand the direction and objectives of the organisation, they are unlikely to deliver their best work. As Solomon puts it, summing up the thinking of many managerial researchers and organisational psychologists:

> What makes a corporation efficient or inefficient is not a series of well-oiled mechanical operations but the working interrelationships, the co-ordination and rivalries, team spirit and morale of the many people who work there and

---

103 Koiranen, M, 'Custopreneur Coalitions in Relationship Marketing' in Nasi, J, *Understanding Stakeholder Thinking*, 1995, pp 184–87.

are in turn shaped and defined by the corporation ... Employees of a corporation do what they must to fit in, to perform their jobs and to earn both the respect of others and self-respect.[104]

If the image and aims of a company do not fit in with those of the most able people for its jobs, the company will not retain the best workers. If working relationships and communication within the company are not personally satisfactory, employees will again be de-motivated and may choose to leave, particularly when the economy is strong. Full-time, long-term employment has been reduced in the UK over the past 20 or so years. People hired on a consultancy basis or those combining a part-time job with other paid or unpaid work quickly need to know the ethos of the company and to feel that they are valued if they are to give their best contributions while working for it.[105]

2.5.3 Supply networks

Between themselves, companies are building up their relationships in ways that challenge the traditional boundaries of the firm.[106] The impetus for this comes from both sides: suppliers who wish to be more responsive to their customers and so gain greater regularity in their business and purchasers who aim for greater quality assurance and price stability. Examples often quoted are the Japanese *keiretsu* system and the German industrial networks, which are said to have produced greater long-term economic success than Anglo-American competitive contracting. If it works well, the network produces the benefits of co-ordination and yet avoids the costly bureaucracy of a single vertically integrated firm.

Technological advances and product improvement can be facilitated by co-operation between companies through the production chain, as the Japanese experience seems to demonstrate well. Professor Ronald Dore has studied the Japanese system in detail and notes three major advantages to long-term relational supply contracting:

> First, the relative security of such relations encourages investment in supplying firms ... Second, the relationships of trust and mutual dependency make for a more rapid flow of information ... Third, a by-product of the system is a general emphasis on quality. What holds the relation together is a sense of mutual obligation.[107]

104 Solomon, R, 'The Corporation as a Community' in Castro, n 96 above, p 195.

105 Handy, C, 'The Coming Work Culture' in n 81 above, pp 23–28.

106 Teubner, G, 'The Many-Headed Hydra: Networks as Higher-Order Collective Actors' in McCahery, Picciotto and Scott, n 42 above, p 41.

107 Dore, R, 'Goodwill and the Spirit of Market Capitalism' in Buckley, PJ and Michie, J, *Firms, Organisations and Contracts*, 1996, p 375.

2.5.4 Economic advantages

Why are jobs with some companies, but not with others in the same sector, eagerly sought after by able graduates and managers? Why do suppliers set great store by the winning and retention of contracts with particular companies and not so much with others? Expectations of reasonable continuity, fair dealing and high standards, usually built up over time, all provide part of the answer. The public company develops a unique personality and an institutional framework that would be extremely difficult for others to replicate.[108]

When a company builds up a relationship with its customers in the retail sector, it is clear that reputation leads directly to added value: branded goods sell for higher prices than their generic alternatives, even where the products are identical for all practical purposes.[109] Where services are concerned, franchises from fast food to photographic processing succeed because a recognised name enables a business to do well in new locations.[110] Differences in the cost of capital between apparently similar firms arise because trust and relationship effects influence lenders. The price and quality of materials also has an obvious impact on financial returns and these may be improved if companies invest in committed relationships with their suppliers and thereby gain better long-term deals than their competitors.[111]

The public company will become far more adaptable if it can expand its labour force quickly to meet demand and can work with other organisations to extend its geographical and technical sphere of operations. If it has a reputation for fair dealing and integrity, the company will be more able to find high-quality workers and partners when it needs them. This will be a great competitive advantage in a fast-changing business world, as Goldberg and Sifonis note.[112] The public company is a set of strategic relationships. When any of them fall down, corporate development may suffer. Professor John Kay has discussed the 'architecture of a company's relationships' as a crucial factor in business success,[113] while the 'inclusive approach', emphasising customer, employee and supplier involvement and community relations has been studied and promoted by the Centre for Tomorrow's Company following the RSA's Tomorrow's Company study.[114]

---

108 Kreps, DM, 'Corporate Culture and Economic Theory' in, *ibid*, pp 246–50.

109 See Clifton, R and Maughan, E, *The Future of Brands*, 2000, conclusion and *passim*.

110 See Klein, N, *No Logo: Taking Aim at the Brand Bullies*, 2000, introduction and *passim*.

111 Deakin, S, Lane, C and Wilkinson, F, ' "Trust" or Law? Towards an Integrated Theory of Contractual Relations between Firms' (1994) 21 Journal of Law and Society 329.

112 Sifonis, JG and Goldberg, B, *Corporation on a Tightrope*, 1996, pp 63 *et seq*.

113 Kay, J, *Foundations of Corporate Success*, 1993.

114 Goyder, M, *Living Tomorrow's Company*, 1998, Chapter 6.

Where does this leave the duties of directors? The board has responsibility for developing the overall policy and strategy of the company. Board members must set the tone for management decisions and the conduct of employees throughout the company's operations. This involves taking account of the interests of all constituencies and acknowledging responsibility for all the impacts of the company's activities. Proper assessments need to be made of relationships and restraint exercised as far as possible where the consequences of proposed changes would be undesirable for a key participant. This is stakeholder management in action.[115]

2.6 CONCLUSION

The nature of the public company has been the subject of controversy for almost 70 years, and indeed since chartered trading companies first emerged with monopoly power and the capacity to raise funds from the public.[116] The leaders of public companies do appear to exercise their freedoms to explore various different routes – some dedicating themselves to shareholder returns by whatever business they can be produced, others devoted to delivery of customer service or technological leadership.[117] In the midst of this diversity and against a fast-changing commercial and social background, the law has given little guidance. The company has been treated as a private domain with incursions to address issues of employee rights, consumer protection, environmental impact and so on as the political climate has dictated. Public companies are designed to provide a reliable investment vehicle and often do so by aspiring to leadership in a particular market. They have, of course, no mandate to carry out charitable activity as such, but they are expected (by many consumers, employees and investors) to set high standards of conduct in business.

Professor Paul Davies, in the latest edition of *Gower's Principles of Modern Company Law*, distinguishes two functions of profit-making companies. On the one hand, there are those formed 'to enable a single trader or a small body of partners to carry on a business' in which 'the members retain control and share the profits.' On the other side are those companies whose function is 'to enable the investing public to share in the profits of an enterprise without taking part in its management' and used 'to facilitate the raising and putting to use of capital by enabling a large number of owners to entrust it to a small

---

115 Freeman, RE, *Strategic Management: A Stakeholder Approach*, 1984, sets out the practical process of stakeholder analysis and management.

116 Davies, PL, *Gower's Principles of Modern Company Law*, 6th edn 1997, pp 21–27.

117 As examples, the Annual Reports of Wassall, House of Fraser, Smiths Industries, Delta, ASDA and Peugeot plcs show different orientations.

number of expert managers'.[118] These two uses of corporate form are different in kind, and quoted public companies (small in number but dominant in economic strength) fall into the second category. The law needs to acknowledge that large, 'open' companies are distinct from small close companies. The latter do behave as real organic entities and depend on lasting relationships if they are to grow and prosper.

The separate legal personality of the company is an aspect of commercial life that deserves to be taken more seriously than it has been. Certainly it means that directors and other executives should not treat the company as 'their' property and it is appropriate for them to be held to strict standards of conduct and prohibitions against self-dealing. Logically, it also means that shareholders have no right to control the company for their own exclusive benefit. The continuing healthy existence of the public company in order to produce particular goods and services is an end in its own right and is best pursued by developing the relationships needed for corporate success.

It is true that contracts of employment, leases of premises and agreements for the purchase and sale of materials and products respectively determine the daily activities of the company to a large degree. However, these arrangements are generally moulded to a predetermined pattern to fit the individual requirements of the company and rely on understanding rather than detailed explanation. Nor can the part played by legal rules, both those of company law and other regulation of business, be disregarded. Thinking in terms of reliance on private contracts alone is a considerable over-simplification of the reality found in public companies.

Companies have their primary economic function and also wider tasks in accordance with the social practices and expectations of their particular period and location. Where shareholding is diversified (by small individual holdings or through the institutions that represent millions of UK investors), the shareholders as a body will be broadly representative of social experience and expectations. They will not wish to see damage to the economy, which may result from supplier or employee maltreatment, nor would most of them want to be party to abuse of consumers or the environment. Stakeholders, in short, frequently deal with companies in more than one capacity and ultimately always respond to them as individuals.

As a reflection of political will, the law could do more to stamp democratic requirements on the deliberations of directors. This has been done with much social and environmental regulation from the Environmental Protection Act 1990 to the Employment Relations Act 1999.

The analysis of relationships with customers, employees and suppliers, whilst also acknowledging the wider social and environmental context,

---

118 Davies, n 116 above, p 10.

provides the best vehicle for understanding the activities of public companies today. These relationships are richer and more complex than mere contractual terms and, over time, they define the individual company as an institution. Shareholders cannot 'own' a public company, whether the latter is conceived of as a hypothetical bundle of contracts or a social entity. It is the trust of all key stakeholders that makes any enterprise a lasting success and this can only be gained by treating them all with respect and justice. The treatment of and payments to different constituencies will depend on the nature of the relationship that has been put in place. There are interests that should not be overridden in the pursuit of profits.

Quantitative, non-financial information, as well as qualitative financial reporting, is relevant to and is needed by both corporate managers and stakeholders in public companies. Some companies' Annual Reports discuss the employees other than in a perfunctory manner, but many do not; some give a picture of customer profiles and demands, while others do not; a few discuss their supplier relationships, so far as relevant, though most do not. Reporting on community involvement and environmental impact is at present largely confined to major retailers and primary producers and seems to be motivated mainly by possible public relations benefits. In a stakeholder approach, managers are seen as the agents of multiple stakeholders instead of the shareholders alone. Directors must monitor progress from the standpoint of all stakeholders and be prepared to engage in open dialogue with many relevant groups. The role of the board of directors will be the subject of Chapter 3.

THE ROLE OF DIRECTORS

3.1 THE FOCUS OF BOARD ATTENTION: STRATEGY VERSUS MONITORING

If legal input to directors' duties is to be relevant and useful, legislators must be clear about what the public company board is intended to achieve. The key to the role of directors is the allocation of their working time. Active involvement by the board in managerial issues has to some extent to be traded off against the independence required to monitor the executive. In the first instance, somebody must give instructions as to the activities of the company and its manner of working. Where there is no 'owner-management' to decide business priorities, it must be for the board to set business targets and plan for the long term. Management is then focused on meeting those targets and keeping company operations running smoothly. Several guides to directorship (for example, those of Professor Colin Coulson-Thomas,[1] Sir Adrian Cadbury,[2] Sir Geoffrey Mills[3] and the Institute of Directors[4]) emphasise that directors are distinguished from management by their longer time horizon and broader strategic outlook. All counsel that directors should not be appointed merely because they have succeeded in management roles or served in executive posts, but because they have the capability for oversight.

That said, a public company board, which meets monthly or 10 times per year can expect to make only a small number of important decisions itself. Most of the time, directors are reliant upon their managers to deliver the outcomes they have set for the organisation. Delegation cannot, in law, become abdication of duty. Responsibility for key administrative and financial matters rests with directors, who face personal liability or disqualification from directorship if filing requirements are persistently not complied with, or if fraudulent or wrongful trading prejudices creditors.[5] The presence of a well-qualified, reliable team of managers is no justification for the neglect of the monitoring task. The theory is that oversight by directors motivates executives to perform well and to follow company policy faithfully. It is also for the

---

1   Coulson-Thomas, C, *Creating Excellence in the Boardroom*, 1993, Chapter 4.
2   Cadbury, A, *The Company Chairman*, 2nd edn 1995, pp 30–37.
3   Mills, G, *Controlling Companies*, 1988.
4   Institute of Directors, *Guidelines for Directors*, 6th edn 1995, pp 19–22.
5   Insolvency Act 1986 ss 213–14; Company Directors (Disqualification) Act 1986.

board as a routine matter to put in place systems that measure progress towards the goals it has set. There is some danger with infrequent directorial meetings of new issues being discussed while ongoing projects are not kept effectively under review.

In any public company, the board as such will not be running daily operations and it would be unrealistic to frame directors' duties in those terms. Nevertheless, the notion that a public company director has no responsibility even to attend board meetings,[6] nor to bring to bear any particular expertise in the service of the company,[7] is no longer supportable (if it ever was). In line with the strictness of their fiduciary duty not to make personal profits from corporate assets (including information), a requirement that all board members, both executives and particularly non-executive directors, be attentive and thorough in supervising managerial action meets modern investor expectations. This supervision clearly includes particular attention to the chief executive, which is unlikely to be forthcoming if he or she is also chairman and the board is filled with compliant executives and ill-informed non-executives.

It is not denied in mainstream management literature[8] that directors must consider and develop all relationships that are relevant to the future success of the company. Managerial systems for analysis of stakeholders have been set out in some detail over the past 15 years or so.[9] They require directors to communicate with the key parties and to ascertain their interests and establish priorities between them. Within a given company, it would be for the board to establish the pattern of stakeholder analysis, just as the directors would take overall responsibility for any strategic management system. Garratt suggests:

> The harder edged aspects of strategic thinking include, for example, the thoughtful positioning of the business so as to achieve an optimum impact on its changing markets. It requires that a significant amount of time be put aside by directors to design and regularly monitor the broad changes taking place in the external environment.[10]

Following the World's Most Respected Companies Survey carried out among business leaders by the *Financial Times* at the end of 2000, it was noted that the 'winners' were admired for widely different reasons. Leadership, innovation, product range, social and ethical responsibility, marketing and focus on customers were all mentioned as important reasons for admiration of different companies (including GE, Microsoft, Sony, Coca-Cola, IBM and

6   *Re Cardiff Savings Bank* [1892] 2 Ch 100.
7   *Re Brazilian Rubber Plantations and Estates Ltd* [1911] 1 Ch 425.
8   Nor by the Hampel Committee Report (see section 3.5 below) paras 1.16–1.17.
9   Carroll, AB, *Business and Society: Ethics and Stakeholder Management,* 2nd edn 1993; Freeman, RE, *Strategic Management: A Stakeholder Approach,* 1984.
10 Garrett, B, 'Directing and the Learning Board' in M Boisot, *East-West Business Collaboration,* 1994, p 16.

Toyota). Returns to shareholders followed from these various attributes. Remaining inventive even while having a substantial market share was perhaps the key factor.[11]

Strategic exercises such as PEST[12] trend analysis and SWOT[13] analysis help to improve the long-range vision of the board and clarify thinking. The board must accept ultimate responsibility for the complaints and concerns of key stakeholders, including customers and employees and suppliers. If directors are extravagant in their own rewards at a time of general 'belt-tightening', or if they do not pay enough attention to corporate product and service quality, it is foreseeable that the company's relationships will be damaged.[14] Accountability towards key groups is therefore an important factor in controlling directorial self-dealing. Monthly meetings and presentations are clearly inadequate by themselves to keep directors in touch with all the relevant constituencies. Non-executive and executive board members need to spend time meeting employees and visiting customers, making themselves available to receive comments.

With no active owner in place, the public company board is the only organ that has the capability and opportunity to monitor the actions of management at the highest levels. Shareholders clearly benefit from this work of directors, but given that customers and employees and suppliers need to be satisfied and the community and the environment protected for the long term, monitoring has to be more extensive and sophisticated than just analysis of financial results. It may be appropriate for specialist input from particular board members and even separate committees to be used (such as standing groups on research and development in manufacturing, or sales and consumers in services). In Chapter 7, the question of whether these constituencies should have their own representatives on public company boards will be further considered. Even without such changes, public company directors are answerable to a wider audience than shareholders alone, as the board members themselves acknowledge in many Annual Reports. If they are to build up the company for the benefit of shareholders and other stakeholders, they must invest in relationships with other parties.

The monitoring task would be enhanced if modernised duties of skill and care and the long-term 'relational' approach were to be reflected in a new Companies Act. While in recent years, the courts' expectations of directors of major firms have gradually been rising, the position is still neither very clear

---

11 Skapinker, M, 'Diverse Qualities Vie for Attention', *Financial Times*, 13 December 2000.
12 Looking at Political, Economic, Social and Technological trends which may help or hinder the company.
13 Examination of Strength, Weaknesses, Opportunities and Threats of and affecting the company.
14 Barclays Bank plc has recently suffered media criticism for announcing the closure of many rural branches at the same time as proposing generous bonus and share option schemes for executives.

nor in line with investor and community expectations of those business leaders. Section 214 of the Insolvency Act 1986 is based on the assumption that directors will exercise the skill and care which are to be expected of a director in their position (the 'objective' element) and also any additional skills and qualifications that that director has (the 'subjective' element). In *Re D'Jan*[15] and *Norman v Theodore Goddard*,[16] the tests from the Insolvency Act were applied to the operations of corporate 'going concerns'. It was emphasised that delegation to competent officers is still permitted so far as regular operations are concerned. Specific standards are not effectively enforced against public company directors in respect of conduct affecting employees and customers, let alone the wider environment and community. The Law Commission's report suggested that the dual subjective and objective test be embodied in legislation.[17] It also recapitulated s 309 of the Companies Act 1985, giving a weak statement of responsibility to employees.[18]

In the US context, the Business Judgement rule protects directors from having their commercial decisions overturned in court if they obtained adequate information before reaching their final decision, had no personal interest in it and acted *bona fide* in what they rationally believed were the best interests of the company.[19] They must show that they made an effort to exercise their judgment and did not neglect their duty, for example by accepting management proposals without question. Advice given to US directors in the light of their law suggests that they should avoid rushing their choices, ensure they obtain and consider all material information, ask questions of management or consultants, keep records of discussions and take appropriate professional advice.[20] It would be beneficial if UK directors similarly knew the procedures they were expected to follow in making key decisions. UK courts are also, in practice, reluctant to interfere in board judgments, but the standard expectations of public company directors are rather less certain. A statement in legislation would make it plain to all boards that entrepreneurial freedom is bought at the price of compliance with directorial processes which inhibit self-dealing and encompass all relevant constituencies.

The so-called 'hypothetical bargaining' model of company law (where it is said that the aim of law is to reproduce the regulations the parties would themselves have agreed if they had had the time and farsightedness to debate

15 *Re D'Jan of London* [1994] 1 BCLC 561.
16 *Norman v Theodore Goddard* [1992] BCLC 1028.
17 Law Commission, Company Directors:*Regulating Conflicts of Interest and Formulating a Statement of Duties*, September 1999, 184.
18 *Ibid.*
19 American Law Institute, Principles of Corporate Governance: Analysis and Recommendations 1992, para 4.01 and notes.
20 Varallo, GA and Dreisbach, DA, *Fundamentals of Corporate Governance*, 1996, pp 33–36.

the issues) is inadequate because in real negotiations, managerial concerns often gain the ascendancy. Utset argues that current corporate structures primarily reflect executive concerns and interests.[21] Even if all parties would like to see a larger corporate pie, they will still disagree as to how the pie should be sliced – and managers, who have the best information and practical control of assets, will try to obtain as much as possible for themselves in salary and benefits.[22] This points once again to the need for a transparent, open system of decision making.

According to the agency theory of the firm (directors being cast as the agents of shareholders), the price the shareholders must pay for hiring managers to run the business on their behalf includes the costs of monitoring the potentially self-seeking behaviour of those managers.[23] It can hardly be expected that chief executives and their managerial subordinates will be able to take an unbiased view as a leadership team unless that team also has strong outside input. Beyond the shareholders, however, there is no reason why other parties affected by the company's deeds should be denied consideration in its regular process of decision making. Non-executive directors, if expected to give more time to their positions and exercise more true independence than many currently do, have an important role to play in enforcing fair dealing and broadening the public company board's outlook.

3.2 THE ACCOUNTABILITY OF THE BOARD: DELEGATES VERSUS CONSCIENCES

The notion that directors are the agents or servants of the shareholders and, as such, are obliged to follow their instructions does not accord with UK company law. Where powers of management are delegated to the board in the Articles of Association, the shareholders cannot usurp that authority.[24] Directors' fiduciary duties are owed to the company as a continuing entity, not to individual shareholders within it.[25] For example, in deciding whether to recommend acceptance of a takeover offer, the board can properly have regard to the interests of the company, which may or may not coincide with producing the greatest profit for current shareholders.[26]

---

21 Utset, MA, 'Towards a Bargaining Theory of the Firm' (1995) 80 Cornell Law Review 540, 546–47.

22 *Ibid*, 608–09.

23 *Ibid*, 550–51.

24 *John Shaw & Sons (Salford) Ltd v Shaw* [1935] 2 KB 113. The present 'standard form' Table A Art 70 provides that the board's power is subject to 'any directions given by special resolution'. This is unlikely to be relevant in a public company.

25 *Percival v Wright* [1902] 2 Ch 421.

26 *Dawson International plc v Coats Paton plc* (1988) 4 BCC 305 (Court of Session (Outer House)).

There is a set of transactions and activities for which the board is obliged by the Companies Act 1985 to seek the approval of members in general meeting. These include: dealings where the directors are encumbered by a conflict of interest (for example, substantial property transaction with a director,[27] long-term executive service contracts[28] and compensation for loss of office[29]) and major events in the company's development (for example, change of name[30] or objects,[31] increase[32] or reduction[33] of the company's capital and voluntary winding up[34]). In practice, however, the likelihood of shareholders rejecting a proposal made by the board is slim. The course of action is set by board members and public company shareholders who disagree with it are inclined to sell out, if they can still do so at a reasonable price, while other interest groups are overlooked.

So far as selection of directors is concerned, the members elect the directors and have theoretically unrestricted powers to dismiss them by ordinary resolution.[35] However, the Institute of Directors[36] and Sir Adrian Cadbury[37] acknowledge that candidates chosen by existing public company board members are almost universally re-elected without opposition. Nor does the power of dismissal carry much weight when executive directors would retain the benefit of long notice periods and substantial compensation under their service agreements. While a 'Just Vote No' campaign (against re-election of directors) may register a lack of enthusiasm for, or confidence in, the current regime,[38] it cannot change the board unless there is sufficient backing for an alternative 'slate' of candidates (and even then only one-third of the board will normally retire at each AGM, making it impractical for a 'dissident' group to gain control at once).[39]

British institutions, unlike the major banks in Germany, have little experience of putting forward names for board candidature, though there are

27 Companies Act 1985 s 320.
28 *Ibid*, s 319(3).
29 *Ibid*, s 312.
30 *Ibid*, s 28(1).
31 *Ibid*, s 4.
32 *Ibid*, s 121(4).
33 *Ibid*, s 135(1).
34 Insolvency Act 1986 s 84.
35 Companies Act 1985 s 303. In *Bushell v Faith* [1970] AC 1099, the House of Lords permitted the use of weighted voting rights in a small private company to enable a director – shareholder to defeat such a resolution. However, the Stock Exchange would not permit the inclusion of such rights in the constitution of a quoted company.
36 Institute of Directors, n 4 above, pp 36–37.
37 Cadbury, n 2 above, pp 58–59.
38 Monks, RAG and Minow, N, *Watching the Watchers: Corporate Governance for the Twenty-First Century*, 1996, pp 142–43.
39 Institute of Directors, n 4 above.

exceptions such as venture capital company 3i plc's practice of recommending experienced directors to support growing companies.[40] The law forbids directors to take decisions in the interests of a nominating shareholder (even a sole owner), rather than the company on whose board he or she serves.[41] On the other hand, a shareholding institution or company that appoints its employee to the board of another company is not vicariously liable for the decisions of that nominated director as such.[42] It is clear that, in law, all directors have the same allegiance and responsibility – to and for the present and future prosperity of the company itself.

By analogy with trustees, directors are not permitted to make a personal profit from their position unless the contrary is agreed in general meeting or allowed by the company's constitution.[43] Any major transactions with the company must be approved by the shareholders in general meeting and the director must declare (in a board meeting) any personal interest in any contract to be concluded by the company.[44] The Law Commission has recommended that the former safeguard should be retained but the duty of disclosure should be subject to exceptions, *inter alia* where a court is satisfied that 'the interest did not give rise to a real risk of an actual conflict of interest' or that 'the rest of the board were aware of the nature and extent of [the director's] interest before the directors approved the transaction.'[45] The Company Law Review Steering Group accepts these qualifications with minor amendments.[46] Lengthy service agreements are also subject to ratification by members and there is no automatic entitlement to remuneration for work done for the company.[47] The requirements for disclosure of remuneration have been made more extensive since the publication of the Greenbury Report in 1995,[48] though presentation of pension and share option arrangements in Annual Reports is often far from easy to follow. The Law Commission recommends that the upper limit on the length of service contracts permitted

---

40 Cadbury, n 2 above, pp 55–56.

41 *Scottish Co-operative Wholesale Society v Meyer* [1959] AC 324.

42 *Kuwait Asia Bank EC v National Mutual Life Nominees Ltd* [1991] 1 AC 187.

43 *Regal (Hastings) Ltd v Gulliver* [1942] 1 All ER 378; [1967] 2 AC 134n; *Industrial Development Consultants v Cooley* [1972] 1 WLR 443; *Queensland Mines v Hudson* [1978] 18 ALR 1 (PC) and *Prudential Assurance Co Ltd v Newman Industries (No 2)* [1981] Ch 257 show a less restrictive approach.

44 *Movitex Ltd v Bullfield* [1988] 1 BCLC 104 (re fulfilment of duty to disclose).

45 Law Commission, *Company Directors: Regulating Conflicts of Interest and Formulating a Statement of Duties* (Report No 261, 1999) paras 16.7, 16.22–16.33, 16.36–16.37.

46 Company Law Review Steering Group, *Modern Company Law for a Competitive Economy – Final Report*, July 2001, para 3.8–3.9.

47 *Guinness plc v Saunders* [1990] 1 All ER 652 (re fees paid to Thomas Ward).

48 At this early stage, the Hampel Committee was understandably reluctant to make further changes to the Greenbury provisions on remuneration.

without shareholder approval should be three years, rather than five as at present.[49] Again the Steering Group agrees with the proposal.[50]

Reference to the board as the 'corporate conscience'[51] emphasises the complexity of moral problems faced by the directors. Again, once a company moves beyond owner management, the board is the only body with the authority, the coherence and the distance from daily operations to handle those issues. Each party involved with the company has its own agenda and will be concerned to promote its own interests. If morality, rather than strict law, is to enter into corporate decision making at all, it will be via the boardroom. Directors are not free to follow their own personal rules of conduct if these do not further the interests of the company – which have been interpreted as equating to the interests of the shareholders, both present and future.[52] Adherence to collective decision making and a variety of experiences among board members will be of assistance in addressing ethical problems.

The actions of managers and employees throughout the company's operations will naturally be guided by the directors' manner and decisions. Codes of corporate aims and values are usually prepared by the board, albeit usually after a consultation process to ensure wide acceptance.[53] Practice that is not in accordance with public statements of aims and values is likely to bring more unfavourable publicity. Investors and consumers are demonstrating that they will make choices in accordance with their ethical expectations and these may make a real financial difference to companies of which they disapprove. The boundaries laid down by directors need to be enforced so that corporate culture is adapted to those ethical requirements. The directors can be personally involved in only a limited number of decisions, but they can ensure that other activity is monitored. As Sir Adrian Cadbury wryly remarks:

> It is helpful to everyone concerned if the board agrees a written social policy, to which ready reference can be made. The test, however, which managers will apply to board statements on social responsibility, is how far adherence to them is recognised in decisions on their pay and promotion.[54]

In the US, the so-called 'other constituency' statutes passes by many states from the 1980s onwards generally permit, but do not require, directors to take

---

49 Law Commission, n 17 above, para 16.34.

50 *Ibid*, 417–18.

51 Institute of Directors, n 4 above, p 15.

52 See well-known comments in *Hutton v West Cork Railway Co* (1883) 23 Ch D 654, *per* Bowen LJ at 672–73; *Parke v Daily News* (1962) Ch 927, *per* Plowman J at 962–63.

53 Hill, P, *Towards a New Philosophy of Management: the Corporate Development Programme of Shell UK Ltd*, 2nd edn 1976, describes an interesting early example of this process.

54 Cadbury, A, 'Rules for a Responsible Company', article reproduced in Rock, S and Kennedy, C, *Power, Performance and Ethics*, 1992, pp 49, 50.

into account the interests of non-shareholder constituents when making their decisions.[55] Their critics have attacked them for reducing management accountability and giving executives the opportunity to 'empire build' and protect their positions under the guise of assisting employees or consumers.[56] If a similar provision were to be introduced to UK company law, as further discussed in Chapter 6, it would require some remedy in favour of named constituencies to ensure its effectiveness. It would give public company boards the opportunity to balance competing interests from their unique position at the centre of the enterprise. Company law deals ineluctably with issues of power and this provides an opportunity for them to be dealt with openly. The board then introduces an ethical dimension into corporate decision making for the benefit of all those affected by company activity.

Stone suggests that, if major corporations are to act responsibly, they need to use some process that is analogous to the decision making of a responsible individual.[57] This entails not behaving in an impulsive or self-centred manner, weighing decisions according to a definite moral code, and considering the consequences of all proposed actions. There is more to ethical conduct than simply compliance with the law – it involves being accountable and setting out priorities. Responsible corporate behaviour will help companies to avoid the costs of rigidity and enforcement which arise from legalism. If stakeholders perceive that corporations are acting irresponsibly towards them, it is foreseeable that they will press for more legislation, though how successful they are may depend on their combined political strength.[58] In order to forestall such campaigns, public companies will have to undergo 'moral development' analogous with that of human persons, a process which can be set in motion and overseen by the directors.[59]

Scattered shareholders do not have sufficient knowledge of or interest in the daily operations of public companies to inject into business the systematic ethical thinking envisaged by Stone. Individual managers are too closely identified with their functional responsibilities to take the necessary overview. If the process described by Stone is to be encouraged, the board as a cohesive group must take the lead. Directors must also be prepared to accept public responsibility for their ethical policies. Stone's own preferred solution is that public directors should be introduced to represent the general interest in very

---

55 Karmel, RS, 'Implications of the Stakeholder Model' (1993) 61 George Washington Law Review 1156.

56 Eg Ward, R, *Twenty-First Century Corporate Board*, 1997, pp 329–32 (the chapter is entitled 'How Many Stakeholders Can Dance on the Head of a Pin?').

57 Stone, CD, 'Corporate Social Responsibility: What It Might Mean if It Were Really to Matter' (1986) 71 Iowa Law Review 557, 559–60.

58 *Ibid*, 567–68.

59 Logsdon, JM and Yuthas, K, 'Corporate Social Performance, Stakeholder Orientation, and Organizational Moral Development' (1997) 16 Journal of Business Ethics 1213.

large companies.[60] Even in the absence of such formal schemes, there seems little doubt that a varied group of able non-executive directors will best equip the board for its moral leadership task.[61]

3.3 CORPORATE STEWARDSHIP

A recent but developing conception of the corporate directorial role is that of the board as stewards of the company's assets, employed to care for and judiciously develop the corporate brand. Like the managers of great country estates in past generations, on this view directors would use the company's property (including its human resources and goodwill) to derive an income and pursue opportunities for growth, while safeguarding the physical and social fabric of the company.[62] The objective of directors as stewards would be to care for the company's property and so benefit the 'owners' (shareholders), the 'labourers' (employees), the 'tenants' (customers), the local community and the natural environment. Where a public company is a major employer or has significant environmental impacts, the analogy with responsible landholding is particularly apposite.

Following the collapse of Barings Bank, proceedings for the disqualification of directors (the deputy group chairman, a product manager, and the head of settlements) highlighted major failures of supervision within the group.[63] Those who should have been overseeing the activities of trader Nick Leeson all too often did not appear to understand what was being done at his Singapore office, or to be concerned about the financial risks he took.[64] In determining the periods of disqualification, Jonathan Parker J stated that directors, collectively and individually, had a duty to acquire and maintain a sufficient knowledge of the company's business to enable them to discharge their responsibilities. Directors' powers of delegation, it was made clear, did not absolve them from the duty to supervise the discharge of delegated functions. There was a link between the position of directors in the management of the company and the expertise and assiduousness of oversight that could be expected from them.[65] Disqualification of directors under the company Directors Disqualification Act 1986 is arguably the most

---

60 Stone, n 57 above, 574–75.

61 Lyndon Griggs and John Lowry point out that non-executive directors 'from much the same social circle' as management, often friends of the chief executive and likely to share a very similar approach; 'Finding the Optimum Balance for the Duty of Care Owed by the Non-Executive Director' in Macmillan Patfield, F, *Perspectives on Company Law* 2, 1997, p 203, at p 212.

62 Goyder, M, *Living Tomorrow's Company* (1998) pp 107–10.

63 *Re Barings plc (No 5)* [1999] 1 BCLC 433 at 528–29, 574–75, 600–02.

64 *Ibid*, 505–08, 570–72, 582–93.

65 *Ibid*, 486–89.

efficacious means in UK law of keeping company directors good stewards and setting minimum standards of competence.[66]

By the time a director falls to be disqualified, however, damage to business, and possibly to customers and employees, has been done. It would, of course, be far preferable to prevent the difficulty altogether. This requires a statement of principle and a clear understanding of responsibility. Relentless pressure for reform and to improve stewardship, not only of money but also of wider social and environmental resources, still proceeds.

'Break-up' takeovers, largely unknown in Japan and Germany but common in the US and the UK, also do not fit with the steward's traditional commitment to places, people and posterity. Profits from the sale of property and reductions in the workforce are 'one-off' windfalls that end the life of a corporate entity. Kay observes:

> Some British companies have seen it as entirely appropriate, in pursuit of shareholder value, to dispose entirely of an existing collection of businesses and buy a new one ... A new vice-chancellor of Oxford University, or trustee of the National Gallery, who suggested that the University should become an international language school or that the Trafalgar Square site would make an excellent shop and restaurant complex, would be seen as having fundamentally misunderstood the nature of his responsibilities.[67]

This does not mean there is no need to update products and modernise practices – a trustee should seek to make effective use of resources and build for the long term. It does mean that the company's core competencies are to be utilised and business values maintained.

Where there is a real culture of commitment and involvement, with shared values and open dialogue, the stewardship approach is most likely to evolve among executives. It can also spread from the board to encourage all staff to safeguard corporate assets, including reputation. The costs of direct monitoring may be reduced if all who have control of company property understand the ethical codes that govern their use. In so far as oversight is still required, in the absence of an effective private 'owner', political representatives are empowered to set out mutually beneficial rules of conduct in legislation. Neither the Law Commission's report nor the DTI's consultation paper mentioned above adverts to the stewardship approach. They seem to posit either a 'shareholders' money' priority or a juggling of incompatible interests with no overall goal in mind, where the stewardship approach offers something distinctive from either of them.

---

66 Walters, A, 'Directors' Duties: The Impact of the Company Directors Disqualification Act 1986' (2000) 21 Co Law 110, 118.

67 Kay, J, 'The Stakeholder Corporation' in Kelly, G, Kelly, D and Gamble, A, *Stakeholder Capitalism*, 1997, p 135.

Directors operating on the stewardship model would need to understand and respect the traditions and priorities of the company and to see its customers, employees and suppliers and the community as partners in an ongoing enterprise. Stewards are not only guardians of another's property, they are obliged to retain it for the long term while producing satisfactory returns from it.[68] It is submitted that many public company directors (both executives who have come up 'through the ranks' and non-executives who accept appointments at 'blue chip' organisations) do see themselves as part of a line of managers building upon and continuing a history. Where takeovers have led to the splitting of asset portfolios, there is little evidence to show they have created extra value for new shareholders in the medium-to-long term.[69]

3.4 BALANCING DIVERSE STAKEHOLDER INTERESTS

Directors need to address the concerns of all whose support they require to stay in business. It is the board that has the ability to take an overview. In the absence of shareholder 'ownership', which is implausible in public companies for reasons that were discussed in Chapter 2, the directors can address all the relevant relationships without presumptions as to the order of priority. The importance of customer relations, of supplier dependability, of community ties and environmental impact, depends on the nature of the business itself.

Within a small group, the board cannot necessarily contain direct representation of all groups affected by corporate conduct. Changes to UK board structure would be a challenge to the national business culture. There must, however, be a range of experience and willingness to listen to the relevant constituencies (including representations made through trade unions, consumer groups and politicians). The Employment Relations Act 1999, the Utilities Act 2000 and European Union social and environmental legislation[70] all emphasise the breadth of accountability. Communication strategies to deal with all these stakeholders are important. It is for directors to take account of these disparate responsibilities and fashion a coherent strategy from them.

---

68 Goyder, G, *The Just Enterprise*, 1993, Chapter 10 (entitled 'The Directors as Trustees') argues that directors should become responsible for carrying out the company's objectives as set out in the new general purposes clause of its memorandum for the benefit of all stakeholders, not solely the shareholders.

69 Jensen, MC and Ruback, RS, 'The Market for Corporate Control: the Scientific Evidence' and Jarrell, GA, Brickley, JA and Netter, JM, 'The Market for Corporate Control: the Empirical Evidence since 1980' are quoted in Romano, R, *Foundations of Corporate Law*, 1993, pp 244 and 251 respectively.

70 Measures under Arts 117–27 and 130r–30t of the EC Treaty (as amended by the Single European Act).

This approach is linked to the stewardship concept discussed above. No one stakeholding group has an absolute right to exploit company property and people for its own benefit. Davis, Schoorman and Donaldson argue that:

> Stewards in loosely coupled, heterogeneous organisations with competing stakeholders and competing shareholder objectives are motivated to make decisions that they perceive are in the best interests of the group ... A steward who successfully improves the performance of the organization generally satisfies most groups, because most stakeholder groups have interests that are well served by increasing organizational wealth.[71]

It is true that increasing wealth gives directors more options to satisfy all constituents, but a group which believes that it has been overlooked or unfairly treated is unlikely to rest content. Just as a government with increased revenue in prosperous times can cut taxes, increase services or try some mixture of the two in an attempt to please voters, so public company boards can exercise their various options as resources allow.

Stakeholding has been downgraded, if not abandoned altogether, as a political slogan of choice since the General Election of 1997, to the chagrin of its proponents.[72] It is certainly no longer a matter of party political rhetoric as it was. However in business debates, consultancy and writing, it has become common currency, as in pensions reform.[73] As the Prime Minister's adviser Phillip Gould points out: 'the language of stakeholding may have withered, but the new approach underpinning it has prospered'.[74]

Lancaster University's Professor of Language in Social Life, Norman Fairclough, in his treatise *New Labour, New Language?* perceptively analyses the use of the stakeholding theme to link together several new Labour concerns. He sums up the central thesis (more concisely than Tony Blair himself): 'being competitive entails entering the quality market (or: the knowledge-based economy); entering the quality market entails the whole country working together ("one nation"); being "one nation" entails everyone having a stake in the economy'.[75] It would be very surprising indeed if the values of the party of government were not reflected in its demands on business, and particularly in its regulation of major companies. As the future of the London Underground and the UK Air Traffic Control system continue to be hotly debated in the summer of 2001, the role of the private sector in national life remains deeply controversial.

The development of stakeholding theory and the identification and classification of stakeholders will be further discussed in Chapter 4. Clearly

---

71 Davis, JH, Schoorman, FD and Donaldson, L, 'Towards a Stewardship Theory of Management' (1997) 22 Academy of Management Review 25.
72 Hutton, W, *The Stakeholding Society*, 1999, pp 263–74.
73 Welfare Reform and Pensions Act 1999, Part 1.
74 Gould, P, *The Unfinished Revolution*, 1998, p 255.
75 Fairclough, N, *New Labour, New Language?*, 2000, pp 91–92.

this role is more complex than the traditional task of profit maximisation and has its critics as a result.[76] Ultimately, however, with large institutional investors representing millions of small UK investors, it is in the interests of capital providers for the corporate sector to be run in an inclusive, investment-orientated way. A new generation of business leaders will have to meet this challenge.[77]

3.5 THE CADBURY AND HAMPEL APPROACHES TO CORPORATE GOVERNANCE

In response to serious apparent failures of financial monitoring by UK boards, the 1992 Cadbury Report and accompanying Code of Best Practice[78] recommended a strengthening of the 'outsider' director's position and a streamlining of directorial work by the use of board committees. The appointment of a separate chairman to counterbalance the power of the chief executive, the introduction of non-executive directors of 'sufficient calibre and number' for their views to carry real weight and the establishment of committees to deal with the audit process and remuneration were all established as 'best practice'. There was no compulsion for public companies to follow all these guidelines. Listed companies do, however, have to report on their record of compliance or otherwise.[79] Peer pressure then develops for all companies to comply if most are doing so. The revised Code of Best Practice discussed below will be monitored in the same way.

In 1998, the Hampel Report's conclusion on corporate and board priorities was clear – directors should focus on shareholder satisfaction and all else is purely incidental.[80] Following the Cadbury Report, the use of committees to make functions such as audit and remuneration more visibly independent of the executive is endorsed in the context of unitary responsibility for leadership and oversight, and the addition of a nomination committee as 'standard' is also advised.[81] Directors are taken to be properly accountable to shareholders alone, so that if board responsibilities were defined to include stakeholders, they would not be effectively accountable to anyone. Leadership and control are said to be vested in the board as a whole, despite the acknowledgment

76 Eg Ward, n 56 above, pp 333–34.

77 Carnall, C and Maxwell, S, *Management: Principles and Policy*, 1988, pp 146–50.

78 Committee on the *Financial Aspects of Corporate Governance* (Chair: Sir Adrian Cadbury), Final Report together with Code of Best Practice, December 1992.

79 *Ibid*, Recommendations 1–4.

80 Committee on Corporate Governance (Chair: Sir Ronald Hampel), *Final Report*, January 1998, paras 1.16–1.17.

81 *Ibid*, paras 4.11–4.12 and 6.3–6.4.

that many use the executive committee structure and so mirror the two-tier board.[82] In general, Hampel leaves the basic governance scheme unchanged in terms of board structure and institutional monitoring. Active attempts to manage potential conflicts of interest within commerce and industry are not openly discussed (unsurprisingly given the membership of the committee concerned).

Where Cadbury attempted to balance out giving directors the freedom 'to drive companies forward' with an assurance that they did so within a 'framework of effective accountability', Hampel is even more concerned to preserve 'managerial freedom' while attempting to ensure that an appropriate standard of conduct is maintained.[83] Little reference is made in the 1998 report to issues of corporate responsibility or the social role of public companies. The agency model of directorial responsibility (that is, that directors are ultimately answerable to members alone) is accepted without much questioning of its relevance to modern public companies. 'Best practice' standards, from which individual companies may derogate, are indicated as the appropriate form of corporate governance regulation on most issues. There is indeed a renewed emphasis on principles, rather than regulatory detail. No change in the non-legal status of recommended standards is proposed. Nor is any real model provided of how effective corporate governance and board processes might look in action,[84] so there may be wide variations even between different companies in the same sector. There is only cursory discussion of audit and accounting standards[85] without much effort to supply an alternative measure of 'good behaviour'.

When compared with Cadbury, Hampel does tighten up some of the proposals: it recommends that non-executive directors should constitute not less than one-third of the board (at Recommendation No 12) and that Annual Reports should state which of the non-executives are considered to be independent (at Recommendation No 9). Beyond that, the later Report introduces few fresh ideas to the debate. It is not proposed that the roles of chief executive and chairman should be split as a matter of regulation or legislation.[86] However, it is recommended that a 'senior independent non-executive director' be named in the Annual Report, whether or not the top roles are separated.[87] Where there is a non-executive chairman expressing 'outsider' concerns openly to the chief executive, as is increasingly the case in

---

82 *Ibid*, paras 3.11 and 3.12.

83 *Ibid*, paras 1.11 and 1.12.

84 Professor Jayne Barnard of the College of William and Mary Law School, Williamsburg, VA, contrasts this with the prescriptiveness of the US SEC (paper given at the Conference 'Beyond Hampel: Theoretical Perspectives on Corporate Governance', Newcastle University, 31 March 1998).

85 Hampel, n 80 above, paras 6.16–6.19.

86 *Ibid*, para 3.17.

87 *Ibid*, para 3.18.

UK quoted public companies, it may seem unclear what value a further 'leader' of the non-executives would add. There is, however, merit for a different reason in having a separate leading and independent director publicly identified. If such a director were available, employees and customers would have a direct channel of communication to the board if dissatisfied with the leadership. Such special responsibility for ensuring that stakeholder concerns were brought to the board's attention would add value to the senior non-executive's contribution.

Relations with shareholders are accorded prominence in the Report and suggestions made for the improvement of Annual General Meeting procedure.[88] Useful ideas about communication, such as the provision of written answers to questions that cannot be answered immediately and the preparation of a resume of the proceedings to be sent to members who are unable to attend, are suggested by way of examples. There is no acknowledgment of the need for directors as policy makers to consult with and listen to the company's employees (despite the advent of European Works Councils in the UK) or indeed its customers (without whom there would obviously be no profits at all). These issues are left entirely to the discretion of each corporate leadership, obviously within existing laws. Stakeholders, when discussed at all, are treated in an entirely 'instrumental' fashion, as means to the end of 'business prosperity.' There is a strong emphasis on the need to make the corporate surplus larger than it might be without sound leadership, but almost no attention to the use or division of the profits.[89]

Another concern of Hampel is the avoidance of mere 'boxticking' – that is, compliance with the letter of a set of governance prescriptions, without real attention to the spirit and purpose of the rules themselves.[90] The number of non-executives, for instance, will not be determinative of their influence on the board, as their calibre and the attitude of the executives will be crucial in this. It is submitted that there is a difference, however, between stating that compliance with rules will not be sufficient in and of itself to ensure good practice and arguing that there should be no absolute rules at all. The Hampel Report at times seems to slide from the first of these positions to the second. While financial audit is tightened to some extent, board information on, and consideration of, broader issues such as corporate social influence and environmental impact are not addressed. In saying:

> Public companies are now among the most accountable organisations in society. They publish trading results and audited accounts; and they are required to disclose much information about their operations, relationships, remuneration and governance arrangements ... [91]

---

88 *Ibid*, Part 5.
89 Riley, CA, 'The Hampel Report: Content and Context' in 'Beyond Hampel', n 84 above.
90 Hampel, n 80 above, paras 1.13 and 1.14.
91 *Ibid*, para 1.1.

the Committee fails to address the concerns of employees and consumers who do not at present share any feeling of involvement or confidence in the public companies that depend on them.

The new Combined Code (Principles of Governance and Code of Best Practice) for listed companies is now part of the Listing Rules, having been annexed to them in 1998. For accounting periods ending on or after 31 December 1998, listed companies must include a statement in their annual report on (a) how they have applied the corporate governance principles of the Combined Code and (b) the extent to which they have complied with the more detailed provisions of the Combined Code. This will place some additional market pressures on quoted public companies to meet Greenbury and Hampel's 'best practice' requirements. There is still, however, no effective sanction if they fail without good reason to do so.

The UK government is very far from satisfied that the Greenbury objectives of accountability, transparency and linkage of rewards to performance have yet been achieved. Compliance with best practice was monitored by PricewaterhouseCoopers for the Department of Trade and Industry.[92] Weaknesses in the independence of board remuneration committees, complexities in disclosure of board remuneration and reluctance to put remuneration to shareholder votes remain common. Strengthening of best practice and potential legislation on these issues, even in advance of a new Companies Act, are indicated. The government states that it does not wish any costs or restraints to make UK companies and listing uncompetitive internationally. However, it argues that business would be improved if pay for top executives were more closely tied to corporate performance.[93]

The role of the Listing Rules remains to be seen, in that there has been little time as yet for its impact to be assessed. In general they seem to have been accepted as having had substantively beneficial effects on the management and the performance of UK quoted companies. Sanctions for failure to comply with best practice at present are weak. Reliance on disclosure of performance is a modest form of performance pressure. There is a group of smaller public companies, not seeking a listing, on which it may be inappropriate to impose detailed rules as to the structure of boards. By contrast, the principles that underpin the duties of directors themselves constitute a subject that needs to be politically debated and made accessible in statute.

It is not practical to deal with matters of managerial detail in primary legislation. Nor should all public companies necessarily be treated alike regardless of their size and financial structure. The role of the Financial Services Authority, which became the UK Listing Authority in May 2000, will be an extremely interesting area to watch. It has been eager in formulating its

---

92 DTI, *Directors Remuneration: A Consultative Document*, July 1999, Chapter 2.
93 *Ibid*, Annex E.

regulations and developing its approach to consult both with former regulators and with financial experts and business people and itself has sought to operate in accordance with stakeholder principles. In so doing it is apparently aiming to operate according to the best of modern management principles. The fact that corporate governance impacts not only on investors but also on the other stakeholders has not been acknowledged by its new overseers.

3.6 PRACTICAL QUESTIONS FOR BOARDS

3.6.1   Board size

The size of any operating group has a profound effect on the nature and effectiveness of its work. Beyond a certain number (Coulson-Thomas quotes 12–15,[94] Cadbury nine–12,[95] Bowen also around 12[96] and Parker anything beyond eight[97]), the possibility of worthwhile individual contributions swiftly diminishes and the quality of the team effort suffers. Inevitably the central figures will become an inner decision making circle when the full group is too big for efficient communication. If non-executive directors are to play a full part in its work, the number of 'automatic' executive appointments must fall to keep the board to a manageable size. In suggesting that six to eight is an optimum size, Puckey draws on practical experience:

> Too many board meetings display verbosity among a few and almost complete silence among the rest. The correct board size encourages all to contribute within a reasonable length of meeting, and this depends greatly on the number of directors present.[98]

Use of executive committees (consisting of executive directors, sometimes with other senior executives, chaired by the chief executive) streamlines decision making between full board meetings. It must, however, be remembered that such groups are essentially senior management sessions reflecting operational concerns. If the full board is too large, it will not function properly in its task of policy oversight. A board that behaves as a 'rubber stamp', dealing perfunctorily with decisions that have substantively already been made, will not escape the attention of liquidators and the courts if things do go badly wrong.[99] Once companies grow beyond 'owner-

---

94   Coulson-Thomas, n 1 above, pp 94—96.
95   Cadbury, n 2 above, pp 42–43.
96   Bowen, WG, *Inside the Boardroom: Governance By Directors and Trustees*, 1994, pp 40–43.
97   Parker, H, 'Re-empowering the Board of Directors', in Monks and Minow, n 38 above, pp 296–97.
98   Puckey, W, *The Board Room*, 1969, pp 85–86.
99   *Bishopsgate Investment Management Ltd. (in liquidation) v Maxwell (No 2)* [1994] 1 All ER 261; *Dorchester Finance Co Ltd v Stebbing* [1989] BCLC 498.

management', there needs to be an effective and cohesive top team in place. A range of specialisms and personalities will be required for it to function effectively.

The board needs to draw on the talents and skills of all its members. This means utilising their individual expertise in an efficient way (and employing other professional support when necessary for sound decision making). A responsible, professional board needs to contain varied specialisms if it is to fulfil its duties effectively and in the case of UK quoted companies, the Stock Exchange's listing requirements help to ensure that there is an appropriate mix of strengths. Nor, with some exceptions, does the traditional US model of a dominant CEO have much influence in the UK. Effective 'technocracy' requires that at least two or three people whose knowledge and personalities are complementary should work together at the head of a company. This also avoids concentration of excessive power in one pair of hands, however safe they may initially seem to be.

3.6.2 Executive/non-executive balance

The balance between executive and non-executive input, between inside knowledge and outside scrutiny, has also been the subject of debate for some years now. Parker in his 'Letters to a New Chairman' suggests that on a board numbering around 12, three qualified and effective non-executives 'is just about the practical minimum'.[100] In order for a public company to comply with the Cadbury Report's recommendations as to remuneration and audit committees composed of non-executive members, three such directors would be required. Six or seven non-executives 'would probably represent the workable maximum'.[101] This is presumably on the basis of needing to leave room for executive contributions and perhaps difficulty in finding sufficient people of the appropriate calibre who are able to devote adequate time to the company.

By the standards of their main employment, pubic company executives are not remunerated particularly well for part-time directorships (though for others their board fees may represent a substantial portion of their income).[102] If all of the non-executive directors are themselves executives in comparable, if not competing, companies, they are not likely to bring to bear any really distinctive and critical views on matters, such as managerial remuneration and audit, where objectivity is crucial. In particular, the practice of executives serving as non-executive directors on the boards of one another's companies

---

100 Parker, H, *Letters to a New Chairman*, 1979, p 19.
101 *Ibid*.
102 *Ibid*, p 297.

in a direct exchange (board interlocks, in the US parlance) is one which clearly diminishes independence and which should be prohibited via the listing rules for quoted companies.[103] Corporate culture may encourage deference to insiders and an unwillingness to 'rock the boat', particularly if current results appear to be satisfactory. The chairing of meetings and arrangements (or lack of them) for *ad hoc* communications between directors are important factors in this connection.

Hampel, following Cadbury, merely recommends that the 'majority' of the non-executive directors should be independent, in the sense of having no financial ties to the company other than their directors' fees (and possibly owning shares). Former executives and professional advisors may therefore be sitting, albeit in a minority, on audit and remuneration committees. This is not acceptable if the true primary function of the board is to oversee management in the absence of effective ownership. The definition of independence does need to be primarily financial and should be tightened to exclude those in receipt of other fees and pensions from the non-executive 'quota'. While the calibre of board members is of the first importance in securing their effective performance, the appearance and actuality of independence are crucial for handling potential conflict of interest situations. Others such as retired executives and legal and financial professionals may have valuable contributions to make, but if the board is already relatively large, one might ask whether provision of a board seat is necessary to secure the advice of the individual.

A further question is whether executives and non-executives should have different legal duties. While the board is unitary in its structure, it is perhaps difficult to see how this would work. A clear majority of the public company directors to whom the author herself spoke were in favour of retaining the unity of the group. Nevertheless, the balance between co-operation in corporate structure and criticism of management when necessary is not always an easy one to strike.

3.6.3 Information

Board members, especially the non-executive directors, are reliant on management to provide them with accurate and timely information, as Hampel clearly acknowledges.[104] This regular information needs to cover financial and social performance of the company and its departments and subsidiaries (if any). Not only are the figures required in a format which will aid ready understanding, but data from surveys of customers and employees, in particular, may be very helpful. A number of organisations provide

---

103 Monks and Minow, n 38 above, pp 188–89.
104 Hampel, n 80 above, para 3.4.

assistance with environmental and ethical auditing and research among stakeholders.[105] If information is to be credible, this is as important as the annual financial audit by independent professionals. As Farrington puts it:

> Non-executive directors are expected to call for information to satisfy themselves as to the propriety of a course of action and that it is in the best interests of the company. They cannot rely on the fact that action is recommended by the executive members.[106]

Directors in large companies are often perceived as being remote from the real issues of the workplace and the market. If the increasingly common division of responsibilities is in place, the chief executive needs to be a respected leader in the company while the chairman takes primary responsibility for conducting external relations. For good performance of both these tasks, and for the proper functioning of other board members, sensitivity to the opinions of key constituencies is essential. Where difficult decisions do fall to be made, the process is made easier if the fabric of relationships woven by the board is a strong one. This points to a need for non-executives to commit to spend at least two full working days per month on company business, aside from reading papers relating to board meetings.

It should be said that reliance upon 'gut feeling' or experience is very important for non-executives in the view of the officers whom the author met. There is no doubt, however, that appraisal and consideration of scenarios and trends are increasingly required.[107] John Micklethwait and Adrian Wooldridge comment: 'globalization has raised the cost of bad government'.[108] This surely applies to major companies as much as to nation states in 2001 and beyond.

The ALI Principles of Corporate Governance, coming from an environment where most public company directors are not 'insiders' and openness is valued, provide that: 'Every director has the right ... to inspect and copy all books, records and documents of every kind, and to inspect the physical properties, of the corporation ... in person or by an attorney or other agent'[109] (exceptions being where information is not reasonably related to the performance of directorial duties or if it is likely to be used in violation of directors' duties to the company). A similar expression of 'informational rights' for directors could be highly significant in the UK, where it is often expected that non-executives will not obtain sensitive documents or 'walk the shop floor' except by prior arrangement with the chief executive.

---

105 Such as ethics etc ..., Business in the Community and the National Centre for Business and Ecology – see n 14 above.

106 Farrington, DJ, 'Universities and Corporate Governance: a Model for the Future' in Robertson, L, *Corporate Governance*, 1995, p 30.

107 Houston, W, *Through the Whirlwind*, 1997, Chapter 14.

108 Micklethwait, J and Wooldridge, A, *A Future Perfect*, 2000, p 297.

109 Principles of Corporate Governance, n 19 above, para 3.03.

3.6.4 Time

The amount of time available for their directorial duties naturally constrains the effectiveness of board members. In addition to monthly board meetings, a non-executive will need at least another day to study reports and time to make his or her own enquiries on site. Equally importantly, an executive has to set aside time from daily managerial tasks to address his or her directorial responsibilities. For a retired executive who is making a career of non-executive directorship, four directorships (averaging out at one board meeting every week) would seem to be a realistic maximum commitment,[110] bearing in mind committee work and the fact that at crisis points, any of the companies may require extra attention. For a heavily committed executive director, two non-executive posts, conscientiously fulfilled, would represent almost a working week each month and more than one would generally be unfeasible. Acceptance of any outside appointment should depend on the principal employer's understanding and approval of the work involved.

When their appointment is first discussed, prospective directors should be clearly informed of the time commitment that will be expected from them. Many well-run public companies have a board calendar showing the meetings and events the board members will need to attend, committee schedules and also the 'cycle' of matters (budgets, accounts, personnel, marketing, etc.) which directors will address through the year. Relatively detailed contracts for both executives and non-executives are common. Would-be non-executives should also bear in mind that unforeseen events in operations or markets might demand additional attendance. Executives invited to join the board are entitled to ask questions about the extra assistance they will receive as they take on more tasks in the context of an existing full-time managerial workload. Once every three years at least, there will be the opportunity to review the time input of each director as he or she seeks re-election.

If there are fewer, but more important, decisions to be made in the board role than in senior management posts, enough support needs to be given to enable those key choices to be made effectively. For large public companies, one suggestion of Drucker's[111] that the board should have its own secretariat to help digest information and research key business issues may be worth considering. Just as government ministers with wide ultimate responsibilities need reliable briefings and assistance from senior civil servants, so many public company directors have too much detail to assimilate without support teams. Bringing experience and judgment to bear on the key issues from a

---

110 Gilson, RJ and Kraakman, R, 'Reinventing the Outside Director: An Agenda for Institutional Investors', paper presented on 14–15 June 1990 at the Saloman Brothers Center and Rutgers Centers Conference on the *Fiduciary Responsibilities of Institutional Investors* quotes six as an upper limit.

111 Drucker, PF, *Management: Tasks, Responsibilities, Practices*, 1974, pp 624–26.

sound basis of policy is the most important function of any board and the assistance of capable staff will help with this.

3.7 EXAMPLES FROM PUBLIC SERVICES

3.7.1 NHS Trusts

National Health Service Trusts are bodies corporate constituted under the National Health Service and Community Care Act 1990. Their structure and proceedings are provided for in some detail by the legislation itself. Following the Cadbury Report, the report of the Corporate Governance Task Force, Public Enterprise Governance in the NHS, contained a Code of Conduct for Trust Directors. Great emphasis was placed here on the independence of chairmen and non-executive directors. When compared with the Cadbury approach, the NHS governance arrangements were far more prescriptive – for example, they provide: 'that there is a clear division of responsibility and boards are required to meet regularly'.[112] Issues of conflict of interest are also strictly dealt with, partly because Trust operations are substantively in the public domain with the addition of some private management techniques.

The Corporate Governance Task Force reported six functions of the Board itself:

* setting strategic direction;
* overseeing and monitoring performance and financial stewardship;
* ensuring high standards of corporate governance and personal behaviour and overseeing employment of senior executives;
* supervising dialogue between the Trust and the community.

While this list is weighted towards monitoring functions (as one might expect in dealing with a body whose funding and responsibilities are essentially publicly determined), the areas of standard setting and communication with the community have lessons for many public companies. The Board itself is designed to provide a balance of inside views, from the chief officer and chief finance officer and also relevant specialists – a doctor or dentist, a nurse or midwife – with non-executives from the relevant area. This is a combination of perspectives from which public companies might learn.

As far as non-executives are concerned, NHS Trusts have absorbed outsider input from business people and community leaders who had little or no experience of medical issues. The Audit Commission in its paper *Taken on*

---

112 Belcher, A, 'Codes of Conduct and Accountability for NHS Boards' [1995] Public Law 288, 292.

Board[113] explored the lessons learned and good practice encountered to date and these may have relevance to non-executive director involvement generally. New NHS non-executives emphasised the importance of induction and training in preparing them for their demanding roles.[114] In business, even experienced managers joining a new company as a part-time independent voice on the board have many of the same needs. In short, during the 1990s it was realised that the complexity of public services such as the NHS could rival that of major businesses. Skills from the development and oversight of one sector could usefully be transferred to the other.[115]

Among the general points raised by *Taken on Board* are the following:

The strategic input of non-executives adds independent judgment to the planning process.[116]

Having a mix of skills among non-executive directors 'is fundamental to the board's effectiveness'.[117]

Non-executives are seen as having a particular responsibility for public consultation and accountability.[118]

The chairman can lead questioning of the executive or can constrain it, while a nervous or defensive chief executive can kill discussion if the board is not persistent.[119]

More specific suggestions include the following:

Sufficient (but not overwhelming) information must be provided to non-executives, in appropriate, manageable amounts and in clear form. 'Away days' to brainstorm aims and priorities can be helpful.[120]

'Walking the shop floor' to obtain independent information is seen as part of the non-executive task and facilitates expression of staff concerns.[121]

Feedback from – and to – the chairman is important and should be a regular process, as should review of the executive's performance.[122]

Non-executive directors 'should be in touch with the concerns of local people' and the board should be prepared to explain its decisions in public, for

---

113 Audit Commission, *Taken on Board – Corporate Governance in the NHS: Developing the Role of Non-Executive Directors*, 1995.

114 *Ibid*, 7–8.

115 Ashburner, L, 'Corporate Governance in the Public Sector: The Case of the NHS' in Keasey, K, Thompson, S and Wright, MJ, *Corporate Governance: Economic and Financial Issues*, 1997, pp 289–90, notes that in an extensive survey, over two-thirds of Trust chairs and almost half of Trust non-executives were private sector directors.

116 *Ibid*, p 19.

117 *Ibid*, p 8.

118 *Ibid*, pp 23–26.

119 *Ibid*, pp 14–17.

120 *Ibid*, pp 19–20.

121 *Ibid*, pp 11–12.

122 *Ibid*, pp 9–10.

example in well-organised local meetings. Community surveys and focus groups may be informative.[123]

For public company boards, there are lessons of openness and diversity to be learned from this. Greater public scrutiny of social and environmental performance is to be expected by those running public companies as well as leaders of public services. The input of directors from a wide range of backgrounds and their genuine involvement in a range of policy issues is to be welcomed in business, not feared. Clear goals, the cultivation of external relationships and the availability of a range of specialist skills are prerequisites for modern business success.

3.7.2 The privatised utility companies

In the utility industries, formerly publicly owned, now in the private sector, regulatory bodies (OFTEL, OFWAT and OFGEM) were established to protect consumer interests (in prices and quality of services) and to enforce the licences under which privatised companies operate. Employee issues and environmental impacts also need to be weighed in the balance by those overseeing such companies. The directors-general of these regulatory authorities are aware that their various responsibilities can conflict, as when expenditure to meet strict environmental criteria may cause price increases. In the absence of full and free competition available to ordinary consumers, there is a need for an independent, publicly accountable body to set the priorities. Utility regulators have viewed their role as a temporary and diminishing one as competition is introduced and strengthened.[124] Their relationship to the major companies has been one of occasional antagonism focused on the directors-general, with disputes ultimately refereed by the Monopolies and Mergers Commission.[125]

Many of the disagreements have arisen because the chairmen of utility companies have wanted to keep the structure intact and free of open competition until modernisation inside the business had been accomplished.[126] If competition is designed only to drive down consumer prices, quality levels and environmental and employment standards may suffer in pursuit of that goal. If the proper goal of competition is seen as being the satisfaction of all participants and the attainment of a sustainable balance

---

123 *Ibid*, pp 23–26.

124 Eg OFTEL, Annual Report 1996, p 2: 'regulation must seek to replace monopolised markets by competitive markets from which regulation can withdraw. ... Our aim is to establish a coherent framework which encourages entry, innovation, efficiency and sustainable competition ...'

125 Bishop, M, Kay, J and Mayer, C, *The Regulatory Challenge*, 1995, p 13.

126 Beesley, ME, *Privatisation, Regulation and Deregulation*, 2nd edn 1997, p 45.

between all their interests, the approach will be somewhat broader.[127] It may never be entirely practical to have unbridled 'free entry' where infrastructure and environmental implications and social and political consequences are significant, but managerial attitudes can be transformed.[128]

The Labour government appears not to be satisfied that the expanding marketplace alone will produce corporate operations which are in the public interest or indeed free of directorial impropriety. It has accordingly brought forward the Utilities Act 2000, which addresses the accountability of utilities companies and declares that the principal objective of gas and electricity regulation is 'to protect the interests of consumers', including disabled or ill persons, pensioners, consumers with low incomes and those in rural areas.[129] The Secretary of State has power to issue guidance regarding the contribution gas and electricity companies can make to governmental social and environmental policies.[130] Those companies are also required to disclose to regulators any remuneration of directors that is linked to levels of performance in regulated services.[131] New legislation can act as a spur to change practice and indeed to justify investment expenditure such as environmental projects and customer service initiatives to shareholders. Other businesses clearly also have major environmental and social impacts and logically should expect to face very similar political demands, while some, such as supermarket chains, appear to be aware of this and emphasise news of community activities in their advertising and publicity material.

In the US, there is a tradition of more inclusive, open decision making, with time and space for the contributions of consumer and environmental representatives as well as management and employees. The expense of such consultation exercises is seen as a price well worth paying in a mature democracy.[132] There are lessons for 'mainstream' public companies to learn from the utilities' experience of public disaffection (for example, at executive pay while the industry faced little competition and the same work had been done at far lower salaries, quite often by the same individuals, before privatisation).[133] The fact that the utility companies now put significant effort and resources into their environmental programmes and into community relations shows what needs to be done.

---

127 Ogden, S, 'Corporate Governance in the Privatised Utilities: The Case of the Water Industry' in Keasey, Thompson and Wright, n 115 above, pp 263–64 notes water companies' innovations in customer relations following regulatory pressure.

128 *Ibid*, p 54.

129 Utilities Act 2000, ss 9 and 13.

130 *Ibid*, ss 10 and 14.

131 *Ibid*, ss 61 and 97.

132 See Harlow, C and Rawlings, R, *Law and Administration*, 1997, pp 332–36.

133 Millstein, IM, 'The Responsible Board' (1997) 52 The Business Lawyer 407, 412–14, points out that this perception extends to the US.

Contractual reasoning underlay privatisation programmes and has dominated political life for almost 20 years. It may sometimes be of quite dubious relevance, for example where employee and environmental awareness issues are involved and the bargaining power of the respective parties is unequal. Political discussion of rights and responsibilities applies to business leaders as much as to other individuals and the discourse of community and co-operation is similarly applicable to business. As social dependency on major business organisations grows, political accountability also needs to develop.

Wherever there is an element of market power and control, it is easy to argue that there is a public interest element to management of a company.[134] Commenting on the utility regulation process as a (quasi-) contract between the companies and the government, Bishop, Kay and Meyer note that:

> The government acts on behalf of consumers and local communities in the case of industries where environmental considerations are of importance ... The contract lays down certain conditions that privatised firms have to satisfy: the provision of services of certain quality for particular groups of consumers [in return for a reasonably certain income stream].[135]

Similar observations could be made of some large industrial and retail UK public companies. Government ministers, particularly in the DTI, are lobbied by various interest groups and attempt to tackle abuses of market power or of the environment.

3.8 CONCLUSION: PRIORITIES FOR DIRECTORS

Without a clear sense of mission flowing from the boardroom, a company is liable to drift or stagnate. Any substantial changes to the activities of the company should be decided by the directors as a body, executives and non-executives alike. The same would apply to substantial acquisitions and disposals it might make. Regular analysis of the external environment is essential to successful board performance. Given the current UK unitary system, there is the opportunity for inside knowledge of the executives to be complemented by outside perspectives from non-executives. Neither group should be (or feel as though it is) excluded from policy considerations.

In addition, the board needs to be well organised and constantly diligent in its monitoring role. The chairman carries a major responsibility for ensuring

---

134 As Millstein puts it in 'The Professional Board' (1995) 50 The Business Lawyer 1427, 1428: 'boards of directors are not only fiduciaries for their respective owners and, less directly, accountable to other corporate constituents, but they are also responsible, in effect, for their nation's economic well-being. The larger and more pervasive the private sector, the greater the responsibility for the national interest.'

135 Bishop, Kay and Mayer, n 125 above, p 6.

that this is so. Non-executives should develop their own information sources within the company and allow sufficient time to become conversant with the organisation, so that they do not depend solely on reports provided by executives. The group of 'outside' directors may find it helpful to meet up for discussions without their 'insider' colleagues. Executives when acting in their directorial capacity also need to feel that they are not constrained by the managerial hierarchy from raising doubts and airing questions. The chief executive must in turn expect and submit to particularly rigorous examination on the company's operations generally.

Public company directors will need to be far more socially, environmentally and politically aware in the future than most have been in the past. Millstein calls: 'efforts to balance societal concerns of employees, customers, suppliers and communities – without compromising shareholder wealth ... central to the board's role.'[136] It is not enough to be adept only at satisfying the investors – there must be a more sophisticated, multi-faceted approach. He points out that: 'any involvement in major policy decisions requires professionals who understand that they need, and are willing to insist upon, the requisite information for each level of involvement, and then spend the requisite amount of time for each level'.[137] A sharp intellect is essential if one is to assimilate complex matters quickly. In order to obtain such a professional service, it may be necessary for public companies to pay high-calibre non-executives rather higher fees than they currently receive, while executive pay will continue to depend on that market.

If stewardship values become prevalent in a board, the details of committee structure and audit procedure may grow to be less important over time. There must first be a clear statement of basic purposes and principles against which decisions and actions can be measured. Directors motivated by satisfaction at the company's achievements and loyalty to the company's approach will align themselves naturally with the company's regular constituents. Balancing the interests of all a company's stakeholders will never be a simple matter, particularly in a diversified transnational organisation. Public pronouncements, at any rate, nevertheless indicate that UK public company directors are paying attention to all constituents and attempting to show fairness to them all. To date, British shareholders have raised few objections to this.

Many years ago, Drucker defined board functions as involving the following elements:

1   A review organ to 'counsel advise and deliberate with top management'.
2   A monitoring body to 'remove top management that fails to perform'.
3   A 'public and community relations' group.

---

136 Millstein, n 133 above, 408.
137 Millstein, n 134 above, 1433.

This corresponds approximately to the strategic, monitoring and stakeholder consideration discussed above, though the terminology was different when Drucker wrote his piece.[138]

For comparison, Tricker's definition of board functions includes these responsibilities:

1   Formulating corporate policy.
2   Developing strategic thinking.
3   Supervising business performance.
4   Accounting to owners and others.[139]

The first two are long-term forward-looking business roles. The second pair of tasks relates to current activity as a whole. None of them are issues that a manager, based in one department and concentrating, quite properly, on efficient daily operations, would have the time or capacity to consider.

Within a unitary structure, non-executive directors have an important contribution to make both to the monitoring of management and to the wide-ranging ethical evaluation of decisions. Senior executives are well able to supply the internal leadership and maintain links to major shareholders and customers, but it is not realistic to think that they can themselves scrutinise executive conduct or critique moral judgments with the necessary detachment. From the realisation that shareholders are not the sole owners follows the observation that financial and social monitoring can be about more than protecting investor wealth. The challenge is to assemble a fairly cohesive group of people who can represent all those with a legitimate interest in the company's success while having the skills to drive it forward.[140]

The major practical issues of board size, executive/non-executive balance, information and time are unlikely to the subject of fundamental legislative or regulatory input, at least in the absence of a radical restructuring of UK public company boards (possibilities for which are discussed in Chapter 7). However, it is suggested that several straightforward measures could usefully be introduced in the context of the current UK unitary board containing 30–50% non-executives:

(a) Individuals should be prohibited by legislation from sitting on the boards of more than four public companies at any one time and it should be understood that a public company executive would normally accept only one additional non-executive appointment.

(b) As a requirement for listed companies, a leading senior non-executive should be named and should make him/herself freely and regularly

138 Drucker, n 111 above, pp 631–34.

139 Tricker, RI, *Corporate Governance: Practices, Procedures and Powers in British Companies and their Boards of Directors*, 1984.

140 Sifonis, JG and Goldberg, B, *Corporation on a Tightrope*, 1996, pp 77–84.

accessible to employees and customers as well as to government-appointed regulators and community leaders.

These steps would emphasise the time commitment involved in public company directorships and provide a stronger formal link between stakeholders and the board itself.

(c) 'Board interlocks' between directors of listed companies should be prohibited by the listing rules.

(d) Directors should be counted as independent and able to sit on audit, remuneration and nominations committees under the listing rules only if they have no financial connections with the company apart from board fees and any shares owned ('pensioners' and consultants would be excluded).

These steps would advance the aim of providing a strong, truly independent, voice on the board as Cadbury and Hampel both suggest.

(e) Directors should be obliged by law to take proper account of all relevant information in reaching their decisions, should not be permitted to vote on matters where they have a personal interest and should exercise their individual judgment on all issues before the board.

(f) As a corollary to the above, all directors should have the right by statute to see and copy company documents, inspect premises and speak to any employee at any time, as required for the fulfilment of their board duties.

Such measures would make it clear to all that directors, including non-executives, are part of the decision making group and entitled to full information accordingly. Specific time commitments in directors' contracts and the availability of well-qualified research staff should also be considered by major companies.

Notable characteristics of those featured among directors nominated as Most Admired Business Leaders by their peers in a *Financial Times* survey at the end of 2000 were 'speed and decisiveness, courage and tenacity, optimism and enthusiasm'. 'Modesty and an ability to listen' stood out. The most respected business leaders invested heavily in their people, motivate and inspire them, Jorma Ollila of Nokia and Lou Gerstner at IBM being cited for their excellent people skills. Many of the most lauded displayed 'a serious concern for society beyond the corporate gates': Ted Turner was admired for his donations to the United Nations, Bill Gates was seen as 'a great humanitarian, concerned about others', while BP's Sir John Browne and Mark Moody-Stuart at Shell were cited for taking leading positions on the global environment and social responsibility.[141]

---

141 Maitland, A, 'Displaying the ability to make a measurable difference', *Financial Times*, 13 December 2000.

Development of strategy, monitoring of executives and the oversight of business relationships are, then, the three essential tasks of public company leadership, which are all performed by the unitary board in UK public companies.[142] Company law, listing requirements and directors' own terms of appointment should all help to make these accountabilities understood. As far as shareholders are concerned, Lord Hoffmann in *O'Neill v Phillips*[143] discussed circumstances in which a promise may affect a person's conscience even if it were not legally binding. The courts will enforce the constitution of a public company but it is not always clear at present how much further its rulings will go in upholding agreements or understandings.[144]

The Cadbury and Hampel Reports and the Combined Code were to a great extent missed opportunities for substantial changes to corporate governance in UK public companies. The standards expected of directors remain uncertain and the ongoing company law reform process is an obvious opportunity to improve matters. Other possible board structures will be considered below, and could, of course, be discretionary rather than mandatory for all UK pubic companies. Short of such measures, it is submitted that greater directorial time commitment and more genuine independence for non-executives would make a great difference to board effectiveness.

---

142 Matheson, JH and Olson, B, 'Relationship Management and the Trialogical Imperative for Corporate Law' (1994) 78 Minnesota Law Review 1443 discuss three board functions: policymaking, monitoring and also relationship management with investors and stakeholders.

143 *O'Neill v Phillips* [1999] 2 All ER 961.

144 *Re Carrington Viyella plc* (1983) 1 BCC 98.

CHAPTER 4

STAKEHOLDING THEORY

4.1 THE CONCEPT OF STAKEHOLDING

The theory of stakeholding in the corporate context posits that those who participate in or are affected by the company, as individuals and groups, all merit consideration and involvement in its decision making – they have a stake in it. This quality of 'membership' entails responsibilities on the part of all involved, as well as the rights associated with 'belonging'. A stakeholder philosophy starts from the premise that inclusion, social, political and economic, is a valuable concept. The mutually responsive connection of persons in the social, economic and political systems, so it is argued, produces better results for all than the depersonalised market. From the management of individual companies, the idea extends to political principles about society as a whole and economic organisation in particular. In the following comments, the concern is with the application of the theory specifically at the corporate level, but the connections and points of comparison with the political system will become evident.

Concerning the label itself, Hutton comments:

> Part of the process of ideological self-definition is finding a word to describe the variety of capitalism one is championing, and stakeholding is an attractive choice. The idea has long been deployed in management literature and various firms have described themselves as stakeholder companies. The best types of overseas forms of capitalism have been achieved by striking the right balance between commitment and flexibility. Stakeholding is a neat way of encapsulating just that.[1]

Regard and respect for individuals as such is the core of the political economy delineated here. The name 'stakeholder' itself implies that the size of a person's stake depends on what he or she has contributed to, or put at risk in, the company. Curiously, the Company Law Review Steering Committee in its Consultation Document avoided the use of the term, preferring to use the expression 'Pluralism' (which was contrasted with 'Enlightened Shareholder Value').[2] The change of wording marks a subtle shift of emphasis from the inclusivity and rights implied by 'stakeholding' to the diversity and conflict emphasised by 'pluralism'.

---

1   Hutton, W, 'The Stakeholder Society' in Marquand, D and Seldon, A, *The Ideas that Shaped Post-War Britain*, 1996, p 300.
2   Company Law Review Steering Group, *Modern Company Law for a Competitive Economy: The Strategic Framework*, February 1999, para 5.1.

Stakeholder awareness poses a direct challenge to a one-dimensional shareholder-centric management approach. Comparably with discussion of 'social inclusion' in politics, it is concerned with drawing out the full potential of all participants. The law provides a framework of minimum standards in specific important areas, for example, on employment rights and environmental protection, to further this process, and here the current UK government, in association with its European partners, has shown itself willing to embrace new development within limits. So far as corporate governance itself is concerned, the present Company Law Green Paper indicates that directors' duties may be altered in a new statute to reflect a stakeholding perspective if it appears that 'best practice' is not achieving the required results.[3] Some major public companies are already employing the stakeholder approach with enthusiasm.[4] Others have leaders who strongly resist the idea.[5]

The idea of organised labour as a full 'social partner' in workplaces is an important principle of the continental European (particularly German and Dutch, also French and Scandinavian) legal tradition, which has been carried over into European Union labour law. The two sides of industry were empowered by the Maastricht Protocol on Social Policy to reach binding agreements which will themselves become part of European law,[6] so both trade unions and business associations are more important than ever before in setting standards at work. The ideal is that all parties work together for a common goal and obtain shared benefits, 'opting in' to the business's project. Employees at all levels will be more productive, so it is asserted, if they understand, and feel part of, the company's plans.[7] More than that, however, if the potential for stakeholder involvement is to be realised, the objective itself must be one that does not damage the interests of the community. If employees, instead of or as well as the shareholders, were put in the position of seeking first their own short-term interests, that would not produce balanced long-termist decision making in public companies.

Suppliers and customers who are involved in dealing with a public company over an extended period also find their prospects entwined with those of the corporation, and in that sense have a significant stake in it.

---

3   DTI, *Modern Company Law for a Competitive Economy*, March 1998, p 10.

4   For example, Sir John Browne of BP, speaking in the BBC's prestigious Reith lectures for 2000 on the theme of sustainable development, set out his strong views on the importance of relationships with employees and customers as well as shareholders and the centrality in those relationships of environmental and social responsibility.

5   Sir Stanley Kalms of Dixons plc has been one such critic of the stakeholder approach generally.

6   1991 (Maastricht) Agreement on Social Policy, Arts 4 and 5. Agreements may be implemented in accordance with the labour law of Member States or by Council decisions on proposals from the Commission at the request of the parties.

7   The European Works Councils Directive 94/45 OJ L254/64 (1994) also reflects the same view.

Japanese networks or *keiretsu*, centred on commercial banks, with significant cross-shareholdings and joint directorial meetings, place these business relationships between firms in different industrial niches on a co-operative long-term footing.[8] In the UK, on the whole, relationships are more atomistic and price-sensitive. Within the same sector, different approaches are taken, for example, of the major supermarkets, Sainsbury's has had a reputation for working with suppliers over extended periods while Tesco has typically used many different providers to maintain price competition. Professor Ronald Dore, who has studied Japanese business practices extensively, notes that commitment in trade relationships is associated with higher quality and better profit margins.[9] At present, small suppliers to UK public companies are at risk of being sent into collapse without warning if the main players experience trading difficulties.

The stakeholder economic system, on the national scale, is said by critics of 1980s Anglo-American individualism to have produced more equitable and sustainable success in the German and Japanese contexts than the less co-operative style of business seen principally in the UK and the US. Differing emphases have emerged through the various commentaries. Will Hutton, Chief Executive of the Industrial Society, believes that the UK financial system is not serving the needs of employees or consumers, nor the aim of business prosperity, very well and that it requires an overhaul, including new companies legislation.[10] Greater commitment by owners of shares and less ease of transfer of control of companies are strongly advocated. Financial commentator John Plender argues, a little more moderately, that companies need balanced long-termist management in order to prosper.[11] Employees, it is asserted, perform best if they feel that their effort is serving a worthwhile common purpose.

Another British advocate of stakeholding, Professor John Kay, views the company not as an asset constantly available to be bought and sold, but an entity to be stewarded and maintained for the long run.[12] Directors' duties in law should set out the appropriate parties for the board's consideration.

---

8   Kim, H and Hoskisson, RE, 'Market (United States) versus Managed (Japanese) Governance' in Keasey, K, Thompson, S and Wright, M, *Corporate Governance: Economic, Management and Financial Issues*, 1997, p 174.

9   Dore, R, 'Goodwill and the Spirit of Market Capitalism' in Buckley, PJ and Michie, J, *Firms Organizations and Contracts*, 1996, p 359, at pp 377–78.

10 Hutton, W, *The State We're In*, 1995 and *The State to Come*, 1997 and articles in *The Guardian* and *The Observer*; Giddens, A, 'After the Left's Paralysis', *New Statesman*, 1 May 1998, 18, 21 simply asks: 'Can government create a stakeholding business culture? Of course it can, through a mixture of incentives and controls, although this will have to be on a transnational as well as a national level.'

11 Plender, J, *The Stakeholding Solution*, 1997, and articles in the *Financial Times*.

12 Kay, J, 'The Stakeholder Corporation', in Kelly, G, Kelly, D and Gamble, A, *Stakeholder Capitalism*, 1997, p 125, at pp 126–31.

Margaret Blair, of US think-tank the Brookings Institution, argues that the 'shareholder ownership' model of the company is outdated and the employees are among the most important players in business. Corporate governance arrangements should reflect that new reality as far as possible.[13] The point has frequently been made that many companies' profits owe more to their employees' abilities and efforts than to physical assets, yet provision of real job security is inconsistent with the flexibility required to compete in a global marketplace.[14] Clear understanding and agreement from a basis of principle are needed to overcome the difficulties caused by this contradiction.

The stakeholder approach requires an enlightened management and a well-trained workforce, drawn together by the board. Public company directors must take seriously views already often expressed in the Annual Report and at General Meetings about 'inclusiveness'. The position taken by the German Constitution (Art 15) is that property rights entail corresponding obligations to promote the general welfare by their use. Shareholders and others, including managers, must come to heed this in the US and UK too if business culture is to change.[15] Harnessing innovative talent is in the collective interest when effort is directed to serving customers and building markets. Market-based capitalism itself works best when there is a framework within which new developments and ideas can flourish.[16]

4.2 THE USES OF STAKEHOLDING

The concept of stakeholding can be seen as one suggestion among many of how things should be done within a public company, whatever the current reality. Alternatively, it could be regarded as a description of matters of fact with no implications whatsoever for the improved conduct of business. The principle of due attention to all parties may be regarded as 'just' part of morality. Otherwise, use of the concept might be 'just' in formation of strategy

---

13 Blair, M, *Ownership and Control: Rethinking Corporate Governance for the Twenty-First Century* , 1995, Chapters 7 and 8; Longstreth, B, 'Implications of the Wealth Maximising Standard in the Law' in Blair, M, *Wealth Creation and Wealth Sharing: A Colloquium on Corporate Governance and Investment in Human Capital,* 1996, p 55, at p 57 says of Blair's suggestions: 'Under corporate law today, directors owe fiduciary duties of care and loyalty to shareholders alone ... So for directors to become representatives of other stakeholders, a statutory change in fiduciary alignment is needed.'

14 Handy, C, 'Are Jobs for Life Killing Enterprise?', in *Beyond Certainty,* 1996, p 87.

15 See generally Alkhafaji, AF, *A Stakeholder Approach to Corporate Governance,* 1989, Chapter 9 (entitled 'The European Model').

16 Clarke, T, 'The Stakeholder Corporation: A Business Philosophy for the Information Age' (1998) 31 Long Range Planning 182.

as a planning tool. It is, ideally, deployed as both.[17] The real strength of the idea lies in the fact that it leads on from a descriptive analysis of how companies function to a suggestion of how to make them operate better, grounded in a principle of fairness and inclusiveness.

Theoretical writings about stakeholding have fallen into the following categories:

(a) Descriptive observations – 'the way things are', interdependence of corporate participants.[18]

(b) Instrumental procedures – focus on business objectives, analysis to aid profitability.[19]

(c) Normative statements – pronouncements on ethics, principles of participation in business.[20]

These distinct uses of the term are not always clearly demarcated in the literature. The real 'job' of stakeholding theory can be seen as the synthesis of ethics and economics, doing well in an economic sense by doing what is right in one's dealings. Public companies need to have leadership that is responsive to all the relevant parties if they are to fulfil their business potential. From the description of facts (for example, associates such as employees are obviously necessary for the business to continue in operation) and the possible strategic benefits (for example, suppliers who anticipate future orders will be more concerned about quality than those who do not), one moves to the normative basis of rights as belonging with responsibilities. Corporate social power and influence legitimate the inclusion of the community and the environment as stakeholders deserving of consideration by boards.

A method set out by Harrington for the ethical analysis of public policy can be applied to management decisions generally. In the descriptive phase: 'stakeholders and stakeholder groups must ... be identified along with the interests of those stakeholders'. In the normative phase, the decision makers then need to ask: 'does a particular ... policy provide disproportionate benefits to certain stakeholders at the expense of others?'. Far from being an additional drain on profits, 'ethical analysis structured in this way can enhance the ability of business entities to meet the needs of their stakeholders',[21] bringing an instrumental advantage. In discovering who their stakeholders are and

---

17 Donaldson, T and Preston, LE, 'The Stakeholder Theory of the Corporation: Concepts, Evidence and Implications' (1995) 20 Academy of Management Review 65.

18 Eg Hill, CWL and Jones, TM, 'Stakeholder – Agency Theory' (1992) 29 Journal of Management Studies 131.

19 Eg Preston, LE and Sapienza, HJ, 'Stakeholder Management and Corporate Performance' (1990) 19 Journal of Behavioral Economics 361.

20 Eg Kuhn, JW and Shriver, DW (Jr), *Beyond Success: Corporations and their Critics in the 1990s*, 1991.

21 Harrington, LK, 'Ethics and Public Policy Analysis: Stakeholders' Interests and Regulatory Policy' (1996) 15 Journal of Business Ethics 375, 379–80.

what each constituency would like to obtain from their dealings with the company, the directors gain the incalculable advantage of a broader and deeper understanding of the business. In determining how benefits and costs should be shared at any time, the board should look to the company's strategic mission and ethical code.[22]

Competitive pressure is not always an absolute or effective restraint on behaviour, especially for large companies. The market generally does not preclude social action, and certainly does not prevent the fair and ethical treatment of employees and suppliers.[23] At the prescriptive level, however, lies the justification for stakeholding on which all others are founded. This analysis goes to the heart of corporate activity and its purpose. Implementation then involves understanding how the firm works and that co-operation as well as competition is needed to allow the company to continue and thrive. The leadership's attention then turns to making it more effective, by applying a system to discover and compare the needs and wishes of the various groups involved.[24]

To the extent that the law restrains the board in looking at any interest other than that of the shareholders as an ultimate goal, it restricts the scope for investment and for the company to play its part in the life of the economy and society to the full. This is a situation the stakeholding perspective could help to change if it were reflected in company law.[25] The board of directors would have greater freedom, in the sense that they would not be confined to looking only at the impact on dividend returns and share prices. In another way, it would be subject to more effective scrutiny as more stakeholding groups were empowered to monitor corporate decisions and protect their expectations. The law has accepted, as noted in the preceding chapters, that the interests of employees and creditors must play a part in corporate decision making on appropriate occasions – as key contributors, they cannot routinely be ignored. There is further competitive advantage to be gained by developing appropriate committed relationships with customers and suppliers in industry, but at present UK law gives little or no support to this where arguably it should do so.[26]

---

22 Clarkson, MBE, 'A Stakeholder Framework for Analysing and Evaluating Corporate Social Performance' (1995) 20 Academy of Management Review 92.

23 Prahalad, CK, 'Corporate Governance or Corporate Value Added? Rethinking the Primacy of Shareholder Value' in Chew, D, *Studies in International Corporate Finance and Governance Systems*, 1997, p 48, at pp 51–54.

24 Freeman, RE, 'Stakeholder Thinking: The State of the Art' in Nasi, J, *Understanding Stakeholder Thinking*, 1995, p 35.

25 Williamson, J, 'The Road to Stakeholding' (1996) 67 Political Quarterly 209.

26 Deakin, S, Lane, C and Wilkinson, F, '"Trust" or Law? Towards an Integrated Theory of Contractual Relations Between Firms' (1994) 21 Journal of Law and Society 329.

One critic of stakeholding has asked:

Should all stakeholder interests be treated equally, along the lines of a utilitarian calculus? Few defenders of the stakeholder approach advocate treating all interests equally. Alternatively, should the stockholders' interests have special priority? If this route is taken, then the stakeholder principle is merely an extension of the profit principle.[27]

It is submitted that neither of these extreme approaches need be accepted. The 'inside' (directly contributing) stakeholders will have priority at different times and all need to be kept satisfied over a term if corporate plans are to succeed, while more wide-ranging considerations (social and environmental impacts) may on occasion be of sufficient weight to rule out a course of action.

'Stakeholder' companies will be better able to build effective alliances between themselves for geographical and operational expansion purposes. They will find it easier to strike satisfactory deals with employee and consumer representatives. They will be at less risk over time of customers or suppliers choosing to deal with another company on price grounds alone. Public companies run in this way will enjoy greater scope to plan for investment in facilities and research.[28] In return, they will have to be prepared to honour their commitments and live up to shared expectations. The competitive, cost-cutting mentality will need to give way to a more co-operative ethos focused on higher performance to benefit all stakeholders.

4.3 THE IDENTIFICATION AND DEMANDS OF STAKEHOLDERS

The original and perhaps the broadest definition of corporate stakeholding refers to a stakeholder as 'any party which can affect or be affected by the activities of a business'.[29] Those individuals and groups who have a direct impact on the productive work of a public company are naturally the most pressing in terms of day to day consideration, while the others come into play at the relevant times and can cause problems to management if mishandled or forgotten. All stakeholders ought to be treated as valuable in their own right, not simply as a means to the end set by others. Nor does any one group have an absolute claim to priority.[30] This is not to say that all their claims are on the

---

27 Fieser, J, 'Do Businesses Have Moral Obligations Beyond What the Law Requires?' (1996) 15 Journal of Business Ethics 457, 460.

28 Casson, M, *Enterprise and Competitiveness: A Systems View of International Business*, 1990, Chapter 5.

29 Freeman, RE, *Strategic Management: A Stakeholder Approach*, 1984, p 25.

30 Sheikh, S, *Corporate Social Responsibilities: Law and Practice*, 1996, p 171.

same level or are relevant in all situations. The interested parties will depend in each case on the actual decision being made.

A narrower definition relates the 'stake' to having time, money or assets at risk as a result of the public company's activities, rather like placing a stake in a casino. Voluntary stakeholders such as capitalists, employees and suppliers agree to invest in the company. There are involuntary stakeholders, perhaps neighbours and communities, who are at risk of harm from the company's actions but have not negotiated with it.[31] Voluntary stakeholders have a moral claim to the good faith fulfilment of their bargains and at present UK law does not always achieve this – for example, employees with long service are poorly recompensed in the event of redundancy. Protection of involuntary stakeholders from abuse is the subject of specific regulation such as environmental and planning law, which is often inadequately understood and enforced. Even on this fairly restricted definition of stakeholding, directors are not in current law made responsible for balancing these risks and safeguarding all investments.

Parkinson suggests that the term 'stakeholder' be reserved for those who enter into long-term relationships with companies and have legitimate expectations of mutual gain from ongoing co-operation. Employees inevitably qualify, as do customers and suppliers who have developed a significant association, not reduced to a written contract, with a company.[32] When considering any right to have board decisions judicially reviewed, it is sensible and practical for potential claimants to be confined to this known group. Their rights, akin to shareholder 'unfair prejudice' claims, would be the result of their particular dealings with the company and the expectations generated by those activities. As far as the directors' strategic deliberations are concerned, however, it is entirely appropriate that they should take into account broader concerns such as the environmental impacts and social consequences of the company's work. Where a major change, such as business expansion or contraction, is planned, the board can and should be held responsible for assessing the outcome for those secondary stakeholders as well as all primary parties.[33]

To qualify as a corporate stakeholder, a party must show genuine grounds for wanting to influence the behaviour and direction of the company. The level of input sought by a contributor might range from daily participation to making comments on major plans. The employees, the investors (of equity and capital) and customers and suppliers (save in competitive markets where

31 Clarkson, MBE, 'A Stakeholder Framework for Analysing and Evaluating Corporate Social Performance' (1995) 20 Academy of Management Review 92.

32 Parkinson, J, 'Company Law and Stakeholder Governance', in Kelly, G, Kelly, D and Gamble, A, *Stakeholder Capitalism*, 1997, p 142, at pp 149–50.

33 Wheeler, D and Sillanpaa, M, 'Including the Stakeholders: the Business Case' (1998) 31 Long Range Planning 201.

they enjoy a ready choice when contracting) will want their voice to be heard in public companies as they make direct contributions, whether of labour, material or cash.[34] In many cases, however, operations will also affect the quality of the environment, the amenity of the area and the broader economic picture. Where recognised bodies exist to represent those interests also, it is undemocratic and unrealistic to shut out their input and deny their interest. In addition to compliance with *ad hoc* environmental and social legislation, it would accordingly be appropriate to mandate public company boards by law to have regard to these factors generally.[35]

Investors need to be provided with appropriate disclosure and are interested first and foremost in dividend returns. Employees need to be developed and encouraged through genuine involvement and are interested above all in their salaries and conditions of employment. Customers can have their feedback heard and expect progress in products and services. Suppliers can be included in co-operation and expect honesty and reliability in dealings. As far as the local community is concerned, relevant information and some monetary returns by way of investment and philanthropy are anticipated from a major business associated with a locality.[36] The most effective public company environmental policies will focus on sustainability and on dealing with campaigns and groups that have drawn attention to specific corporate problems.[37]

The mission of a public company may well be best served if it can enter into carefully selected agreements to exchange technical information or for the distribution of its products. Risks can be dealt with explicitly and shared between the parties who stand to gain from success.[38] This produces a greater incentive for all involved to be innovative and diligent. In recent years there has been a growing trend towards joint ventures, though it is not one that every public company has joined. A concerted effort to communicate with all business partners and keep them informed is in any event a matter of good business sense. Research and development projects may be too large to be funded by one company alone (as developments in the European aircraft and defence industries show), in which case progress depends on the ability to

---

34 Zingales, L, *Corporate Governance*, 1998, p 5.

35 US state legislatures have made efforts to do this by means of 'constituency' statutes enabling directors to have regard to the interests of non-stockholder groups.

36 As far as consultation with employees is concerned, Roger Lyons, General Secretary of MSF, gave the example of the sale of BOC, a major British company, without any discussion with trade unions, in contrast to what would have been required in Germany (speech to Young Fabians on 'The Ethics of Good Business', 17 July 1999 at KPMG London, at p 8 in transcript report).

37 Bill Eyres of the Co-operative Bank, *ibid* , p 31 in transcript report, discussed the bank's pledge of 'ecological sustainability' and how performance is assessed.

38 Mariti, P and Smiley, RH, 'Co-operative Agreements and the Organisation of Industry' in Buckley, PJ and Michie, J, *Firms Organizations and Contracts*, 1996, p 276, at pp 284–87.

construct satisfactory arrangements whereby the stakes of all parties can be clearly established.

More generally, there is the danger of a company losing its 'Licence to Operate' – its informal social approval, in the wording of the RSA Tomorrow's Company inquiry report[39] – if public confidence is not earned and maintained. The political climate, public opinion and media coverage are important in creating this legitimacy, as are industry contacts and reputations. Defining one's 'Success Model' – the long-term stakeholder-centred plan, as the Centre for Tomorrow's Company labels it – for the company and thinking about balanced measurement of its various parts are key leadership functions, as discussed by the Centre for Tomorrow's Company.[40] However large the organisation, the directors need to be involved in this essential work. Management and board openness to the greatest degree possible is 'both right and sensible' (per Sir Adrian Cadbury).[41] Interest in what public companies make and market is widespread among investors and suppliers, as well as workers and consumers who want to gain a rounded picture of the business.

Inside a given company, the emphasis placed upon the various stakeholder claims will depend to some extent upon the type of business it runs – whether or not it is labour intensive, uses costly raw materials, requires substantial research funding and so on. The impact of operations on consumers, on employment, on technology, on society, on the industry and the environment must be examined in the round.[42] One may be dealing with any one of a host of stakeholder combinations. Public interest will naturally be greater if the company has significant environmental impacts or is a major employer. The corollary of separate corporate personality should be that the company, or more particularly the group at the apex of it, is responsible for the consequences of its actions.[43] It is top managers and directors who must take the personal risk of having their decisions examined, in the last resort, by the courts.

Management expert Charles Handy suggests that core employees are the real 'citizens' of the corporate 'community.' Other workers brought in as 'associates' also need to be treated with fairness and respect. In addition:

> [Partnership or associateship] are ... terms that are easier [than citizenship] to apply to two other stakeholders – the suppliers and the customers. It is important for any company to win the trust and co-operation of the largest and most important of these groups, along with the most significant of their investors. Were citizenship to be formalized in any way, it would be

---

39 Goyder, M, *Living Tomorrow's Company*, 1998, pp 92–94.

40 *Ibid*, pp 95–101.

41 Cadbury, A, *The Company Chairman*, 2nd edn 1995, p 121.

42 Blair, M, 'For Whom should Corporations be Run: an Economic Rationale for Stakeholder Management' (1998) 31 Long Range Planning 195.

43 Alkhafaji, n 15 above, Chapter 10 (entitled 'The Stakeholder Model').

appropriate to see these other stakeholders as associate citizens, with at least the right to be kept informed, to be consulted whenever appropriate. This form of associate citizenship should help to bond these crucial players into the long-term aims of the organization and to build a degree of mutual trust by the sharing of information.[44]

The possible legal expression of this associative status vis à vis a public company will be examined in Chapter 6. In addition to the rights to be informed and consulted, it should also encompass provision for some compensation when expectations born of long association are breached.

4.4 THE CLASSIFICATION OF STAKEHOLDERS

Stakeholders can be divided fairly naturally into what have been called their 'Primary' and 'Secondary' groups.[45] Primary stakeholders are all those who count on a 'strictly business' basis, without whom the business simply could not function. They consist of managers (who are at the hub of the whole network), customers, employees, shareholders and suppliers. These participants all require day to day and month by month attention from directors and legally, this needs to be acknowledged in any new Companies Act. Secondary stakeholders have influence and effect in specific, important situations of concern to them. The national and local media (central to corporate external communications), the community and the environment, all of which can be essential to success at critical times, fall into this category. No major change in the operations of a public company can be conducted without attention to those vital constituencies. Information systems serving the board of directors need to provide relevant and clear briefings on the aforementioned areas of concern.

Another division, suggested by Professor David Wheeler and Maria Sillanpaa, both formerly of the Body Shop plc, is that between the 'social' and 'non-social' classes of stakeholder. These are said to be distinguishable by the fact that the former can be communicated with directly by the company while the latter cannot. Future generations, the natural environment and non-human species, plus environmental pressure groups and animal welfare organisations acting as their representatives, are included in the category of 'non-social stakeholders'.[46] This raises the question of how widely 'society' is

---

44   Handy, C, *The Hungry Spirit*, 1997, p 181.

45   Goldenberg, P, 'Shareholders versus Stakeholders: the Bogus Argument' (1998) 19 Co Law 34, 37 speaks of 'groups that have market relationships with a company' who are 'on the inside track' and 'public pressure' and 'interest groups' to which directors may view it as in the company's interests to respond.

46   Wheeler, D and Sillanpaa, M *The Stakeholder Corporation: A Blueprint for Maximising Stakeholder Value*, 1997, pp 167–68.

to be defined (past and/or future; local and/or global). The difficulty with listing the stakeholders in such an all-encompassing manner is that it brings to prominence groups which can rarely have a direct bearing on decisions to be taken by directors and managers 'here and now'. This is not to deny that major choices of location and production, which will have an impact on an area for a considerable time, should be subject to rigorous analysis of their physical and economic impacts. Few UK public company directors are presently qualified to assess such factors, as opposed to making financial projections. There are, however, independent advisers and consultants who can assist in carrying out the necessary studies.

Public companies wield power and enjoy social and economic influence to an extent that makes it credible and appropriate to regard the wider polity as a stakeholder in them. The tax contribution of major businesses is, of course, very substantial, though governments are aware of the danger that multinational companies may relocate if their tax rates are too far out of line with those of other states.[47] Employment policies cannot be delivered in market economies without the support of the large-scale private sector. Economic factors, such as inflation rates, are also determined to a considerable degree by the prices set by public companies. It was argued in Chapter 2 that directors as the leaders of such businesses are in a position of substantive autonomy and social and political power. As a *quid pro quo* for this privilege, they owe an obligation to respect the law and to give consideration to the social interest as expressed primarily by elected representatives.[48]

Stakeholders can also be rated according to their economic and political power. As between investors, clearly those who have contributed most have the loudest voice. Where employees are concerned, if a particular group (such as providers of professional or technical support) could damage or stop the company's work if it withdrew its co-operation, that group will have corresponding influence. Among customers and suppliers, those with the longest and closest ties to the company will have priority.[49] This is not simply a pragmatic issue for the management. Where a particular stakeholder has the power to harm or exclude others, it may be appropriate for the law to address this (in the 1980s, presumably on these grounds, trade union rights to strike and picket were curtailed; in the 2000s, major institutional investors may face compulsion to vote at company Annual General Meetings).

Another type of stakeholder comprises the 'normative groups' who lay down the rules by which public companies must carry out their work. National and local government, regulatory agencies and also the influential

---

47 Picciotto, S, *International Business Taxation*, 1992, in particular Chapters 4, 6, 8 and 10.

48 Solomon, RC, *Ethics and Excellence: Cooperation and Integrity in Business*, 1993, pp 184–85.

49 Mitchell, RK, Agle, BR and Wood, DJ, 'Toward a Theory of Stakeholder Identification and Salience: Defining the Principle of Who and What Really Counts' (1997) 22 Academy of Management Review 853.

consumer and environmental groups fall into this category. Trade and professional associations, the Stock Exchange and increasingly the Financial Services Authority also set standards by which public companies must operate.[50] Individual companies will benefit if they have good relations with, and good reputations among, these bodies, which, in the last resort, have the power to restrict or stop business operations.

Campaigning groups and others (including journalists) who take an interest in the work of a company where it impacts on their concerns are what may be called 'diffused groups.' The name may not be attractive (though it does avoid the slightly pejorative connotations of 'special interest groups' or 'lobbyists') but these stakeholders are indeed widely dispersed in that their remits may cover many aspects of corporate life. Their attention may well come during times of corporate difficulty or crisis.[51] Again, it will be helpful at such times if familiarity with and the confidence of relevant people have already been established.

The regulation of utilities, as the *New Statesman* magazine's treatment of the subject indicated, is not an exclusive example of public companies being required to show more far-reaching concerns than returns to shareholders:

> In reality public authorities have long struck bargains with private concerns in order to meet wider social criteria: planning gain is one example – build a supermarket in return for a road/creche/new park; the 'polluter pays' principle is another. The 'natural' operation of the market is frequently constrained or distorted in the wider social interest.[52]

Social and environmental measures are not left to general legislation and enforcement – they are introduced as part of the internal strategic processes of the public company. The privatised utilities also illustrate the potential for controversy when directors and shareholders are perceived to be benefiting disproportionately from corporate performance compared with customers and employees.[53]

Explaining major business decisions to all those parties who may otherwise raise 'misguided' objections is a board function and often one for the chairman in person. Market capitalist economies vary in the power wielded by the various groups: American shareholders, German employees and Japanese managers are all pivotal within their respective systems. Arguably the most effective combination of all is an 'insider' system involving committed investors, matched by robust competition in the consumer market.[54] The labour market and supplier arrangements are also inextricably

---

50   Dowling, GR, *Corporate Reputations,* 1994, p 26.

51   *Ibid,* p 27.

52   *New Statesman,* Special Supplement, 'The Bare Necessities', 24 July 1998, III.

53   Simpson, A and Bingham, K, *ibid,* XII–XIII.

54   Mayer, C, *Corporate Governance, Competition and Performance,* 1996, pp 15–16.

linked to varying national governance arrangements and economic performance. We may be witnessing some convergence of advanced industrial systems as they all attempt to find an appropriate balance between the interests of the major parties, acknowledging shareholder rights while respecting the rights of employees and expectations of consumers.[55] Certainly it is increasingly difficult for one national government alone to establish and enforce social, environmental, consumer and labour standards when business is operating on a multinational basis.[56]

4.5 RELATIONS WITH AND BETWEEN STAKEHOLDERS

Stakeholders do not exist, nor do they deal with companies, in isolation they interact and communicate between themselves. Social network analysis deals with these interconnections (the amount of overlap between interests) and the centrality of particular parties (the figures at the hub of the connections and those out on the periphery) and can be helpful to companies in understanding stakeholder relations.[57] To complicate analysis further, people as individuals often deal with public companies in more than one capacity – employees may also be customers, while many shareholders are pressure group members, for example – and expect to see a consistent corporate approach. It is certainly not satisfactory today to give one 'message' about the company's plans to a meeting of major investors and a different impression to trade union representatives, and the same applies to other corporate communications.[58] The board should examine not only the workforce, but also the customer and supplier bases, to see whether the maximum advantage is being extracted from existing connections and whether there might be costs benefits to reducing the number, and increasing the strength, of contacts. A full corporate 'stakeholder mapping' exercise for the directors' use will also include public bodies and community and environmental issues and will take into account relevant Non-Governmental Organisations.

Multiple stakeholders inevitably present conflicting demands at times and the board as the ultimate arbiter of policy matters must come to a final

---

55 Price Waterhouse, *Converging Cultures – Trends in European Corporate Governance*, 1997.

56 Galbraith, JK, *The Good Society*, 1996 goes so far as to say (at p 119): 'The economic and social responsibilities are a transitional phase. The ultimate goal is a transnational authority with the subsidiary powers, not excluding the raising and spending of revenue, that go with it.'

57 Rowley, TJ, 'Moving Beyond Dyadic Ties: A Network Theory of Stakeholder Influences' (1997) 22 Academy of Management Review 887.

58 Smythe, J, Dorward, C and Reback, J, *Corporate Reputation*, 1992, assert (at p 8) that:
'* The traditional public relations role must be buried for ever, and
*   The promise offered by the organization to the outside world must match reality.'

decision about them. The power, legitimacy and urgency of each source of pressure must be carefully weighed.[59] Where there is a clash between the interests of the key groups – for example, shareholder dividend requirements and employee pay demands – the balance has to be one that serves the continuing prosperity and development of the corporation as an entity. Other 'single issue' pressure groups which take an interest in the company's development must be paid due attention and reasons given for the refusal or acceptance of their proposals, but their special interests must be set in the context of an overall framework of responsibilities for the company. An organisation that receives many requests for donations, most of which it has to turn down, will be best equipped to deal with matters efficiently and to show it has behaved fairly, if it has an agreed policy as to the types of cause it will normally support. In the same way, economic demands from stakeholders are best dealt with in the context of a predetermined business strategy and code of ethics.

Trust is a link between companies and stakeholders that does not require negotiation of elaborate contracts. The decision to trust, in business as elsewhere, centres on interpersonal expectations, the willingness to accept temporary vulnerability and optimism about one's partner's behaviour. As the Prisoners' Dilemma game shows, trust and dedication to duty are the way to go beyond immediate self-interest and provide a forum for advantageous exchanges to happen.[60] The company's most important intangible asset, its reputation, crucially determines its ability to achieve the benefits of trust. Nothing can replace the interpersonal flows of information in a small company and the larger a corporation grows, the more difficult it is to ensure accurate transmission of messages. Integrated systems of communication for insiders and outsiders need to be arranged to tackle the problem.[61] The more fast-moving and complicated the external commercial and technological environment, the greater the benefits of trust are likely to be. The law can act as a failsafe mechanism to provide some recompense for actual loss caused by detrimental reliance on promises.

The choice to trust leaves open the possibility of abuse as well as gain; those who have invested their time and money in the expectation of a satisfactory relationship may find that their faith proves to be ill-founded. Without detailed contractual terms, expectations can be founded on misunderstandings. In a public company, top management, overseen by the board, is continually responsible for preventing this. Relationships are often worth more than short-term gains, for example, the international success of

---

59 Rowley, n 57 above, pp 896–901.

60 Prodhan, B, *Corporate Governance and Long Term Performance*, 1993, pp 2–3.

61 Scholes, E and Clutterbuck, D, 'Communication with Stakeholders: An Integrated Approach' (1998) 31 Long Range Planning 227.

Germany and Japan has partly been built on implicit contracts.[62] Confidence in the integrity of the top team is vital, as it will need to respond to crises quickly and appropriately. The Johnson and Johnson Tylenol poisoning incident[63] and British Airways' dispute with Virgin Atlantic[64] are frequently-cited examples of near-instinctive responses, which enhanced or diminished companies' images with all their stakeholders. If other key constituencies had access to procedures, comparable to shareholder actions, to question board decisions they believed had been made in bad faith or unfairly, the temptation of directors to opt unquestioningly for quick profits would be lessened. Chapter 6 will explore the practical implications of this approach.

Managerial flexibility and attention to stakeholders can, happily, go together, comment Sifonis and Goldberg:

> An organisation with a reputation for honorable behavior toward its employees, shareholders, customers and the community is an organisation that can be flexible, because it can attract the kind of workforce and strategic allies it needs when it needs them. Such an organisation also has the ability to do new things, introduce new products and services more easily because people trust that an organization with a good reputation will stand by its products and services, even those it has never offered before.[65]

Commitments, once made, should be honoured if the organisation's image is to be protected. At the same time, that image can help the company to build new alliances.

The company must have a distinctive essence and purpose at its core, if it is to remain adaptable but coherent. Blurred boundaries will characterise new relationships with customers and suppliers as they exchange information, share costs and become more technologically dependent on one another. Greater flexibility comes from having a good reputation for integrity, as arrangements can be more open-textured. When there is a changing workforce and shifting supplier alliances, new partners welcome the reassurance of knowing that the central organisation does operate on a basis of principle. If the board had to consider the interests of all relevant stakeholders and the standards expected of directors were more clearly defined in law, the position would become simpler overall. The most retrogressive public company leadership needs to be stimulated to achieve the standards of the most progressive.

---

62 Kay, J, 'The Stakeholder Corporation' in Kelly, Kelly and Gamble, n 32 above, p 125, at pp 133–34.

63 Monks, RAG and Minow, N, *Watching the Watchers: Corporate Governance for the Twenty-First Century*, 1996, pp 42–44.

64 Kitson, A and Campbell, R, *The Ethical Organisation: Ethical Theory and Corporate Behaviour*, 1996, Chapter 3.

65 Sifonis, JG and Goldberg, B, *Corporation on a Tightrope*, 1996, p 59.

Some individuals and groups, as well as being stakeholders themselves, act as opinion leaders. They spread information about a company's goods and services, and about how it treats its workers and suppliers, through the groups that may deal with the company in the future. Formal announcements will have little effect if such 'word of mouth' adversely contradicts it. Directors are generally aware of their influential stakeholders and spend time communicating with them.[66] The level and quality of board contacts with trade unions and consumer groups will greatly influence the likelihood or otherwise of conflict and disruption. Good relations with such official representatives of stakeholder groups are greatly to be desired by any board.

In the final analysis, as long as the shareholders hold the power to replace the directors, they will receive attention and communication to keep them satisfied. Senior employees known to have skills and knowledge that are valuable to the company (and potentially useful to its rivals) will also be high on the list for board contact. Greater public knowledge and scrutiny of corporate plans should be part of the routine price for the capacity to raise funds from the public. While Department of Trade and Industry inspectors have near-draconian powers to act if wrongdoing is suspected,[67] disclosure provisions except in such crises are weak. Improved links between different stakeholder groups (for example, employees receiving information about customer requirements, shareholders being informed about environmental work) would also lead to less misunderstanding and confrontation between constituencies. It is for directors to build and maintain those bridges.[68]

4.6 CORPORATE STAKEHOLDERS AND ECONOMIC PERFORMANCE

The basic philosophy of the responsible public company, like that of the individual businessperson, is centred on honesty, maintaining personal integrity, not cheating, never stealing and honouring commitments. If these principles are not seen to be valued at the highest levels of a large organisation, they will very likely be disregarded lower down the hierarchy. If the majority of the employees would not be happy to be treated as they are expected to treat others during their working time, to tell their spouses and children about business decisions and see them discussed in local or national

---

66 Mitchell, NJ, *The Generous Corporation: A Political Analysis of Economic Power*, 1989, Chapter 8.

67 Companies Act 1985 Part XIV (ss 431–53).

68 Porter, M, 'Capital Choices: Changing the Way America Invests In Industry' in Chew, n 23 above, p 5, at pp 13–16, speaks of measures to: 'Better align the goals of capital providers, corporations, directors, managers, employees, customers, suppliers and society.'

newspapers, there may be difficulties of morale and commitment.[69] Rigid ethical separation of professional life and private life is both unrealistic and unsatisfactory for the well-educated, thoughtful workforce needed by most public companies today. Other stakeholders, including consumers and investors, are becoming increasingly aware of their ethical influence on directors. If they wish a particular set of social and environmental standards to be upheld, customers and institutions can, in effect, vote for it with their cash.

There are several possible stances for a public company in relation to corporate social responsibility issues:

- reactive – fight all the way to avoid non-financial questions;
- defensive – do what is required to avoid trouble but no more;
- accommodative – be progressive in attitude;
- proactive – lead change in the industry concerned.[70]

It is primarily for the management, under the guidance of the board of directors, to establish the position that will be taken by a public company, and there is considerable variation among competing businesses at present. Legal rules simply lay down minimum standards for business, which are socially accepted and endorsed by the democratic process. They do tend to lag behind the standards set by the most advanced public company leaderships for themselves. Businesses must, of course, be distinguished from charitable or social welfare bodies, but can contribute a great deal of expertise to the non-commercial sector and to social progress. Above all, having decided on its commercial objectives, a company should be concerned to address the direct impact of its activities and treat all those who come into contact with it with justice and decency.[71]

Fostering a general atmosphere of stability and loyalty brings benefits in terms of reduced transaction costs and increased participant commitment. Permitting the greed and ambitions of a business elite to carry the day would benefit only those at the top of the corporate hierarchy. The law can play a part in introducing moral responsibility to public company operations. Processes used naturally by morally responsible individuals can be adapted for the public company boardroom.[72] Rational choice for individuals involves a lack of impulsiveness, care in examining the alternatives and consequences and clarity of purpose. If directors were required to show that they had considered all the available materials and exercised their judgment in the

69 Mueller, RK, *Anchoring Points for Corporate Directors: Obeying the Unenforceable*, 1996, pp 102–05.
70 Carroll, AB, *Business and Society: Ethics and Stakeholder Management*, 1989, pp 41–45.
71 cf Sternberg, E, *Just Business*, 2nd edn 2000, pp 80–87, which starts from the assumption that 'the definitive purpose of a business is to maximise long-term owner value'.
72 Maclagan, P, *Management and Morality*, 1998, Chapter 11.

interests of the company, that would put such a process at the heart of corporate deliberations. Respect for the lives and interests of others as valuable in themselves is a further element of morally responsible decision making. The stakeholder approach enshrined in law, listing relevant parties and protecting their interests, would go some way towards promoting this.[73]

In 1960, McGregor indicated that so-called 'Theory X', the traditional management view of direction and control (that people in general have an inherent dislike of work, must be coerced or threatened to push them to make an effort, wish to avoid responsibility and have little ambition) could more profitably be superseded by 'Theory Y' (that the expenditure of physical and mental effort at work is just as natural as rest or play, that people will exercise self-direction in the service of objectives to which they are personally committed, that such commitment is a function of the rewards associated with attainment of the objectives, that the average person learns to seek responsibility under suitable conditions and has the capacity to exercise a high degree of imagination and creativity in solving work-related problems).[74] In the customer service and technology-related businesses that play an ever-larger part in the economy, these observations are increasingly relevant. In addition, there is a 'Theory X' of relations with suppliers and partner firms (which assumes that they will do a poor job if not formally checked, that they cannot usefully show initiative or make suggestions and that they will cheat given the opportunity), as opposed to a newer 'Theory Y' (which assumes professional standards of conduct, a willingness to work hard and the possibility of co-operation towards a common goal). The latter view is evidently not as widespread in the UK as in some other industrialised economies.[75]

At present, it is only shareholders in the UK who can legally challenge board decisions if they feel that their interests have been unfairly prejudiced and their legitimate expectations not met. They may well do so if, for example, dividends have been low while management remuneration has remained generous. Other groups which have also 'invested' in the company's activities by co-specialising in them, including employees and major suppliers and dependent customers, ought to have a similar ultimate right of veto.[76] As Teubner puts it:

> To privilege one group, whether shareholders or management, that acquires flexibility through contractual arrangements would be bound to be sub-optimal in the interest of the corporate actor ... 'Organisational surplus value' arises (1) through the building up of long-term cooperative arrangements

---

73 Goodpaster, KE and Matthews, JB (Jr), 'Can a Corporation have a Conscience?' (1982) Harvard Business Review 132, 134–35.

74 McGregor, D, *The Human Side of Enterprise*, 1960, Chapters 3 and 4.

75 Plender, n 11 above, Chapters 6 and 12.

76 Maclagan, n 72 above, pp 148–51.

which would be continually destroyed by contractual flexibility; (2) through the diffuseness of 'commitments' in the organisation which by comparison with rigid, sharply defined contractual obligations produce more situational flexibility and finally (3) in the orientation towards the organisation's interest which provides stronger orientation than mere linkage to a contractual purpose.[77]

The benefit of doing business through an ongoing firm, as opposed to relying totally on one-off contracts, is that transaction costs are saved by not having to spell out in advance all the work that will be required, for example, of employees and suppliers. The board is charged with bringing together the various elements of the business mix in order to produce goods and services that will be profitable for the company and they can best do this by paying adequate attention to all of these constituents.[78]

Some of the most important facets of a responsible, successful business are its value as a long-term investment, innovativeness as an enterprise, the ability to attract, to develop and retain talented people, general awareness of community and environmental matters, the provision of goods and services to high standards and philanthropy that fits in with the corporate mission. These elements all interact and satisfy various stakeholders while contributing to sustainable business growth.[79] A solid business reputation will attract additional custom, encourage good performance from suppliers and assist in building a strong team. As far as donations are concerned, these need to be carefully targeted and managed according to a policy that relates to the company's purposes.[80]

4.7 STAKEHOLDER MANAGEMENT

In order to be able to serve its stakeholders well, the successful public company must undertake a process of studying and mapping its relationships – that is, assessing who its main participants are and who has an interest in its activities. The question 'Who can stop your business operating?' is a good one for directors to examine, remembering required inputs, desired outputs and issues of public interest. They must go on to ask 'What will the reaction of those parties be if we take this particular step?'. 'Constituency' statutes like those in the US only follow basic public relations imperatives in this respect.

---

77 Teubner, G, 'Enterprise Corporatism: New Industrial Policy and the "Essence" of the Legal Person' (1988) 36 American Journal of Comparative Law 130, 154.

78 Leader, S, 'Private Property and Corporate Governance Part I: Defining the Interests' in Patfield, F, *Perspectives on Company Law*, 1995, pp 85–88, 104–07, 112–13.

79 Sternberg, n 71 above, pp 87–90.

80 Carroll, AB, 'Stakeholder Thinking in Three Models of Management Morality: A Perspective with Strategic Implications' in Nasi, n 24 above, p 47, at p 70.

The public company board in future will need to consider hiring independent auditors, not just of financial results but also of social and environmental impacts, and the production of clear, attractive reports and accounts of relevance to all the main parties. The companies that make such efforts will reap many rewards in smoother co-operation and new opportunities.

Powerful and influential stakeholders, who may well include core employees and suppliers and lenders, must be given priority, albeit in differing measures according to the circumstances, and if important decisions do not go in their favour, the reasons need to be explained in order to retain their support. Persuasive and interested stakeholders, such as community and environmental groups, who are not direct participants in the business but may be concerned about its major decisions, need to be informed and consulted in order to avoid costly errors of judgment. The board has a responsibility to ensure that it sees adequate information from data and surveys, preferably conducted by experienced independent persons, to keep it up to date with the views of all parties.[81] Personal communications with employees, major customers and suppliers and relevant interest groups, also need to be maintained by the board. A duty upon directors to obtain and consider relevant information before reaching their decisions, failing which any key party aggrieved could seek review of the outcome, would contribute greatly to this process. The framing of such directors' duties in legislation will be examined in Chapters 5 and 6.

The public company Annual Report contains accounts for evaluation of financial performance, details of board membership and remuneration, (usually perfunctory) statements of employment policy and (even shorter) accounts of payment times for suppliers. Independent environmental audit, full disclosure of all charitable and political donations and customer and supplier profiles could usefully be added to this compendium in the future.[82] In cases of good corporate performance, such reports would enhance the company's public image. It must be for each company to decide how then to use the Annual Report to set out details of its products and services and its overall plans. It should keep in mind that individual customers and consumer groups, community leaders and environmental organisations, may all refer to the document and gain positive or negative impressions from it. Attractive presentation is also important for this reason. Under the proposals of the Company Law Review Steering Group, public companies would be compelled to provide a far fuller and more 'rounded' review.[83] Some compulsion in this respect would make comparisons between different public companies rather easier without causing significant difficulties.

---

81 Wheeler and Sillanpaa, n 46 above, Chapter 12.

82 Monks, RAG and Minow, N, *Corporate Governance*, 1995, pp 67–74, cite the examples of Atlantic Richfield and Eastern Gas and Fuel Associates in the US.

83 Company Law Review Steering Group, *Modern Company Law for a Competitive Economy – Final Report*, July 2001, Chapter 8.

Another opportunity for communication with the whole range of stakeholders is the company's Annual General Meeting. As noted in Chapter 3, the Hampel Committee have commended the practice of some public companies in making business presentations, having all board committee chairs as well as the chief executive and the chairman available to answer any questions and producing a summary of the proceedings for distribution afterwards.[84] The meeting is already the company's largest public examination and yearly opportunity to set out its aims and objectives. It should be recognised that customers, long-term suppliers and *bona fide* community representatives and environmental groups have a legitimate interest in the progress and plans of a public company too and arrangements should be made to enable them to attend. For reasons of practicality and time, it may be necessary to stipulate that questions from these stakeholders be submitted in writing in advance or to limit them in number, but there seems no good reason to exclude them altogether. An exchange of views might inform all stakeholders of each other's priorities. The Steering Group considered whether public company Annual General Meetings achieve anything of value, but concluded that the time was not yet right to abolish them.[85] Extending the meeting to provide a wider forum for debate could help to revitalise the event.

Within a framework of stakeholder relationships, the board will be looking to build up a stable core of investors and, in practice, will do this by communicating regularly with the institutional shareholders. More strategically, it may investigate which major investors might be expected to hold its shares but currently do not.[86] Pension funds, in particular, often have a 30-year span between receiving contributions and making payments to a given client, so they are the most natural long-term investors. However, the purpose of investment and research and development needs to be set out clearly in order to gain institutional support. Where the corporate situation warrants it, the major equity holders who wish to exercise their rights as long-term stakeholders may consider establishing a formal shareholder committee as a means of dealing with the directors on important corporate issues. The tradition in the UK has been for discussions with large institutions to take place privately, which itself leads to allegations of favouritism and even insider dealing.[87]

The question of whether stakeholder groups should have representation on the board will be further discussed in Chapter 7 and is linked to possible

---

84 Committee on Corporate Governance (Chair: Sir Ronald Hampel), *Final Report*, January 1998, Part 5 section IV.

85 Company Law Review Steering Group, n 83 above, paras 4.25–4.50, 4.61–4.64.

86 Useem, M, 'Shareholders as a Strategic Asset' (1996) 39 California Management Review 8.

87 Cadbury, n 41 above, p 134, suggests more open, businesslike presentations for interested investors, and fewer private briefings ('free lunches') for a select audience.

changes in public company structures. *Prima facie* it seems more valuable to stakeholders for them to have substantial input in the strategic and planning process than in review after the event. Within a unitary board system, both stages are the responsibility of all the directors, the executives and non-executives. The board cannot avoid the task of balancing relevant interests as it seeks to drive the business forward. The question is whether it will have in place a sensible and defensible framework for taking those decisions. A group which has little knowledge of customer and supplier bases and which is all of much the same mindset as far as community and environmental issues are concerned is not likely to perform as well as a more balanced team.

The Institute of Directors in its initial response to the Company Law Consultation Paper stated that:

> Company law should highlight that in making decisions, both collectively as part of the board and individually, must act in the general interests of the company ... However, company law should not attempt in any way to prescribe how boards of directors should carry out their decision making function.[88]

While private sector organisations such as the Institute of Directors can play an important part in spreading best practice and providing training for directors, it is surely unsatisfactory that the law itself should give no guidance in statute on the routine behaviour expected in the boardroom. There is a great deal of possible middle ground between leaving public company directors subject to no regulation at all and being excessively rigid in prescribing their conduct and how they spend their time at work.

It should be remembered that managers, including the executive directors, are themselves corporate stakeholders whose time and reputation, as well as their income prospects and often some of their capital, are bound up with the company. They therefore have a powerful incentive to ensure that the organisation consistently performs to high standards, especially as pride and prospects are boosted when the individual's association with the company generates a positive response. So far as the financial rewards for the managerial contribution are concerned, these need to be as fair and reasonable, in the light of market conditions and the situation of the company, as the treatment of the other primary stakeholders. Independent assessment by objective, experienced non-executive directors and submission of each 'package' for shareholder approval are changes which are becoming widespread and are welcome. More explicit ties to treatment of other stakeholders include making assessment of any bonus conditional on improving customer service and satisfaction[89] and even capping top executive

---

88   Institute of Directors, *The Government's Company Law Review: Modern Company Law for a Competitive Economy – The IoD's Initial Response*, 1998.

89   Some of the privatised utilities companies, for example, including Scottish Power and Anglian Water have adopted this approach.

salaries to a fixed multiple of those of the lowest-paid workers in the company.[90] If management rewards continue to behave in a manner which is out of line with the benefits which other stakeholders are deriving – and there is little sign that non-executive board remuneration committees have yet made much impact on this – the legislature may proceed to introduce those measures in sectors where they are perceived to be needed.

The ethos of stakeholding, particularly as regards attention to customers, employees and business partners, needs to pervade the management team and appropriate training for all employees in social and environmental policies needs to be provided if change is to be effective and lasting. Customer care and quality criteria, which are integral to the management philosophy of efficient public companies,[91] are natural parts of a stakeholder organisation. Legal advice should be sought where doubts arise and always followed precisely – any sense that directors and management are happy to 'bend' the rules may translate in time to unethical conduct by employees. Ethical codes can be prepared which are sufficient in most cases and can be augmented by the availability of an advisor to assist employees in cases of doubt.

The effect of the stakeholding philosophy is to turn relationships of many different kinds which are usually temporary into more lasting arrangements for the benefit of the company. Supermarket and garage customer 'loyalty cards' and retailer and manufacturer main supplier lists are straightforward, commonplace ways of trying to achieve this. Even without the agreement at the outset of precise terms, the law can act where necessary to uphold the bargain struck by the parties where broad arrangements for future business dealings were in place.[92] In the event of a takeover, relationships which had been envisaged as enduring ones are broken and there is a case for parties which had planned in the expectation of continuity to be protected, as the Transfer of Undertakings (Protection of Employment Rights) Regulations 1992 safeguard employees.

4.8 CONCLUSION: PRINCIPLES IN PRACTICE

It is in the business as a workplace that stakeholding principles can make an immediate impact, as those who invest their time in the company's life see their status as participants increase. Business partners dealing with the corporation should also notice a real difference in prompt payments and

---

90 As suggested by the Channel 4 Commission on Poverty in Britain in their published report, 1996.

91 Oakland, JS, *Total Quality Management: Text with Cases*, 1995, quotes examples including Esso, EXXON, CarnaudMetalBox plc and Pirelli Communication Cables.

92 McKendrick, E, 'The Regulation of Long-term Contracts in English Law' in Beatson, J and Friedmann, D, *Good Faith and Fault in Contract Law*, 1995, pp 305, 316–21 and *passim*.

negotiations for long-term partnerships. It is for governments to set social priorities, but large companies need to 'fall into line' if they are to be treated as part of the solution to social and environmental problems and accorded political respect. The change to an inclusive approach will not happen without the understanding and permission, at least, of institutional fund managers, who themselves ought to be planning for long-term growth, especially where pension funds are concerned. Motivation and effectiveness are likely to improve dramatically when people (both employees and suppliers and customers and neighbours) understand the aims of the company. If difficulties nevertheless arise in a competitive environment, there is no *a priori* reason why one constituency should always bear the costs.

Stakeholding has rather modestly been described as a matter of 'taming' the 'harsher aspects of capitalism',[93] but could provide something more positive by supplying a model for good companies to aspire to without being overly prescriptive. It has the potential to be a more humane, yet more flexible, alternative to traditional management, a kind of 'Third Way' for large-scale business,[94] one which neither relies on excessive contractualism nor invites over-regulation to correct its imbalances. No group that has made a contribution to corporate success should find itself going unrecognised. The stakeholder model is highly adaptable in that, outside the core area of employees and managers, each company will have different groups that follow its fortunes and affect its activities. Where appropriate, the opportunity to build constructive relationships with customers and suppliers ought to be seized. Directors need to be alert and accessible to make it work well, but when it does, the foundation for truly sustainable growth is constructed.[95]

The demarcations between customers and suppliers and internal operations, and between permanent employees and casual labour, are becoming less and less clear.[96] The overall responsibility of the public company board, with its top management, for the conduct of its operations should not be put in doubt by this. Treatment of labour providers, whether core staff members or not, and of suppliers, those within the inner circle and others outside, of customers both large and small and of investors in debt and equity, is ultimately the responsibility of the directors jointly. Standards that will not be compromised need to be agreed and promulgated by each individual board to suit the circumstances in which it finds its organisation. The role of the law is to provide a framework for the level of care and attention expected of public company directors, providing that their business

---

93 Plender, n 11 above.

94 Roddick, A, 'A Third Way for Business, too?' *New Statesman*, 3 April 1998, 24.

95 Giddens, A, *The Third Way and its Critics*, 2000, pp 151–53, gives a cautious analysis of contrasting national systems.

96 Fruin, WM, *The Japanese Enterprise System*, 1992, Chapters 7 and 8 discusses interfirm networks and corporate interdependence in the Japanese context.

judgment will be respected if they have considered all the relevant evidence and made their decision in the best interests of the company. This means greater freedom than is possible in a relentlessly shareholder-driven system, but liberty exercised within a zone of responsibility.

A blinkered view of what constitutes 'business success' restricts opportunities for worthwhile business development and leads to unfairness in the treatment of important stakeholders. The economy and polity suffer when short termist views prevail in public company strategy.[97] Traditional UK accounting rules have encouraged such a limited outlook, counting employees only as a cost and putting no value on the company's network of connections. Human resources and investment in customer and supplier bases should at least be reflected in the Annual Report and statements of the directors. There is also the alleged bias of UK public company management and boards towards accounting expertise, which may be contrasted with German emphasis on technical specialisms and perhaps a Japanese regard for personnel skills. This further strengthens the argument for a more representative board of directors.

All stakeholders must count with directors, but none too much. Investors whether of loans or equity are of course vital, but if a board has confidence in the corporate direction it wishes to pursue and some of the shareholders or the lenders think it excessively risk-taking, the directors should ultimately be capable of 'selling' their plans to other financial backers. The top management team itself is one of the primary objects of board attention (along with product and stock market performance which shows the external verdict on those people and their decisions) and is neither irreplaceable nor unaccountable in a stakeholder setting. Directors should indeed communicate to management the company's responsibilities to its constituencies and ensure that departments and functions play their part. Both corporate finance and executive appointments are ultimately matters for the directors in the light of the plans they have formed for the company – neither more nor less. Board decisions will be much easier to make and defend in the light of a clear set of corporate responsibilities.

Many UK public company boards currently do not know enough about the views of all stakeholders to avoid serious and costly errors nor to plan for future prosperity. This is in part a function of the fairly narrow social group, with much shared and similar experience, from which directors of those companies have traditionally been drawn.[98] It also comes from the narrowly financial focus of reporting and audit with which the directors must deal. As

---

97 Tylecote, A, Doo Cho, Y and Zhang, W, 'National Technological Styles Explained in Terms of Stakeholding Patterns, Enfranchisements and Cultural Differences: Britain and Japan' (1998) 10 Technology Analysis and Strategic Management 423.

98 Paxman, J, *Friends In High Places*, 1990, gives an illuminating account of the social milieu that produces British leaders, for business and for other areas life.

the Hampel Report pointed out, a great deal of attention has been given to ensuring the financial probity of public companies and less to finding new means of enhancing their performance. It is here submitted, in contradistinction to the Hampel Committee's view, however, that improving communications with and attention to all the stakeholders can best advance the latter aim. The company will develop a stronger identity and greater loyalty from its customers, suppliers and workers.

Responsiveness to the concerns of all parties interested in the business is the key to corporate success in the new Millennium. A statutory formula specifying the many stakeholders to whom directors must have regard would lead to a change of approach, where needed, and provide this advantage. Not all the stakeholders in any public company can be satisfied with business decisions all of the time, but proper explanations must be given by directors to pre-empt, as far as possible, unnecessary disaffection and damage to the corporate reputation. In the final analysis, primary contributors, be they core employees, relational customers and suppliers or investors, merit protection from exploitation as a matter of fundamental principle.[99] Companies legislation can assist this development by spelling out the primary stakeholders and giving them capacity in the last resort to question board decisions which are, or appear to be, seriously inequitable. Public companies are not in any realistic sense the property of any one group, and it is outmoded for them to be treated as such.

Speaking to business leaders in Singapore, Tony Blair stated during the run-up to the 1997 General Election:

> We cannot by legislation guarantee that a company will behave in a way conducive to trust and long-term commitment. But it is surely time to assess how we shift the emphasis in corporate ethos from a company being a mere vehicle for the capital market to be traded, bought and sold as a commodity, towards a vision of the company as a community or partnership in which each employee has a stake, and where a company's responsibilities are more clearly delineated.[100]

If this is to be made a reality, legislative change in the context of a new Companies Act is an obvious place to start. If employees and major customers and suppliers and others with a stake in a public company had a statutory right to information and consultation and in certain circumstances to seek review of corporate decisions, the rhetoric of stakeholding would be given substance in Britain.

---

99 Solomon, RC, *Ethics and Excellence*, 1993, pp 179–86.

100 Blair, T, speech to the Singapore Business Community, 8 January 1996, quoted in *New Britain*, 1996, p 291 at p 295.

CHAPTER 5

DIRECTORS' DUTIES IN LEGISLATION

5.1 PROPOSALS FOR CHANGE

The political climate is currently favourable both to fresh discussion of the responsibilities of directors and to treating public companies as a distinct business medium for the purposes of regulation. The government's stated priorities are to ensure that the legislation emerges in a modernised, more 'user-friendly' state than the present lengthy amalgam of detail and to enhance the competitiveness of British industry. The Green Paper 'Modern Company Law for a Competitive Economy' left open the question of changes to the formulation of directors' duties. It specifically noted that one issue for review was whether board members' fiduciary responsibilities should take account of interests other than those of the shareholders.[1] The possibilities for clarification and modification of directors' duties were also addressed. While the work of the previous Committees on Corporate Governance, most recently the group chaired by Sir Ronald Hampel, was praised, the Labour government, which has used the rhetoric of inclusion and partnership in society and in business,[2] considers that the stakeholding approach should be examined. This was not followed up by the Company Law Review Steering Group, which, as was noted in Chapter 4, used the term 'Pluralism'.[3] In the subsequent draft statement of directors' duties, ultimate primacy for shareholder interests was deliberately retained.[4]

The Law Commission Consultation Paper entitled 'Company Directors: Regulating Conflicts of Interest and Formulating a Statement of Duties'[5] was intended to connect with, and feed in to, the company law review process.[6] The document examined in some detail Part X of the Companies Act 1985, which deals with directorial 'conflict of interest' situations. The objective was to consider whether the existing requirements were appropriate and whether they could be simplified. The second part of the paper dealt with the advantages, disadvantages and problems of codifying directors' duties. The

1   DTI, *Modern Company Law for a Competitive Economy*, March 1998, p 10.

2   Blair, T, *The Third Way*, 1998, pp 3–4, 8–11.

3   Company Law Review Steering Group, *Modern Company Law for a Competitive Economy: The Strategic Framework*, February 1999, para 5.1.

4   Company Law Review Steering Group, *Modern Company Law for a Competitive Economy- Final Report*, July 2001, Annex C.

5   Law Commission Consultation Paper, *Company Directors: Regulating Conflicts of Interest and Formulating a Statement of Duties*, September 1998.

6   *Ibid*, 2.

project was, however, specifically expressed to exclude such matters as 'the question whether directors should owe duties to persons other than the company such as employees and the community' and 'any duties of good citizenship the company may owe to the community'.[7] The Law Commission was therefore concerned with the form and presentation of directors' duties under 'the current general law', rather than with a fundamental re-appraisal of the legal position.[8] In the final report, following empirical work by the ESRC Centre for Business Research, a brief (non-exhaustive) statutory statement of directors' duties was proposed, which reflected the existing common law.[9] This was largely accepted by the Steering Group.[10]

The current scheme of regulation of directorial conduct is, in form, a mixture of traditional common law, recent legislation[11] and City-based self-regulation.[12] Individual cases are still very important when an overall understanding of board responsibilities is required, although key judgments are not conveniently accessible to and useable by directors. There are procedural requirements, designed to avoid self-dealing, which must be met where an individual director is making commercial contracts with the company on whose board he or she sits.[13] In addition, where the company is in some financial difficulty, legal advisers to directors must draw their attention to the risks of personal liability, not only for fraudulent trading but also for 'wrongful' continuance of trading where there is no likelihood that debts can ultimately be paid.[14] The relevant part of the common or statutory law depends on the financial stage of the company's life that has been reached. Fiduciary duties (to the company and its stakeholders) and rules against self-dealing are related in practice and should be addressed as part of a coherent package.

As to the content of the existing rules, there is some discrepancy between the stringency of formal procedures designed to counter directorial self-dealing[15] (for example, as regards employment contracts and compensation for loss of office) and the lack of specificity where corporate decision making processes are concerned. On the one hand, even where its utility is dubious,

---

7   *Ibid*, 19.
8   *Ibid*, Chapter 16.
9   Law Commission Report, *Company Directors: Regulating Conflicts of Interest and Formulating a Statement of Duties*, September 1999, Part 16 and Appendix A.
10 Company Law Review Steering Group, n 4 above, para 3.40.
11 Eg Company Directors Disqualification Act 1986.
12 Eg Combined Code (*Principles of Good Governance and Code of Best Practice, annexed to Listing Rules*).
13 Eg Companies Act 1985 ss 319–20.
14 Insolvency Act 1986 ss 213–14.
15 Companies Act 1985 Part X contains detailed rules on employment contracts, payments to directors on loss of office, substantial property transactions and loans or quasi-loans to directors, but no effective control over annual remuneration packages.

the current law requires disclosure to the board of individual directors' interests in contracts made by the company.[16] On the other hand, executive and non-executive directors of public companies can be appointed without ensuring that they have a clear understanding of their accountability in law or their place in what might be called 'public life'.[17] The promulgation and enforcement of stricter standards for board decision making would do much to ensure probity while making public companies more 'inclusive'. Both of these areas have been matters of public concern, as press coverage of privatised utilities in the 1990s illustrated. Business leaders are now expected to show social awareness in their 'core' work even as they are invited to help solve social problems.[18]

The courts have employed various analogies (with trusteeship,[19] partnership,[20] employment[21] and agency,[22] to name four examples) in formulating their conceptions of the duties of company directors. As commercial and social expectations have progressed, and despite the doctrine of precedent which has been restrictive in other areas, the courts have changed their expectations. They are also less inclined to show leniency to a public company director or one who professes special expertise than to a person of relatively modest means running a small business through the medium of a company.[23] Nevertheless, the interpretation of concepts such as 'duty not to make a private profit' or 'duty to act in the best interests of the corporation as a whole'[24] has been a matter for the individual judge in each particular situation. This has made possible a wide range of interpretations of

---

16 *Neptune (Vehicle Washing Equipment) Ltd v Fitzgerald* [1996] Ch 274, relating to a sole director, is called by Davies (in *Gower's Principles of Modern Company Law*, 6th edn 1997, at p 629) 'the apotheosis of meaningless disclosure'. *Runciman v Walter Runciman plc* [1992] BCLC 1084 effectively disregarded the omission to disclose an interest which was known to other directors, but as Davies remarks (p 630) this 'does nothing to put in place effective disclosure provisions'.

17 The CBI's PROBE set of 'benchmarking' tools includes CONTOUR, which focuses on Environment and Health and Safety Best Practice, Stakeholders and Organisation and Culture (www.cbi.org.uk).

18 Education Action Zones and urban regeneration projects such as those in Hulme, Manchester and Easterhouse, Glasgow, seeking private sector involvement alongside local authority strategic planning are two prominent recent examples.

19 *Selangor United Rubber Estates Ltd v Cradock (No 3)* [1968] 2 All ER 1073.

20 *Clegg v Edmondson* (1857) 8 De GM & G 787.

21 *Lister v Stubbs* (1890) 45 Ch D 1.

22 *Great Eastern Railway Co v Turner* (1892) 8 Ch App 149.

23 Eg compare *Re Barings plc (No 5)* [1999] BCLC 433, which concerned the collapse of Barings Bank and expressly emphasised that the greater the remuneration of a particular director, the greater the responsibility that may be expected, with cases such as *Secretary of State for Trade and Industry v Rosenfield* [1999] BCC 413 which emphasised public protection and commercial necessity.

24 See eg the subtle change in rhetoric between *Heron International Ltd v Lord Grade* [1983] BCLC 244 and *Dawson International plc v Coats Paton plc* [1991] BCC 278 where the board's duties in the event of a takeover are concerned.

directors' duties. Taking the case law as a whole, there has been cautious judicial deference to the decisions of board members and their right to manage the company's affairs.[25]

There is, however, a core set of basic duties and fundamental responsibilities attaching to fiduciary positions in general and to all those who are, as Adam Smith described company directors, 'managers rather of other people's money than of their own'.[26] The Law Commission identified a core of 'reasonably clear' basic duties for fiduciaries: the 'no conflict' rule', the 'no profit' rule, the 'undivided loyalty' rule and the duty of confidentiality.[27] Where a director makes a profit on his or her own account, using knowledge possessed by reason of the office, the director is liable to account for that profit to the company.[28] The director must not put him- or herself in a position where his or her duties conflict with those of the corporation as an entity.[29] While it may generally be true, as the Law Commission has suggested, that the 'fair dealing' rules are well understood, their enforceability is threatened if directors are not effectively monitored.[30] There is a relatively stringent regime of procedures to involve shareholders in controlling contracts in which they directors are interested as individuals and loans to them.[31]

A statutory list that brought together the duties of directors would provide a much clearer focus for both directorial and judicial attention than the existing law. The knowledge that one may have to demonstrate the basis of one's strategic decisions and the information used in arriving at them is likely to be a powerful incentive for measured, well-planned corporate behaviour.[32] Should there be any dispute of fact about the matters which had been taken into account by a company board, that is the kind of issue which judges are experienced in assessing. The collection and assessment of evidence that may dispose of a matter before trial, or in the courtroom if necessary, is a feature of the British legal process. If the role of the private sector generally, and public companies specifically, is to serve the public's demands and interests as responsibly and efficiently as possible, primary legislation must be the place

---

25 Eg *Re Tottenham Hotspur plc* [1994] 1 BCLC 655 where Nicholls VC said (at 660): 'Whether Mr [Terry] Venables' dismissal [as Chief Executive] was in the best interests of Tottenham is not a matter for the court to decide. That is a matter for the Tottenham board to whom the decision is entrusted under the company's constitution ...'

26 Smith, A, *The Wealth of Nations* (1776), 1910, Vol ii, p 229.

27 Law Commission, *Fiduciary Duties and Regulatory Rules*, December 1995, p 2.

28 *Regal (Hastings) Ltd v Gulliver* [1967] 2 AC 134.

29 *Aberdeen Railway Co v Blaikie Bros* (1854) 1 Macq 461.

30 The CBI published a guide entitled Fraud: Risk and Practice, 2000, and states: 'Corporate fraud costs business hundreds of millions of pounds each year. Ignoring the risk is not an option.'

31 Companies Act 1985 Part X ('Controlling Self-Dealing by Directors').

32 Commission on Public Policy and British Business, *Promoting Prosperity: a Business Agenda for Britain*, 1997, p 107 recommended that UK company directors be empowered by legislation to take a broader view.

to determine how this is to be done. Where, historically, UK public companies have paid greatest attention to returns on capital, and German and Scandinavian employees' rights have imposed high costs on business in those countries, genuinely forward-looking legislation should seek a sustainable balance of interests.[33]

More fundamentally, if responsible conduct is to be demanded of corporate business, there is a problem of locating in a real person the accountability for producing that behaviour.[34] In a volume edited by the consumer activist and US presidential candidate Ralph Nader, the matter is expressed as follows: 'Much of the deterrent effect of heavy fines on individual businesspeople comes from the social stigma of a criminal conviction. But individuals within a corporation may feel shielded from any stigma that attaches to the corporate entity ...'.[35] The reconnection of managerial leadership with corporate responsibility is crucial to restoring faith in large-scale enterprise and rests on identification with directors.[36] They must, of necessity, delegate responsibility for daily operations, but they need to establish decision making processes that reflect contemporary political demands on business. The incremental development of the law through precedent is inadequate by itself to send the clear signals that are needed.

5.2 ARGUMENTS AGAINST CHANGE

In 1995 the Law Commission's report on fiduciary duties concluded that legislation in this area as a codifying measure should not be recommended, as it was thought to be both impractical and undesirable.[37] The options of complete or partial codification of trustee-type duties were re-examined in 1998 and the 'arguments against' legal change were again well canvassed.[38]

---

33 Loredo, E and Suarez, E, 'Corporate Governance in Europe: is Convergence Desirable?' (1998) 15 International Journal of Management 525.

34 Gobert, J, 'Corporate Criminality: Four Models of Fault' (1994) 14 Legal Studies 393 argues (at 409): 'Companies should bear responsibility for crimes occurring in the course of their business without the need for the Crown to attach fault to specific persons within the company. It should be the company's responsibility to collect information regarding potential dangers possessed by its employees, collate the data, and implement policies which will prevent reasonably foreseeable risks from occurring.'

35 Nader, R and Shugart, C, 'Old Solutions for Old Problems' in Nader, *No Access to Law: Alternatives to the American Judicial System*, 1980.

36 *Williams v Natural Life Health Foods Ltd* [1998] 2 All ER 577 reasserts the principle that an individual is not liable for negligence committed as an officer of a company through which he exercises corporate business. Following the Zeebrugge ferry disaster, no individual member of the hierarchy was sufficiently senior to be identified with the P&O corporation: *R v P&O European Ferries (Dover) Ltd* (1990) 93 Cr App R 72.

37 Law Commission, n 27 above, p 89.

38 Law Commission, n 5 above, pp 275–77.

The critics of codification examined two possible approaches: the use of broad, general language which itself 'would not make the law accessible' and would 'still need a professional to mediate [for the lay user]'[39] or the use of comprehensive codification with 'a loss in flexibility' and 'a real risk that a situation occurs which is outside the statutory code but where the law ought to have applied'.[40] Other methods of bringing legal duties to the attention of company directors, such as 'authoritative pamphlets' and prescribed forms were also considered.

As far as the substance of board members' day to day responsibilities is concerned, there has been (and remains) resistance to the notion of developing any separate duty to examine the interests of parties other than the shareholders.[41] It can be argued that UK public company boards are subject to efficient markets (for their products and their shares) and examination of stakeholder interests to the extent necessary to further performance in those markets is not a concern that should be demanded of private sector management.[42] If markets do not produce socially acceptable results (for example in the level of employment generated or the use of small suppliers), that is a matter for direct government action (for example, Welfare to Work programmes, legislation on prompt payment of debts). Any provision that might be more prescriptive as to the structure of board operations is resisted as potentially detrimental to 'entrepreneurial drive'.

Turning to the practicalities of prescribing matters for directorial attention, it has been argued that if the board had to consider factors other than wealth maximisation for shareholders, it would lose its focus and business performance would suffer, to no constituency's benefit.[43] Board members, so it is asserted, need the 'North Star' of shareholder value alone[44] to set their course in their business judgments. Results and benefits other than profit may be diffuse and relatively difficult to quantify. Many UK public company directors would not consider themselves qualified to analyse social and environmental data, for example. Economic efficiency feeds into social benefits through a combination of taxes, wages, demand for materials and returns to shareholders as the market dictates. The place for redistribution of the wealth created, if rebalancing is needed, is through the activities of governments.

The issue of adjudication between the different groups of constituents is also presented as a difficulty. Where the claims of, for example, employees

---

39 *Ibid*, n 5 above, p 277.
40 *Ibid*, n 5 above, p 276.
41 Company Law Review Steering Group, n 4 above, paras 3.25–3.30.
42 MacIntosh, J, 'Designing an Efficient Fiduciary Law' 43 University of Toronto Law Journal 425.
43 Sternberg, E, *Just Business*, 2nd edn 2000, pp 32–35, 257–62.
44 Ward, R, *Twenty-First Century Corporate Board*, 1997, p 334.

and shareholders conflict, a statement of duties that adverts to both while giving no guidance as to their 'rankings' is of little practical assistance to the public company director.[45] Each primary stakeholding group (as discussed in the previous chapter) has a legitimate expectation of fair and reasonable treatment from the board. Where choices have to be made between groups, the long-term well-being of the organisation must be at the forefront of the directors' minds. The chosen course of action must be the one that secures and promotes the future of the company with the minimum of present difficulties to the participants. The duration and extent of the relationships between the company and stakeholders (for example, key customers and suppliers) will also be relevant.

The collection of information and its analysis by a fairly small team of directors is relevant to the practicality of extended fiduciary duties. If they are to remain a coherent group, the directors can only discuss a finite number of factors in their regular meetings. Both executives and non-executives have a range of duties outside the boardroom. The point is made that directors are therefore best held to the pursuit of profits alone, since they do not have the expertise or the resources to scrutinise employee requirements, supplier and consumer links and so on to adequate levels. Better, it is said, that they address one key issue, which they fully comprehend and handle well, than that they attempt to pay attention to several groups and deal with none of them satisfactorily.[46]

Deregulation in the interests of national competitiveness has also been presented as an argument against more specific legislative 'interference' in executive 'prerogative', both under UK governments of the 1980s and within the present administration.[47] The example often quoted is that of US corporations choosing to locate in Delaware, which is perceived to have the most liberal rules from the board standpoint.[48] However, during the 1990s the federal regime has in fact become somewhat more regulatory, from the increased minimum wage level and tougher environmental standards to yet greater openness on accounts and compulsory institutional voting in corporations. The perception that legislation would enforce undesirable uniformity is also advanced as an argument against new laws directed to corporate board activity. In the free market economic system (and undeniably 'capitalism has triumphed for the moment in the great battle with socialism –

---

45 Van der Weide, M, 'Against Fiduciary Duties to Corporate Stakeholders' (1996) 21 Delaware Journal of Corporate Law 27.

46 Fischel, D, 'The Corporate Governance Movement' (1982) 35 Vanderbilt Law Review 1259, 1285–86.

47 DTI, n 1 above, pp 12–13.

48 Romano, R, 'The State Competition Debate in Corporate Law' (1987) 8 Cardozo Law Review 709 discusses other reasons for the success of Delaware, such as the 'stock' of company law precedents and experienced corporate counsel, which the UK could attempt to emulate in the European setting.

if socialism is understood to mean a planned economy, extensive public ownership, negligible private property rights and a directed society',[49] even though the 'End of History' argument[50] downplayed fundamental socio-political differences between different forms of capitalism), if companies have different management styles, that is welcome, as the market will determine the success of each of them.

Turning first to the point about directorial capacity, practical steps could quickly be taken to increase the skills of boards that at present lack confidence in dealing with multiple constituencies. Their own membership could be diversified to include the necessary areas of expertise and if new wording encourages movement in this direction, it will be beneficial to business. Investigations and reports to the board by individual directors, often with the assistance of suitably qualified executives, are already featured in public company board meetings. Directors in large, complex organisations might consider the engagement of a small, intellectually able support team (discussed in Chapter 3).

Without some explicit and authoritative guidance as to the identity and status of all the protagonists in the corporate drama, the danger is that UK public company directors will continue to be too limited in their outlook. The formal listing and acknowledgment of all relevant stakeholders in the primary legislation could therefore be a matter of some significance in itself. The fundamental expectations of each of the groups can be noted in the same place and the principle of monitoring constituents' views established. These provisions will not be exhaustive for any company, since each has its own set of relationships and concerns, but it will set out the essential issues. Each board will then need to ensure that it has in place adequate systems for communicating with and monitoring the views of relevant groups. This 'Stakeholder Mapping' exercise is itself a valuable business discipline, as shown by well-documented incidents such as the Nestlé boycott[51] and the Shell Brent Spar[52] dispute (both of which could have been handled more effectively with earlier consideration of corporate responsibility and consumer reaction).

It has been asserted that ethical investment funds perform well[53] precisely because their managers have to get to know the business policies and

49 Hutton, W, *The State To Come*, 1997, p 4.

50 Fukuyama, F, *The End of History and the Last Man*, 1992.

51 Frederick, W, Post, J and Davis, K, *Business and Society*, 7th edn 1992, pp 560–73.

52 'Greens Claim Victory as Shell Recycles Brent Spar', *The Independent*, 29 January 1998, Environment section; 'All at Sea over Disposal of Oil Rigs; Industry and Environmentalists Remain as Far Apart as ever Despite Solution for Brent Spar', *Financial Times*, 29 January 1998.

53 McCallin, J, 'The Engagement Ring: How Shareholders are Starting to put Pressure on Management', *The Guardian*, 6 May 2000, Money section; Papworth, J, 'Ethical Investment Keeping Pensions Free from Pollution: Moves to Bring in Socially Responsible Investment', *The Guardian*, 6 May 2000, Money section.

operations of the companies in which they invest, rather than simply relying on past 'bottom line' figures. In a similar fashion, boards that have to investigate the needs and wishes of consumers and employees will be in a better position to plan for successful future operations.[54] The awareness that long-term corporate strategy will be reviewed and criticised not only by investors (including institutions) but also by employees, customers and perhaps suppliers may also lead to a sharper and more balanced programme. Public scrutiny of accounts has historically been accepted as part of the price to be paid for use of the corporate form[55] and there is no reason to doubt that greater openness about plans will come to be accepted. The very knowledge that corporate strategy will be open to discussion by parties from a range of perspectives means that board members are less likely to put into operation plans with unintended and damaging consequences.[56] New ideas for the business itself may also emerge from wider communication with stakeholders.

Constituency statutes in many of the United States have indeed been perceived by critics as an 'executives' charter' to block mergers which would be profitable to shareholders but would threaten managerial security or privileged lifestyles.[57] While self-dealing by directors still needs to be firmly tackled, it is true that there is a social interest in putting damage to employees and suppliers and customers on the agenda in all discussions of strategy. US public corporate directors, moreover, are subject to a more investigative business press and a greater culture of freedom of information.[58] It is appropriate that a broader range of board accountability be accompanied by a fresh culture of scrutiny inside boardrooms.

The Company Law Green Paper discussed the use of Codes of Practice, as appended to the reports of the Cadbury and Greenbury Committees and consolidated by the Stock Exchange post-Hampel, as an alternative to legislation in the corporate governance field. Among the advantages of the non-legislative approach were said to be the following:

> Best practice is more flexible: individual companies can apply it in a way that best fits their own circumstances and it can be kept up to date more easily. The government does not intend to replace the use of best practice by legal rules, provided best practice is seen to be working.[59]

---

54 Centre for Tomorrow's Company, *The Inclusive Approach and Business Success: The Research Evidence,* 1998, discusses relevant research material.

55 The Limited Liability Partnerships Act 2000 provides for disclosure of comparable financial to that required of small companies.

56 Wilson, A, 'Business and its Social Responsibility' in Davies, PWF, *Current Issues in Business Ethics,* 1997, p 50, speaks of 'discerning' customers, investors and employees.

57 Ward, n 44 above, p 331.

58 Barnard, J, 'Hampel: A Transatlantic Critique' (1998) 19 Co Law 110.

59 DTI, n 1 above, p 9.

The inconsistency of approach between competing companies can make it difficult for those which wish to pursue a managerial policy other than one of maximum short-term returns to shareholders to survive in the capital market; paradoxically, then, lack of regulation can restrict freedom of action for managers. 'Best practice' does not in reality produce the intended results if it does not set a timetable for specific action (the length of time taken to eliminate 'rolling' or long directors' contracts is one example of this).

The volume of business activity in the economy produces a tendency among corporate executives perhaps comparable to that seen and documented among investment managers, in that there is irrational overreaction to promises of prosperity and excessive panic whenever the horizon seems to be clouded.[60] Indeed the phenomenon of 'boom and bust' in investment projects by public companies is connected to the behaviour of the Stock Market, which is not in fact a logically predictable, self-correcting system but a chaotic and unpredictable ebb and flow of funds. By giving recognition to other parties, which want to see productive activity and economic stability, fresh wording would reduce the pressure to be seen to expand the business at a time of rising prices and to contract rapidly after the peak in the economic cycle. The process of consideration of the whole range of interests in the company is a discipline which would be likely to lead to steadier but more sustainable progress.

5.3 CONSTITUENCIES FOR CONSIDERATION

Given the unsustainability of the 'shareholders as owners' argument in public companies and the recognition that leaders of such organisations do not base their decisions solely on the production of maximum returns by way of dividends (if nothing else, they are also concerned about their own long-term security and prospects), any statement of duties which did not reflect the responsibilities of directors to a range of participants in corporate life would be less than intellectually honest. Nevertheless, the programme of 'privatisation' in the UK in the 1980s and into the 1990s was founded on a belief that a leadership focused on running a core business as efficiently as possible would produce greater satisfaction for consumers than an anonymous executive with a vague responsibility to 'society'. There must be a clear sense of purpose at the head of a company, and this may best be achieved by including the relevant groups in understanding and acceptance of that mission. In the age of internet access and email networks, shutting employees or customers out of the planning process becomes difficult.[61]

---

60 See eg Bulow, J and Klemperer, P, *Rational Frenzies and Crashes*, 1991, and Campbell, J, *Media, Mania and the Markets*, 1994.

61 Fabian, C, 'Answering Hard Questions in the Stakeholder Age', *Marketing*, 17 February 2000, 24.

There is a delicate balance to be struck between breadth of approach and realism in the number and kind of constituencies that can routinely be taken into consideration. If the law is overly prescriptive, it will risk damaging the competitiveness of UK business and creating resentment among managers. If it is not sufficiently inclusive, it will cause an unwarranted balance in favour of too narrow a sectional interest, be it shareholders or employees or others. A manageable, coherent list, with clear statements of their rights, is the most useful way forward. The Law Commission, at the start of its discussion of 'Economic Considerations' in lawmaking, referred to 'technical efficiency' (rules to minimise costs such as agency costs) and to 'allocative efficiency' (rules to allocate scarce resources in a way which maximises their value to society).[62] The remainder of the Consultation Paper concerned itself with producing the most 'user-friendly' version of the rules, while largely ignoring the social impact of corporate activities, an approach that has filtered through to the remainder of the company law review.

The demise of the corporate *ultra vires* rule, firstly by the expansion of objects clauses[63] and ultimately by removal of shareholders' rights to challenge acts beyond the scope of the company's objects unless the latter are discovered before they become binding commitments,[64] left the directors accountable for delivery of dividends, but not for the development of core businesses. Particularly in the 1980s, public company boards seemed to hesitate little before switching markets and activities in order to utilise the capital-raising power of the corporate name and its assets to greatest revenue-producing effect.[65] Without a 'main object' and a constituency monitoring adherence to it, the identity of a public company was divorced from any specific line of business. A fresh legislative reminder that large business operations create a relationship of mutual interdependence with employees (this is ever more the case as 'knowledge work' replaces unskilled tasking) and customers and suppliers, would help to refocus board attention on serving a market rather than 'betting' on various activities at will.

Both Kay[66] in his discussion of the interests of the company and Goyder[67] in his proposals for a new 'general purposes' clause (as set out in Chapter 1) include customers, employees, shareholders and the community; environmental responsibility could appropriately be added, as could a

---

62 Law Commission, n 5 above, pp 33–34.

63 Eg through the devices seen in cases such as *Cotman v Brougham* [1918] AC 514 and *Bell Houses Ltd v City Wall Properties Ltd* [1966] 1 QB 207 and latterly with the option of incorporation as a general commercial company (Companies Act 1985 s 3A).

64 Companies Act 1985 s 35.

65 The Maxwell and Polly Peck affairs demonstrate the ease with which loan capital was available for expansion of activity by a 'proven' managerial 'team' (or leader).

66 Kay, J, 'The Stakeholder Corporation' in Kelly, G, Kelly, D and Gamble, A, *The Stakeholder Corporation*, 1997, p 137.

67 Goyder, G, *The Just Enterprise*, 1993, p 56.

reference to suppliers where relevant. The main concerns of each group are not difficult to articulate in general terms: fair prices and good products in the case of customers, fair wages and good conditions for employees, fair returns and good profits to investors. All share an interest in consistent and improving corporate performance and are usually willing to accept the consequences of genuine market pressure. If they lose confidence in the central decisionmakers, they may, however, begin to mistrust the corporate system as such.[68] A simple statement that public company directors are obliged to take into account the interests of these essential groups would make it impossible for board members to disregard the representations of those groups. The recognised office of Senior Independent Non-executive Director (discussed in Chapter 3) would provide a channel through which named groups could 'feed in' their views directly to board discussions.

The danger in producing a statutory stakeholder list is that it will come to be seen as exhaustive of corporate management's responsibilities, rather than as a guide to an appropriate managerial approach. There is certainly a *prima facie* case for close scrutiny of any corporate activity and expenditure that does not benefit any of the core stakeholding groups. There is already a requirement for the amount of charitable donations made, if they are in aggregate above a very low baseline, to be disclosed in the Annual Report.[69] Party political involvement is already against the policy of many major companies[70] and, in principle, there seems no reason why company members should not enjoy the same rights as trade union members to 'opt out' of making political contributions. It should, however, be emphasised that the current level of general charitable giving in the UK is way below that in the US and has caused no evident concern to shareholders so far.

The emphasis placed on satisfaction of particular groups of constituents will vary between public companies in different sectors. Some participants are a *sine qua non* of success in any business (the customers, the employees and often the suppliers, as much as shareholders).[71] In other instances, public

---

68 Glasbeek, H, 'The Corporate Social Responsibility Movement' (1988) 11 Dalhousie Law Journal 363 points out (at 385): '[I]t is part of the popular understanding that the adoption of the corporate form is a convenient means by which to dodge responsibility ... the large corporations' claim [in Canada] that they deserve respect and should be left as unregulated as possible because of their utility to the economy is spoilt by the fact that a huge number of organisations – which have the same legal form but are much smaller in size – are seen to serve no socially useful purpose.' One might add that public companies, individually and as a whole, obviously serve a whole range of purposes and a focus on a main object as discussed above might help directors in conveying the utility of their company.

69 Companies Act 1985 Sched 7, para 7(3) – the limit below which disclosure is not required is £200.

70 *Ibid*, para 7(5) – in the case of payments for political purposes the recipient has to be identified.

71 Brooks, R, 'Why Loyal Employees and Customers Improve the Bottom Line' (2000) 23 Journal for Quality and Participation 40.

companies can be expected only to adhere to standards set out in specific legislation.[72] Environmental improvement and social welfare burdens cannot be shouldered by (even large) companies on a voluntary basis in a competitive market. It is important to legitimise the inclusion in boardroom discussion not only of direct contributors but also of proper examination of the social and environmental consequences of company activities. Without such a statement, the tendency is for companies to attempt to adhere (or at least aim to be able to document adherence) to statutes but treat as taboo any discussion of proceeding further in pursuing social and environmental responsibility.

5.4 BOARD DECISION MAKING MODELS

Companies legislation has been silent, and the courts generally quiet, on the decision making practices of, and matters for consideration by, company directors, provided only that fraud is avoided. Executives are often elevated to board level in consideration of their achievements as functional or departmental administrators, with little clear conception of the distinctive role of the board. The best 'passport' to a non-executive directorship, in turn, is still executive board membership in a prestigious company.[73] As a result of these traditions, a narrow pool of talent is used in public company boardrooms and there is a clear mismatch between current social demands on business and the understanding of many boards. What developments in law might improve public company performance in this respect?

The nexus of directorial accountability to the company ('Enforcement of Fair Dealing' as the Companies Act 1985 entitles it) with standards of decision making is found in answering procedural questions such as what information directors need to seek, and whose views they should take into account, when determining company policy. The variation in approach between companies within the same sector, as referred to in Chapter 4, has been found to be related in general terms to their respective long-term performances.[74] The use and distribution of the profits made by a given enterprise in turn reflects its investment and time horizons. Training for board service, as long discussed by the Institute of Directors and others, is also relevant here.[75] If it were

---

72 Many corporate leaders protest against these: for example, the Institute of Directors publishes RegAlert, highlighting new regulatory burdens, and the author Richard Baron said in the 27 April 2000 issue: 'Jobs will only be secure if directors can concentrate on developing their businesses.'

73 Mason, E, 'The Problem of Legitimacy in the Modern Corporation' in Sutton, B, *The Legitimate Corporation*, 1993, p 148 discusses 'fit' and 'togetherness' as featured in board selection.

74 Centre for Tomorrow's Company, n 54 above, summarises the current state of knowledge in this field.

75 The Institute of Directors has launched a 'Chartered Director' qualification for Members and Fellows, which is designed to promote high professional standards.

possible for new directors to be given, as part of their induction, a copy of a set of principles for board service, that would be a helpful innovation in itself.

The fact that even a listed public company could still legally be run by two directors[76] shows how far removed the major companies legislation is from the reality of life in these large and complex organisations. The delegation of many board functions to an executive committee, which knows the detail of daily business operations and can conveniently meet between monthly 'full' meetings, is common, while the input of non-executive directors varies widely from company to company. Any efforts to obtain a broader perspective from the full board are defeated if the executives have determined matters before all the directors meet. The proposed statement of individual responsibility on the part of each director to all of the primary stakeholders would give non-executives a tool to assist them in engaging with management and challenging the institutional ways of thinking. Both internally promoted candidates and outside experts can and should be concerned with taking a broad and balanced view of the organisation's role and responsibilities.[77]

In future, significantly more time will need to be spent on board duties by many public company directors if they are to become aware of the implications of their decision making from the points of view of primary stakeholders. Given the pace of change in business life, full meetings less often than monthly will probably prove to be inadequate, while even more frequent gatherings could allow insufficient time for reflection and slip to the status of routine administration rather than strategic planning. The number of non-executive directorships held by individuals and the size of the regular agenda will obviously have an impact on the time dedicated by an individual to each board assignment (see the discussions in Chapter 3). The prospect of having to justify the chosen decision making process should act as an incentive to directors to put in place a clear structure for all board meetings and reports. While the frequency and agenda of meetings of individual organisations cannot sensibly be prescribed, benchmark standards can be set by legal rules.

Techniques such as SWOT[78] analysis and PEST[79] trend analysis can usefully include systematic consideration of the company's primary stakeholders. Inclusion of key constituents was piloted in a *Tomorrow's Company* scheme, arising from a report of the Royal Society of Arts, which showed that employees and customers welcomed the chance to contribute their ideas and businesses that engaged in such communication were more commercially successful than rivals who did not. Direct involvement in decision making is likely to reassure even those constituencies who may not

---

76 Companies Act 1985 s 282.
77 Stiles, P, 'Corporate Governance and Ethics' in Davies, n 56 above, p 39.
78 Strengths, Weaknesses, Opportunities and Threats of and facing the company.
79 Political, Economic, Social and Technological trends.

agree with the conclusion reached on a given matter that the relationship is nevertheless worth pursuing. It is for directors as part of their decision making processes to listen and also to explain their understanding of and vision for the corporate entity.

The possibility (noted in Chapter 3) of a 'Business Judgement Rule' as in the United States was discussed by the Law Commission[80] with reference to the 'safe harbour' provided for directorial decisions. There was also reference to the draft Australian provisions in a similar vein. If directors are to be required to make complex analyses of interests and effects, they should know how they are expected to come to those conclusions. Good practice can be spread by enforcement of these standards. Both in terms of 'easing uncertainty in the minds of directors about a statutory statement of the duty of care' and 'encouraging [directors] to make appropriate enquiries', the Law Commission noted the possible utility of such a rule.

The full board of a large public company will not necessarily be an efficient body to consider all the possible implications of a suggested course of action, and indeed the use of specialist committees to advise and report to the whole membership is already widespread.[81] On the political 'select committee' model, it could become commonplace for a public company to have one group, including directors and managers, addressing itself to the needs of each of the key constituencies and taking evidence from those involved. The employee committee, the customer committee, perhaps the business partners committee and the public affairs committee could monitor corporate progress from the point of view of the relevant groups and report on specific key issues of their own motion and report to the full board. While there has been some attempt in transnational corporations across the European Union to make progress with employee representation in the shape of European Works Councils, these are unlikely to gain influence unless they have links to the board. Other groups, including customers and suppliers, also merit systematic attention from directors.

A strategy of measuring likely impacts and deciding in what circumstances a given result will be accepted has produced only modest gains in the environmental arena but it is an integral part of successful public management. In the employment field, it is not encouraging that many public company leaders have been publicly hostile to the limited protective measures introduced in the UK since 1997.[82] In consumer markets, the competitive retail

---

80 Law Commission, n 5 above, pp 296–98.

81 Aside from the independent nomination, remuneration and audit committees recommended as best practice by Committee on Corporate Governance (Chair: Sir Ronald Hampel), *Final Report*, January 1998, paras 3.19, 4.11, 6.3.

82 Commenting on the CBI's Employment Trends Survey (23 May 2000), John Cridland said: 'Firms are working hard to balance business and employment needs, but more legislation could tip the scales in the wrong direction.'

sector in the UK has not stopped customers from being far more heavily squeezed for profits than their neighbours in France.[83] The need for appropriate impact assessment is one which can sensibly be met only in an integrated fashion for all key groups. Where non-executive directors do not have the time or expertise to construct such programmes *ab initio*, there are models to which they can turn,[84] just as they have traditionally worked within accounting rules on financial affairs.

5.5 FORMULATION OF NEW LEGAL DUTIES

The primary statutory wording dealing with directors' duties needs to be sufficiently clear and precise to be readily understood and followed by board members themselves. If it is not to be counterproductive in effect, however, it cannot be so specific as to bind directors in a straitjacket of procedure, which risks becoming formalistic rather than enhancing the quality of board decision making. The Hampel Report's disparaging reference to 'box ticking' (arranging for all the formal requirements of new regulation to be met while continuing to make substantial decisions much as before) is very pertinent here.[85] New legislation needs to flow with the most progressive managerial movements and the tide of opinion while carrying the more retrogressive elements in some public companies along in its wake. It is right to have extensive prior consultation and would be erroneous to grant the wishes of any one group (including 'business leaders' themselves) automatic primacy.[86]

The legislative drafting process in the UK is biased towards the reproduction of traditional statutory forms of wording.[87] It is also subject to shortage of time for production of the final wording, against the backdrop of political demands.[88] The Company Law Green Paper attempts to deal with

---

83 MacShane, D, 'The Great Supermarket Rip-off', *New Statesman*, 4 September 1998, p 14.

84 Kaplan, R and Norton, D, 'Using the Balanced Scorecard as a Strategic Management System' (Jan 1996) Harvard Business Review 75 (a book is forthcoming by the same authors from Harvard Business School Press on *How Balanced Scorecard Companies Thrive in the New Business Environment*).

85 Hampel, n 81 above, para 1.12.

86 O'Sullivan, M, 'Sustainable Prosperity, Corporate Governance, and Innovation in Europe' in Michie, J and Grieve Smith, J, *Globalization, Growth and Governance*, 1998, p 203, writes that: 'If sustainable prosperity is the objective, proposals to reform the corporate governance system must be based on a theory of the innovative enterprise. Without such a theory, stakeholder arguments run the risk of encouraging other groups, besides shareholders, to become claimants in a given, and even diminishing pool of returns.'

87 Zander, M, *The Law-Making Process*, 4th edn 1994, quotes Francis Bennion, a senior legislative draftsman who was roundly criticised for attempting to use 'tried his best' in place of the time-honoured 'used his best endeavours' (at p 20).

88 *Ibid*, pp 15–19, quoting Sir Granville Ram and Sir Harold Kent who had also worked as draftsmen.

both of these constraints. It speaks of Table A's being 'rewritten using plain English' and emphasises a clean break with the past in terms of style.[89] It also set out a lengthy timetable with the intention of providing ample opportunity for consultation and scrutiny[90] (political pressure, or lack of it, within Parliament will obviously depend on its members following the General Election of 2001).

Some past attempts to reform UK rules in line with European Union law principles have not been successful in achieving their intended effect, nor in producing wording which was easy to understand (one thinks of the reform of *ultra vires*[91] and, outside the corporate context, equal pay provisions).[92] More positively, British judges, though schooled in literal statutory interpretation, have shown themselves able and willing to adopt a more teleological approach when handling statutes produced to implement European Union obligations.[93] Lack of prescription as to outcomes should not therefore be a barrier to the effectiveness of legislation in practice. As the effort to graft European Union requirements on to a traditional British company law framework is reconsidered,[94] the place for an overarching statement of directors' duties looks more secure.

The aims of the company as an entity, its survival and prosperity, would be central to the board's thinking under a new Companies Act. However, corporate financial results are not ends in themselves – they are produced in order to benefit individual people, as consumers, employees, investors (including holders of pensions) and citizens of communities. Parties may not have invested equity capital, but instead may have contributed in another way to public company results. They accordingly merit respect and a statement of their entitlements.[95] Stakeholders will also benefit by being able to call to account the individuals who are responsible for the policies of what

---

89 DTI, n 1 above, p 6.

90 *Ibid*, p 21.

91 Now at Companies Act 1985 s 35.

92 *Marshall v Southampton Area Health Authority* OJ 152/84 (1986).

93 Eg *Litster v Forth Dry Dock Co Ltd* [1990] 1 AC 546; *Webb v EMO Cargo (No 2)* [1996] 2 CMLR 990.

94 One of the disappointments of the Hampel Report was the almost total failure to address the responsibilities emanating from and the models available from European Union partner states: see Villiers, C, 'Do Employees have a Role in Corporate Governance?' (Paper delivered on 31 March 1998 at University of Newcastle Law School).

95 McNulty, M, 'A Question of Managerial Legitimacy' in Sutton, B, n 73 above, 160 again relates this to business prosperity: 'The injustice perceived by the individual when his contributions to the organization are not appropriately recognized and rewarded normally might be reflected in a homeostatic process whereby inputs become curtailed to restore the balance ... It is suggested that there exists a parallel with the political sphere in that the underlying basis of these theories and their manifestation in the business world rests on the extension of the contractualism within the traditionally autocratic bureaucracy of the corporation.'

seem to be 'faceless' corporations. While specific laws on, for example, environmental standards will change as society and technology move on, the fundamental principles of inclusiveness in corporate dealings are likely to stand the test of time.

Bearing all of this in mind, new wording along the following lines is suggested:

> A director of a public limited company shall in all his/her conduct and decision making so act as to advance the development of the company in the interests of its customers, its employees and its shareholders and with proper regard for the effect of its operations on the environment and on the community. The interests to which a director of a public company should give due consideration include:
>
> - the provision for customers of safe and effective goods and services of good quality at fair prices
> - the provision for employees of fair remuneration and secure work with reasonable opportunity for their interests to be heard within the company and for their promotion and development of skills
> - the provision for shareholders of fair returns to remunerate past investment and encourage future investment in the company
> - the provision for key business associates including suppliers of goods and services of secure relationships and ongoing co-operation where such connections offer advantages to both parties
> - the provision for the community of programmes to monitor and minimise the environmental impact of the company's operations and advance responsible conduct towards the company's neighbours.

This would apply to all UK public companies.

As compared with the Company Law Review Steering Group's wording, this gives much more detail as to what can be expected by participants in 'business relationships'.[96] It also makes clear that the company is to be run with a view to its success benefiting all the participants, rather than exclusively for 'the benefit of its members as a whole'.[97] Put simply, any company director needs to ensure that customers are satisfied and employees treated fairly, for without repeat and referral business and enthusiastic staff commitment, there is little long-term future for development of a business. Perceived irresponsibility in social action and environmental performance is likely to damage the organisation in that customers will choose alternatives, good potential employees will not apply and investors will avoid the company, if not on principle, then from self-interest because of those other effects.

---

96 Company Law Review Steering Group, n 4 above, Sched 2, para 2, note (2)(a).
97 *Ibid*, Sched 2, para 2(a).

The Company Law Green Paper emphasised the need for deregulation of the small company and for greater distinctions in law between companies of different sizes, which fulfil distinct economic functions.[98] It is submitted that this is the correct approach. While it would be wholly unrealistic to subject every individual who decided to incorporate his or her business to the scrutiny of employees and customers beyond specific protective legislation, it is equally inappropriate for persons appointed to boards of public companies simply to seek to behave like start-up entrepreneurs. They have advantages in the marketplace that should be tied to expectations of genuine public service. Public companies have the resources to ensure that within the boardroom 'team' there is an appropriate mix of skills including the financial, the technical, the market-related and the employee-focused. The ultimate responsibility for 'pulling together' these strands rests with the chairman who, appropriately, will usually be the public face and voice of the company.

Furthermore, the courts have recognised that there is a clear practical distinction between the role of the executive on the public company board and that of the non-executive director. In preliminary investigations, Braes found that non-executives themselves quite often viewed their position as a means of providing an external perspective and an independent voice.[99] Interestingly, he discovered that non-executive board members themselves in discussion mentioned the possibility of taking a broader view and becoming more involved in more than financial audit work.[100] The view that the 'inside' and 'outside' directors ought to have formally different duties is one that has been advanced as a means of enhancing clarity. Against this, it is suggested that if executives were perceived to be orientated towards efficient operations and annual profits, while non-executives represented assorted 'constituency' or 'non-financial' interests, the lack of coherence would be most unhelpful for corporate prospects. All directors need to focus their attention on the same issues and the author finds this argument more persuasive.

5.6 RELATED LEGAL PROVISIONS

The Hampel Report's further suggestions for substantive changes to company law were centred on the position and power of shareholders, both private and institutional. Useful ideas for increasing the accessibility of general meetings and the general involvement of large and small investors were noted.[101] Like UK government departments, public company boardrooms have operated in

---

98 DTI, n 1 above, p 7.

99 Braes, D, *Corporate Governance: Company Responses to Cadbury and a Review of the Issue*, Kingston University Master's Thesis, 1996, p 92.

100 *Ibid*, p 93.

101 Hampel, n 81 above, Part 5 section IV.

a culture of enclosure and defensiveness that is proving difficult to challenge. Somewhat ironically, formerly publicly owned utilities now in private ownership are, if anything, more exposed to public scrutiny, whether by regulators and consumer groups or through Annual Reports and accounts, than when they were run by civil servants reporting to government ministers.[102] In general, though, the possibilities offered by new technology for direct communication with stakeholders have not yet been fully explored. A comprehensive codification of directors' duties would be a signal to the courts to take a somewhat more interventionist line on dealings by directors with property owned by a company. The vigilance of 'watchdogs', including not only shareholders but also employees and customers (who may in many instances have a greater proportionate stake in the honest and effective management of the public company), may then be expected to improve standards of managerial propriety and performance.

Clear, accurate, up to date financial information is of importance to all concerned with a company and is far from being guaranteed by current accounting rules.[103] The present Directors' Report for public limited companies[104] contains a long but unco-ordinated list of issues on many of which most companies evidently say as little as they feel they legally can. More generally, board policy for the corporation's future cannot effectively be challenged if it is not known until specific plans are at an advanced stage. Greater consultation as a part of information gathering before decisions were made would also indicate to the parties contacted the possible direction of corporate change. Consumers could better communicate their requirements, employees prepare to adapt to change and investors be appraised of the cost and timescales for expenditure if all were included in discussions, rather than being viewed as outsiders to be compelled to deal with any plan chosen by the management. Holders of 5% of shares in a limited company[105] have the right to circulate resolutions and comments on agenda items prior to general meetings, while large European-based corporations will have to 'consult' with their employees on issues such as plant closures and reconstructions.[106] Even so, while shareholders risk having to meet the costs of such a campaign and employees have no automatic right to board discussion of their views, the appearance of openness is not much more than illusory.

---

102 Ogus, AI, *Regulation,* 1994, Chapter 13 discusses the issues.

103 The fact that public companies are allowed up to seven months between year end and filing and laying of accounts is in itself a constraint on the usefulness of full accounts (Companies Act 1985 s 244).

104 Companies Act 1985, Sched 7.

105 Companies Act 1985 s 376.

106 European Works Councils Directive 94/45 OJ L254/64 (1994).

The whole climate of respect for employment rights is important in setting the tone and context for the board's work.[107] Acknowledgment in company law of corporate responsibility towards employees as a class cannot be a substitute for the provision of satisfactory individual employment rights, but may support them. Productivity improvements, for example, can be a matter of negotiation and co-operation.[108] Unlike much employment law, the relatively detailed consumer protection legislation of the 1970s survived the 1980s process of deregulation unscathed (though access to remedies for contravention is rather more difficult to achieve in practice). This does not contradict the principle of corporate responsibility to customers. Many companies have already learned that they have much to gain from building mutually trusting relationships with customers.[109]

As far as corporate environmental and social responsibility is concerned, there is great scope for more precise definitions of expected outcomes and for more effective enforcement of those regulations. A pan-European approach would help to avoid the danger of differential costs and competition driving down performance standards across the European Union. On a still broader scale, there is some international consensus emerging on the seriousness of world environmental threats and the desirability of minimum labour standards.[110] Without the provision for fines of an amount which impacts seriously on the corporation's wealth and a real likelihood of transgressions being punished, it is too easy for managers of companies to conclude that observing stringent rules is not worth their while. Only good enforcement and better boardroom understanding of the issues involved can solve the problem of mismatches between apparent corporate concerns and broader public opinion. Non-Governmental Organisations from Friends of the Earth to Public Concern at Work have expertise in monitoring and publicising these issues.

Public companies' Annual Reports vary greatly in what might be called their 'production values' (colour, glossiness, use of graphics, readability of text) but very few are really suited to the needs of the whole range of key participants discussed above. In a modern context where the UK government is itself publishing Annual Reports to show progress towards its goals in key areas, the bare publication of a selective set of figures and 'policies' appears all the more inadequate.[111] For public elected authorities and appointed agencies

---

107 Eg Employment Relations Act 1999.
108 Trade Unions such as MSF and the AEEU have found that the UK's accession to the European Social Chapter, negotiated partnerships with management have become more popular.
109 Companies such as InfoQuest Customer Relationship Management Ltd and Market Elan Ltd are specialist in advising businesses on customer retention.
110 See comments of European Commissioner Chris Patten on Governance in the Year 2000 Reith Lectures, text at www.bbc.co.uk.
111 Leonard, M, 'Why the Annual Report might just Restore Faith in Politics', *New Statesman*, 7 August 1998, p 18.

alike, the articulation of sets of targets across a range of operations and measurement of outcomes have become a fact of life and public companies need to respond to this. This does not mean vaguely aspirational 'Mission Statements', but broader discussion of business strategy and long-term objectives for the whole organisation.

Provisions for 'inclusive' reporting would cover attention to employee conditions and to customer satisfaction, as well as company environmental and social policy.[112] For public companies, which already expend large sums on publication and dissemination of the Annual Report and which should (as a matter of good modern business practice) already be collating information on its workforce and business partners, the burden would not be great. Coupled with the provisions for enforcement of wider directorial responsibility (which will be explored in the next chapter), rules as to reporting are central in ensuring compliance with the new decision making process. The senior executives can themselves explain the 'trade-offs' made between the demands of different participating groups and their understanding of environmental and social responsibility in the setting of a report that is both readable and wide-ranging.

5.7 COSTS AND BENEFITS OF LEGISLATION

In considering further legislation, the Company Law Review Steering Group asked the ESRC Centre for Business Research to report on the regulatory bodies operating in company law and corporate governance. The possibility of moving to more 'non-statutory regulation' was highlighted. Cook and Deakin prepared a literature review and commentary on the subject, which was published on the DTI website. In this context what is called 'enforced self-regulation' is normally regulation by private sector organisations of themselves, but subject to the discipline of possible legislation as a last resort.

The ESRC report quotes Ayres and Braithwaite's[113] summary of the strengths and weaknesses of enforced self-regulation of business, as opposed to legislation:

(i) Strengths

- *Rules would be tailored to match the company ...*
- *Rules would adjust more quickly to changing business environments ...*
- *Regulatory innovation would be fostered.* By allowing a variety of approaches to be adopted by firms and commercial actors, the conditions for innovative solution ... would be enhanced.

---

112 Company Law Review Steering Group, n 4 above, Chapter 8.
113 Ayres, I and Braithwaite, J, *Responsive Regulation*, 1992.

- *Rules would be more comprehensive in their scope.* Self-regulation encourages companies to deal with a wider range of hazards and abuses than legislatures can efficiently consider.

These points seem to the present author to be important reminders of the inherent limitations of lawmaking by statute.

- *Companies would be more committed to the rules they wrote ...*
- *The confusion and cost from having two rulebooks (the company's and government's) would be reduced ...*

  In terms of internal corporate procedures, these observations may well be accurate. However, as far as third parties are concerned, statute may well be more accessible to and carry greater weight with, those who deal with public companies.

- *Business would bear more of the costs of its own regulation ...*
- *More offenders would be caught more often ...*
- *Compliance would become the path of least corporate resistance.* Companies would have powerful incentives to avoid public exposure and enforcement ...

These factors are not, in the present author's view, inevitable distinctions between systems of self-regulation and legislation.

(ii) Weaknesses

- *Regulatory agencies would bear the costs of approving a vastly increased number of rules ...*
- *State monitoring would sometimes be more efficient than private monitoring ...*

These factors clearly speak in favour of legislation.

- *Co-optation of the regulatory process by business would be worsened.* There would be an increased risk of insider control of the regulatory process ... but this would depend on how far other affected groups were given representative status in relation to the rule making process.
- *Particularistic rules might weaken the moral force of laws that should be universal.* How far this was a problem would depend on the degree to which what Ayres and Braithwaite refer to as 'overarching standards' could be enforced, in the last resort, by public agencies.

It is for government to take into account all the relevant parties. The political process provides the means for an appropriate policy balance to be struck.

- *Companies would write their rules in ways that would assist them to evade the spirit of the law ...*
- *Companies cannot command compliance as effectively as government ...*
- *The independence of the internal compliance group could never be fully guaranteed ...*

These last three matters, in particular, demonstrate the unique status of legislation in changing corporate and managerial behaviour.[114]

Professor Brian Cheffins invented text company law. They structured operation discusses the advantages and disadvantages of self-regulation within the UK corporate governance system.[115] Cook and Deakin quote the arguments:

Advantages of Self-regulation

i   Flexibility

Cheffins identifies two aspects of flexibility derived from self-regulation:

- *responsiveness* to changing circumstances from being able to make changes quickly and through access to information from informal sources; and

- *flexibility* in rule making and enforcement from a co-operative, consensual style of supervision; being able to rely on warnings or informal sanctions; and from being in a position to interpret rules in the spirit, rather than the letter, of the law.

These characteristics may sound positive enough, but also have disadvantages.

Some of the negative outcomes of flexibility in regulation are:

- the potential for arbitrary treatment arising out of vagueness of rules or a lack of openness;

- concerns over procedural mechanisms for adjudication ...

- concerns over procedural mechanisms for rule-making ...

ii Expertise ...

iii Cost ...

As far as fundamental aspects of directors' duties are concerned, involvement of affected parties is a public good, a fact to be taken into account in discussing staffing and funding.

Disadvantages of Self-Regulation

i   Bias

Cheffins reiterates the point that self-regulatory bodies may unduly favour the interests of their own members at the expense of other interest groups (and cites the composition of the Cadbury and Greenbury Committees as evidence of this effect) ...

At the same time, he notes that self-regulatory bodies are likely to experience pressures from the threat of government-imposed supervision

---

114 Cook, J and Deakin, S, *Regulation and the Boundaries of the Law*, 1999, www.dti.gov.uk, Chapter 9, pp 8–9.

115 Cheffins, BR, *Company Law: Theory, Structure and Operation*, 1997.

and from the attentions of the financial press to act in a balanced fashion, and argues that frontline regulators have been making efforts to distance themselves from the enterprises being supervised ...

This is perhaps the most important difficulty with enforced self-regulation, from which primary and secondary stakeholders other than shareholders and managers are generally excluded.

ii   Insufficient co-ordination of government policy ...

iii   Enforcement problems

Enforcement problems were characteristic of the situation prior to the mid-1980s when the Takeover Panel, the Stock Exchange and the ASB all operated without any direct statutory backing. This meant that they were without any statutory backing to investigate, prosecute or punish misconduct. Subsequent legislation has devolved various forms of enforcement authority to these bodies. For instance, the Financial Services Act 1986 gave some enforcement powers to self-regulatory bodies, the Companies Act 1985 gave the DTI powers to investigate company affairs, and the Criminal Justice Act 1987 provided for the Serious Fraud Office.[116]

The impact of the Financial Services and Markets Act 2000 and the input of the Financial Services Authority remains to be seen.

The Company Law Review Steering Group itself made a distinction between those parts of 'the company law framework ... so fundamental [or embodying] such significant elements of public policy that they should be enshrined in primary legislation', on the one hand, and 'policy areas which are subject to rapid change'[117] or 'implementing detailed technical requirements'[118] on the other hand. The line between the two is not always easily drawn. However, there is a clear distinction in principle between directors' duties and governance structures. The former are suitable for change by legislation, while the latter are impractical to prescribe in that form.

5.8 THE IMPACT OF NEW LEGISLATION

Parkinson sees reformulation of directors' duties as part of a process of cultural change 'so that managers place greater weight on the development of the company's relationships and pay increased attention to the welfare of groups affected by corporate activity'. He stresses that in his formulation 'the intention is not to give an expanded role to the courts'.[119] Where the stated

---

116 *Ibid*, pp 22–24.

117 Company Law Review Steering Group, *Modern Company Law for a Competitive Economy – Completing the Structure*, November 2000, p 247.

118 *Ibid*, p 248.

119 Parkinson, JE, 'Company Law and Stakeholder Governance', in Kelly, Kelly and Gamble, n 66 above.

aims and objectives of companies in the same sector vary greatly, a tightening up of legislative duties to bring all into line with the best is in tune with developments in the public sector. Accountability for a range of targets and to a range of stakeholders is now expected by those in senior positions in hospitals and schools, for example. Those at the head of public companies are responsible for the stewardship of even larger sums, ultimately provided by the general public (mainly via institutional investors) and, as such, should expect to face performance targets and 'benchmarking'.

Explosion of the myth of shareholder ownership of public companies, discussed in Chapter 2, would be another potentially powerful effect of stakeholder constituency legislation. Where the same people, or members of the same family, have headed a company from its earliest days to a Stock Market flotation, there is, understandably, a particular tendency for them to regard the company as subordinate to the wishes of its long-standing members. If a different set of priorities is in reality more appropriate, a new UK Companies Act for the 21st century will best serve society[120] if it reflects that point of view. While Richard Branson, Alan Sugar and others may decide that the reduction in personal control outweighs the benefit of a Stock Exchange listing, most leaders of public limited companies are happy to take a more collegial view in return for the benefits of public status. It is managerial folly, as a business grows, not to take on board (quite literally) the range of expertise needed at its head and a non-executive team can also provide valuable insights into the views of customers and suppliers as well as investors.

For such non-executive directors, the fact of a statutory and systematic reference to all key corporate constituencies would give them a lever to open up discussion about extending the board's outlook and utilising expertise in the consumer and employment areas. A small, well-qualified committee in consultation with external auditors carries out detailed scrutiny of accounting records and performance in listed companies. Where there is a dominant figure (be he or she titled chief executive, a founder promoted to the chairman or holding both titles) this can leave the full board without a clear focus. A specific list of stakeholder groups and issues for consideration could revitalise directorial discussion in many such cases. It may be that the current board members are not the right people to play the new role, whether from a lack of time or expertise or otherwise. The Takeover Code's principle of fair treatment for all participants and the Stock Exchange's insistence on full, timely information are not discredited but, on the contrary, extended, to cover all those with a stake in the company's performance.

---

120 Dworkin, R, *A Matter of Principle*, 1985, Chapter 12 (entitled 'Is Wealth a Value?') distinguishes increases in social wealth from improved value and argues that a society with greater wealth is not for that reason alone better or better off and hence the law should operate on grounds of principle, not policy.

Turning to public company executive officers, they are in an even better position than the part-time board members to assess the needs and wishes of customers and employees. As the interviews extracted in Chapter 8 make clear, however, most feel that their performance is judged principally on the share price achieved by the company and the support or otherwise of institutional investors. A wider set of legal responsibilities and business objectives is in harmony with most executives' perception of their own proper task, as the interviews revealed. Not surprisingly, most expressed full commitment to product quality and service delivery and to their workforce and believe that profits will flow from the focus on these fundamentals.

What might be called the 'democratic control of capital' argument posits that, if company law is to be about more than the financial results, its formulation of responsibilities of directors needs to deal with more than the enforcement of financial propriety. Primary legislation passed by Parliament and applied by the courts is able to reflect the interests, not only of capital, but also of other groups deemed to be worthy of proper attention and protection. The law can be stated in a form suitable for enforcement by parties who have an appropriate interest, in the expectation that the existence of such powers will normally produce the desired conduct. The very fact that, once in place, a legislative rule would be expected to last for a generation[121] would give it an authoritative status lacking in codes, which are designed to be procedural and flexible.

The Institute of Directors, in the context of discussing recruitment to and training for boards, has sometimes expressed concern that the status of company director has been tarnished, or at least 'downgraded', by the easy and cheap availability of corporate status and the activities of a miscreant minority.[122] If only from a public relations perspective, the ability to point to a set of directors' duties that reflected common social concerns would in fact be an asset to responsible business leaders. In time, it would shape the expectations of a new generation of managers with ambitions to head public companies. By emphasising skills other than financial expertise, legal change may in time encourage a wider range of able young people to embark on careers in business in the UK.

---

121 As the Companies Acts of 1908, 1929 and 1948 did.

122 On 11 May 2000, the Institute of Directors published the results of a MORI survey, which showed that in the UK only 29% of adults and 22% of 11–15 year olds admired people who started their own businesses.

5.9 CONCLUSION

Public companies are part of long chains of capital manipulation, as Cotterrell points out:

> Corporations own the shares of other corporations in complex chains in which the agency of human beings seems dwarfed by the structures of capital holdings. The twentieth-century discussion of a collapse of shareholder power over the management of corporations – the divorce of ownership of capital from control of capital – seems to suggest a recognition that the corporation is to be seen as the modern holder and embodiment, in itself, of capital; that capital is the actor whose instrument is the corporation.[123]

The obvious candidates for the task of controlling that economic power and humanising and socialising the use of capital are the directors – a point noted by many commentators ever since Berle and Means commended the idea of the corporate board as a 'neutral technocracy' during the 1930s.[124] In the UK, however, the tendency has been for the board to be permitted to operate without direct intervention from its shareholders[125] and without specific reference to the interests of employees[126] or trade creditors.[127] The various statutory incursions into this directorial freedom[128] have not yet succeeded in changing the culture in UK public companies.

The line between the public and private sectors has in any event become somewhat blurred where economic regulation is concerned. The question therefore arises: 'For whose ultimate benefit is the state regulating the management of corporations?'. Once the misunderstanding of shareholder ownership has been cleared up, there is no compelling reason why shareholders alone should benefit from consideration by public company boards. The functions of regulation when it is used to correct market defects are varied: to provide more information, to open up markets, to mimic competition in natural monopolies and so on. If the market tends to lead to a myopic focus on short term shareholder returns, a multi-stakeholder statement in statute of their duties could provide a necessary corrective lens for public company directors.[129]

---

123 Cotterrell, R, *The Sociology of Law: An Introduction*, 1984, p 137.

124 Berle, A and Means, G, *The Modern Corporation and Private Property*, new edn 1997, and see Stokes, M, 'Company Law and Legal Theory' in Twining, W, *Legal Theory and Common Law*, 1986, 'Implications for the Study of Company Law'.

125 *John Shaw & Sons (Salford) Ltd v Shaw* [1935] 2 KB 113; *Breckland Group Holdings Ltd v London & Suffolk Properties Ltd* [1989] BCLC 100.

126 *Parke v Daily News Ltd* [1962] Ch 927.

127 *Re Horsley & Weight Ltd* [1982] 3 All ER 1045.

128 Companies Act 1985 ss 309 and 719 and Insolvency Act 1986 ss 213 and 214 among them.

129 Ogus, n 102 above, Chapter 3.

The fact that major economic and corporate systems are interdependent and that many of the main public companies operate in several nations across and beyond Europe does not mean that there is no scope for appropriate national regulation. As far as specifically financial regulation (focused on raising capital) is concerned, a system which is clear in its objectives and is well administered is likely to command respect and improve the standing of the state concerned as a good place to do major business. Again the global trend, supported by the UK, is towards greater regulation to ensure transparency and fairness in international capital flows.[130] Piloting the extension of similar principles to cover the concerns of other stakeholders is an effort that would benefit the UK as it modernises its system of company law.

There are many other issues to be addressed in the process of reforming company law as a whole (among them the rules dealing with share capital and accounts), many of which concern board members. In addition to the specific responsibilities and technicalities in which the UK has remained somewhat heavier than many other common law jurisdictions, there is a need for a more general statement of responsibilities such as the one described above. That the primary company law statute should not even address the responsibilities of the public company board is simply an anachronism in 2001. While there may be flexibility as between different companies when it comes to determining how to fulfil their duties to stakeholders (for example, the use of committees or delegation to individuals), core responsibilities of directors as such should not be left in doubt.

The objective of such legal change is not simply to protect existing standards and to promulgate good practice but also to set a course for future development. The interests of a majority of mainstream opinion can be reflected through the political process as a counterweight to the traditionally narrow background and approach of board members. Cotterrell notes the foundation of legal change generally is that:

> The basic assumption which underlies the view that law in contemporary Western societies can operate as an instrument for inducing widespread change in citizens' behaviour patterns and beliefs or attitudes is ... clear. It is that the organisational and power resources of government in contemporary Western societies and the technical resources associated with modern legal institutions are such that law can confront mores and overcome them.[131]

The legislature of a state can impose its will even when not directly reflecting 'democratic opinion'; attitudes and practices can be changed through laws.

---

130 See speech by the Chancellor of the Exchequer Gordon Brown at the Council for Foreign Relations in New York on 16 September 1999 (text at www.treasury.gov.uk) and Department for International Development, Departmental Annual Report 2000, Chapter 5 (text at www.dfid.gov.uk).

131 Cotterrell, n 123 above, p 71.

This is not to say that the practical needs of public company directors should not be carefully considered in formulating rules that will govern their decisions and actions. The present situation in which many key duties are set out in cases decided many generations ago and relevant statutory provisions are almost equally inaccessible and unwieldy is clearly unsatisfactory. A consensus seems to have emerged to the effect that codification of the duties is possible and desirable. The challenge, taken up in this chapter, is to produce a statement that reflects best modern practice and social values while leaving the necessary scope for business judgment.

In drafting new legislation, the aim should always be to produce a document that can be used by public company directors themselves. Those who attain such positions are, one assumes, experienced and intelligent people who should not require constant expensive, professional interpretation of what the law demands in their decision making. At the same time, the legislation should be sufficiently precise for use by judges (as a last resort) in the event of a dispute. Public company directors are at present not seen to be effectively accountable for their business judgments where there is a diffuse shareholding, although some institutional shareholders are becoming more assertive.[132] While, as suggested above, they may delegate responsibility for investigation of specific shareholder demands to a kind of 'select committee', the full company board under the guidance of its chairman must look at the whole picture.

The purpose of legislation is to set collective standards sanctioned by a majority in society for the conduct of individuals. Considerations of fairness (particularly in procedural terms) and for the morality of the marketplace are evident in existing company law.[133] Privatisation has somewhat clouded the distinction between operations run for private gain and those organised for public benefit. It cannot seriously be argued that running corporations on which large groups of people are dependent for investment, for employment and for goods and services is purely a private contractual arrangement[134] – there is already too much state regulation in Britain for such a statement to be credible. The crucial point is whether the central legislation acts as a clear introduction to the terrain and sets a context for the more detailed rules in a comprehensible manner.

---

132 Cadbury, A, 'What are the Trends in Corporate Governance? How Will They Impact Your Business?' (1999) 32 Long Range Planning 12, 17; B, Garratt, 'Developing Effective Directors and Building Dynamic Boards', *ibid* 28, 30.

133 Cheffins, n 115 above, pp 142–58.

134 Frederick, RE, *A Companion to Business Ethics*, 1999, highlights International Business Ethics, Business Ethics and Work, Business's Environmental Responsibility and Social Responsibility and Business Ethics (Part III).

CHAPTER 6

REMEDIES FOR BREACH OF DIRECTORS' DUTIES

6.1 RIGHTS AND REMEDIES

Any right without a corresponding remedy will be of little real value, except perhaps as an instrument to allow the 'right-holders' to exert moral pressure. Nor would it be meaningful to speak of company directors as having a 'duty' towards stakeholders who could not take action to defend their own position, though the board may have moral responsibilities towards such persons. For reasons discussed in Chapters 2 and 4, it has been asserted that board members should have regard to the interests of a range of participants in, and contributors to, the life of a public company. The legal consequence of this essentially political judgment is that there should be some possibility of action by those key stakeholders when directors fail to follow the correct procedure in reaching their decisions. This chapter will consider the legal form such stakeholder intervention might appropriately take.

Liability in the common law tradition has generally been assessed and discussed in relation to causes of action.[1] Knowledge of potentially available court orders will affect the conduct of parties between themselves, even without reference of disputes to the courts. Out-of-court compromises in business are coloured by awareness of the remedy likely to be available if the claimant were successful in a legal action (this has been termed 'bargaining in the shadow of the law'). Standing to pursue a legal claim is, therefore, an important bargaining weapon in the armoury of complainant stakeholders and will have an impact on board strategy. It can be argued that the possibility of shareholder claims is one reason for the priority traditionally enjoyed by shareholders in UK public companies.

The law in the UK has traditionally recognised two sets of limitations on the powers of the directors to run the company as they see fit. One is the rights of shareholders, who are given the ultimate power in respect of several important events in the life of the company (for example, allotment of relevant securities,[2] changes to its constitution[3]) and the ability to oversee dealings between the company and the directors as individuals (such as any long

---

1   Samuel, G, *Sourcebook on Obligations and Legal Remedies*, 1995, pp viii–ix; a cause of action, in turn, has been described by Lord Diplock as: 'a factual situation the existence of which entitles one person to obtain from the court a remedy against another person.'

2   Companies Act 1985 s 80.

3   Companies Act 1985 ss 4, 9, 17, 28, 43, 53, 121.

service contract[4] or substantial property transaction[5]). In addition to their collective right to regulate the activities of the board, the shareholders have individual rights as members, emanating from the constitution of the company, which they can pursue in a personal capacity.[6] However, the scope of these personal rights has not been clearly defined in legislation and only members acting as such have been treated as corporate 'insiders' for the purpose of legal action.[7] Even directors, in their board role, have been regarded as outside the scope of constitutional protection,[8] while shareholders have taken action under the common law to prevent employees benefiting from corporate 'generosity'.[9]

The second source of restraint on corporate leaders is the growing volume of regulation by and under statute (primary and delegated legislation). This extends far beyond 'companies' legislation in the narrow sense. Directly or indirectly, company board members have been made responsible for supervision of employee health and safety, consumer protection, supplier payments and accounting compliance, among many other matters. Whereas a company, as an artificial legal person, can be held liable for strict liability offences,[10] the officers as individuals can also be held personally responsible in law for many of its actions (or inactions).[11] It follows the example of current statutes that directors should be accountable for the supervision of stakeholder interests.[12]

To these constraints upon the activities of UK public company directors may be added self-regulatory systems, including the Listing Rules (incorporating the Principles of Good Governance and Code of Best Practice, known as the Combined Code, which draws together provisions suggested by

4   Companies Act 1985 s 319.
5   Companies Act 1985 s 320.
6   Eg the right to have one's votes counted: *Pender v Lushington* (1887) 6 Ch D 70; a right to receive dividends in cash: *Wood v Odessa Waterworks Co* (1889) 42 Ch D 636.
7   *Eley v Positive Government Security Life Assurance Co Ltd* (1876) 1 Ex D 88.
8   *Beattie v E & F Beattie Ltd* [1938] Ch 708.
9   *Parke v Daily News Ltd* [1962] Ch 927 (a result since overturned by Companies Act 1985 s 719).
10 Eg a manufacturer under Part I of the Consumer Protection Act 1987; Trade Descriptions Act 1968 (but see *Tesco Supermarkets Ltd v Nattrass* [1971] 2 All ER 127); Environmental Protection Act 1990 (as to which see *Alphacell Ltd v Woodward* [1972] 2 All ER 475).
11 Eg Companies Act 1985 s 35(3) (personal liability for *ultra vires* transactions); s 221(5) (duty to keep proper accounting records); s 399(3) (duty to register charges).
12 Home Office Consultation Paper, *Reforming the Law on Involuntary Manslaughter: The Government's Proposals* (Home Office, May 2000) proposes a new offence of corporate killing and states (at p 21): 'the Government is of the view that: Any individual who could be shown to have had some influence on, or responsibility for, circumstances in which management failure far below what could reasonably be expected [sic] was a cause of a person's death should be subject to disqualification from acting in a management role in any undertaking.'

the Cadbury, Greenbury and Hampel Committees), to be supplemented by the Financial Services Authority.[13] There is little evidence that, in the short run, voluntary codes and recommendations lead to widespread changes in corporate practice.[14] However, the ultimate sanction for breaches of the Takeover Code, for example, is that those who do not abide by the rules of the market can be denied use of its facilities.[15] Institutional investors, in particular, have the financial influence, if they choose to use it, to demand that companies meet recommended standards of governance. Collective, voluntary standard-setting can work well to 'level up' standards if the required conduct is encouraged by the prospect of commercial penalties, including ostracism (or 'cold shouldering', in the language of the Stock Exchange), for non-conformity.

Directors may also face personal liability in the event of corporate insolvency if they have patently misjudged whether to carry on trading in the hope of escaping difficulty.[16] There is also the prospect in these circumstances of disqualification for the director, the court's decision in this respect being based upon considerations of public protection rather than punishment.[17] This provides a strong incentive for directors to focus attention on the creditors if trading conditions appear threatening. The number of directors subject to disqualification proceedings in any year is, however, small and the provisions say nothing of how well, and for whose benefit, companies are to be run so long as they remain solvent. Prompt internal correction of any breach of duty is always likely to be more speedy and cost-effective than reliance on 'policing' by an outside agency.

Executives of public companies normally have connections with legal and financial advisers of the highest quality and board members are accustomed to seek assistance when the qualifications and expertise of the directors do not equip them to meet a particular regulatory requirement. There should be no greater difficulty in principle with boards obtaining advice on potential new claims from stakeholders. There is, of course, nothing to prevent executives from seeking to take on board as non-executive directors individuals who have expert knowledge of particular areas of concern for their company (for example, customer relationship management, trade union links). There is a growing body of evidence that public companies will gain economically in the

---

13 Under the Financial Services and Markets Act 2000.

14 Eg Martinson, J, 'Half of Top Companies Fail to Comply with Hampel', *Financial Times*, 1 December 1998, 10 (on the same page, see also Buckby, S, 'Ethical Codes of Practice not being Implemented').

15 Introduction to Stock Exchange Code on Takeovers and Mergers.

16 Insolvency Act 1986 ss 213–14.

17 *Re Sevenoaks Stationers (Retail) Ltd* [1990] BCC 765.

long-term from addressing the development and management of their relationship networks.[18]

Issues of principle and of practicality surround the availability of legal remedies to stakeholders. So far as company auditors are concerned, the courts have been eager, for reasons of policy, to define their responsibilities precisely, so as to avoid the imposition of liability 'in an indeterminate amount for an indeterminate time to an indeterminate class'.[19] However, board members, for sound business reasons, need to pay attention to their primary stakeholders and their statutory responsibilities. The provision of remedies in these connections should not, therefore, be seen as adding to the board's burdens, but as reinforcing good management practice.[20]

6.2 THE DERIVATIVE ACTION MODEL

A minority shareholder is permitted to take legal action to defend the interests of a company in a limited range of situations, notwithstanding the fundamental principle of 'majority rule' in corporate affairs. Where the alleged wrongdoers are in control of the company's general meetings[21] and have in some sense committed a fraud,[22] for example by misappropriating corporate property, a derivative action by a minority shareholder will be allowed to proceed. This puts into the hands of individual members a weapon with which they can defend the interests of the company from those who are abusing their managerial powers. The action is taken to benefit the company, not the claimant personally. The court will need to be persuaded that the case is a suitable one for overturning the normal rule (majority decision) and a judge may look to the view of 'the majority of the independent minority' in

---

18 In addition to such established sources as Collins, JC and Porras, JI, *Built to Last*, 1995, and Peters, TJ and Waterman, RH, *In Search of Excellence*, 1992, one might add the evidence of MORI (paper by Hutton, P, Director of MORI, 'Using Research to Improve Quality and Service Provision' at SMI Conference, 28 January 1997) and that of International Survey Research Ltd (Maitland, R, *Employee Morale in the High Performance Organisation*, 1994)).

19 *Caparo Industries plc v Dickman* [1990] 1 All ER 568; cf *Morgan Crucible Co plc v Hill Samuel Bank Ltd* [1991] 1 All ER 142 (*per* Lord Bridge, quoting Cardozo CJ).

20 Levine, D, *Working in the Twenty-First Century*, 1998, argues that, in particular, employee consultation mechanisms encourage problem-solving and increase product quality and customer satisfaction (reviewed in *Financial Times*, 13 January 1999, p 10); see also DTI, *Working for the Future – The Changing Face of Work Practices*, 1999.

21 *Prudential Assurance Co Ltd v Newman Industries Ltd (No 2)* [1980] 2 All ER 841 makes the point that *de facto* control in a large company cannot be assessed simply by reference to the voting rights - the pattern of shareholding needs to be taken into account.

22 Negligence will not suffice to permit a minority derivative action: *Pavlides v Jensen* [1956] 2 All ER 518 but matters will be different where a director has personally benefited from alleged misdeeds: *Daniels v Daniels* [1978] 2 All ER 89.

deciding whether or not to allow the action to proceed.[23] If the case is not pursued *bona fide* in the interests of the company, but for some ulterior personal reason, the court may strike out the action.[24]

In respect of shareholders, the Company Law Review Steering Group consulted specifically on the creation of a new statutory derivative action in order to improve upon the current position in two key respects: first, to cure the uncertainty that surrounds the position of minority shareholders; secondly, expressly to permit derivative actions in cases of alleged directorial negligence or breach of duty (including breach of trust and a director putting him- or herself in a position where his or her interests conflict with those of the company).[25] This would avoid the problem of lengthy, costly preliminary trials to determine whether a particular situation fell within the exemption. It would also emphasise the standing of the shareholder as a valid guardian of the corporate interest if the management fails to meet its fiduciary obligations. It would not, of course, solve the problem of the shareholders' lack of sufficient committed interest or commercial incentive to monitor management in widely held public companies.

There seems to be no *a priori* reason why others with a direct stake in the financial health of a public company should not enjoy similar access to the courts to protect the company from harm, under a regime of judicial supervision similar to that envisaged to 'manage' shareholder actions.[26] Where negligence or fraud is being perpetrated on a company, its employees, and suppliers and customers who have a relationship of trust and interdependence with it, are often as likely to suffer financially as the shareholders and creditors. If misdeeds come to the attention of any of the primary stakeholders, it should arguably, therefore, be permissible, with the leave of the court, for them to take action in the name of, and to protect, the company itself. Any funds that have been misappropriated will have to be returned to the company. However, where employees and suppliers are in a contractual relationship with the company and the shareholders benefit from residual profits, it is the members who would gain by any increase in value above the solvency level.

The traditional arguments against extension of the right to bring derivative actions are essentially that this would lead to a multiplicity of cases and that the majority of the members, as owners, should have the right to determine the course of action taken by the company. Once the latter argument is dispensed with in the case of public companies, practical difficulties (not least of cost and co-ordination) still remain. Institutional shareholders have been

---

23 *Smith v Croft (No 2)* [1988] Ch 114.

24 *Barrett v Duckett* [1995] 1 BCLC 243.

25 Company Law Review Steering Group, *Modern Company Law for a Competitive Economy—Final Report*, July 2001, paras 7.46–7.51

26 Law Commission, *Shareholder Remedies*, Report No 246, October 1997, Draft Civil Procedure Rules (Derivative Claims).

discouraged from bringing actions, even where directorial wrongdoing had apparently been uncovered, on the grounds that it was for the company itself (that is, the corporate membership as a whole, acting by majority vote)[27] to decide whether or not to issue proceedings. One would expect this to have the effect of reducing the monitoring and scrutiny to which public company directors were subjected.[28] Whether such scrutiny by members is ever likely to increase under the present system must be open to serious question, given the lack of financial gain to shareholders from carrying out monitoring.

Bearing in mind the severe limitations on the information provided to shareholders (and their limited incentive to use such facts and figures as they are given),[29] other participants may sometimes have greater opportunities to protect the corporate interest where those in control have been committing fraud or have been negligent. Employees, for example, may be in a far better position to observe how directors are performing than shareholders. Through the Public Interest Disclosure Act 1998,[30] the legislature has already recognised the value to the public of encouraging those who become aware of wrongdoing within a company to 'blow the whistle' on employer malpractice by protecting the 'whistleblower'. Established customers and suppliers who have doubts about the financial practices or competence of those running a company with which they deal may also wish to take action. In the event of corporate insolvency, it is unsecured creditors who would be likely to suffer financial hardship. In any such case, there would need to be a preliminary process to ensure that there were genuine grounds for the suspicions aired and that the action was not being brought out of personal malice.

As at present constructed, the derivative action is treated as a procedure to be utilised 'for the good of the company' and is not available where the action is brought from personal motives or where there is an alternative remedy available (including, it seems, winding-up).[31] Where employees were involved, it can be imagined that courts would often need to question the reasons of those who had been dismissed or bore some grievance for bringing an action. So far as customers and suppliers are concerned, if the wrongdoing

---

27 *Prudential Assurance Co Ltd v Newman Industries Ltd (No 2)* [1982] Ch 204.

28 More recently this approach seems to have been confirmed in *Re Astec (BSR) plc* [1999] BCC 59 (see note, Copp, S and Goddard, R, 'Corporate Governance Principles on Trial' (1998) 19 Co Law 277).

29 Members have no right to see accounting records and may have to wait for seven months in a public company before the final accounts are laid before them in a general meeting: Companies Act 1985 ss 222, 242.

30 This new legislation protects the employee who discloses a breach of environmental, health and safety or other legislation from victimisation or harassment and renders dismissal on the grounds of disclosure automatically unfair.

31 *Barrett v Duckett*, n 24 above.

is affecting the company's performance of contractual obligations, they will normally have the option of commencing an action for breach of contract or presenting a winding-up petition. The restrictions on the use of the company's name in any litigation (put in place for understandable policy reasons where minority shareholders are involved) would usually apply with equal or greater force so far as the other stakeholders are concerned.

It is, perhaps, unrealistic to expect that stakeholders, including employees and long-term business associates, would negotiate all of these technical and procedural hurdles simply to defend the position of a public company where they were employed or with which they did business. To make matters worse for claimants, as Davies points out, the form of the (current shareholder) derivative action is misleading in two key respects, in that 'it is required to be brought in the representative form, even though it is the company, rather than the other shareholders, whom the plaintiff represents' and, even more confusingly, 'the company appears as a defendant' even though its rights, and not those of shareholders personally, are being enforced by the action.[32]

Easterbrook and Fischel assert: 'A dominating characteristic of the derivative action is the lack of any link between stake and reward – not only on the judge's part but on the plaintiff's.'[33] The authors also comment that: 'Paucity of information frequently makes it difficult for either plaintiffs or judges to determine which actions promote maximum value for the firm.'[34] Where claimants do have a financial stake in a company, their fate is linked to it. What might be called the 'respect for business judgment' point is unconvincing where derivative suits are restricted to cases of directorial wrongdoing. Where such misfeasance is found to have occurred, the costs of proceedings ought to be borne by the wrongdoers themselves; where it is not, but the action was brought *bona fide* in defence of the company's interests, it is not unreasonable that the company should meet the expenses. Procedural rules as suggested by the Law Commission[35] should help to ensure that costs do not escalate unjustifiably.

The main difficulty, then, is that in most public companies, there is no sufficient financial incentive for individual shareholders to take action in respect of wrongdoings that harm the company. The possible increase in the value of their own shares will simply not repay the time involved and the risk of having to pay costs if litigation fails.[36] Employees and customers and

---

32 Davies, P, *Gower's Principles of Modern Company Law*, 1997, p 666.

33 Easterbrook, F and Fischel, D, *The Economic Structure of Corporate Law*, 1991, p 101.

34 *Ibid*, p 102.

35 Law Commission, n 26 above, Draft Civil Procedure Rules 50.4–50.11.

36 See, however, *Wallersteiner v Moir (No 2)* [1975] QB 373 – the plaintiff can seek indemnity for costs from the company but it is for the minority shareholder to persuade the court that it has a reasonable case to bring at the company's expense.

suppliers who have contracts with the company are only likely to lose personally from managerial wrongdoing if the solvency of the whole operation is put at risk so that debts cannot be paid. Their priority will quite understandably be the security of their own position. Channels of communication with genuinely independent non-executive directors should provide an alternative means of expressing concerns and having them addressed at a much earlier stage. In summary, it is submitted that there are more satisfactory alternatives to the derivative action model, so far as non-member primary stakeholders are concerned.

6.3 THE 'UNFAIR PREJUDICE' MODEL

The most widely used remedy by minority shareholders in smaller companies today is s 459 of the Companies Act 1985 (as amended in 1989). This demands a demonstration that the affairs of the company are being/have been conducted in a manner which is unfairly prejudicial to all or some part of the membership. The judicial view of events will depend on the arrangements that were in place within a given company and the expectations of the participants before the difficulties arose. Once unfairly prejudicial conduct is established, the court has a broad discretion to address the situation and has been prepared to be quite innovative on occasions in its use of its powers.[37] Such action can only be brought by a company member (or one to whom shares have been transferred or transmitted by law) but the member's standing to petition is clear.

One proposal for change to the current legislation, made by the Law Commission and adopted by the DTI in its recent consultation, would strengthen the link between the s 459 remedy and small private companies. It would do so by enacting that, where a member who holds at least 10% of voting rights in a private company where all (or substantially all) of the members are directors, is removed from directorship, unfair prejudice to the member who was removed will be presumed. It had already become clear from the jurisprudence that the 'unfair prejudice' provision was construed as being intended mainly for the benefit of members of small, 'quasi-partnership' companies. Public company shareholders, it seems, will find it difficult (if not almost impossible) to establish that they held legitimate expectations beyond the bounds of the company's written constitution.[38] As long as the letter of the corporate constitution has been observed, the courts have generally taken the view that there is no further legal cause of action for investors in the stock market.

---

37 Eg *Re HR Harmer & Sons Ltd* [1958] 3 All ER 689.
38 *Re Astec (BSR) plc* [1999] BCC 59.

It should not be forgotten, then, that while investors in public companies may indeed act on an 'impersonal' or 'transactional' basis, and so may realistically be presumed to know little or nothing of the company's management beyond the matters set out in formal documentation, the employees and suppliers and customers may develop their own 'legitimate expectations' as to the conduct of a public company. At the very least, a norm of consultation and information with these contributing groups when major business decisions were contemplated could readily be envisaged. Development of such safeguards could build upon the existing legal principles concerning legitimate expectations and detrimental reliance.[39] If other stakeholders, together with shareholders, are to enjoy a strong position in the context of directors' and executives' work, other primary constituents' rights in law should surely be comparable to those of members. As with company shareholders at present, one class of stakeholder might complain of being treated unfairly by the controlling executive (for example, by lack of consultation) or individual participants might allege that they have been treated unfairly vis à vis others in their group.

Apart from the dismissal of a director who had a 'legitimate expectation' of remaining involved in company management, a variety of circumstances have been accepted as good grounds for a claim of 'unfair prejudice'. The conduct of the company's affairs other than for the corporate benefit,[40] impropriety on the part of management[41] and non-payment of dividends (albeit in exceptional circumstances)[42] have been regarded as 'unfairly prejudicial'. In an analogous fashion, the other key stakeholders could be permitted to take legal action where the directors were gleaning personal advantages from their corporate position rather than acting in the interests of the primary contributors. The categories of 'unfair prejudice' should not be regarded as closed,[43] as they will depend on each individual company and its relationship with its stakeholders. The appropriate balance of interests will vary at different stages in the company's life.

The range of remedies available under the auspices of s 459 to 'do justice' in the case in question has contributed greatly to the provision's popularity. The courts have shown flexibility in using their discretionary powers to improve unsatisfactory management situations for the future[44] or to correct what appears to be a clear maldistribution of assets.[45] The primary remedy so

---

39 But see the apparent restrictions applied by the House of Lords in *O'Neill v Phillips* [1999] 2 All ER 961 (noted by Goddard, R, 'Closing the Categories of Unfair Prejudice' (1999) 20 Co Law 333).

40 *Nicholas v Soundcraft Electronics Ltd* [1993] BCLC 360.

41 *Re Elgindata Ltd* [1991] BCLC 959.

42 *Re Sam Weller Ltd* [1990] Ch 682.

43 *Re BSB Holdings Ltd (No 2)* [1996] 1 BCLC 155.

44 *Re HR Harmer & Sons Ltd* [1958] 3 All ER 689.

45 *Re Sam Weller Ltd* [1990] Ch 682.

far as the shareholders are concerned has, however, always been the purchase (by the company or the directors) of the plaintiff's shares so as to give them an 'exit route' from the company when this may not otherwise be available. A flexible approach to compensation for lost employment or broken contracts would be welcome but would naturally be guided by the level of existing remedies in contract law and employment law if 'specific performance' of agreements were impossible or unrealistic. As far as other primary stakeholders are concerned, the intervention in the conduct of company business by injunction or directions at the suit of the members is envisaged under the current s 461. Employees or long-term suppliers could, in theory, be granted similar powers to petition the court, to ensure that public company boards acted fairly towards them as well as to shareholders.

Orders in respect of unfair prejudice are not directly linked to proof of specific financial gain to directors or others.[46] It is proof of the wrongful behaviour itself, rather than the actual cost to the claimant, that is the focus of attention. The remedy is in general compensatory (in the sense of improving the position of the unfairly prejudiced stakeholder in the most effective manner), rather than penal to those who had made an inappropriate decision. Even so, directors whose companies were repeatedly in court for unfairly prejudicial treatment of their stakeholders would damage their reputations and might find themselves at risk of removal from office, just as they would for repeated breaches of other legislative requirements.

As a practical matter, how would one deal with the situation where action that was favourable to one primary stakeholder was apparently prejudicial to another? This might occur, for instance, where cost-cutting redundancies were planned, which would inevitably 'prejudice' the workforce for the benefit of shareholders and customers who wish to see the business remaining 'competitive' (on price and cost). In cases of insolvency, there is already a precedent to the effect that the directors are not bound to give absolute priority to obtaining the highest possible cash sum for the company's assets above consideration of the impact of the transfer or closure of the business on employees.[47] The courts would, over time, become accustomed to assessing whether the board had properly balanced the rights of different stakeholders. If it had done so in any case, a claim of 'unfair prejudice' by a particular stakeholder would not succeed.

Objections might be raised to the effect that, under the proposed regime, judges would be substituting their decisions for those of the directors themselves. In reality, the courts would be doing no more than assessing the proper treatment of stakeholders and quasi-contractual arrangements between them and the public company, a role for which judges are well suited

---

46   *Re HR Harmer & Sons Ltd* [1958] 3 All ER 689.
47   *Re Welfab Engineers Ltd* [1990] BCLC 833.

by training and experience. Standards of 'reasonable' conduct and decision making (including in the context of directors' duties)[48] are defined, refined and frequently adjudicated upon by the courts. The action to be taken in respect of unfair prejudice, furthermore, need not involve a forced reversal of company policy (any more than the forced 'buyout' of a dissenting shareholder frustrates the will of the majority in the shareholder context). It might simply provide compensation for the stakeholder who has suffered a breach of legitimate expectations.[49]

The prospect of employees, suppliers or customers taking legal action because the company had been making large profits and not using or distributing them in an appropriate manner might seem somewhat controversial. There is, however, already a 'floor' on competitive behaviour to mitigate the perceived negative effects of the market, and with the introduction of the national minimum wage,[50] legislation to outlaw abuse of dominant market position[51] and the Late Payment of Debts (Interest) Act 1998,[52] the trend towards moderate intervention by way of legislation seems fairly consistent. Executives in public companies should be aware of the need to maintain a sustainable commercial and economic base for their future operations. This entails a proper balancing by the board of the rights of primary stakeholders.

6.4 PERSONAL RIGHTS OF ACTION

The basic right of the majority of a company's membership to control the use of its name in legal actions[53] has not prevented individual members from suing in their own names, for their own benefit, when their rights have been violated and they have suffered loss. Where a personal right of action is demonstrated, it is said that the principle of 'majority rule' has no application. Unfortunately, much confusion has been caused by the lack of any clear distinction in the authorities between those rights which count as 'personal' rights, attendant on the status of membership, and those which were for the

---

48 Eg *Dorchester Finance Co Ltd v Stebbing* [1989] BCLC 498; *Bishopsgate Investment Management Ltd (in liquidation) v Maxwell (No 2)* [1994] 1 All ER 261.

49 Arrangements between shareholders themselves are not properly the subject of actions under Companies Act s 459 at present: *Re Leeds United Holdings plc* [1996] 2 BCLC 545.

50 National Minimum Wage Act 1998.

51 Competition Act 1998 Chapter II.

52 This provides that, initially, small businesses can claim interest at 8% over base rate from public companies and the public sector if payments are overdue, with the regime set to expand to cover all business contracts; in practice public companies still have the upper hand in setting the contractual arrangements with their smaller contractors.

53 *Foss v Harbottle* (1843) 2 Hare 461.

company as a whole to enforce.[54] If the courts were, in addition, to pronounce separately on the rights of employees and those of customers or suppliers beyond the bounds of strict contract, the picture would become less clear.

As far as the primary constituencies (other than the shareholders) are concerned, the principal right which they would enjoy by virtue of their association with a public company, on a stakeholder analysis, would be the procedural right to have their position duly examined and considered by the board. As with dissenting shareholders, once relations have clearly broken down between management and the long-standing employee or the long-established customer or supplier, there is often rather little the law can usefully do, except to facilitate a reasonably harmonious and fairly recompensed exit.[55] It could, however, do that much and sometimes might be able to produce a *modus vivendi* between parties, which would allow a mutually profitable association to be resumed. If the concept of primary stakeholders (other than the shareholders) as participants in the company's life is to be taken more seriously, it is certainly arguable that the law should provide this supervisory facility (or 'backstop') to each of them.

The law needs to make clear both to public company directors and to stakeholders the legitimate expectations the latter can have of board members and of legal protection. There will be cases where the interests of the different primary groups will conflict, notwithstanding the managerial arguments that the long-term interests of the shareholders will be best served by paying attention to the requirements of customers and employees. It is not sufficient simply to identify the responsibilities of the directors with attention to the interests of 'the company', interpreted as those of the totality of members at present and in the future.[56] Other participants have rights, arising from contractual provisions and from legitimate expectations, in relation to the activities and decisions of any public company executive.

Quantification of losses would also be a barrier to pursuit of many complaints of directorial breach of duty where the principal grievance was that the board had not paid proper attention to the interests of a specified constituency. It would be problematic either to calculate the pecuniary costs of such neglect or to insist upon satisfaction of the rights of one stakeholder in isolation. Personal actions have led to injunctions to prevent company resolutions in general meeting from being put into effect, but it would be

---

54 Eg compare *Salmon v Quin and Axtens Ltd* [1909] 1 Ch 311 with *Mozley v Alston* (1847) 1 Ph 790 (both cases concerned decision making contrary to procedures set out in company's articles but the outcomes differed).

55 It could be argued that compensation for unfair dismissal and claims for breach of contract already fulfil this function in part but both are limited in their sphere of application.

56 *Hogg v Cramphorn Ltd* [1967] Ch 254; *Howard Smith Ltd v Ampol Petroleum Ltd* [1974] AC 821.

inappropriate for other stakeholders to enjoy that power. Clearly, where no one stakeholder is to have automatic primacy, the court must consider the fairness and reasonableness of the board's decisions in the light of the concerns of all affected parties.

In the context of judicial review, the courts have attempted to deal with breaches of legitimate expectation and detrimental reliance and have proceeded with flexibility to act according to the circumstances.[57] Thus a public body's discretion cannot be fettered by reason of an incorrect or *ultra vires* decision of one official, but where a change of policy adversely affects a party who had reasonably relied on its continuance, that party may be awarded compensation. The courts could, in principle, safeguard the rights of those dealing with public companies in a similar manner. Where directors were to be allowed to exercise commercial freedom while a principal stakeholder suffered an injustice as a result,[58] the claimant could be awarded compensation in a comparable manner to public law claimants.

Personal rights enforceable by individual shareholders have been those arising from the 'statutory contract'[59] between the company and the members, as set out in the memorandum and articles of association.[60] The entitlements of employees are also settled by contract at the beginning of the parties' association with the company,[61] but after a period the employment relationship may also encompass *de facto* bargains that have developed. Supplier and customer links also raise the issue of the scope and completeness or otherwise of legal contracts. Given the complexity of the legal issues surrounding the boundaries of the s 14 'membership contract', there is no real reason to suppose that judges would be unable or unwilling to tackle the issues involved in enforcing the rights of other constituents. The concern on a stakeholder analysis of the public company is whether automatic enforcement of one party's expectations would lead to other key participants being excluded from their proper consideration.[62]

Without adequate information systems, there would be great difficulties in practice for stakeholders seeking to exercise any personal right of action. As a starting point, suggestions that the Annual Report and Annual General Meeting be more accessible and useful to stakeholders would make it easier

---

57 *Western Fish Products Ltd v Penwith DC* [1981] 2 All ER 204; *Lever Finance Ltd v Westminster (City) Council LBC* [1971] 1 QB 222.

58 As set out in Wade, W and Forsyth, CF, *Administrative Law*, 7th edn 1994, pp 372–78.

59 Companies Act 1985 s 14.

60 The 'model form' of which is Table A, Companies (Tables A to F Regulations) 1985 (SI 1985 No 805).

61 The contract in writing or particulars of it delivered to the employee within two months of the commencement of employment: Employment Rights Act 1996 s 1.

62 Stewart, R, *Managing Today and Tomorrow*, paperback edn 1994, Chapter 5 summarises 'common stakeholder groups for all organisations ... providers of finance, employees ... clients or customers and the community'.

for all to appraise management performance. Employee rights of information and consultation are gradually being strengthened, thanks mainly to the intervention of European Union law.[63] Customers requiring consumer goods would be better protected if labelling were more informative than it is now. The rule that public companies have to disclose their supplier payment policy in the Directors' Report could appropriately be expanded in the light of the Late Payment of Commercial Debts (Interest) Act 1998.[64]

A separate issue concerns the right to pursue litigation connected with breaches of environmental legislation or other criminal law. This is, of course, not for the personal benefit of the litigant, but to secure that the legislation is upheld. Any body, including a Non-Governmental Organisation, which can show that it has a good arguable case and a particular expertise in the topic under discussion, should be able to bring a prosecution. This does not have the effect of extending managerial responsibility beyond its current bounds but merely ensures more effective enforcement of the existing rules. As such it is a form of 'public interest' action *par excellence*. This argument will be further developed in the following section.

6.5 THE AVAILABILITY OF REMEDIES

Having considered some possible structures for stakeholder remedies with a view to choosing between the alternatives, one must then ask: to whom should redress be available and by whom should the process of seeking that recompense be managed? On grounds that were discussed in Chapters 2 and 4, it is both anomalous and *prima facie* unjust to make distinctions between the different groups which contribute to the financial well-being of a public company. As a further issue, there are matters of public concern, particularly relating to the environment and public health and safety, where legislation is in place but enforcement and penalties are arguably inadequate to secure the desired standard of conduct. Could stakeholder involvement help to solve this problem in future?

It has been argued that management, headed by executive directors, needs to be able to conduct the affairs of the company (within basic bounds of commercial morality) as it sees fit, with a minimum of interference from statutory bodies or from officials. It is certainly true, as was remarked in the *Prudential Assurance* case,[65] that 'monitors' who can set in train an action costing hundreds of thousands of pounds and taking up weeks of court time are not necessarily acting in the best interests of the company if the cost is not

---

63 Eg Directive 94/45 OJ L254/64 (1994) on the establishment of European Works Councils.

64 n 52 above.

65 [1982] Ch 204.

justified. Judges in civil proceedings will, however, become accustomed to taking a more active role than before in case management under recent provisions, which followed the recommendations of Lord Woolf.[66] The danger in requiring too much 'front loading' of evidence (as opposed to presentation of argument at trial) is that this may increase the initial costs beyond the reach of stakeholder groups.[67]

Limitation of standing to bring an action on the basis of the conduct of the company's internal affairs to those with a direct financial interest in performance would deter generalised interference in management by individuals and groups with personal grievances or ulterior motives. This is not to say that UK public companies should not be required to be more open than they are now with information as to their environmental and social, as well as financial, performance. Pressure groups ranging from Greenpeace to UNICEF have had a major impact on the policies of large multinational companies by organising consumer boycotts and disseminating adverse publicity. As noted in Chapter 5, the experiences of Shell over disposal of the Brent Spar oil platform and Nestlé over their baby milk sales policy are cases in point. The reality in many instances is that the public authorities do not have the resources to pursue all known or suspected 'offenders'. Where this is so, as in public law,[68] a person or group with a sufficient interest and a good arguable case on the face of it should have standing to proceed with an action as in substance a 'private prosecution' for alleged breaches of existing legislation.

In public law terms, *R v Inspectorate of Pollution, ex p Greenpeace Ltd* (No 2)[69] established a modern approach to pressure groups. Otton J (as he then was) said in that case: 'I consider it appropriate to take into account the nature of Greenpeace and the extent of its interest in the issues raised, the remedy Greenpeace seek to achieve and the nature of the relief sought.'[70] After examining those factors, the learned judge added: 'I regard the applicant as eminently respectable and responsible and its genuine interest in the issues

---

66 New Civil Procedure Rules replacing the former County Court Rules and Rules of the Supreme Court came into effect from 26 April 1999; their impact will become apparent over time but it is intended that judges should seek to control the length of hearings and the evidence that is presented.

67 In the US, it is the availability of contingency fee arrangements for legal advice that facilitates much shareholder and consumer activism and similar developments may be observed in the UK in the future – information such as 'The Shareholder Action Online Handbook' (Craig Mackenzie) on the internet also facilitates shareholder campaigns.

68 Contrast *R v Inland Revenue Commissioners, ex p National Federation of Self-Employed and Small Businesses* [1982] AC 617, which appeared to indicate that if a good case were made out, standing would not be examined separately, with *R v Secretary of State for the Environment, ex p Rose Theatre Trust Co* [1990] 1 QB 504, which emphasised the importance of establishing a 'sufficient interest' in the matter in dispute.

69 [1994] 4 All ER 329.

70 *Ibid*, 349.

raised is sufficient for it to be granted *locus standi.*' The issues in question concerned the licensing of BNFL operations at its Sellafield nuclear reprocessing plant. If public bodies do not take appropriate action, their practice is thus subject to judicial review on the suit of such 'respectable, responsible' bodies. Public companies (including those in the 'privatised' sector) could, in principle, be made subject to similar legal challenge. This would certainly help to counter criticisms that large corporations were not publicly accountable for actions with public health or major social impacts.

Once society, via Parliament, has laid down a prescribed standard in legislation,[71] there should be no real objection of principle to an interested and responsible party taking legal steps to enforce it. Many key constituencies already enjoy channels by which their complaints could be pursued in law against a public company. Employees can bring actions in the Employment Tribunal (though at present these are hampered in practice by the fact that affordable advice and representation may often be difficult to find). As far as protection of customers and suppliers is concerned, there is the possibility of action for breach of contract, but these will largely be confined to agreements which have been reduced to documentation. Such specific rules are, it is submitted, no substitute for the ultimate threat of civil proceedings by one of those parties if those in charge of conducting a public company's business do so in a manner which unfairly damages the stakeholder.

In this context Pettet argues that:

> [S]ome thought could usefully be given to extending section 309 of the Companies Act 1985 so that it requires that directors should have regard to the interests, not just of the employees, but also the company's suppliers, customers and the community in which the company is located ... [I]f the constituencies are to be extended beyond shareholders at all, then why just to the employees?[72]

To this one might usefully add, if all of these stakeholder groups are proper objects of the board's attention, why should they not be permitted to take action directly on their own account?

In the case of shareholders in public companies, they at least have the 'remedy' of selling their shares where there is an open market. Employees may find it much more difficult to replace their jobs, while customers and suppliers may have relatively little choice in the market where a major public company decides to change its terms of business. Shareholders also control the market for corporate management and will determine whether a takeover bid succeeds or fails.[73] In most public companies at present, a dispute over

---

71 Eg in consumer or environmental protection legislation.
72 Pettet, B, 'The Stirrings of Corporate Social Conscience' (1997) 50 Current Legal Problems 289.
73 *Hogg v Cramphorn Ltd* [1967] Ch 254; *Howard Smith Ltd v Ampol Petroleum Ltd* [1974] AC 821.

their future direction will *de facto* be settled by a relatively small group of investment managers from the major institutions. The prospective new management needs only to convince the investors that it can increase returns in order to succeed in its bid. If all prospective arrangements were subject to an overriding duty to be responsible to all key constituents, there would be less room for 'asset stripping' after takeovers in Britain.[74]

Increased clarity of rules as regards *locus standi* or otherwise of stakeholders would help to reduce expensive uncertainty in litigation. As with all known legal obligations, the risk of actions under the new provision would be actively managed by procedures in well-run public companies.[75] In the event of a dispute, negotiation and accommodation would be more common than a trial. Armed with appropriate disclosure and the ultimate possibility of sanctions in law, constituencies could defend their interests more effectively.[76] As far as existing legislative requirements are concerned, it is surely a matter of environmental and social priority to see that the rules are effectively and consistently enforced.

6.6 THE RANGE OF AVAILABLE REMEDIES

The courts have available to them in 'unfair prejudice' cases a whole range of possible awards, including injunctive relief and specific provision as to the future conduct of the company. A derivative action will simply restore to the company's accounts funds that should have been in its possession at the start of the proceedings. Personal actions are for the individual benefit of those who feel they have been wrongfully deprived of some advantage that was due to them. The distinction between the different types of circumstances has not always been clearly drawn in jurisprudence, while the minority shareholder has been left in an uncertain situation (which the Law Commission's proposals, discussed above, may ameliorate to some degree). To the extent that particular groups are prejudiced because of action taken to benefit other stakeholders, it would seem to be justifiable that compensation should come from the company's resources. Where the performance of directors has been manifestly inadequate, some personal reparation from them to the company would appear to be equitable.

---

74 Cosh, A *et al*, *Takeovers and Short-Termism in the UK*, 1990, discusses the phenomenon from the perspective of the 1980s.

75 Coulson-Thomas, C, *The Future of the Organisation*, 1997, emphasises customer relationship management, the supply chain and quality of working life.

76 The higher level of shareholder activism in the US, for instance, may in part be attributable to a greater culture of openness – see eg Monks, RAG and Minow, N, *Watching the Watchers: Corporate Governance in the Twenty-First Century*, 1996.

Where the board is found to have made an error of judgment when trying to balance the interests of the stakeholders, this may be rectifiable, for example by the amendment of business plans. If the board members have not acted in good faith while exercising their duties, an order that they compensate the company for the cost of reparation to the stakeholder may also be appropriate. An order to provide that civil proceedings may be taken (by any party and in any manner as the court may direct) in the name of the company would also continue to be a useful possibility, particularly in the event of misappropriation of assets. Direct compensation from the company's funds is, however, likely to be the most frequently sought remedy. In effect, this would amount to a redistribution from the shareholders (profits available for distribution) to others where the correct balance had not been achieved by directors. That is one purpose of the liberalisation of access to the courts in favour of the primary stakeholders.

Reinstatement of employees who have been wrongfully dismissed, in the sense that their interests were not properly considered by the company's board, will frequently not be practical (one may compare the situation with unfair dismissal claims where, although available, reinstatement is rarely sought).[77] Similarly, where customers and suppliers perceive that a company has reneged on a long-standing commitment, an order for future specific performance may be commercially unwarranted where alternatives are available. Compensation could, however, be awarded in recognition of the breach and to deter directors from similar behaviour thereafter. If directors had not reached the proper standard in making their assessment, it might even be considered appropriate to order that they should reimburse the company. Where protection of existing jobs or business connections was still feasible at the time of a hearing, and the alternative was unemployment or decline for the claimant stakeholders, the courts could become more interventionist in combatting the unfair prejudice directly.

Shareholders usually require an 'exit route' if they are dissatisfied with management. In listed public companies, they have that option of departure if they can sell their shares for a satisfactory price in the open market (this being one probable reason for the fact that plaintiffs using s 459 have overwhelmingly been members of small companies founded on personal relationships). Other stakeholders may want to remain involved with the company, perhaps on amended terms, if only because their economic future is bound up with that of the organisation (this applies most obviously to employees, but customers and suppliers can also become 'dependent'). There is scope for the future conduct of the company's business to be regulated more closely using a procedure analogous to the existing s 461. Past relationships

---

77 The Employment Relations Act 1999 s 34(4) increased the maximum compensation payable for unfair dismissal to £50,000.

between the company and the stakeholder will be important in this respect and directors' knowledge of that fact should encourage the cultivation of lasting associative relationships where any difficulties can be resolved without recourse to litigation.

If the objective of permitting 'stakeholder' legal action is to ensure that directors pay proper regard to the interests of all those who should be treated as part of the corporate network, there are two elements to the assessment of final orders. One is to compensate the person whose interests have been wrongfully disregarded; the other is to ensure that directors are deterred from breaches of duty in future. Where directors' actions were taken in pursuit of shareholder value (and in the process involved a breach of clear understandings previously reached with employees or suppliers), the company's resources can, with justification, be used to compensate those who were injured. The remedy against board members who were personally responsible for the situation and hence for costing the company compensation payments, at present lies in the hands of the shareholders who can remove the directors from office.[78]

Shareholders, like creditors, currently also have open to them the possibility (as a last resort) of petitioning to wind up the company on the ground that it would be 'just and equitable' to do so.[79] Where an alternative remedy is available to a member, however, and it appears the petitioner is being unreasonable in pressing for a winding-up rather than pursuing an alternative strategy, the court will not wind up the company.[80] Since creditors (including providers of equity) will be the parties who stand to benefit when a company is dissolved and are the parties who suffer when trading goes on for too long, it is appropriate that they should enjoy this power. In any reform of insolvency provisions, however, consideration should be given to allowing or requiring other parties who would be affected by a winding-up to be heard and their views considered in court. So far as employees are concerned, European Union provisions on information and consultation (for example through European Works Councils, discussed below) already go part of the way along this route. Customers whose business interests are interdependent with those of the public company that faces winding up should arguably also enjoy some right of input into the decision as to its fate.

Furthermore, in discussions of corporate amalgamations and reconstructions[81] and arrangements with creditors,[82] it would be desirable from the stakeholder perspective to encourage interaction between

---

78 Companies Act 1985 s 303.
79 Insolvency Act 1986 s 122(1)(g).
80 *Ibid*, s 125(2).
81 Companies Act 1985 ss 425–27A.
82 Insolvency Act 1986 Part I.

shareholders and creditors and others. Where jobs are put at risk or existing arrangements called into question in the name of financial restructuring, there could at least be warnings to those who would be affected (and again European Union requirements point in this general direction). A further interesting possibility is then opened up, which is that workers or those in the supply chain might be able to raise funds to challenge a plan that would be contrary to their interests by proposing an alternative. UK financial services and structures would arguably need to be more flexible than they are now for this to have very much practical effect[83] but in a climate of lower interest rates (directly or indirectly influenced by the conditions set for European Monetary Union and 'Euroland' economies),[84] it could have a significant impact.

6.7 SHAREHOLDER ACTIVISM

The focus in law on shareholder rights would be explicable as a means of disciplining management if it were proved that shareholders were likely to remove directors in case of poor performance. Franks and Meyers' study for the Company Law Review Steering Group showed little evidence of such an impact of membership. Nor does the presence of non-executives, often supposed to reflect the interests of members, appear to make a significant difference to turnover of executives (though separation of chairman and chief executive posts apparently does). In more formal terms:[85]

> The overall conclusion from the regression results is that although there is a strong relation between performance and board turnover, concentration of ownership and the category of owner play a limited role in the disciplining of management. The exceptions are inside ownership, which is used to entrench existing management, and industrial companies, which acquire stakes in poorly performing companies and precipitate high executive board turnover. Capital structure is important in explaining high levels of board turnover and the significance of new equity issues points to an important role for shareholders in disciplining boards of poorly performing companies when they are forced to seek additional equity. Board structure has little influence on overall executive board turnover but is important in the CEO regression with separation of the position of CEO and chairman leading to higher CEO turnover.

83 Hutton, W, *The State We're In*, 1995, Chapter 6.
84 Eg *The Observer*, 24 January 1999, front page, comments that: 'Interest rates in the 'eurozone' are half those in Britain. Barclays say the saving on a £100,000 mortgage taken out in euros is nearly £250 a month.'
85 Franks, J and Meyer, C, *Governance as a Source of Managerial Discipline*, www.dti.gov.uk, p 18.

Letza, Hardwick and Ashton investigated the UK impact of corporate governance and updated the Franks report. They write:

> The main conclusions to be drawn from this study may be summarised as follows:[86]
>
> 1   The link between CEO and executive board turnover and company performance is weaker than suggested by the Franks study and by previous US studies.
>
> 2   Our research supports the Franks study's finding that non-executive directors on boards perform only a weak monitoring or disciplining function. Their role appears to be advisory, rather than disciplinary.
>
> 3   While large corporate shareholders may exert some pressure on CEOs when the share price is under-performing, we generally support the Franks study's finding that outside shareholders have little or no influence on either CEO or executive board turnover.
>
> 4   Our results provide strong support for the Franks study's finding that inside shareholdings help to entrench management by having a significant effect in reducing the rate of CEO and executive board turnover. Thus, we agree with Franks *et al*'s conclusion that 'the main source of block holder control comes from those in the hands of insiders and these are used to entrench rather than discipline management'.

The takeover process in the UK is, of course, the ultimate expression of the power of the shareholders. While they are immediately beneficial for target shareholders, the evidence for the predator investors who ultimately fund the bid premium is far less favourable. Cook and Deakin report:[87]

> Generally, event study evidence from both the US and the UK indicates that takeovers generate the greatest returns to target shareholders and modest, if any, returns to bidding company shareholders.[88] ... It has also been shown that the larger the wealth effect, the greater the likelihood of the bid being successful.[89]

There is a more fundamental issue, as the reporters comment:[90]

> While a critique of the disciplinary effect of takeovers may shake our faith in the promise of performance improvements from an active market for corporate control, it does not question *why* only shareholders have the authority to monitor management and, therefore, does nothing to dislodge the primacy of shareholder interests within the Anglo-American corporate governance model.

---

86   Letza, S, Hardwick, P and Ashton J, *Who Disciplines Management in Poorly Performing Companies? An Updated Study*, www.dti.gov.uk, pp 19–20.

87   Cook, J and Deakin, S, *Stakeholding and Corporate Governance: Theory and Evidence on Economic Performance*, www.dti.gov.uk, Chapter 1, p 27.

88   MacKinlay, AC, 'Event Studies in Economics and Finance', (1997) 35 Journal of Economic Literature 21.

89   Holl, P and Kyriazis, D, 'The Determinants of Outcome in UK Takeover Bids', 3 International Journal of the Economics of Business, 1996, p 165.

90   Cook and Deakin, n 87 above, p 26.

This can only be done by questioning the association between shareholder value-maximisation, on the one hand, and economic and social welfare maximisation (defined in terms of both efficiency and distributional criteria), on the other hand. More specifically: do the observations of target company share price premiums imply productive efficiency gains in the companies concerned? What about for the economy as a whole?

Legal action protects shareholders if directors try to 'rig' the results of a bid, for example by using their power to issue fresh shares to friendly potential holders. Such share issues have been set aside as unlawful, even when members of the board were acting in 'good faith'.[91] The formulation of duties derived at common law thus supports shareholder primacy. In addition there is, at present, under s 309 of the Companies Act 1985, a duty to consider the employees as a class. While this explicitly does not give the employees any right to take action themselves, it may at least be a shield for directors who take steps which are not value-maximising for shareholders.[92] Politically there is no prospect of retreat from this approach, and indeed it is likely to be extended to customers and suppliers who are in a close relationship with a public company.

The rise of the institutional shareholder, most often a pension fund or insurance company, has been inexorable in the UK. One should remember that these shareholders, in turn, represent many other stakeholders. Pension funds are the investment vehicle for the majority of UK employees; insurance companies receive payments from almost all homeowners. At present there is no obligation for this power of shareholders to be exercised in a responsible manner. The voting record of institutions has remained poor. While improvement in this is to be encouraged, the present situation strengthens the case for direct involvement of other stakeholders.

The distribution of profits to the benefit of shareholders is also protected and furthered by takeovers. The potential for action by shareholders may lead to less favourable treatment of others:[93]

> Non-value maximising behaviour by management of hostile targets largely consists of 'transferring corporate wealth from shareholders to other non-management constituencies, such as employees, suppliers and customers'[94] Therefore, much of the observed wealth gain to shareholders must represent a redirection of rents from stakeholder groups.

While target shareholders gain from bids, acquiring shareholders and many other groups lose out:[95]

---

91 Eg *Howard Smith Ltd v Ampol Petroleum Ltd* [1974] AC 821.

92 Eg *Re Welfab Engineers Ltd* [1990] BCLC 833.

93 Cook and Deakin, n 87 above, p 28.

94 Jensen, MC, 'Takeovers: Their Causes and Consequences', (1986) 2 Journal of Economic Policy 21–48.

95 Cook and Deakin, n 87 above, p 28.

Supplier relationships, relationships with local communities, etc. may also be compromised as a result of a change in ownership along with a change in management. The discontinuity in implicit contracts is one of the hidden costs of takeovers that Shleifer and Summers[96] directly address. ... While this is value-maximising for shareholders, it is destructive of valuable corporate culture and of reputational capital, the consequences of which may be felt in the long run. Observed shareholder value increases may not be indicative of real efficiency gains so much as of rent extraction from stakeholder groups, redistributed to shareholders.

Shareholders in public companies have not been inclined so far to use the rights they have under the Companies Act and the common law. 'Exit', preferably following a takeover bid, rather than active monitoring, remains the preferred option. From the point of view of individual private shareholders or indeed institutions, this policy may be entirely rational, even if all the members collectively would benefit from exercising their rights. Other stakeholders may have different views and in many cases a stronger interest in active monitoring.

6.8 THE IMPACT OF LEGAL REMEDIES

There is little reason to suppose that the possibility of shareholder legal action very often causes concern to the directors of UK public companies. As has been noted, s 459 is, in practice, seldom available to members of public companies and the likelihood of 'wrongdoer control' being proved, so as to bring into play the exception to *Foss v Harbottle*,[97] is remote. The possibility of embarrassing litigation by pressure groups (which may create highly damaging publicity whatever the eventual result) is perhaps more often in the minds of board members, depending on the nature of the company's activities. Directors' main contact with shareholders is likely to be with the institutions; the priority of board members in those communications is to guard against the company's share price being reduced by sales of equity and to bolster confidence.

If the same duty were owed to all primary stakeholders and any of them could potentially recover damages or other recompense from the company for losses caused by a breach, the position would in fact be a good deal clearer from a managerial perspective than it currently is. The accountability of directors for failure to pay due attention to all appropriate constituencies would indeed have become a reality in the public company boardroom. This responsibility extends beyond adherence to formal contracts. As Harris puts it:

---

96 Shleifer L, and Summers, H, 'Breach of Trust and Hostile Takeovers' in Auerbach, AJ, *Corporate Takeovers: Causes and Consequences,* 1998, p 33.
97 (1843) 2 Hare 461.

The traditional law of contract is ill-suited to a long-term relationship where not all future contingencies can be anticipated, and even if they can be, the appropriate modification of the relationship will not be clear until the contingency occurs ('bounded rationality' in economic terms). In a long-term relationship the parties need to preserve flexibility to enable them to respond to new circumstances in ways which maximise their joint welfare.[98]

If public company directors knew that all key participants were in a position to take action in the event of directorial breaches of duty, one would expect this to increase their vigilance for the interests of all those stakeholders. In time use of the 'select committee' system (discussed in Chapter 3) might spread, initially as a kind of defensive response and subsequently because it had proved to be useful to executives in their strategic planning. Negotiated claims are certainly preferable to legal actions from the point of view of business efficiency. The senior independent non-executive with particular responsibility for stakeholder relations (building on the idea set out in the Hampel Report)[99] could also help to provide 'early warning' of potential complaints. If, furthermore, primary stakeholders were granted *locus standi* in legislation to protect their expectations of information and consultation and compensate for detrimental reliance on unfulfilled assurances, those parties would at last have a legal status commensurate with their economic importance.

Following on from the inclusive statement of directors' duties it is suggested that wording such as the following (based on s 459) be added:

A customer, employee, shareholder or key business associate of a public company may apply to the court for an order on the ground that the public company's affairs are being or have been conducted in a manner which is unfairly prejudicial to the interests of the applicant or the customers, employees, shareholders or key business associates of the company generally or that any actual or proposed act or omission of the company is or would be so prejudicial.

As under the present s 461, it should be clear that the court can make such orders as it sees fit to provide suitable relief if it finds the claim proven and, in particular, may regulate the affairs of the company for the future, require the company to refrain from doing or continuing to do an act or to do an act which it had omitted to do, authorise proceedings to be brought in the name of and on behalf of the company by such persons and on such terms as the court may direct or provide for payments by the company to the claimant.

Under a European Union Directive, which has effect in the UK under the 'Social Chapter', directors of companies which operate in more than one Member State are going to become accustomed to interaction with employee

---

98   Harris, D, *Remedies in Contract and Tort*, 1988, p 16.

99   Committee on Corporate Governance (Chair: Sir Ronald Hampel), *Final Report* (January 1998), para 3.18.

representatives on European Works Councils.[100] There will also be a requirement of Trade Union recognition where a majority of the workforce so wishes, a measure which will alter the dynamic of industrial relations in a modest way in favour of employees.[101] At the same time, new technology and market forces are combining to change the relationship between producers and customers. A standardised approach is no longer adequate if competitors are offering 'tailored' goods and services for their customers. Changes in employment law mean that the relationship between management and employees is being placed on a more formal and procedural footing than has traditionally been the case in Britain, while customers are inclined to be more more assertive as economic growth slows. The formal provision of remedies for these parties would simply confirm on a secure basis trends that have been apparent to alert executives for some time now.

The dynamic as regards environmental and social 'watchdogs' is a different one, albeit one that feeds in to the financial health of the company.[102] Insofar as government agencies and passive or 'interested' primary stakeholders are failing to ensure that directors keep corporate activities within legal bounds, these groups ought to enjoy legal standing to pursue proceedings. There will be those who argue that the possibility of litigation from so many quarters might lead directors to adopt an unduly 'defensive' management style. It is surely reasonable that the boards of public companies should be expected to show that their procedures have been in order and they have taken into consideration all relevant factors in reaching their conclusions.

In addition to the US corporate law analogy,[103] there is again a similarity to public law, given the impact of public company activities and the fact that funds from the public (in the form of pension contributions, insurance premiums and subsidies from central and local government sources) are so heavily involved. One would not wish to pursue this comparison too far, since the ultimate goal of the public company is to produce profits (however these are to be distributed), but it is pertinent. Of necessity, many environmental and labour standards are becoming the subject of international agreement, a development that helps to counterbalance the economic strength of the multinational companies. Considerations of human rights and of ecological protection are important both for multinational corporations and for national governments.

---

100 European Works Council Directive 94/45 OJ L254/64 (1994).

101 Employment Relations Act 1999 s 1.

102 PIRC, for example, makes available via its website (www.pirc.co.uk) reports on the activities of qouted companies with comments on their social and environmental performance and corporate governance generally.

103 American Law Institute, *Principles of Corporate Governance: Analysis and Recommendations,* 1992, para 4.01 and notes.

Increasingly open and genuinely global competition, particularly in manufacturing industries, means that directors must offer attractive deals to their customers while seeking to train and retain the best workforce they can and build mutually advantageous business partnerships. That is precisely what the protection discussed above would require. With another round of international mergers in progress,[104] executives in different jurisdictions will have to find ways of working together to pursue common aims and lasting prosperity. It is submitted that a UK legal regime that mitigates some of the least desirable effects of shareholder hegemony and encourages the building of sustained relationships will, if anything, increase UK inward investment prospects.[105]

6.9 CONCLUSION

There are a number of possible models available from the existing law to strengthen the position of stakeholders in a public company. Each strikes a slightly different balance between the interests of the company as an entity and the powers of the stakeholders. If the statement of directors' duties is to be reformulated (as was suggested in Chapter 5), that change needs to buttressed by a power to protect stakeholder expectations in court. In reality, the 'best interests of the company' cannot be separated from the benefits to its various participants. Nor can one evade the issue that the interests of these groups will be in conflict on occasions. The most satisfactory form of action would, accordingly, be one that recognised the importance of all primary stakeholders while acknowledging the need for directors to make business decisions that ensure the survival and prosperity of the business in the future.

The 'derivative action' model is designed to protect the integrity of the company's finances and produces no direct reward for the claimant. Its scope has always been disputed, though the Law Commission's proposal would alleviate this uncertainty to a considerable extent. The 'unfair prejudice' model, on the other hand, is more directly accessible and 'user-friendly' to the stakeholder, giving a better incentive for monitoring and reflecting the reality that sometimes the interests of the participants are irreconcilable and choices must be made by directors. This form of action also provides valuable flexibility as to choice of remedy. Discussion of personal rights of action raises the issue of what claims each primary stakeholder group might have that are

---

104 Eg BP-Amoco-Arco-Castrol in the oil industry (1998–2000), Ford-Volvo in the car industry (announced January 1999) and AOL/TimeWarner in the media/communications industry (completed January 2001).

105 Belanger, J, Edwards, P and Haiven, L, *Workplace Industrial Relations and the Global Challenge*, 1994, in their Conclusion draw attention to a gradual convergence in industrial relations practice to co-operative and participatory management methods.

not satisfactorily protected in other ways at present. One does not wish to lose sight of the fact that, if the stakeholder analysis is accepted, the directors cannot properly give absolute priority to the rights of one primary group above all others.

Of the various possibilities, the most promising, therefore, seems to be the form of the current 'unfair prejudice' (s 459) action. Ultimately, there may be irreconcilable differences between the interests of different groups of stakeholders, such that the directors could not please all of them. In addition to showing they had suffered 'prejudice', claimants would, therefore, need to demonstrate that the choice finally arrived at was 'unfair' in order successfully to challenge the board's decisions. If board members could show that they had properly examined all the relevant options with appropriate reference to stakeholder interests, those individuals and the company would escape liability. If, on the other hand, directors had proceeded in flagrant disregard of the rights and expectations of the customers or suppliers, the employees or investors, a suitable court order could be made for reparation in the circumstances.

In addition, the company's existing social and environmental legal duties would be more effectively enforced if public authorities were more generously funded and staffed to deal with monitoring. Insofar as Non-Governmental Organisations are 'filling the gaps' at present where such public provision falls short, their status to bring private prosecutions should be recognised accordingly. This would not in itself expand the content of directors' duties and responsibilities. It would simply increase the prospect of these duties being enforced in law.[106] In many cases responsibility for breaches would come to rest with the directors personally. Where it is the management system within the company that is at fault (and particularly where a company is known to be operating in an area that poses particular environmental or public health risks), this is entirely proper.[107]

In the event of such new legal actions being introduced, there would inevitably be commercial pressure on public company boards to put in place internal mechanisms to avoid the prospect of their organisations being taken to court by stakeholders. Where a relatively small group of shareholders (normally the institutional investors) currently holds the effective power of removal of directors, it is not surprising that executives invest so much time

---

106 Eaglesham, J, 'Directors Face Prospect of Greater Duty of Care', *Financial Times*, 31 March 2000, p 8.

107 Cannon, T, *Corporate Responsibility*, 1994, Chapter 9, discusses 'Safety Standards and Security' and the importance of managerial responsibility and corporate standards, using the Union Carbide (Bhopal, India) and Piper Alpha disasters as instructive case studies.

and energy in communicating with them.[108] This could be extended to embrace other players in the corporate field. If a greater risk of litigation improves internal 'relationship consciousness' and management, it could enhance UK public company performance at less cost than that of pursuing hostile takeovers.[109] It should be remembered that many company boards, at least if their own statements are to be believed, are already operating in the way the new remedies would seek to enforce (and some are frustrated when competitors fail to do so).

Board members' legal responsibilities, if extended in the manner proposed, would inevitably give rise to a demand for appropriate advice, in order for directors to be able to demonstrate that good practice had been adhered to. This would be linked to the existing requirement for an independent element on the board and for a lead non-executive director, whose role could be to take responsibility for stakeholder communications. The current isolation of many executives from the needs and wishes of primary stakeholders is an undesirable, even dangerous, situation from a managerial perspective. Structural changes should flow from the objective of giving different corporate constituencies a voice.

The common law tradition has a practical basis and has been concerned not with abstract rights, but with the provision of remedies.[110] Access to the courts for shareholders has been tightly controlled on the basis that excessive judicial interference with commercial freedom was undesirable.[111] In an era of greater accountability in the public sector and wider access to education and information than were known a generation ago, this is no longer adequate. Other stakeholders, too, are coming to demand their share of directorial attention within the UK system. At present, many may feel morally aggrieved but legally impotent when faced with a sharp directorial focus on short-term returns to shareholders.[112]

The effectiveness of the new remedies would depend on the willingness of the stakeholders themselves to take up active roles and seize the new opportunities they were given. Trade unions and supplier and consumer organisations could play a vital role in co-ordination and education. Funding

---

108 Eg 'When Prudential Wavered and MAM [Mercury Asset Management] went for Royal [Bank of Scotland], BoS [Bank of Scotland] knew that NatWest was Lost: How RBS [Royal Bank of Scotland] Won the Battle Between the Scottish Banks for the Hand of the Embattled English Clearer', *The Independent*, 10 February 2000, p 21.

109 Parkinson, JE, *Corporate Power and Responsibility*, 1993, pp 395–96.

110 In this respect the Human Rights Act 1998 may presage a major shift in UK legal thinking.

111 *Stein v Blake* [1998] 1 All ER 724 is a recent example of the survival of the 'proper plaintiff' principle.

112 The AA 1000 foundation standard in social and ethical accounting, audit and reporting launched by the Institute of Social and Ethical Accountability in 1999 aims to set process standards underpinned by accountability to stakeholders (see www.accountability.org.uk).

of legal actions will, however, continue to be a problem for many stakeholders. Ultimately, the experience of being rewarded for vigilance may lead to demands for more direct participation in the management structure as a quicker and cheaper check on executive discretion. First, however, stakeholder monitoring and empowerment by the processes outlined above need to be experienced by both sides.[113]

113 Luoma, P and Goodstein, J, 'Stakeholders and Corporate Boards: Institutional Influences on Board Composition' (1999) 42 Academy of Management Journal 553, a study of firms listed on the New York Stock Exchange concluded that 'in larger corporations in particular, stakeholder representation on corporate boards has assumed a degree of legitimacy as a means of responding to stakeholder interests.' The same could not be said of companies listed in London.

CHAPTER 7

EUROPEAN CORPORATE GOVERNANCE MODELS

7.1 CONTINENTAL EUROPEAN MODELS AND ANGLO-AMERICAN CAPITALISM

In the US and the UK, efforts to reform company law in general, and governance of public corporations in particular, have centred on making corporate executives more responsive to the demands of shareholders – reinvigorating 'shareholder democracy', as it is often termed. This can be seen in the Hampel Report[1] in Britain and in the activities of organisations such as the LENS fund[2] in the United States. It is argued that institutional investors, by virtue of their financial expertise and the size of their holdings, are becoming well placed to take up a monitoring role over management.[3] Where monitoring has been entrusted to non-executive directors, in the UK they usually come from the financial side of business life (frequently with accounting qualifications) and often from the same type of company as the executive directors they supervise. Other stakeholders in UK public companies, including employees and suppliers, have in general not been treated as business partners, but as instruments to be used in the production of profit.

The UK governments of the 1980s and 1990s insisted that they would not allow UK business to be made 'uncompetitive' by the importation from continental Europe of systems and structures for public companies that were unfamiliar (and unwelcome) to British executives.[4] In the European Union, harmonisation of company law has been delayed in part because of British resistance to German-inspired corporate models. This is not to suggest that there have been no debates between other European states as to the best structure for company law and many of the detailed rules. Each wishes to protect what it sees as the virtues of its own system and Germany and the UK have simply been particularly forceful in this. This has arguably led to

---

1   Committee on *Corporate Governance* (Chair: Sir Ronald Hampel), *Final Report*, January 1998.

2   The 'active shareholding' organisation run by Robert Monks and Nell Minow, authors of *Corporate Governance*, 1995.

3   See, for example, 'The Economist Survey: European Business: Good Heavens, Good Governance', *The Economist*, 29 April 2000, S13; 'Shareholders are Grabbing the Reins in Europe', *Business Week*, 29 November 1999, 30.

4   Brown, K, 'Byers to Calm Fears on Company Law Review', *Financial Times*, 7 June 2000, p 2.

something of a missed opportunity to transmit high corporate governance standards across the European Union.

The stock market-driven model seen in the UK and the USA is, of course, not the only form of technologically advanced capitalism that has succeeded on the world stage. In Germany, as also in Japan, high post-Second World War rates of personal savings facilitated bank lending to, and investment in, major industries. 'Patient capital' and the desire for high and stable rates of employment combined to make effective systems in which workers had a more central role than in the UK.[5] Economic progress on the continent of Europe may have been unspectacularly steady (particularly compared with the USA, which combined substantial capital with a mobile and educated workforce), but it has generally been sustained. Globalisation undeniably puts pressure on social market systems. One of the key questions to be answered in the new era is surely whether different forms of capitalism can still co-exist as they did during the latter half of the 20th century.[6]

Corporate boards are becoming more alike in practice across major industrial economies, for example in their use of non-executive representation and committees. This does not necessarily mean that a nation such as the UK cannot impose its particular corporate governance requirements on companies registered in its jurisdiction. It simply demonstrates that, with increases in global capital movement, legislatures and regulators in many countries were dealing with many of the same problems and issues in the 1980s and into the 1990s. Where requirements as to information and transparency are not so strict in less developed economies, moves are now underway by means of the World Bank and the International Monetary Fund to spread good commercial practice. If non-executives are seen principally or exclusively as monitors, it is appropriate for them to be on a separate panel in a supervisory capacity. If they are to contribute to the formulation of policy and the strategy of the company, it is more acceptable for them to sit in a single group with managers.

Whatever the formal structure of the board, Charkham suggests that it be judged by two key measures: the extent to which it permits the leadership to 'drive the business forward' and the extent to which the executive is effectively supervised.[7] He is reluctant to 'award the palm' for the 'best' national system, but after his research in France, Germany, Japan, the US and Britain, he inclines towards the German model.[8] Certainly the important issue

---

5   Giddens, A and Hulton, W, *On the Edge: Living with Global Capitalism*, 2000, pp 31–38.

6   Fukuyama, F, *The Great Disruption: Human Nature and the Reconstitution of Social Order*, 1999; Gray, J, *False Dawn*, 1998 are among many comments on this complex process.

7   Charkham, J, *Keeping Good Company: A Study of Corporate Governance in Five Countries*, 1994, pp 354–62.

8   *Ibid*, pp 363–64.

is not whether the board formally has one tier or two. It is whether it can and does act as an effective supervisor and whether people of an appropriate calibre and outlook are literally 'on board'. Protection for a particular social system under the guise of companies legislation may carry a cost in loss of flexibility in the international market. However, a fixation with the interests (and, specifically, short-term gains) of shareholders may, somewhat paradoxically, be a handicap in the globalised economy. With increasing global competition, the same key stakeholders are crucial for success throughout the capitalist world.

There are several ways in which company law could give stakeholders the opportunity to contribute to decisions in public companies. Apart from the possibility of direct representation on the board, separate mechanisms for consultation and legal rights to challenge unfavourable board resolutions may also be valuable. It is not surprising, given the nature of the common law as compared with civil codes, that UK protection of stakeholder rights depends on jurisprudence rather than legislation. Greater attention to procedure is warranted in the UK, as on the continent of Europe, and may result in a higher quality of decision making. The shareholders' conduct in selecting, and where necessary removing, the board will not then reflect a concern with short-term dividend payments alone. Taking over ownership and taking over the board appointment role are to some extent alternative methods for stakeholders to exercise influence. Different industries may lend themselves to different methods of participation by stakeholders, depending on the mix of factors of production involved in each case.

The general trend in manufacturing industry is that the balance is shifting from mass-produced goods towards more 'tailored' products that meet the specific and individual requirements of customers. Where multinational companies own plants in many different countries, significant local autonomy for branches is fast becoming the norm. Within Europe, clearly there are important national differences, not only of language and culture, but also of climate and income, which affect customer requirements. On the supply side, too, there are essential differences between nations, which governments can affect, as Phelps points out:

> Perhaps the most salient area in which there is a continuing and vital contribution to industry embeddedness and competitiveness at a national level is in terms of education and vocational training as a key input to production. Here it becomes apparent that UK government policy over a long period has contributed to the poor vocational skills available to manufacturing industry in the UK.[9]

There are two competing definitions of national state jurisdiction over corporate entities – the 'incorporation' doctrine, favoured by the UK, and the

---

9   Phelps, N, *Multinationals and European Integration*, 1997, p 18.

'*siege reel*', real seat model, which is preferred in continental Europe.[10] The former grants control to the place where legal formalities of incorporation were completed while the latter favours the site of the company's head office. Rights of taxation, in particular, are a crucial issue for national governments.[11] As far as the administration of the company is concerned, there is no doubt that the state of incorporation is pre-eminent in discerning the company's and officers' duties. Whether diversity is seen as a positive factor depends on one's view of competition between states in the matter of producing corporate law where there is free movement of capital. The supreme example of this is the United States, where Delaware has without doubt 'won' the 'race' to be the state that attracts the largest number of major companies to incorporate there.[12]

In principle, UK business leaders have indicated that they would support greater European economic integration and availability of more measures along the lines of the European Economic Interest Group[13] (which is designed to promote partnership ventures across borders) just as they, in general, support the principle of the UK joining the single currency.[14] Much of UK opinion, however, is not well informed about the real opportunities for progress arising from European co-operation. Having completed the single market in legislative terms, the European institutions need to publicise the merits of different corporate systems and so to spark an informed debate about further integration. If the interests of the Union's economy would be best served by allowing the various states to compete to develop the most popular system (as in the USA), this would be a powerful argument against further integration. Linguistic, cultural, political and educational factors are, however, still highly diverse as between different states and are likely to have a strong influence on investment decisions. Even comparatively high rates of taxation in a given nation need not deter investment in the aggregate if revenue is used to increase skills and encourage research.[15]

Changes to the laws affecting companies have a commercial cost, and this has to be balanced against the gains which it is alleged that the alterations will bring. The UK government has already made clear that its priority is to produce legislation and regulation which is in a modern and accessible form

---

10 *Centros Ltd v Ehrvervs-og Selskobsstylrelsen* C-212/97 [1999] BCC 983 (ECJ).

11 As to German tax reforms see: Smith, M, 'Proposed Tax Reform in Germany for 2001/2002' Corporate Finance, May 2000, in supplement 'Germany Meets the Challenge' 37; 'Germany's Tax Reform', *Business Europe*, 30 June 1999, 6.

12 Romano, R, *Foundations of Corporate Law*, 1993, Part III A deals with 'State Competition for Corporate Charters'.

13 Council Regulation 2137/85 OJ L199/1 (1985).

14 CBI news release, 'CBI Members reaffirm Support for EMU Membership in Principle', 20 July 1999.

15 Currie, D, 'Does EMU Need Political Union?' (June 1998) Prospect 60, 62; Taverne, D, 'Europe and the Tax Question' (July 2000) Prospect 54 .

and does not place unnecessary restraints on managerial freedom – hence the title of the DTI's 1998 Green Paper, *Modern Company Law for a Competitive Economy*. The compulsory introduction of unfamiliar ideas such as employee representation on boards is, therefore, unlikely to be welcomed. Economically and politically, different systems of company law may well suit different nations in Europe.[16] On the other hand, there is much to be said for making the process of movement of capital and of managers themselves across the European Union as open and straightforward as possible. What follows in this chapter is a (necessarily brief) account of the corporate governance systems in the largest European corporate economies other than the UK, namely Germany and France, and of the progress and pitfalls of European Union integration and regulatory harmonisation.

7.2 THE GERMAN SYSTEM AND CO-DETERMINATION

Under the German constitution,[17] the use of property is said to be a matter of legitimate social concern that should 'serve the common good'. Employee involvement is part of the structure of all large German corporations. This has lead, so its supporters assert, not to industrial strife, but to co-operation which has proved to be highly productive.[18] In large German companies, there is a formal separation of executive decision making by the *Vorstand* and monitoring of management by the *Aufsichtsrat*. The other distinctive feature of the German system is that of long-term bank investment in major manufacturing industries. Flotation of shares on the German stock market (which is much smaller, in both absolute and relative terms, than that of London) has tended to come at a later stage in a company's life than is usual in the UK – a state of affairs which may be changing, but slowly if so.[19]

The post-1945 German *Wirtschaftwunder* ('economic miracle') has been the subject of comment and praise:

[O]ne should credit above all the energy and work habits of the defeated Germans. In 1945 their currency was worthless ... The years that followed were marked by hard winters, food and fuel shortages, endless cleanup of rubble,

16 Business leaders are sceptical of any increased regulation – see Institute of Directors press release, 'The IoD says the Queen's Speech is Mixed for Business', 17 November 1999.

17 Article 14(1) of the Federal Constitution of Germany.

18 Addison, JT, Siebert, WS, Wagner, J and Wei, X, 'Worker Participation and Firm Performance' (2000) 38 British Journal of Industrial Relations 7, found that mandatory Works Councils did not impair, and might even improve, the performance of larger German establishments.

19 Such a trend would expose German companies to international competitive pressures: see 'Business: Germany Unlocked', *The Economist*, 8 January 2000, 62 and Bushrod, L, 'Private Equity – Continental Buyouts Surge as Small UK Deals Face Squeeze', *European Venture Capital Journal*, 1 May 2000, 1.

and political repair, if not retribution. And then in 1948 the new Germany issued a new currency, exchanging one deutsche Mark for 10 Reichsmark. ... In twenty years, the deutsche Mark, along with the Swiss franc, became the strongest currency in Europe. New plants sprang up and German goods sold everywhere, enjoying a nonpareil reputation for solidity and design.[20]

In a new generation, it is competition from the Far East in manufacturing industry that has posed perhaps the greatest fresh challenge.

An expert in industrial relations and corporate governance from a German perspective, Professor Wolfgang Streeck, writes:

[T]oday's growing markets for diversified quality products can only imperfectly be served by an economy that is not also a society, that is, one which is not in a particular way regulated and supported by thick, non-economic social institutions ... among the possible institutional arrangements on the supply side that may sustain diversified quality production are some that are highly compatible with traditional social-democratic objectives like high wages, a low wage spread, workplace participation and full employment.[21]

In other words, investment in training and the pursuit of strategic alliances may best equip an economy to compete in a global market that demands flexible responses and high levels of skills.[22]

There is in corporate governance systems a trade-off to be made between flexibility (to cut costs and workforces promptly in an economic downturn) and stability (in the labour market and the wider economy). Competition on grounds of quality, rather than of price, is not an easy option. It is, however, the UK government's favoured prescription for sustaining a prosperous, high-wage economy.[23] The investment and scale of production required in high-technology industries may also mean that one organisation cannot succeed in isolation in a developing market. On the global scene, business partnerships are crucial and growing in salience. A system that seems to 'outsiders' to be complex and bureaucratic may deter potentially useful corporations from investing in a national economy.

A critic of stakeholder theory, Patrick Minford, comments: '[Under] the leadership of Erhard and Adenauer ... West Germany decided to pursue policies of radical liberalisation ... while conceding some social partnership to unions that were in practice highly docile and co-operative for some two decades.' He concedes that during this period, between 1938 and 1979, German productivity growth was on average 3.9% per annum, the UK's 1.8%

20 Landes, D, *The Wealth and Poverty of Nations*, 1998, p 471.

21 Streeck, W, *Social Institutions and Economic Performance*, 1992, p 10.

22 See proceedings of conference 'The Economics of the Knowledge Driven Economy', jointly organised by the DTI and the Centre for Economic Policy Research, 27 January 1999.

23 DTI White Paper, *Our Competitive Future: Building the Knowledge-Driven Economy*, 1998.

per annum.[24] After 1979, when growth trends in productivity reversed, trade unions in the UK were indeed forced into 'docility' by being stripped of the legal rights they had enjoyed. During this time, however, the UK's relative economic decline continued and average income fell further behind that of Germany.

Further criticisms of the *Aufsichtsrat* system have centred on the fact that even employee-elected members are alleged to 'go native' and focus principally on profitability and that supervisory directors may lack the information, or indeed the training, to act as a counterweight to the *Vorstand*.[25] It is certainly difficult for stakeholder board members to put aside their constituency interests and think in terms of the company's good when acting as board members. The German experience shows that it is possible. If anything, there has been more criticism from the labour side that board members elected by the workforce have not been vociferous enough in support of employees. This is, however, perhaps to misunderstand the point of stakeholder inclusion on supervisory boards. Communication with the stakeholder group via its representative and appraising the stakeholders (in the German case, the workers) of long-term business plans are seen as important in themselves.

Some capital-intensive industries such as telecommunications and pharmaceuticals requires international capital investment, which in turn demands both transparency from management and liquidity of investment. Traditionally, however, as Cioffi points out, the interests of management and labour and banks have reinforced each other in Germany:

> Management has remained substantially shielded from takeover threats and shareholder pressures by long-term relationships with banks, cross shareholdings with other firms, and the ability of labour to reduce the short-term rents that can be appropriated from post-takeover restructuring. The result is an informal 'governance coalition' that embraces the principal actors and interests in the German governance debate and straddles the political divide between the CDU-CSU and the SPD.[26]

There is some concern about the effects of this 'coalition'. Charkham and Simpson comment:

> In principle there [in Germany] the shareholders appoint the non-employee members of the *Aufsichtsrat*, [which] in turn appoints the members of the management board (*Vorstand*). In reality the *Vorstand* usually has a great say in the choice of members of the supervisory board and its own composition.[27]

---

24 Minford, P, *Markets Not Stakes*, 1998, p 70.

25 Centre for Law and Business, University of Manchester, *Company Law in Europe: Recent Developments*, 1999, p 30.

26 Cioffi, JW, 'Governing Globalization? The State, Law and Structural Change in Corporate Governance', 27 Journal of Law and Society, 2000, p 596.

27 Charkham, J and Simpson, A, *Fair Shares*, 1998, p 230.

Despite such practical reservations, German fears of reductions in their standards of social protection and worker participation have clashed at European Union level with UK opposition to employee involvement in management.[28] The original Draft Fifth Directive on public companies was based squarely on the German model, with a two-tier board and worker representation on the supervisory tier. This has now been much 'watered down' to permit very different systems to be chosen by different nations. Where the capital structure of large companies also varies between major economies, this is probably sustainable. However, with increased capital mobility in the European Union, there are opportunities for foreign as well as domestic takeovers in Germany. As the cohort of post-Second World War entrepreneurs retire[29] and the work ethic gives way to a culture increasingly reluctant to trade leisure time for more disposable income,[30] the possibilities for more 'efficient' management and cost-cutting are increased.

It has been persuasively argued that the main benefit of the German 'bank-dominated' system is not that this, in itself, has provided cheaper capital, but that the absence of the threat of takeovers enables management to pursue longer term goals.[31] This also facilitates the development of long-term relationships with stakeholders; as Pugh put it:

> In Germany, to move towards the UK's ease of transfer of corporate control would hinder commitment to relationships of trust and co-operation between business 'stakeholders'. This would tend to deracinate Germany's 'social market economy'.[32]

To the extent that stakeholder relationships are fruitful in a business sense, any legal change that might undermine them would also be economically damaging. Germany, it seems, does not wish to lose its competitive advantage in this respect.

Where investors are 'passive', there may be particular merit in the functional clarity offered by the separate two-tier board as an alternative means of keeping the executive in check. Within the Anglo-American system, it seems that investors have recently been 'flexing their financial muscles'[33] and have succeeded in securing management changes in a few major

---

28 Andenas, M, 'European Company Law Reform and the United Kingdom' (2000) 21 Co Law 36.

29 Randlesome, C, 'The Business Culture in West Germany' in *Business Cultures in Europe*, 1990, p 54.

30 *Ibid*, p 39.

31 Pugh, G, 'Financial Systems and Industrial Performance: Germany in Comparison with the UK' in Lange, T and Shackleton, J, *The Political Economy of German Unification*, 1998, Chapter 11.

32 *Ibid*, p 177.

33 For recent examples see Emmett, A, Levine, S and Slepicka, M, 'Shareholders Strike Back', *America's Network*, June 2000, Telecom Investor supplement, 14 and Feldman, A, 'Shareholders of the World, Unite!' (2000) 29 Money 1333.

corporations. From a stakeholding perspective, one could argue that this needs to be balanced by somewhat stronger labour rights than have been enjoyed in the US or the UK during the 1980s and 1990s. Competition law is similarly important to give customers a genuine choice as to the supplier they use. With all these checks in place, there is still a need for objective, long-termist input into board decision making. Whether it takes the form of a 'strong non-executive element' within a unitary board or as a separate tier is far less significant; indeed the unitary board may give its members more access to information and better communication with the executives.

It is possible for the two-tier board system to be used in a rather different way from that which German law provides. In Holland, for example, the supervisory boards are self-selected from recommendations made by the employees and the shareholders.[34] As in Germany, it is the supervisory board, rather than members in general meeting, which has the right to appoint and remove executive directors and in Holland directors are charged with considering the welfare of all stakeholders.[35] Indirectly, therefore, employees and shareholders of major Dutch public companies are both exercising powers over the composition of the management team. In Germany and Holland, the quality of supervision by employee representatives is enhanced by the provision of information to Works Councils and in fact the great majority of worker directors are also Works Council members. This is arguably a logical extension of recognising that, in a public company, shareholders are effectively passive investors rather than active members, while employees have a daily commitment to the company's activities.[36]

It has been said by du Plessis, an expert in continental European corporate governance, that: 'most German writers are reasonably satisfied with the two-tier system' and that: 'through such a system a broader spectrum of interests in the company are formally recognised and it ensures that exclusive shareholder control is not the norm anymore'.[37] If shareholders are not, in fact, reliable monitors in most public companies, the supervisory board certainly provides one answer to the problem of keeping the executive in check. However, the effectiveness of the monitors depends on the information they are given and their personal commitment and ability. They will inevitably be partisan to the extent that they are representing different constituencies. The German experience has shown that they can work

---

34 *Per* Dutch Civil Code Book 2, *de Structuurvennootschap* (large/widely-held company) – see Maitland-Walker, J, *Guide to European Company Laws*, 1993, pp 300–05.

35 Centre for Law and Business, n 25 above, p 50.

36 On defensive tactics in takeover bids, such as use of 'crown jewels' and 'poison pills', see Wymeersch, E, 'The Effects of the Regulation of Securities Markets on Company Law within the EEC' in Drury, RR and Xuereb, PG, *European Company Laws*, 1991, p 61.

37 Du Plessis, JJ, 'Corporate Governance: Some Reflections on the South African Law and the German Two-Tier Board System' in Macmillan Patfield, F, *Perspectives on Company Law 2*, 1997, Chapter 8.

together for the long-term goals of the company. To this needs to be added the recognition that, without proper attention to customer requirements, and in many cases good relationships with suppliers as well, the public company is highly unlikely to prosper.

7.3 THE FRENCH SYSTEM AND LEADERSHIP

The option provided by French law for large corporations to adopt a two-tier board structure, closely modelled on the German system, is not much used in practice, nor is trade union membership at significant levels. The social security system and employment law rights in France are, however, more generous and comprehensive than in Anglo-American or Asian states. Perhaps this helps to explain why business 'leadership' has been left in the hands of relatively few executives, while employees have shown little appetite for participation in management as such. The large number of privately owned and state-owned businesses of substance in France also helps to account for its management culture. Even after major privatisation of financial institutions and manufacturing organisations during the 1980s, close links between government and business still remain.

As a more rural society than either Britain or Germany, there is a sense that France still takes a longer term perspective and puts more emphasis on 'quality of life' issues than the longer urbanised societies. Some ways of life, for example in agriculture, are regarded as being worth preserving for the future, even if they are not the most profitable now. The individual's expectations of reasonably secure employment and good social security provision if it is needed are seemingly held in higher regard than competitiveness for its own sake.[38] This challenges the free market orthodoxy which seems to have 'won' politically in the Anglo-American world (despite the election of centre left leaders in the UK and the US in the 1990s), for example, there are still fierce debates around reform of the European Union's agricultural policy. It also means that France has the highest indirect (non-wage) employment costs of any major economy.

As Professor David Landes (of Harvard University) comments:

> One sticking point, source of weakness as well as strength: the French are proud. They have their way of doing things and, unlike the British, do not take easily to loss of power. This makes them poor learners of foreign ways. They have their own way ... Such countries as the United States persuaded of the value of free markets and committed to survival of the fittest, shower the French with advice. The French reply: Get lost, we don't need any lessons from you.[39]

---

38 Gordon, C, 'The Business Culture in France' in Randlesome, n 29 above, p 63.
39 Landes, n 20 above, p 470.

As if to prove the point, the French, maintaining their social security net and excellent health care and transport, enjoyed one of the highest standards of living in Europe, and indeed the world.

The French response to international moves towards minimum standards for monitoring public company executives has been somewhat unenthusiastic. In 1995, the Vienot Report on corporate governance, commissioned by the Conseil National du Patronat Francais and the Association Francaise des Entreprises Privees, accepted similar overall principles to those set out in US and UK reviews (the ALI Principles of Corporate Governance in 1994 and the Report in 1995, respectively). Similar committees were proposed to deal with nominations and remuneration and audit to those recommended as 'best practice' across the Channel and the Atlantic. There was, however, no real challenge to the hegemony of the PGD in major French companies and no statement that there should be an independent Chairman, while the notion of a separate monitoring board was rejected. No new information rights for non-PGD board members, in line with the US position, were introduced.[40]

Business leaders in France, it was reported in 1998, had woken up to the importance of corporate governance 'chiefly as a means to placate (mainly foreign) institutional investors' and were voluntarily adapting to international standards. The law was said to be progressing 'towards more transparency and a more balanced equilibrium between the powers of the board and those of the PDG' in line with international trends.[41] French shareholders are becoming more active. For managers, there is an increasing threat from foreign 'predators' to consider.[42]

On the international scene, French companies have been taking advantage of the opportunities offered by the privatisation of UK utilities.[43] In the financial sector, France's own 'privatised' banks have been staking out a strong position in the new European market created by the single currency. Like the UK, however, France has found that 'national champions' are often too small to compete effectively in the global marketplace.[44] Its business leaders, therefore, need to learn to co-operate effectively with their European counterparts from other nations. Its corporate leaders are becoming more dependent on the capital market and less reliant on French public sector contracts.

---

40 Tunc, A, 'Corporate Governance a la Francaise: the Vienot Report' in Macmillan Patfield, n 37 above, Chapter 7.
41 Letreguilly, H, 'France' (1998) International Financial Law Review, Corporate Governance supplement 18, 22.
42 Rossant, J, 'En garde, French shareholders', Business Week, 8 May 2000, 18.
43 O'Connor, M, 'Global Capitalism and the Evolution of American Corporate Governance Institutions' in Macmillan Patfield, n 37 above, Chapter 5 refers to the possibility of a 'neutral referee' to arbitrate between shareholders and employees.
44 Gordon, n 38 above, p 103.

The French as consumers have traditionally been patriotic (and protectionist) and more concerned about high quality in 'commodities' such as food and drink than their Anglo-Saxon neighbours. At the same time, the perception has been that quality of life is valued more highly than 24-hour, no-wait-service culture.[45] In the high technology industries, mergers for reasons of scale will bring some rationalisations. Where the service sectors are concerned, American and to some extent Anglo-Saxon cultural influences will have their impact, particularly on the younger generation. Nevertheless the French have pride in their own way of carrying on business, as in their national culture generally, which is unlikely to be dented even by further integration in the European Union.[46]

Paris has never enjoyed the same status as an international financial centre as London, nor has the stock market in France exerted such an influence over industrial decisions as in the UK. This has arguably allowed more individuality at the expense of some 'efficiency':

> Another criticism, the lack of entrepreneurial leadership, in particular in the question of the rationalization of industry, has been stronger in Britain, reflecting in a way the difference between the merchant banks and the *banques d'affaires*. While the former have their origins in the financing of world trade, the latter are heirs to the Credit mobilier, and direct control of industrial companies has from the start been an essential part of their strategy.[47]

France has also tended to favour national solutions to its manufacturing problems, often with state support. Wholly or partly in the private sector, French corporations are holding their own in a number of key sectors – the car industry and telecommunications being particularly instructive from a British perspective.

Successive French governments have acted as a watchdog for some major industries with the intention of furthering consumer interest, with somewhat limited success. Efforts to co-ordinate industrial planning and organise supply chains have also proved difficult, perhaps because they have not sat easily with prevailing French culture. In common with Germany, there is usually less pressure for flotation at an early stage than in the UK. The takeover market has, however, grown substantially as investors have learned their power. Many large French companies have themselves engaged in acquisitions at home and elsewhere in Europe in order to reach a size required to compete in global markets. This has contributed to pressure for greater

---

45 Minford, n 24 above, p 182.
46 See Guehenno, J-M, 'The French Resistance' (June 1998) Prospect 31 and Henley, J, 'Vive La Belle France', *The Observer*, 25 June 2000, p 19.
47 Cassis, Y, 'Divergence and Convergence in British and French Business in the Nineteenth and Twentieth Centuries' in Cassis, Y, Crouzet, F and Gourvish, T, *Management and Business in Britain and France*, 1995, p 27.

flexibility in French company law to make it more attractive for international business.[48]

The market for corporate control has certainly become more active. This does not mean that the state has relinquished any responsibility for managing events and maintaining national distinctiveness, as Cioffi points out:

> Foreign institutional investors hold 35–40% of the French equity market, but the French government retains extensive powers to block control transactions and intervenes selectively in merger and acquisition activity. Hence the state has combined liberalizing and interventionist policies in overseeing the process of sectoral consolidation to ensure that French industry remains largely in the hands of French managers as a deliberate policy choice.[49]

The two-tier board model has been adopted by some privatised French corporations as a means of giving 'voice' to stakeholders after direct state ownership. Even though they expect it to be little used in Britain, Charkham and Simpson write:

> We see no reason to object to UK shareholders having the option, as they do in France, of voting in favour of the company having a two-tier board rather than a unitary one. To introduce such an option would require a definition in law of the functions of the management board and of the supervisory board.[50]

The traditional SA (*société anonyme*) structure for companies is also seen in Southern European countries such as Spain. The power of shareholders to appoint and oversee the 'administrators' is undiminished by many obligations to consider the other constituencies. Indeed in the Spanish *sociedad anonima*, there is a proportional representation system whereby substantial shareholders can appoint individual directors.[51] In general the line between private or closed companies and open public companies is much more blurred than in Germany or Holland, or indeed the United Kingdom, with the SA form of incorporation straddling large, medium and even small business.[52] A unitary board structure is used for Spanish SAs, very few of which are listed.[53] France is the home base of significantly more multinational companies than its Southern European neighbours but shares the same (civil law) legal tradition.

The whole leadership of French society, in the public and private sectors, is still very much in the hands of products of the *Grandes Ecoles* system. This means that there is a real 'public service' ethos among those running the largest businesses, and that they have close contacts with those who pursue

---

48 Centre for Law and Business, n 25 above, p 26.
49 Cioffi, n 26 above, p 591.
50 Charkham and Simpson, n 27 above, p 230.
51 Maitland-Walker, n 34 above, pp 386–88.
52 Rojo, A, 'The Typology of Companies' in Drury and Xuereb, n 36 above, pp 41, 45.
53 Centre for Law and Business, n 25 above, p 57.

prestigious careers in the civil service. It also means that there is a certain deference to the education and attainments of those in high-ranking positions. There may be little internal debate or challenge until suddenly, a strike is upon the company, for example. This elitism also fosters a sense of distrust between workers and executives. This in turn makes European Union company law integration difficult, as Franzmeyer has observed:

> While German trade unions see an element of industrial democracy in 'co-management', which should in addition be underpinned by profit-sharing with employees, this kind of strategy is regarded in other countries, especially by the big Italian and French unions, as a capitalist 'confidence trick' which runs counter to the fundamental interests of workers. In this instance integration cannot be pushed through according to plan – for example, in connection with the completion of the internal market.[54]

7.4 EUROPEAN UNION LEGISLATION AND PUBLIC COMPANIES

Germany, with France and other continental jurisdictions, appears unwilling to accede to any lessening of the protection enjoyed by employees in a systems it feel has generally served its citizens well. The United Kingdom government has been, and remains, equally opposed to any suggestion that employees should have seats on the board of public companies, either with the executive or on any second tier monitoring body. Proposals for the Draft Fifth Company Law Directive on the form of public companies were stalled as a result of disputes concerning worker representation.[55] In its latest draft, the Fifth Directive allows for so many options as to permit the continuance, *de facto*, of national jurisdictions with only minor changes of substance.

Corporate governance has, however, been influenced by EC Directives, which have required significant changes to UK companies legislation. The First Company Law Directive,[56] for example, provided that third parties dealing with companies should not be affected by any internal limitations on the objects of the company or the powers of the board. The Second Directive[57] introduced the principle of a minimum capital requirement for UK public companies, though this has been set at a relatively modest £50,000 (of which £12,500 must be paid up at the outset). Other company law directives that have dealt with information issues are the Fourth Directive on the contents of

---

54 Franzmeyer, F, 'Economic, Social and Political Costs of Completing the Internal Market' in Bieber, R, Dehousse, J, Pinder, J and Weiler, JHH, *One European Market*, 1992, p 55, at p 67.

55 Latest amendments: 34 OJ C321, 12 December 1991.

56 68/151/EEC OJ Special Edition 1968 (1), 41–45.

57 77/91/EEC 20 OJ L26, 31 January 1977, 1–13.

annual accounts[58] and the Eighth Directive[59] on the qualifications and independence of company auditors. All of these issues, insofar as there is a common theme, seem to be designed to increase the free movement of capital by promoting investor confidence in European company projects outside the prospective shareholder's own nation. Whether this has made much difference in practice to mobility of companies or capital around the European Union is questionable.

The Draft Fifth Directive on the structure of public companies is by far the most ambitious of the EC projects and has failed to make any progress for many years, mainly because of controversy surrounding the issues of worker participation and board structure. As provided in the latest version, which remains the subject of negotiation, there must be supervision of executives within the board structure, but this could be provided by either the second tier or by non-executives inside a unitary group. There must also be employee participation in public company decisions where there are 1,000 employees or more, but this could be provided by Works Councils or other 'collectively agreed' structures, rather than by direct board membership. Nothing in the Draft Fifth Directive as it currently stands would, therefore, require the UK government to do very much more than ensure that the recommendations of Hampel were complied with as regards participation by non-executives and to apply the concept of Works Councils, discussed below, to United Kingdom public companies. The degree of discretion left to nation states means that the ultimate product will achieve relatively little 'harmonisation', let alone 'approximation', of legal requirements across the European Union. In a modest way, by furthering the principles of independent supervision of central management and participation by employees, it may be said to be spreading 'best practice'.

The European Union's website in its information on company law gives an interesting insight into current philosophy. It says:

> This setback [regarding the Fifth Directive], together with the difficulties of incorporating into national law legislation which, while attempting to remove disparities between Member States' laws, leads to the adoption of extremely detailed and stringent rules and regulations has led the Community legislature to leave national legislatures more room for manoeuvre and to allow economic operators more scope for exercising freedom of contract. Growing competition on world markets is furthermore prompting it to impose the minimum constraints necessary on European firms, while providing them with the legal instruments they are lacking.[60]

Aside from the controversial worker participation issue, the Fifth Directive would introduce other changes of substance to UK company law. For

---

58   78/660/EEC 21 OJ L222, 14 August 1978, 11–31.

59   84/253/EEC 27 OJ L126, 12 May 1984, 20–26.

60   SCADplus (European Union database).

example, contrary to the rule in *Foss v Harbottle*,[61] 10% of shareholder votes would carry an automatic right to take legal action on behalf of the company.[62] This is broadly in line with the recommendations of the UK Law Commission as regards shareholder remedies.[63] There would also be a tightening up of directors' duties to end the system whereby directors can ratify their own wrongdoing using their own votes in general meeting.[64] For smaller companies, this may be thought to be somewhat rigid as a general approach. Where listed companies are seeking public capital, a more stringent approach may be regarded as entirely appropriate.

In the field of corporate takeovers and mergers, there has been an element of 'protectionism' on the part of the UK in refusing to compromise on the voluntary status of the Stock Exchange and the Takeover Code. As the largest marketplace for shares and the most active takeover arena in Europe, London has a vested interest in not losing the advantages of speed and flexibility that are said to flow from allowing self-regulation. At the same time, the benefits of ensuring a 'level playing field' grow as European Union businesses consolidate. Political agreement between ministers on a Draft Thirteenth Directive on Takeovers and Mergers[65] was reached in June 2000 and focused on protection of and full information for shareholders, in line with existing practice in London. It would introduce compulsory bidding for all shares once an offeror has gained voting control of a company.

The proposed Tenth Directive, dealing with cross-border mergers,[66] has so far foundered on the issue of ensuring that current levels of worker participation are maintained and 'social dumping' (that is, the relocation of business to states where social costs are low) is avoided. It is nevertheless important that investor confidence be maintained. This failure does not seem to have acted as a significant brake on European-wide mergers in the most capital-intensive industries, such as the oil and aerospace businesses. Even so, the less 'high-tech' manufacturers and retailers might be assisted in efforts to pursue consolidations that seemed commercially justifiable if there were a single European Union system for regulation of takeovers.

Consumer regulation at European Union level is justified by the fact that trust facilitates a single and genuinely free market in goods and services. The impact of new technology is also significant:

> The Internet offers the opportunity to re-establish the communication loop between manufacturers and customers. It has the potential to put these parties

---

61 (1843) 2 Hare 461.
62 Amended version, n 55 above, Art 16.
63 Law Commission, *Shareholder Remedies*, Report No 246, October 1997.
64 *Ibid*, Art 18.
65 32 OJ C64, 14 March 1989.
66 28 OJ C23, 25 January 1985.

back in the position they were in before the Industrial Revolution, but, in this case, they are not bound by the confines of a village.[67]

There are, of course, economic losers as well as winners from the completion of the single European market. Many companies suffer losses of income and even complete closure; many workers suffer increased job insecurity and possibly loss of income as a result of increased competition.[68] Given the current size of the European Union's total budget,[69] these are largely matters that national governments will have to deal with, by paying unemployment benefit temporarily if nothing else. The medium to long-term benefits of European competitiveness with American and Japanese companies may be bought at a high price for the nation states.

The areas in which the European Union has legislated to date have been largely in the realms of administrative detail, rather than managerial priorities. As regards information provision, for example, minimum standards have been assured in principle across the Member States. This gradualism is almost inevitable given the divergence of attitudes towards business leadership and entrepreneurship generally and the role of the private sector in different nations. Nevertheless, multinational companies are increasingly treating the European Union as a unit. An individual state whose legal framework for businesses diverges too far from what is familiar or acceptable to Europeans and investors in Europe generally risks losing major investment to more congenial surroundings. The Union also has a role in setting a floor on regulation, to avoid a competitive 'race to the bottom' between states.

Many UK company directors may not be aware of the fact that much of the regulation that affects their operations every day (such as employment and environmental legislation) is derived from European Union directives. Many of them are quite enthusiastic about the principle of being able to set up a single legal entity which could do business in any part of the European Union, just as they tend to like the idea of the convenience and transparency of a European currency. At the same time, many are still reluctant to adapt to different ways of doing business. Mutual recognition of Member State rules provides one way to unblock the legislative impasse but can only fulfil a limited function in keeping up regulatory standards across the European Union.

The European Union has also had a major impact in the area of worker participation and trade union involvement and recognition in particular. The UK government, in its UK Presidency of the Union conference 'Working for the Future – New Ways of Organising Work'[70] (Glasgow, 28–30 April 1998)

---

67 Wiegran, G and Koth, H, *Custom Enterprise.com*, 2000.
68 Franzmeyer, n 54 above, p 56.
69 Currently capped at 1.27% of GDP.
70 As reported in a follow-up brochure, *Working for the Future*, 1999.

emphasised work partnership structures and training. These were tied in to customer satisfaction and negotiation with unions over flexible work practices.[71] The managerial prerogative of directors was not challenged and there is no mention in the conference document of employee participation on the board. It is the European Works Council Directive which currently provides for information of and consultation with employees in transnational companies.[72] There is also in negotiation a draft Domestic Works Council Directive which would provide minimum standards for information and consultation in purely national companies that have at least 50 employees.[73]

The European Company Statute, after a lengthy period of contention, stalled on the basis that 'mutual recognition' of companies across the European Union would be sufficient. Instead of being incorporated centrally, without attachment to any particular state, the *Societas Europea* (SE) on the latest plans would be subject to differing rules depending on its location. The disadvantage of this is that a great deal of reference would still have to be made to the national law of a state in which a *Societas Europea* is registered to ascertain the detail of the relevant regulation. Political agreement has finally been reached on the outline of the SE legal structure (the European Parliament's views are awaited at the time of writing). Given the existing European Union law on free movement of goods and services,[74] the use of the SE form arguably adds little to the existing advantages of major European businesses. Companies registered in Member States as legal 'persons' also have rights of freedom of establishment within, and can freely transfer their capital around, the European Union.[75]

SCADplus, the European Commission's internet information commentary on Company Law, states that:

> Everything holds out hope that the idea of the European company, which was first mooted nearly thirty years ago, is shortly to become reality. It appears that a decisive step forward has been made, with discussions focusing less and less on comparisons between a 'European' model and the different national models and more and more on the search for a flexible formula that would leave the essential features of the different national systems intact.[76]

This view may prove to be excessively optimistic.

---

71 *Ibid*, 5 and *passim*.

72 94/45/EC OJ L245/64, 22 September 1994.

73 European Commission, 'Proposal for a Council Directive Establishing a General Framework for Informing and Consulting Employees in the European Community' COMM/0612/EC (1998).

74 EC Treaty Arts 28–31 (formerly 31–37) and Arts 49–55 (formerly 59–66).

75 EC Treaty Arts 42(2) and 48 (formerly 52(2) and 58); *R v Daily Mail and General Trust plc* C-81/87 [1988] ECR 5483 (ECJ).

76 SCADplus, Company Law – current position and outlook, updated May 2000.

The US has, of course, succeeded economically in the 1990s without a single system of company law (or indeed a uniform tax structure) while having a single market and a single currency. It is not likely that in the near future or the medium term the states of the European Union will cease to have very diverse systems of company law. The challenge is to ensure that minimum standards of regulation are maintained and that the nations learn from one another. It has also been pointed out that enlargement of plant sizes in order to pursue economies of scale may not, in fact, lead to more vigorous competition and hence to increased productivity. There is a danger that markets will become more oligopolistic, leading to reduced consumer choice and competitive pressure.[77] Pursuit of increased size for its own sake was somewhat unfashionable as a business credo by the end of the 1990s.

Labour markets appear to be rather more diverse than financial regulatory systems. One should not forget that 'confounding the theory that globalization is driving convergent liberalization [of corporate governance systems] is the EU's adoption of the [European] Works Council Directive...' The introduction of works councils to major European corporations 'devolves power and legal authority within the corporation downward to the employees and their representatives'.[78] This indeed runs counter to arguments that globalisation is forcing all countries are adopting the 'Anglo-American' shareholder model.

On a strict interpretation of the principle of subsidiarity (as incorporated in the EC Treaty[79] and amplified by the 1992 Edinburgh Council declaration[80]) it is arguable that further harmonisation of company systems is not necessary to complete the Single European Market nor further the goals of the European Union. What does require co-ordination, and has received it, is control of takeovers, with the objective of ensuring that capital flows and Union-wide competition become a reality. As Drury puts it:

> The programme for the harmonisation of company and capital market laws seems to have based ... on two premises. The first is that companies are the most important economic actors within the Member States, and that they are becoming increasingly active on a wider transnational stage. The second premise assumes the existence of a substantial connection between the harmonisation of company and capital market laws on the one hand, and the advancement of economic integration on the other. One can readily subscribe to the first premise without much convincing, however the second does become something of an article of faith.[81]

---

77 Phelps, n 9 above, p 50.
78 Cioffi, n 26 above, p 597.
79 EC Treaty Art 5 (formerly 3b, as amended in 1992).
80 Edinburgh Heads of State or of Government Conference, December 1992.
81 Drury, R, 'A Review of the European Community's Company Law Harmonisation Programme' (1992) 24 Bracton Law Journal 45.

According to the legislators, European Union legislative and regulatory harmonisation is not an end in itself; it is a means to economic goals.[82]

7.5 EUROPE IN THE WORLD

The European Union is large enough to exercise global economic and commercial influence with the United States and Japan. In international fora such as the World Trade Organisation, it can speak with a powerful voice to argue for its standards – which of course include free trade – to be promulgated more widely.[83] The introduction of the European Single Currency has the potential to consolidate the market strength of the main European economies (though the UK remains outside it). However, a leadership role in setting rules of business conduct has so far eluded the European Union, in large part because of disagreements over retention of national models of regulation and governance. US multinationals have taken the lead in treating the European Union as a single trading area and Japanese management techniques have proved to be popular among European business leaders. A single European market has arguably not benefited Europeans themselves as much as it might otherwise have done because of cultural barriers to transnational co-operation and labour mobility.[84]

As a general rule, it is true that social and labour costs are higher in the European Union than in the Americas or Asia. Investors who want good returns regardless of where production is actually located will need to be convinced that these higher costs are justified by improved workforce skills, better technology and infrastructure, proximity to markets and other countervailing advantages.[85] Common standards on information for investors are an important source of reassurance, hence the relevance of the apparently extremely technical European Union directives on Listing Particulars and Company Accounts. General economic stability and a reputation for integrity among public sector officials are also major advantages for Western European states.[86]

---

82 The SLIM initiative – Simpler Legislation for the Internal Market – as far as Company Law is concerned emphasises this (Report from the Commission – *Results of the Fourth Phase of SLIM* dated 4 April 2000).

83 The European Commission under instructions from Member States negotiates with their global trading partners on their behalf in trade discussions.

84 Graham B and Hart, M, 'Cohesion and Diversity in the European Union: Irreconcilable Forces?' (1999) 33 Regional Studies 259.

85 Wallace, W and Zielonka, J, 'Misunderstanding Europe' (1998) 77 Foreign Affairs 65.

86 Kaltenheuser, S, 'The Best Place to do Business' (2000) 13 World Trade 28.

US state 'constituency statutes' governing duties of directors[87] and Japanese corporate networks or *keiretsu*[88] will demand a response from Europe if their benefits are not to handicap Europeans by comparison. Executives of multinational corporations have great power to move capital to where they believe it will be most productive. Corporate governance regimes that march out of step with such management teaching may positively discourage investment. The trend is certainly for multinational companies to devolve more administrative detail to the level of local management while simultaneously exercising control from the centre as far as issues of corporate principle are concerned.[89] So long as the national legislation is clear and is perceived to reflect the social consensus, there is no need for countries to assume that the executives of multinational companies will object to restrictions imposed by national laws. In the end, however, the aim must be to produce a clear guiding vision for leaders of businesses.

Styles of legislative drafting vary between common law and civil law jurisdictions, further complicating efforts at supranational lawmaking.[90] UK judges, through their fast-growing experience of European Union law, are becoming more comfortable with interpreting broad statements of principle that lack the detail of typical British legislation. If business people in the Anglo-American world are inclined to think in terms of 'profit maximisation within the law' while continental European executives perceive themselves more as guardians of a social institution, this may in some part be attributable to their attitudes to regulation. In Britain the general principle of 'whatever is not expressly prohibited will be permitted' holds firm, while in other European Union states the experience of state regulation has been much more pervasive. Clearly the standardisation of an area as complex and detailed as 'core' company law is only practicable in the context of a shared legal culture. It is doubtful whether this exists across the European Union as yet, though it may be in development.

The administrative efficiency of public bodies (such as companies registries) in a given jurisdiction and the quality of contractual and commercial law are factors which play a part in the location decisions of

---

87 Eg IND CODE ANN 23 23-1-35-1(f) (1995) (Indiana statute which allows for a broad interpretation of stockholder interests); CONN GEN STAT ANN 33-756(d)(3) (1997) (Connecticut statute which requires that employee interests be taken into account in a takeover situation) in addition to well-known Pennsylvania and Ohio statutes.

88 See Ming-Hong Lai, G, 'Knowing Who You are Doing Business with in Japan: A Managerial View of Keiretsu and Keiretsu Business Groups' (1999) 34 Journal of World Business 423; Oliver, RW, 'Killer Keiretsu' (1999) 88 Management Review 10.

89 Handy, C, 'Subsidiarity is the Word for It' (1999) 36 Across the Board 7; Schwab, C, 'What's Best for your Customers?' (2000) 17 Executive Excellence 20.

90 Lewis, X, 'A Common Law Fortress under Attack: is English Law being Europeanized?' (1995) 2 Columbia Journal of European Law 1; Legrand, P, 'Structuring EC Law: Tacit Knowledge Matters' (1998) 21 Hastings International and Comparative Law Review 871.

multinationals. 'User-friendliness' of local laws and the availability of high-quality legal (and financial) advice are attractions.[91] The extent to which regulatory requirements and legal duties placed on directors are effectively 'policed' may also be a positive factor for potential investors (though a negative one in the eyes of some executives, one suspects). In all of these considerations, the UK 'scores' relatively highly, though the adoption of greater codification and more 'plain English' (as in Canada and New Zealand) would help to give a modern feel to UK company law. There are signs of an emerging consensus among major industrial nations as to the requirements that should be imposed upon publicly held corporations. Europe has played a part in this, as Grier recognises:

> Reputable companies should not be ashamed to publish their accounts, and companies that try to avoid doing so may have something to hide ... Suggestions that within the trading block of the EU there might be a race to the bottom are therefore unrealistic and if anything, the EU directives are encouraging ever higher standards of accountability and disclosure, at least as far as public companies are concerned, in order to encourage quality business and fair competition.[92]

Directors of transitional companies, no matter where they are based, do face many of the same functional tasks. Dallas indicates that the board is charged with two main responsibilities – conflicts monitoring (for which independent directors are essential) and business review (for which useful connections are certainly a key attribute for a director) which should be carried out by distinct groups.[93] This definition rather underplays the task, brought back to prominence in the UK by the Hampel Report, of driving the business forward and the place of technical expertise. It does, however, highlight the point that the board of a global corporation will have to be of suitable calibre to maintain a hands-on approach while devolving administrative work to the lower ranks of management.

When they are competing on an international level, the main rivals of European Union public companies are clearly US corporations (which have a greater degree of independent director input and information output) and Japanese corporations (which have large and relatively inactive boards but include employee input and are often in close relationships with others in the supply chain). When they invest in European Union states, while adapting to local requirements, the executives of such global companies will, so far as they are able, continue to exercise their preferred style of management. If either

---

91 Charny, D, 'Competition among Jurisdictions in formulating Corporate Law Rules' (1991) 32 Harvard International Law Journal 423; Levine, R and Ahmed, S, 'The Legal Environment, Banks and Economic Growth' (1998) 30 Journal of Money, Credit and Banking 596.

92 Grier, N, *UK Company Law*, 1998, p 648.

93 Dallas, L, 'The Global Corporate Board of Directors: a Proposal for Reform' in Macmillan Patfield, n 37 above, Chapter 6.

executive jurisdiction or employee contributions 'add value' to a business plan, they will be adopted whether the law requires them or not. If other national companies are not matching those standards, they will lose out in competitive markets. There is some argument, then, for saying that it is the role of a national government to promote best practice within its own jurisdiction.

There is no real consensus at European Union level either on the purpose and nature of companies themselves or on the proper aims for those who control them. It is hardly surprising, therefore, that efforts to take into account the various views have been described as 'accommodation rather than harmonisation' and this 'a polite way of describing a fruitless dissipation of energy.'[94] It is suggested that the stakeholder model in fact provides a more realistic and useful model of the public company than either the shareholder ownership paradigm or the neo-corporatist standpoint. Unless all the major European governments can agree on a single impetus for company leadership, however, further efforts in the direction of unified provisions are likely to prove ineffectual.

As has been noted (7.2 and 7.3 above), if a two-tier board system is to be adopted, several important questions remain. Chief among them are: who should appoint the supervising directors and what powers should those directors have over the management? Clearly if constituencies other than the shareholders win the power to appoint supervisory board members, who can, in turn, dismiss executives, a shift in stakeholder rights will take place. Since the Anglo-American system is so heavily dependent on stock markets for its capital, it is unlikely that plans to alter their powers to dismiss executive directors would be politically acceptable in the foreseeable future. Allowing other constituencies to nominate some non-executive board members would be a possible compromise. The requirement that executives give an account of themselves if they did not accept the recommendations of non-executives could also be upheld, if shareholders had the will to do so, under the current corporate governance regime

The Anglo-American system is heavily reliant on takeovers and the ultimate threat of removal of executives on change of ownership as a spur to good management ('good' in this context inevitably meaning successful from the point of view of shareholders, whose votes determine the outcome of takeover contests). Merger and acquisition activity is still spreading internationally, leading to investor pressure for more transparent accounting standards and greater liquidity of shareholdings.[95] As continental European

---

94 Du Plessis, JJ and Dine, J, 'The Fate of the Draft Fifth Directive on Company Law' [1997] JBL 23, 45.

95 Reed, S and Matlack, C, 'The Big Grab', *Business Week*, 24 January 2000, 130; Rothnie, D, 'M&A Commentary: From One High to Another', *European Venture Capital Journal*, 1 February 2000, 1.

models have demonstrated, however, there are well-tried alternatives to this is somewhat drastic and expensive method of 'policing' management. These include, as set out above, 'second tier' supervisory boards and monitoring by committed, influential investors such as banks. The current UK law does not, of course, actively prohibit steps in such directions but more could be done by way of formalising the role of non-executive directors and facilitating substantial long-term investment (for example, by amending the mandatory bid requirement, which occasioned some of the political objections to the Draft 13th Directive on Takeovers). This could empower executives to drive projects forward while ensuring that they had to give a regular and precise account of themselves.

As far as the UK itself is concerned, it is something of an exaggeration to say at the present time, with the authors of *Farrar's Company Law*:

> The membership of the EU means that there has been a complete parting of the ways with the USA and a growing detachment from Commonwealth company law reforms. Even if it wished to follow those reforms, the UK has lost the right to do so.[96]

The DTI's Green Paper, 'Modern Company Law for a Competitive Economy', made it clear that the UK 'modernisation' process may borrow ideas, particularly for simplifying procedure and language, from Commonwealth systems – and as noted above, there is little sign of national regulatory systems being superseded by a common European system of company law.

7.6 CONCLUSION: CONVERGING CAPITALISMS?

The latest round of transnational mergers emphasises that, as markets become global, complementary skills and products can exist across boundaries in Europe and beyond.[97] The largest corporations will be exporting their management styles and bringing the same values to work in many different states. The law needs to respond to this trend by reflecting the core management values that are shared across the world. For corporations that have enjoyed widespread, lasting success, these appear to include focus on the customer and development of employees. In a global economy, flexibility of the labour force is important and so is co-operation on supplies. Executives on the board need to see themselves as co-ordinators of the work of skilled labour and managers of relationships with others, rather than as 'experts' in all relevant areas.

---

96   Farrar, J and Hannigan, B, *Farrar's Company Law*, 1998, p 749.

97   For examples in the motor industry, see *The Economist*, 24 June 2000 'The Global Gambles of General Motors' and 'Car Making in Asia – Politics of Scale'.

The extent of active investor involvement in the major companies varies a great deal between the different legal systems. In those states where the ownership of large enterprises is still largely in the hands of private owners or of the state, control of and access to business information may matter less than in the UK. Where the public market for capital is more significant, as in this country, it is all the more important to ensure transparency. As consumers come to have a greater choice of goods and services with free cross-border trade, their wishes will need to be taken into consideration. Small and medium enterprises, which include many of the suppliers of European public companies, have also been recognised as having an important role to play in social policy and provision of employment and wealth. The thrust of European Union policy is towards encouraging greater recognition of all these factors, as well as facilitating managerial movement and flexibility.

European countries such as France, Germany, Spain and Holland have had to deal with similar corporate governance issues to those which have been the subject of debate in the UK and the US. Freedom of capital movement was one of the 'four freedoms' included in the original EEC Treaty. As capital has become more mobile, the expectations of investors are being transferred with it from one jurisdiction to another. At the same time, the European Union is still expanding its activities in the social field, including setting some common employment standards. It is natural that there should be demands at a European level for comparable participation (or at least consideration) in the decision making of the company. As enterprises grow larger when transnational consolidation takes effect, there is a common problem of control of executives at the centre.

Without a strong social fabric and the intangible but essential bonds of trust between employers and employees and between business associates, businesses will lack the necessary flexibility to succeed in the modern post-Fordist world. Co-determination by investors and workers is clearly an attempt to maintain that fabric. So, in a different way, is community involvement by large corporations in the US. The UK has hitherto tended to rely on exhortation of 'big business' to act responsibly. In future, this may not be enough to sustain competitive advantage and meet political demands in Britain. Greater employee share ownership and increased vertical integration may reduce the clash between different stakeholder interests but ultimately each political entity (still the nation state in Europe) has to determine, through its political processes, the extent to which it wishes to maintain or develop a social market economy.

Where European integration is leading to strategic alliances, these will be unlikely to achieve their potential unless the management teams and the employees from both or all organisations concerned are convinced of the desirability of the scheme. Other stakeholders also need to back the co-operation, as Lorange and Roos indicate:

Are relevant ownership groups convinced that the venture will be desirable from their stockholder viewpoint? What will be the effect on their reputation and the response of the stock market? How will customers, suppliers, existing alliance partners, financiers and and competitors react? it is important to carry out initial preparatory efforts to increase the likelihood that major stakeholders will accept and promote the idea of a particular co-operative strategy.[98]

Financial institutions are far more likely than ever before to operate across national borders. With them travels their habit of intervention in the case of American institutions, their patience with good industrial ideas if they are German, their public service ethos if they are French. They will not expect to be sidelined in UK businesses. Nor can high-technology, capital-intensive investment really succeed without them today. Shareholder rights and remedies are, therefore, inevitably set to converge between states. The opportunity afforded by the single European currency for financial products to be marketed outside their state of origin gives the potential for the most successful institutions to pool small investors' fund from across large parts of the Union. The businesses in which the managers of those funds choose to invest will be the companies that appear to be the best-managed and most competitive organisations. Moreover it has been said that:

> It is the UK, with its financial services industry, that should have the most to gain from company law harmonisation. The models of English company law are generally accepted as the better [sic] suited for the development of modern financial markets.[99]

Both geographically and culturally, the UK sits between Europe and the US. There has at times been a regulatory dilemma, arising from the fact that Britain had economic affinities with the US but was bound by legal ties to EEC, then European Union, partners. If the UK is to influence best practice and avoid being left behind in its system of corporate regulation, it needs to take its European neighbours seriously. It can also find much to learn from their traditions. The suggestion has been that in recent generations the UK has suffered the 'worst of both worlds' by trying to pursue Europeanism and Atlanticism at the same time, benefiting neither from the low taxes and labour mobility of the US markets nor by the social partnership and internal monitoring seen on the European continent. Instead it could act as a bridge to help each side learn from the other's best practice.[100]

Uniformity for its own sake is not the object of European Union reforms today. One must look to see the advantages of each system and the best way of realising these within each political and legal culture. Streeck has argued that:

---

98 Lorange, P and Roos, J, *Strategic Alliances*, 1992, p 33.

99 'Only mad cows and Englishmen' (1997) 18 Co Law 65.

100 David, P, 'Britain: A Power in the World', *The Economist*, 6 November 1999, S15; Nicolle, L, 'UK.com Leads Europe' (2000) 125 Accountancy 70.

Management in co-determined enterprises is exposed to constant pressures to provide information and to give reasons for its decisions. This has forced it to consider decisions more thoroughly, to take more factors into account, to communicate more freely within the organisation in general and with the workforce in particular.[101]

This seems to have served German industry well up to the 1990s and it has been as much to do with works council consultation as with employee board participation. In the new global economy, however, responsiveness to customers and external communications are surely as important as internal communication. Transnational business arrangements are politically desirable to those who wish to advance the cause of European federal structures. In reality, they should be seen by business people as possible means to serve their specific commercial ends.[102]

Little would be gained by imposing on business leaders a detailed structure with which most of them disagreed. The provisions which have succeeded on the continent of Europe have done so because the employees have been involved in delivering, and have been personally committed to, high standards of productivity and quality. Focus on external stakeholders including customers and suppliers is also essential for directors and senior managers. All those who join a public company board should have the capacity to take a long view of matters. So long as shareholders are solely responsible for electing and removing the directors, however, that is where their principal loyalty will lie. To counterbalance this, it is important that other stakeholders have legal rights such as those described in the previous chapter.

There has been a tendency among those who favour employee representation and controls on takeovers and mergers to see the European Union as a source of legislation to further their aims whilst the UK government was reluctant to take action, particularly during the 1980s. It has now become clear that the detailed adaptation of UK public companies law via the European Union is not a realistic option for the foreseeable future. The Hampel Committee report was particularly disappointing in its failure to recognise implications of the UK's existing obligations under European Union law, let alone the lessons to be learned from other European models. The Company Law Green Paper, while discussing developments in other common law jurisdictions such as Australia and Canada, New Zealand and South Africa, also had disappointingly little to say on the subject of European common ground and co-operation.[103] If the DTI, in particular, is prepared to

---

101 Streeck, W, n 21 above.

102 Lorange and Roos, n 98 above, Chapter 9.

103 Company Law Review Steering Group, *Modern Company Law for a Competitive Economy: The Strategic Framework*, February 1999, and Company Law Review Steering Group, *Modern Company Law for a Competitive Economy: Developing the Framework* (DTI, March 2000) similarly overlook this issue. The Steering Group's *Final Report* (July 2001) at Annex B, 'The European Dimension', largely repeats the critique of European measures.

seize the opportunities offered by closer engagement with Europe, there will be more chance to influence world affairs. The European Union as a whole has the potential to set standards of investor protection, of employee treatment and consultation and of customer service and supply chain relationship management to which others would have to respond.

At the European Council meeting on Employment and Social Policy on 6 June 2000: 'the Council recall[ed] the overall objective to raise the employment rate from an average of 61% today to a rate approaching 70% by 2010 and to increase the female employment rate from 51% to more than 60%'.[104] It went on to comment that: 'Special attention should be given, in this context, to the improvement of employability and lifelong learning, exploiting the complementarity between lifelong learning and adaptability through flexible management of working time and job rotation, bearing in mind in particular the challenges and opportunities arising from a knowledge-based economy.' This is in line with the policy accepted by the majority of Member States. Company law in the European Union will need to fit in with this agenda in future.

---

104 Minutes available at www.europa.eu.int.

CHAPTER 8

PUBLIC COMPANY OFFICERS AND COMPANY LAW REFORM

8.1 THE COMMERCIAL CONTEXT

The discussion of the appropriate legal form for directors' duties must take into account the views of those who would have to work within the new rules if the debate is to produce results that enjoy general support from business. The process leading up to revised legislation may itself have 'business value' insofar as:

(a) it leads business people to reflect upon their own practice and the issues they consider to be important in the context of their business;[1]

(b) it provides an opportunity to argue for 'levelling the playing field', that is, that the social and environmental standards of the best performers should not be put at risk by those content to operate at a lower level in these areas;[2]

(c) it provokes fresh discussion of the UK's current position relative to laws of other major states;[3]

(d) it creates new opportunities to examine the economic impact of legal rules on directors and shareholders, companies and third parties.[4]

Issues of public company board structure are also pertinent, in that an appropriate team of directors needs to be assembled and to be organised so as to make the best use of its skills. While few people have direct, in-depth experience of more than one corporate law system, most of those operating at public company board level have clear views of what works for them. Most of this chapter is given over to a record of the views of a few of these business leaders, using their own words. Extracts given are from transcripts of tape-recorded conversations. The choice of language is often very revealing in itself. Some deep ideological divisions between individuals were revealed, as

---

1   Among current issues of concern are: Secretan, L, 'Customer Connections' (2000) 10 Industry Week 25; Drucker, P, 'Knowledge Work', (2000) 17 Executive Excellence 11; Moss Kanter, R, 'Are You Ready to Lead the E-Culture Revolution?' (2000) 22 Inc 43; Wong, A, 'Integrating Supplier Satisfaction with Customer Satisfaction' (2000) 11 Total Quality Management S427.

2   Zadek, S, 'Balancing Performance, Ethics and Accountability' (1998) 17 Journal of Business Ethics 1421; Monaghan, 'Warts and All Reporting' (1999) 124 Accountancy 61.

3   Company Law Review Steering Group, *Modern Company Law for a Competitive Economy: The Strategic Framework*, February 1999, Chapter 4.

4   Law Commission, *Company Directors: Regulating Conflicts of Interests and Formulating a Statement of Duties*, Report No 261, September 1999), Part 2.

were areas of common concern. Implications of these views for the UK company law review process are also noted. The range of views may also be of interest to business practitioners and students.

8.2 KEY ISSUES FOR DISCUSSION WITH PUBLIC COMPANY OFFICERS

These emerged from the preceding chapters and included the following:

(a) Primary responsibility of directors: to whom does (and should) the board owe its principal allegiance?

(b) Which groups are taken into consideration in decision making (for example, customers, employees, shareholders, suppliers, the community, the environment)?

(c) What is the 'ranking', if any, of these various groups (does the board see the company as being particularly oriented to one 'internal' group and how important are 'external' considerations)?

(d) How are stakeholders considered: what are the mechanisms of accountability?

When and at what stage in the decision making process does consultation occur?

Where – at board meetings, whenever expert opinion is sought?

Changes to the law:

(e) How does interviewee react to the prospect of a stakeholder-inclusive statement of directors' duties and quasi-derivative enforcement actions?

(f) Is the approach that such laws would require different from current practice in the interviewee's company and if so, how?

The overriding priority in the discussions was to relate managerial practice to actual and potential legislation for UK public companies.

Within each company contacted, the writer spoke to the officer who was best prepared to discuss these issues. Many larger public companies have legal directors on the main board in addition to the company secretary who deals with administration. In some medium-sized companies, the company secretary sits on the board with key executive colleagues. The smaller the organisation, the more weight the chief executive's own priorities and opinions are likely to carry. The perception in some corporations that 'legal matters' are the concern of the company secretary or the legal director alone, while board colleagues show little interest, is itself a matter for concern. Legal language and concepts are certainly perceived to be arcane or impenetrable by many lay people, including public company directors, at present.

8.3 THE INTERVIEWEES

A total of 21 individuals, many of whom held executive and several non-executive positions, took part in meetings over the summer and autumn of 1999 and autumn 2000. Their respective roles at the time of the interviews were: three chief executives, plus one former chairman/chief executive who remained an executive chairman and one recently retired chairman/chief executive; two finance directors (one of whom was also company secretary); two directors of business development (one of whom also covered legal affairs); two company secretaries and two group legal directors who were on the main boards in their respective companies; two company secretaries and one group legal director who did not have 'main board' seats but worked closely with senior colleagues; one personnel director with a board seat and four very experienced non-executive public company directors. The individuals concerned had a wide variety of professional backgrounds, from accounting and law to science and technology. Only two were female (both were company secretaries, one of whom had a main board seat), which reflects the proportion of women on public company boards in 1999. All had responded to a letter outlining the research proposal and requesting their assistance that was sent to some two hundred directors and secretaries (given at Appendix One). The key sectors represented were energy and primary products, manufacturing, both traditional and high-technology (including computing and pharmaceuticals) and retailing and information about companies and individuals was principally obtained from the *Kompass Company Information Register*,[5] the *Hambro Company Guide*[6] and companies' own Annual Reports and websites.

Within the group of interviewees, representation from a broad spread of sectors (primary, for example, oil; secondary, for example, consumer goods, high-tech manufactures; and tertiary, for example, retail, leisure) was obtained. It was felt that financial service providers and privatised utilities, while raising interesting issues of governance, were subject to other regulatory regimes than standard Companies Act, Stock Exchange and Financial Services Authority rules.[7] Even excluding those sectors, public companies whose goods and services are consumed directly by members of the public may be expected to have a rather different set of priorities from those which 'sell' to other corporations. Similarly, it might be anticipated that industries (such as oil) which are capital-intensive would rate human resources less highly than those (such as leisure) which rely more directly on the initiative of members of

---

5   Published annually.

6   Published quarterly.

7   The Financial Services and Markets Act 2000 and the Utilities Act 2000 have recently been passed.

staff.[8] Of the 20 companies that provided the officers' main workplaces, six were listed in the FTSE 100, seven in the middle 250, three were 'FTSE Fledglings', two had full listings but were not in an index and two were public companies without Stock Exchange listings. While this was not a large nor a 'scientific' sample, there was, therefore, experience of a cross-section of public company sizes within the sample, a fact which is reflected in the comments.

The companies whose officers were interviewed ranged from a retailer with over 300 stores from Aberdeen to Plymouth, to a shoe producer with a single UK manufacturing base. One manufacturer's oldest business dates from the origin of the Industrial Revolution, when the process of smelting iron using coke was discovered, whereas another company was founded 18 years ago and is at the leading edge of palmtop computing and wireless data transmission. Many of the companies, such as market leaders in oil and pharmaceuticals, are of international standing. None of those interviewed felt that current UK company law entirely reflected the realities with which they had to deal every day. All of them were speaking in a personal capacity, rather than as representatives of their particular current main employers. Indeed, many interviewees consciously drew on experiences from previous workplaces and several executives also referred to work in part-time non-executive posts.

Each semi-structured interview lasted between 40 minutes and one hour. The outline schedule of discussion topics is set out at Appendix Two, though issues relevant to each interviewee's experience were explored in greater depth as time permitted and the interviewees were encouraged to give practical examples from their own careers and companies. The following is a selection of extracts from interviewees' comments on some of the main issues explored in previous chapters. They reveal a range of attitudes and opinions, with issues of priorities in decision making at board level and directorial accountability producing the greatest divergences of view. All of the interviewees are thanked for sparing time from very busy schedules to take part and share their experiences. As they were promised, they and their companies are not named in this report of what was said.

8.4 THE BOARDROOM ROLE

When asked how they perceived the role of a director, and how this differed from management, interviewees highlighted the strategic questions that are determined in the boardroom. For example:

---

8   Corbridge, M and Pilbeam, S, *Employment Resourcing*, 1998, discuss the importance of staff as a business asset.

The role of the board is to be primarily concerned with strategic direction and control. To be concerned with what the company intends to do, how it intends to achieve it and how it's setting about that task. What it shouldn't do is get involved in the minutiae of day to day management tasks – that should be left to managers. It needs to ensure that managers are competent to carry out the strategy and policy the board has agreed. The board also needs to ensure that the company has sufficient resources for its plans, and that implies both money and people. The board also needs to establish the tone of the business, that is to say its general attitude towards trading, its attitude to its responsibilities towards the environment, its staff, and to the community at large.

Another comment expressing similar views was:

The role of the board as a whole is to determine what the strategy of the business will be, the areas the business is going to operate in, the steps the business needs to take to grow either by organic growth or by acquisition, whether that is to be confined to one specific area or to diversify, to have regard to the overall control of the business and see that there are policies and structures in place to ensure the board's strategy is implemented. The board's role is as a force giving direction to the thousands of employees who work to produce the profits for the people who own the business, that is the shareholders.

Two other contributors used comparable wording.

One interviewee summed up the issue as follows:

The responsibility of directors is to direct the company, the responsibility of others below board level is to execute the policy of the board and to manage the projects that result from that policy and the employees who carry out those processes ... It is the responsibility of directors to examine, identify and develop the strategy of the company, to identify the policies and framework of the group of companies and then to arrange for the execution and proper operation of those strategies and policies.

Strategy and planning are clearly of vital importance. They seem to be at the heart of the distinction between 'management' and 'direction'.

A further common observation was that, in practice, the line between board activity and senior management was often quite difficult to draw. As one participant said:

The management committee of executive directors and myself (the company secretary) look after the day to day running of the business and the board meets monthly to discuss wider issues, big investments, and review the ongoing business and how we're doing against our budgets and forecasts. In terms of management, I wouldn't say there's a great deal of difference. In terms of responsibility, being a director obviously carries with it greater responsibility to the company.

Similarly, another director remarked:

I'm not sure you actually see any material distinction in the way you approach things at all. Being on the board means you have more decisions to make but a lot of people are given a lot of executive responsibility in any case.

One interviewee put forward his views about this continuity between different levels of corporate activity somewhat more trenchantly:

> It's a common fallacy to believe that managers occupy one universe and directors another and in some mystical way one is transmogrified from being a mere manager to being a director and a lot of consultants make a lot of money from pretending that they can in some way help with this transformation. It is of course, like a lot of the rhetoric in this area complete and utter garbage, one is merely an extension of the other ... There are plenty of people in this organisation doing very senior and responsible jobs who don't happen to be on our board and the notion that their role and responsibilities and compass are in some way minor compared with the board is nonsense.

An officer from a large multinational company did, however, draw a clear distinction between the nature of board members' duties and those of other executives:

> You have to realise that the board is there to set the general checklists, the hurdle rates within those checklists, and then somebody else sits down and does the specifics ... By choosing a board of directors who are people of wide experience, we get the right sort of perspective at the top and by having executives who are required to interact across the whole of society and think about the society in which they're living, we get the specificity at the bottom.

Other interviewees noted the public and representational role of directors. One said:

> I think the main differentiation of the directorial role is the higher profile it has, particularly from an institutional investor perspective. It is the directors, executives and non-executives in different ways, who are contemplated by shareholders and they're not concerned about the others. This is reflected in the fact that the remuneration of directors is public knowledge and the benefits package, incentive plans and so on come up for approval at the Annual General Meeting.

Not all new public company directors have felt very well prepared for this public aspect of their role. Training in communication and media-handling is, however, becoming more widespread.

With regard to the law, another director commented:

> Obviously the board of directors has legal and very serious responsibilities. They are responsible for the management of the business and every decision made. They are collectively responsible as we have a unitary board system in this country. People further down the business, unless they do something dishonest, as far as I know, are basically sheltered. If they are carrying out the policies of the board they are in a relatively protected position. And obviously directors have responsibilities, some would say principally, to the shareholders who have invested their money in the company. They also owe responsibilities to the staff and for compliance with legislation, whether health and safety or anything else.

Two other participants highlighted board responsibilities to shareholders, one saying:

> As a director you have to be driven in your decision making by the creation of shareholder value and wealth – that is the single most important consideration that comes into your mind when you look at the issues facing the company. The other responsibility is concerned with the fiduciary duties and, in simplistic terms, making sure the company's behaving itself!

The other director who had similar views stated:

> Directors have specific responsibilities quite separate from the role they may have as managers. Currently they are answerable solely to the owners of the business, ie the shareholders, and they have, in law, no other responsibilities.

It was, perhaps, surprising that more participants did not address the constituency – or constituencies – issue at this stage, particularly given the later remarks in many interviews concerning the power of institutional investors.

Finally, one company secretary, who was in the midst of dealing with a takeover, pointed out:

> If you're involved in a lot of corporate activity, you're very much involved with directors' responsibilities, particularly when you've got to sign statements. That helps to concentrate the mind! Aside from corporate activity, issuing new shares and so on, most boards would meet once a month. Then there will be more informal meetings on board matters – for example, if there are appointments to be made, interviewing people, succession planning, those sorts of issues.

Good professional advice was clearly regarded as important in these situations. The director's commercial experience also counted for a great deal.

As to the roles of non-executives within the unitary board, there were interesting comments from two experienced practitioners. The first commented that:

> One is concerned that a company does its best to ensure the company creates value for shareholders and shareholders have a good understanding of what the company is about. The key to it is that when investors invest in good faith, there are no surprises. To this end, the Chairman is the leading non-executive, but broadly speaking what non-executives expect is that in this process of value creation the company has a strategy which is credible, and that underlying this strategy is a business model which will make money, that you can buy things, transform them and sell them at a sensible profit, in an ideal world a profit that will grow with volume ... In a strategic session, the non-executives can only approve or not – I like to think the executive proposes and the board disposes. If the non-executives don't like it they can ask for it to be done again, but you don't expect them to be strategy makers.

The second interviewee asked:

> What are non-executives for? I think their most important role is to provide a combination of support and challenge to the chief executive. That's quite

difficult for some chief executives to understand because a lot of them would like just supportive non-executives. They may say: 'Have you thought of this?' but that's supportive. To say: 'Why aren't we doing something about this? Are we as good as the competition? Shouldn't we be doing something about this?' without being threatening, is important.

On occasion, where there are insurmountably serious problems, the chief executive may need to be removed and it is then that a strong chairman or lead non-executive may be most valuable.

It became clear in discussions that the line between executive action and directorial oversight is not always clear-cut in practice. The officers interviewed nevertheless see the board as providing strategic direction and managerial leadership and carrying ultimate legal and public accountability for corporate actions. There was some difference of emphasis as to the extent to which non-executive directors should involve themselves in monitoring operations in detail and their proper input into strategy. Most of the executives are very conscious that they are, in practice, reliant upon a large number of people to carry out their strategies each day – and the larger the corporation, the more this is so. However, if management systems prove to be inadequate, all of the company's directors may suffer consequences in UK law.[9] While the Hampel Report emphasised the importance of 'driving the business forward', the Turnbull Report's recommendations have turned the spotlight back on the management of risk.

8.5 WHOSE INTERESTS DO DIRECTORS TAKE INTO ACCOUNT IN MAKING DECISIONS?

The question was asked without mentioning 'stakeholders' or any particular interest groups, so as not to bias or 'lead' responses, though most interviewees noted that it related to the 'stakeholder' issue. One director's opinion was representative of several others:

Without a doubt the primary interest group would be the shareholders. At the end of the day, if you've got two ways to do things and they're both equally shareholder-friendly, you might do things that would be better for your customers or employees if you've got a choice. At the end of the day, the reason you want to keep the customers happy is because of the impact they have on shareholders. The reason you want to keep employee morale up and give them a good career is because that is the future of the business for the shareholders.

Another interviewee said in response to the question:

9   As in, for example, *Re Purpoint Ltd* [1991] BCLC 491; *Secretary of State for Trade and Industry v Baker et al (Re Barings plc (No 5))* [1999] 1 BCLC 433.

The answer to that primarily has to be the interests of the shareholders, the owners of the business, and I don't think any director of a listed company can really give a different answer to that as the prime responsibility. However, I'm conscious that there is, if I've remembered my Companies Act right, a statutory duty to have regard to the interests of employees – it's still there isn't it? I suspect I'm one of the few company directors who does remember that it's there, it's virtually unenforceable, but to my mind it is meaningful ... I personally also think that we as a board ... should have regard to wider community interests ... Our first duty is to our shareholders, but I do mean all our shareholders large and small, though of course in the last resort it is the big institutions who dictate the outcome of shareholder votes.

There was further support for the view that the board should aim for shareholder value, but with some qualifications:

Our main interest is making a profit, so you could say we're considering the interests of shareholders. Having said that, I would obviously take a broader interest in all the elements that make up the profit. Disgruntled employees because they're not paid properly, shoddy products and dissatisfied customers aren't very good for profits! While trying to make profits is the end result, you do that by running a business properly and ethically.

Another director explained in greater detail:

When all is said and done, it is shareholders we are reporting to and we have to keep them satisfied, otherwise they start selling shares, the share price goes down, we start getting bad write-ups from the analysts and life is not rosy! If you're referring to wider stakeholders – customers, employees, etc. – all those issues have to be borne in mind, because if your company gets a bad press and a bad image, that reflects on the share price and the desirability of the company as a business for people to invest in. I would say that those are secondary issues compared to the shareholders who are the owners of the business. It's good business practice that you run your business as effectively and profitably as possible and that will encompass environmental issues. We happen to be in a chemicals business. We have to make sure that's run properly, that it meets all the health and safety requirements, that we don't pollute the local river and upset the local inhabitants ... I do think that that is part of the management of the business rather than why you are ultimately running the business, which is for the shareholders, to make sure that people who've entrusted their funds to your business get the returns they want.'

A similar point was also put forward in more blunt terms in another interview:

These days, the pressures of the market are never far away. A company would be very foolish if it decided to ignore its shareholders and not worry at all about its share price, because it would then come under pressure ... If it doesn't consider the interests of its other – the modern word is stakeholders, it can't look after its shareholder interests. If you rip off your customers, pretty soon you won't have any customers! If you maltreat your employees, they'll leave! If you don't pay your suppliers, they'll offer their best lines to other people! In order to look after your shareholders' interests, you've got to make sure you're looking after the interests of all these other people.

On this view, then, the shareholder is supreme. Attention to other stakeholders is instrumental, that is, for the purpose of increasing returns to investors.

Shareholder value was perceived by at least three participants to have become more prominent in recent years, as the following extract states:

> Over the last ten or twelve years, following the concept of shareholder value, there was a change of attitude through the mid-1980s. There was a re-focusing of management, and of executive directors towards this fulcrum of shareholder value and responsibility to shareholders. I think there was a kind of oligarchy back in the Fifties, Sixties and Seventies. A lot of British companies were extremely poorly run, they weren't getting proper returns on capital and the directors were appointed by themselves not so much on the basis of merit but on the basis of clubs ... There undoubtedly has been, though the mechanics have often not been attractive, a re-focusing on shareholder value, proper returns to the company, proper shareholder returns and so on.

The performance of a corporate group as a whole may be adversely affected by underperformance of one part, which may lead to tough choices for main board directors. In one case redundancies by a brewing company were discussed:

> If profit (for one company in a group) depends on the internal price, which isn't related to the market price, you can't go on like that. The internal wholesale price for beer was 25% more expensive than the price we started buying for (outside of the group) ... We've provided generous compensation and outplacement services where employees have met people who would write CVs and so on. 30% of the redundant employees have already found jobs.

Nevertheless, many directors did see their role as to some extent that of balancing a number of important demands for the benefit of the company. A legal director described the process as follows:

> First and foremost come the shareholders. When we're looking at major moves for the company, we have to look at shareholder value, are we doing the right thing for the shareholders, because we are ultimately responsible for what we are proposing ... They do come first.

> Secondly, the company is enormously important – it's not about the directors' personal ambitions, it's about where the company is going to go, in terms of market share and new products, and obviously that has an impact on shareholder value ... The company as a separate legal entity, how it is positioned, how it is to grow, how it is progressing, its impact against competitors ... comes a close second.

> The third set of concerns would be customers and employees – I'm hesitating as to which comes first, they perhaps rank equally. Without customers you haven't got a business, so they're extremely important. Most companies rely on their employees to produce the plans and carry out the strategy.

Another group we must never forget of course is the suppliers ... If we grow larger and therefore have better buying power and therefore can dictate better terms with our suppliers, that will have an impact on our suppliers.

Broader corporate responsibilities can also, in the stated opinion of two participants, be compatible with the delivery of shareholder value, one of them saying:

The prime interest of a director is in the owners of the company, that is the shareholders, and we have to act in the best interests of all the shareholders – the minority shareholders, the public shareholders, and the others, who could be industry players. There are other responsibilities which I think are very important. People talk about responsibilities to the environment, to the community, to employees, and I think you have to be very clear what is meant by that ... You can either choose to take a pro-active policy on the management of safety or you can choose not to ... If you take a pro-active policy towards safety which results in fewer lost time accidents, fewer injuries to your employees, you will improve the efficiency of the plant and your ability to service the market ... Similarly with the environment. The way legislation is going, you have to take damage to the environment seriously. The costs of not doing so can be extremely high. You can be prosecuted. The reputation of the company can suffer. Public attitudes to the company can have a major impact on whether or not they are prepared to buy its goods and services – we saw the Shell example (the Brent Spar controversy and subsequent consumer boycott) which had a serious impact on the company's financial performance and shareholders. But ultimately those things have to be driven by what creates value for shareholders.

It was interesting that two other commentators independently referred to Shell's public relations difficulties.

Questions of reputation are widely regarded as having financial impacts, as this comment from a large building materials company showed:

Fundamentally what we're looking to do is to grow the company and to develop it and that's got to be in the prime interest of the long-term shareholder ... We're acting on their behalf, essentially, to improve the investments they've made ... If you get a bad reputation you're not going to have a good business, therefore it's essential that you take everyone whose interests are directly affected into account ... A lot of our involvement is with local communities. We need their support to be able to get planning permission to run our business. We've got to extend our quarries and run trucks all over the place ... Fundamentally the strategic decisions are taken in the interests of the shareholders but at the end of the day, you have to take everyone else's interests into account who is directly involved in whatever activity you're talking about. Employees, customers, the community etc. are all relevant.

The board had to monitor all those issues.

A striking example of the possible consequences of environmental neglect was given:

In the broadest sense, we're looking at what is in the interests of the company and the principal measure of the interests of the company is the impact on shareholders. Having said that, one has to qualify it. We're a drug company. We're selling off some old sites, and quite a lot of old drug company sites are quite seriously contaminated ... Someone may come and say that there's a big environmental risk there. Rather than having an ongoing liability to the purchaser, we'd like it cleaned up and that's going to cost a lot of money, say x million pounds. We don't say: 'How does this relate to the interests of the shareholders?' ... We look at that in terms of: 'What should a responsible company do in those circumstances? What's the right thing in terms of minimising our ongoing obligations? What's the right thing in terms of our reputation as an environmentally responsive company?' ... If we buy the argument that we should clean up the site, that's self-interest ... In some ultimate sense you're asking, is this good for the long-term health of the company, and that involves the reputation of the company. Corporate reputation links the share price with broader stakeholder concerns.

Behind the interests of different factions, the public company has a life and image all of its own. Directors of long-established corporations seemed to be particularly conscious of themselves as guardians of their particular brands.

It is interesting to note that those with retail experience saw the need to balance the interests of various stakeholders in stronger terms than most other participants, as the following extracts indicate:

In retail, the most important constituencies we have are shareholders, first and foremost because they own the business and we are in the business of making money, secondly our customers, without whom we wouldn't have a business, thirdly our suppliers, on whom we are dependent for the products we sell to our customers to generate a return for our shareholders, and fourthly, our employees, who again are absolutely vital because without them we wouldn't have a business. In any big strategic decision we take, we always have regard to those different interests. It's interesting that our board reflects all those various interests. We have the Chairman and non-executives who can be said in many senses to be representing the interests of the shareholders, although I think all the directors collectively have to represent those interests, as they are servants in legal terms of the company but in real terms of the shareholders. Then we have very strong representation from the buying and merchandising community, we also have the interests of the retail part of the business ... through the MD, who's a retailer. We also have a Personnel Director who is on the board representing the interests of all the employees across the business ... Most enlightened businesses in this country recognise what is, I think, an obvious fact, which is that you cannot grow a business and sustain a business into the future unless you have regard to these various interests. I'd in fact go further and say I consider it to be a legal obligation of directors to have regard – to have regard, as opposed to owing a duty – to these various interests in carrying out their primary duty, which is their duty to the company.

Similarly, another outstandingly experienced retailing executive said this:

I don't think that any one of the views on the matter would suggest that all three groups (shareholders, customers and employees) aren't very important. They all get top priority treatment but at the end of the day, the shareholder lobby believes that ... everything you do must be done with first and foremost the shareholder in mind. I'm not in that camp. I'm not of that view, any more ... I think with today's growing short-termism of the institutional investor, who himself is being monitored as to his performance in managing the fund, it's much more difficult for him to take a long-term view ... I've come to the conclusion that the shareholder is entitled to enormous priority, but if you haven't got customers satisfied with your product, you've got a problem, and frankly, you won't have customers if you don't employ good staff producing the good product or the service they're going to buy from you and interfacing with them properly, efficiently, and in such a way that those customers will stay loyal to you. I'm of the view now that you've got to have a very well-motivated, efficient staff and after that, they will serve the customers well and in a manner that pleases them and the benefits will flow to the shareholder. I'm very much of the stakeholder approach, but it is all very marginal because it would be totally wrong to take other than very seriously the needs of shareholders who, after all, are investing in your company.

In a public company that was still in governmental ownership (albeit preparing for the sale of part of its equity) and a private sector corporation concerned with delivering contracts for formerly 'public' services to local authorities, the stakeholder viewpoint was strongly endorsed. The comment of the legal directors of the former organisation was simply:

There are many stakeholders, not just the shareholders. A company like ours, or virtually any major company, has many employees and legal responsibilities to creditors ... There are local communities in which companies operate, companies can be dominant in particular geographies and they have responsibilities ... Some towns are one-company towns. You also have all kinds of responsibilities, to other stakeholders, to the environment. The precise set of stakeholders will include shareholders, employees, the community, the ones I've mentioned, but other companies will have additional stakeholders.

The Managing Director of the latter company said:

Obviously as an organisation which sees itself as being very customer-orientated, we have a very strong focus towards our clients. So they come very high on our list of priorities. Our staff are very important to us and form part of what we are offering, because the bulk of them are ex-public sector employees. But in any event you can't deliver a strong or good service without having a strong affinity to your employees and involving them strongly. So I think these are two very strong areas but in addition, one cannot forget the shareholders, not least because I am one – from a self-interest perspective, that's important to me. I think if you get the customer focus right, if you employ people who are dedicated to the organisation, then shareholders' interests will follow. But if all you do is say: 'I will only look narrowly at satisfying shareholders' interests', ultimately you lose the plot.

Some public company officers would reject the contention that they were 'stakeholder managers' but nevertheless were clear about the importance of customers and employees to business:

> There's a very funny view of stakeholders which says the board sits round at planning time and says: 'We'll have to share this company between the stakeholders, so we'll give this to the shareholders, this to the customers, this to the employees.' That's a totally unrealistic view, you don't do anything like that at all. You're always trying to find formulae which enable you to sell a product at a price the customer can afford, which will be competitive against the next product, which you can get your people to happily make in terms of what you pay them and what they are required to do, and which at the end of the day produces enough profit to satisfy the shareholders. You're very conscious of these dynamics and they are reconciled in every product and every service a company sells.

Maximisation of shareholder value itself requires attention to other groups, as one director explained:

> I think there is a virtuous circle here. Whatever the law may say about employees, communities etc., if you say to yourself: "My job is to create value for shareholders," the first thing you do is to think about customers, how you satisfy them. If they are dissatisfied they'll go somewhere else and employees will lose their jobs. Suppliers, employees, communities are all very important but my personal, rather old-fashioned view is to say the thing to do is to think about creating value for shareholders by communicating effectively with those other groups.

The extent to which shareholder returns are or should be prioritised, if at all, is obviously a matter which still ignites great controversy in management circles. It is fair to say that if asked expressly for their views of the stakeholder approach, around half of those taking part in the discussions would have expressed extreme scepticism. Even so, almost without exception they would have acknowledged that primary stakeholders are key to corporate financial success. Planning for medium and long-term profitability and growth is a concern for all boards. Some public company leaders make explicit that they regard themselves as agents of investors in making and executing those plans. Those directors who see themselves as stewards or guardians of the interests of the company as an ongoing institution are somewhat closer to the 20th century judicial understanding of directors' duties.[10]

8.6 WHICH STAKEHOLDER(S) HAVE PRIORITY?

Many of the most difficult decisions for directors come when there is an apparent clash between the interests of different interest groups, for example,

---

10   Eg *Percival v Wright* [1902] 2 Ch 421; *Stein v Blake* [1998] 1 All ER 742.

employees who wish to protect their tenure and remuneration and shareholders who demand what they see as acceptable profits. One company secretary said:

> I think we would see this very much as a situation where we have been given investors' money to use, in the best way possible – but 'best' has got a wide, large, liberal interpretation. We seek the best use of those funds in their interests to give them the best possible return, because those people need and are indeed relying on us to provide them with future growth and future economic welfare. We clearly have to ensure that those funds are put to the best use in the ways in which we have declared we will use them. We have declared we will use them in three markets and some sectors of those markets.

Another interviewee spoke of financial pressure from investors:

> People always look to their own individual long-term interests. If they feel they're under pressure from shareholders, it's not surprising that people will act in a manner which will try to assuage the demands of shareholders. At the end of the day if institutions said: 'We don't care, do what you like and if you lose money, you lose money' directors wouldn't have to worry would they? That's not what the investing public actually demands. The investing public is not just the institutions – the institutions are investing on behalf of a significant proportion of the people who live in the UK. At the end of the day, if companies don't perform, the institutions won't get the returns they need to be able to pay their pensions.

Loss-making activities cannot be sustained indefinitely.

A corporate reputation for responsibility can affect the views of potential shareholders, as one interviewee explained:

> We wouldn't invest in just anything, however socially unacceptable it was, because we have a reputation for being a traditional, well-established, respectable business and I think we would be careful to guard that. To give an example of something we wouldn't necessarily invest in – genetic engineering maybe, if it were thought to be unacceptable; on the other hand it's a growth area and we may look at it in time. I don't think we'd want to be seen to be involved in a business that was blatantly breaking every corner of the health and safety regulations or seen to be abusing its workforce in any way ... We've got no existing problems and as far as I'm aware the investment community doesn't regard us as a potentially sensitive business.

Investor impressions of the corporate brand are a strong consideration for directors.

One director clearly expressed the view that shareholders were entitled to priority as they were accepting the risks of failure:

> In law, you would have to look at what happens when a company goes bankrupt. The pecking order then gives some indication of the government's viewpoint. Tax I think comes first, the shareholders come at the bottom, suppliers are next bottom, banks I think come next – and I'm not sure where employees come as regards back pay they may be owed. If you reversed those,

it would give you some idea of what the government thinks are the stakeholders in any big business – how they split up the spoils when it goes bust. If you take any business, the people who have an interest in the success of that business, apart from the shareholders, are employees, customers, suppliers and the local community that provides the environment for the business and where people's wages get spent. If the government wants to change the responsibility from being to shareholders, they have to put in place not only privileges but responsibilities ... If the government is going to expect shareholders to put their money in to a risky enterprise, they have to think about what's going to happen when things go wrong.

An experienced director commented very straightforwardly:

I have very simple, traditional views here – the shareholders' money is at risk, and the Companies Act requires that we put their interests first. The structure of the company is based around that – you can't serve two masters. I can't imagine creating a Companies Act that qualified the responsibilities to the shareholders. Who would invest? In terms of so-called company stakeholders, there are a number of people whose relationship to the company is defined by contract, contracts with customers, contracts with suppliers and contracts with employees.

This simple approach does not take into account the question of relationships that go beyond formal contract terms.

The treatment of employees who are made redundant in the interests of assuring profitability was cited as significant in the following comments:

In the very short-term, the interests might be in conflict, because you would be perceived as putting people out on to the streets ... The argument that is counter to that is that if you don't have a competitive business, in the long-term you won't survive and a lot more people will be out on the streets. Telecommunications has created, as it's grown, more jobs than it has eliminated through someone like BT having to downsize because of competitive forces and changes in technology ... What you've got to do as a company, and this is a choice directors can make, is to choose how you treat those employees when you've got to lay them off and that's really tricky – there's no right or wrong answer to that. Some companies are totally ruthless in the way they do it, others are more respectful of what people are going through, in the way it's handled and the terms and conditions ... You can decide what sort of behaviour you want to have in a company, take a personal view that you've got to take hard decisions but you can treat people with the respect they deserve.

From another industry which has suffered many job losses came these remarks:

We were known as metal bashers (though we had interests outside of metal and we did a lot of things with metal other than bash it!), we had steel mills and iron foundries and we have disposed of most of those. When you are focusing, enhancing results, a major part of the response tends to be curtailment of costs ... and you cut costs by reducing numbers ... That I wouldn't myself see as setting up a situation of conflict. Why not? Because we're conscious of our responsibilities, for example under the redundancy payments legislation, we have always complied with that and more. In our relationships with unions and individuals, providing outplacement services for those being made redundant, we have done far more than the statutory requirement.

Another commentator highlighted a different way of aligning the interests of employees and shareholders:

We've had a profit-sharing scheme for over 20 years, which gives full-time employees a shareholding in the company. We look after employees by making them stakeholders, that is owners of the company. It's a good way of retaining loyalty and commitment. I'm in favour of that and very much in favour of the things that successive governments have done to make that more tax-efficient and sensible, I think that's been beneficial. I wouldn't be in favour of legislation which would make people behave in a certain way ... Anything that suggests that companies shouldn't conduct their activities in a way which will produce the greatest profit would be very unhelpful.

Many of those interviewed, however, took as their lodestone the long-term good of the company as a whole as the following shows:

It comes back to the basic premise of doing what's best for the company. You owe a duty to all stakeholders to take them into consideration. If you've got two different stakeholders pointing East and West, diametrically opposed, you've got to think what's best for the company. That will involve upsetting one stakeholder if you agree with the other one, but you've got to manage that disagreement and explain why you've taken that decision.

To quote another example of balancing different interests in practice:

Let's assume we are closing factories to produce more efficiently at the expense of some jobs. You take a view on what you believe is good for the long-term health of the company... Implicitly you are saying a few employees will lose their jobs, but that is a sacrifice (quite brutal as this sounds) they have to make in order that the ongoing viability of the business can be assured. If we are to stay a successful and efficient drug company, we have to develop new drugs. That's a difficult and risky business, you need all the money you can get for that, so if you can stop money being dissipated in surplus factories and bring it behind researchers and their equipment, that's what you are going to do. So the test would be, what is in the interests of the health and future prospects of this company? Another way of saying that would be, what's in the interests of the majority of its employees? ... You look at the impact on a whole range of constituencies from public opinion, at the most abstract end, to employees and the stock market and you come to a conclusion based on what is in the interests of the ongoing success and prosperity of the enterprise. If you want to say that the principal indicator of that, in a broad sense, is the share price, then I wouldn't disagree.

As for priorities between different stakeholders, one director said this:

I don't have a ranking order in that at times one [stakeholder group] may be very relevant, at other times it may be less relevant. I do have a ranking order in that the business of a company is to create value for its shareholders. The way you get there is to put enormous efforts into helping suppliers and employees to do a great job for customers.

Another participant summed up his response as follows:

It's not a question of either/or, you have to think about them all, all the time, but on a particular issue, you may have to give somebody preference. For instance, if it becomes perfectly clear that you need to increase the wages of a large part of your staff in order to be competitive – the Health Service found this recently in relation to nurses' pay – then you must do it, and if it comes off the bottom line, that's tough. At that moment in order to look after the interests of shareholders in the long-term, you have to diminish their expectations in the shorter-term. On the other hand, you could easily have a situation where you've formed the conclusion that a particular plant is never likely to produce a satisfactory level of profitability, it can never be remedied, and you'd have to close it.

A different perspective on the question of redundancies came from a more service-orientated business:

The reality is that we need to look at the long-term in decision making. It's no use letting go of 10% of the employees when they transfer [to the private sector] and then finding we haven't got enough [people] ... It's much better to keep these people. The point about fleecing the customers – that could lead to better short-term profits but not in the long run ... With the long-term relationships we have with clients, our minimum contract is five years and we have contracts up to 15 years. It would be very shortsighted to fleece the customers. So in both instances I have answered in what is the long-term interest of the organisation. Once we've started seeing it in a medium or long-term, the interests of the shareholders, customers and workforce actually converge.

Other directors agreed that the conflict between shareholder value and stakeholder interests was false. As one put it:

What is this idea of 'the company'? It's evolved over the last 200 years to a construct where, in my opinion, a company is a structure in which capital, management, employees, customers and suppliers come together to effect ends which supersede any of the specific or particular interests of those groups ... The company is apparently a very successful machine, or structure, which brings these things together to achieve something greater than each of them can achieve alone ... There are new kinds of structure developing now which supersede the company and Silicon Valley is an illustration of that ... But if we stick to my definition of 'the company', there are four or five different interest groups or stakeholders coming together to achieve those ends. Company law is partly buried in history here and doesn't actually deal with the reality. Having said all that, companies in this capitalist world we live in survive or flourish, or alternatively die or get acquired, according to their success as measured in financial and accounting terms. That, if you like, is the scorecard, the end-of-term report for a company ... A modern, intelligently-run company is extremely conscious that to deliver the shareholder returns, to be effective, they have to have very positive, progressive policies for their employees, for their customers, for their suppliers ... These things correlate – if they didn't correlate, the company wouldn't be a successful form.

This medium to long-term convergence of interests was the subject of another discussion:

I think companies do increasingly bear in mind that short-term decisions which might seem to be for the benefit of shareholders are not always a sensible way forward because in order to make short-term profits, that might involve, for example, sacrificing a segment of the workforce and have longer- term consequences that might affect profitability in the future ... I'd certainly like to dispel any myth that the boards of British companies are concerned only with producing a profit and returns to shareholders – I don't believe that's the case and had it been the case, British business would be radically different from what it is now ... There's a separate issue, which is, does British business feel constrained by thinking that the City has a short-term approach? I think British business sometimes kids itself that the City is short-termist and the City is considerably less short-termist than most British business people say. The stock market value of a company such as this is not judged on what our current profits are or what people expect in the current year. We are valued on what the market believes we will be producing in the future, and it can only come to an assessment of our future profits based on our proposals for investment going forward ... In the retail business, by the very nature of what we do, we have to have regard to all those constituencies or we wouldn't have a business. I think the same could be applied with equal force to an industrial concern.

One director was in favour of permitting different corporate models:

I think to ask people to choose between shareholder value and pluralism is wrong – I don't think shareholder value is necessarily different from the pluralist view. I think if you pursue it to its ultimate conclusion, you end up with the same thing. If you pursue shareholder value, you treat all these other interest groups well ... There's no reason why you can't have two different types of company, PLC pluralist and PLC shareholder, with different articles of association. If you have a shareholder value corporate shell and a pluralist corporate shell, let the market develop and let people decide whether they want to work for PLC pluralist or PLC shareholder, let suppliers decide who they want to supply, let shareholders decide where they want to invest their money. It's typical of government, saying we've got to choose one or the other ... You could just say: 'Here's an alternative structure, anyone who wants to adopt it can do so', and if no-one's adopting it, that means companies don't want it. If there's no pressure form suppliers, no pressure from customers, no pressure from shareholders, to adopt this second structure, then what's the government rattling on about?

Despite the popularity of management literature on the topic,[11] it was notable that only one participant thought that customers had top priority and he explained his reasons:

> Customers are number one. They pay my salary ... It's customers first, employees second and shareholders third. The reason for that is straightforward. If you put shareholders first, I as a shareholder receiving my dividend do not guarantee I will reinvest in your organisation. I'll invest where I can get the best return. Also we've got to look, particularly in the UK, at investments for the long journey. The Japanese approach is for long-term investments, whereas if there is a complaint against the US, it's that many investments are for very short-terms. We mustn't be too short-termist. Decisions to stay in markets and trade into other markets are often made because people do not see how they will produce returns quickly enough and we could be, in terms of technology, having to deal with situations which last for years.

A small but significant group of public company officers interviewed perceived themselves as primarily agents of the shareholders. Equity investors in their view would always have ultimate priority. The remainder took the view that they had a more complex set of responsibilities, all of which had to be addressed if their respective businesses were to be successful. Unsustainable activities may have to be terminated but all those affected needed to be treated considerately. Perhaps the most important argument advanced by those who are in favour of shareholder primacy has been the need for a single goal by which directors could measure their decisions (though as seen above, some also use arguments around shareholder 'ownership rights'). Those directors who claim to make their assessments by reference to the long-term 'good of the company', however, do not appear to feel that they lack a guiding principle in their daily work, though they may weigh other considerations in the balance against returns to shareholders.

8.7 MANAGING RELATIONSHIPS WITH STAKEHOLDERS

There were some very detailed responses to this general question, revealing comprehensive and sophisticated communication strategies. For example:

> We have regular contact with shareholders, one-to-one meetings. Through the analyst community, we have meetings at least twice a year with our group of analysts ... We're also setting up an internet site so we'll be able to communicate more rapidly. Our small shareholders will be able to tap into that, because there's always the dichotomy between the big institutions where there are one-to-one meetings and they have the benefit of analysts' research and private shareholders ... Of course by Stock Exchange rules you can't

---

11   Eg, Patricia Seybold's *Customers.com*, 1998, has been in Amazon.com's business books bestseller list (1999/2000).

divulge information that's material or price-sensitive to one class of shareholders without telling everyone else ... Obviously we have the AGM so our private shareholders have the opportunity to ask questions of directors there. This year we did a presentation, which went down very well.

The customers – obviously we get feedback via the branches on how customers are thinking, but we have also just done a large amount of independent research into what our customers and suppliers think of us ... We also do market research, so when we've done TV advertising we'll do market research to see what the audience thinks.

For employees – we have a regular newsletter. Also any announcements we make go all round the group immediately. Again, hopefully people will get used to looking at the website so they can get information on the report and accounts and so on. We also have a European Forum, which is effectively a Works Council. Not many companies have that in place yet.

Another example of this systematic, integrated approach was the following:

If we start with the shareholders, we're a small plc and there's been a lot in the press about availability of finance for smaller public limited companies. What you have to do is keep the interest of the shareholders in what you're doing. Obviously we have the AGM and put out statements. We also had two meetings at the Barbican where we put our products out, did a presentation and invited shareholders. We also are involved with the Guild of Shareholders, which is a guild for smaller plcs ... In a smaller plc, institutions aren't very interested, so we have a lot of smaller shareholders. We have a lot of dialogue with our shareholders one to one, where you talk about what you're doing. You have to be careful you don't stray from the guidelines about what you can say to one shareholder alone but they will telephone us and say: 'How are things going?'

As far as staff are concerned, we have built up here a very loyal, generally young staff around the world. We do have different systems in different parts of the world because different regulations apply, but in the UK we have development plans for individuals, encourage them to get training and get involved in the business and also encourage them to move on in the business.

For customers, you have to look at quality – we've just got ISO 9000 and that's an indication for customers of the quality of what we're doing. For suppliers, again it's about contact.

From the retail sector came the following example:

We have the usual Annual Report, a half yearly report and a series of investor newsletters ... We have Stock Exchange announcements ... We have an AGM like all companies and we use the opportunity to sell our philosophy to shareholders ... We also have a programme of institutional shareholder meetings where we see institutions on a regular basis, usually the Finance Director and the Chief Executive make presentations outlining our strategy, so there's quite a good flow of information, subject to the usual constraints of price sensitivity.

We regularly have meetings with our suppliers where we invite suppliers to come and see us and discuss our plans ... We used to have thousands, we're now down to seven hundred world-wide and we've had conferences with suppliers ...

We have a series of regular communications with employees, an in-house quarterly magazine, a glossy one, which we encourage people to contribute to and which we put things in to explain what's going on. Whenever we announce trading results or make any other announcement we circulate it by e-mail. We have focus groups, discussion groups where we encourage employees to participate ... We are also setting up a European Works Council.

On the customer side, we produce a magazine, which is free to customers, on a half-yearly basis. We have a lot of contact with our customer base through the fact that a large proportion of our customers is store card holders, so they get direct mailings.

Other respondents focused on shareholder relations:

Institutional investor relations have long been the prime responsibility of the Chief Executive and the Finance Director ... In the 1980s we consciously set out to develop an institutional investor relations programme ... Apart from the main board directors I've mentioned ... our group treasurer and corporate planning manager have also been involved. My own links with shareholders, which go back to my time as group secretary, have been with ... the individual shareholders.

Clear communication with shareholders must be a priority for the whole board, according to one interviewee:

The investors will have a concept of how much money the company is going to make ... It's on the basis of ... analysts' reports that people buy shares. So you have a delicate set of expectations in the marketplace about your profit potential, profit expectations and your ability to deliver those results, and it's very much the duty of the board to make sure expectations in the market are reasonable and the company is set up to deliver them. If the executive team can't deliver those results, that's a real problem which has to be addressed at the executive level.

Two respondents highlighted increasing pressures from shareholders, particularly institutions:

Shareholders are increasingly demanding on short-term returns. Quarterly reporting has made that much tougher. I think if you communicate openly and regularly about the issues you're dealing with, you can begin to manage this short-term/long-term trade-off. If you're a company that's doing the right thing, there shouldn't be any major conflict between the short-term and the long-term.

One finance director commented:

In terms of the institutions, we see them face-to-face at least twice a year ... Last week and this week I've seen 15 of the top 20 shareholders. They are primarily concerned with profits. On a scale of one to 10, profit is 10, the next thing is about two. They're not interested in employee relations unless suddenly we have a strike, they're not interested in the environment unless we have an environmental issue, and customer relationships are about: How can you make money? It all comes back to the same thing.

One director, however, emphasised that directors retain substantial control over corporate decisions, at least as long as they are seen to be producing consistent financial results:

We believe that [the shareholders] would expect us to run the business for its overall long-term health, as measured by the long-term value of the capital and the payments we make twice a year. I don't believe that anybody buys a share ... so that we can say: 'Sorry, you've put ten quid in here and it's only worth eight quid and we've halved the dividend, but we've got some happy customers and lots of employees who would otherwise be fired... and the community is delighted because we've been giving your money to art galleries. You haven't made any more money but we've looked after all the constituents except you.' ... Do we ask them about charitable giving, do we say: 'Do you mind if we give £x million to charity?' No we don't ask them that. It's none of their business, they're only the owners! ... If we said: 'Do you mind us giving £x million to charity?', most of them would say: 'No, we don't mind that, it's *de minimis* compared with the totality of funds of which you're stewards, as long as you're looking after us and the share price is rising.' ... If we didn't spend £2.1 billion on R&D, there'd be more money to give to the shareholders, but that's the business ... Similarly you could say: 'Why do you have such generous redundancy terms?' We could halve our redundancy terms tomorrow and they'd still be much better than anybody else's ... so why don't we do that and leave more money for the shareholders? ... The answer is – we do believe in the right to human dignity ... but also treating people properly, and in financial terms generously, is part of what [the company] is all about.

The sense of duty to the company as an institution, rather than to individual current shareholders, emerged here.

The board can influence the perceptions and expectations of shareholders:

If you play fair with shareholders, there's a reasonable chance they'll play fair with you. The first thing is to try to shape your shareholder register so you've got there people who understand what you're trying to do and feel that fits in with what they are trying to do. The second thing is to find ways of explaining what you're trying to do in the long run and explaining that you need their support over the next three to five years ... So, share your long-term plans, don't just do the set pieces, the AGM, not even just the once or twice a year when you're reporting results, but find out who are the key institutional shareholders and try to spend some time with them when you're not trying to prove something.

One comment emphasised that in many large companies, much responsibility must still be devolved to the operational level:

We have an environmental report once a quarter, supplied to the board.

Formal decisions and approvals are notified to the board. By the same token, where we've got fined – for discharges and things like that, you can't avoid it completely – that sort of information goes up to the board ... We've got 400 sites ... but we try to avoid fines as much as possible ... We've got a general environment policy and general health and safety policy but we have directions which are far more detailed and far more onerous at the operational level. You have to, they are dangerous places to work, quarries and brick factories ... There's no way we can set those standards at Head Office, we have to leave that to the local level ... There are industry statistics all the time about injuries and to be perfectly honest, it's financially advantageous not to have accidents happen, because it means your insurance premiums are significantly less.

Internal control systems and risk analysis are increasingly important in public companies.

Other companies rely chiefly on the board making deductions from the figures presented to it:

I don't think the board sees any information concerning customers or employees. The board sees financial figures and it will make deductions from those figures – obviously if you're not selling well, there's something wrong with your customer link. The board assesses management by their financial returns, but uses the financial performance to draw other conclusions. We don't have customer surveys or employee surveys.

In a similar vein came the following comment:

With customers, you can look at your sales figures and see if your market share is decreasing or increasing. If your market share is decreasing, your customers love somebody else better! Top line, so to speak, tells you quite a lot. Some companies have procedures for giving people reports on complaints, press reports – these things have a habit of getting back to customers. As far as employees are concerned, you can look at what the turnover rates are and how these compare with those of your competitors. Among your senior managers and directors, you will know who's resigned and why.

There appears from the wide range of comments to be a broad spectrum of policies concerning stakeholder communication and relations. Satisfying and informing the institutional shareholders is understandably a priority for public company directors whose positions may depend on the votes of those major investors, but many are also conscious of the needs of the smaller shareholder and all are aware of Stock Exchange rules on disclosure of information. As far as customer and employee relationships are concerned, however, policies and procedures differ, with retail and associated businesses often at the forefront of new thinking.[12] Insofar as the UK has traditionally had a poor reputation for employee development and customer satisfaction compared with continental Europe and the USA, an updating of the Directors'

---

12 Goyder, M, *Living Tomorrow's Company*, 1998, sets out the so-called 'inclusive approach' to management of companies.

Report to include simple measures of, for example, employee turnover and customer complaints might focus directors' minds on those areas. The Operating and Financial Review, which it is proposed that public companies would have to prepare under a new UK Companies Act, covers many of these issues. As drafted, however, the proposal leaves much of the judgment as to which matters are 'material' (and therefore need to be disclosed) to directors, giving considerable scope for variation of standards between reports.[13]

8.8 CHANGES TO COMPANY LAW

Of the officers interviewed, many were firmly against the notion of directors owing legal duties to constituencies other than shareholders. For example, one said:

> My view is that if people wish to organise and form an institution of any kind, then there is the freedom and flexibility within the current Companies Act for them to do so ... If they can show that they cannot do what they want under the present system of company law, then it's for them to make their case ... What is clear is that there needs to be, within that range of options ... a type of company, in which the members clearly have the right of control over the people at the top and in which the directors are accountable to them and them alone, which is the normal kind of company which is used for business purposes and which will continue to be necessary for business purposes. If they change the law in such a way as to deny those companies behaviour which ... gives shareholders exclusive control, exclusive accountability, then business will simply move, people will go to other jurisdictions.

Another interviewee also spoke of illegitimate wealth transfers:

> Firstly, to change the law to force directors of companies to take other interest groups into account at the expense of shareholders is a bad idea because, at the end of the day shareholders will leave and take their money away. If you force them to act at the expense of shareholders, then you've got a wealth transfer away from shareholders towards some other part of the business. It's a tax if you do that, and you're taxing some people on a different basis than others, for example shareholders in a business with a lot of employees. There's a principle of equality. Secondly, if you're going to have this sort of pluralist view, there has to be some basis on which to make decisions. Otherwise what do you aim at? You're giving directors carte blanche to do what they want and say: 'It's in the interests of this group or that group'.

The concern about potentially conflicting obligations was raised by others, including the following commentator:

---

13 Company Law Review Steering Group, *Modern Company Law for a Competitive Economy – Developing the Framework*, March 2000, paras 5.77–5.92.

To have as your overriding focused objective the interests of shareholders, taking into account all the other things and it being of course legitimate to have regard to those things, but subordinating them to the overall objective, in other words the status quo, does seem to me the only realistic and practical way of formulating directors' duties. If you said you've got a whole series of duties, all spelled out, shareholders are one group, employees another, would that make any difference to the way we ran our business? I don't think from a practical point of view it would improve the way we run our business. We'd either take no notice of it, which is what I'd be inclined to do, or we'd get ourselves thoroughly confused! ... At the end of the day we're a business, not a charity or an academic institution, we're a commercial enterprise, and it seem to me it's an illusion to pretend that we're running the business other than in the interests of its owners. Of course that's a simplification and it's not to the exclusion of the other people. If you pursue and facilitate those interests you are likely to be pursuing the interests of the owners, not the current owners necessarily, the current and future owners (and the share price is only a crude measure of those interests), but unless what you're doing is directed to the overall health, strength and prosperity of the business, as measured principally by the interests of the owners, I don't see how you could run a business, other than by paying lip service to all these fashionable lists of stakeholders. If you're doing things out of fashionable deference, I'm not sure that's a good reason for doing them at all!

Clear constraints on what a state could impose by way of regulation were set out here. The limits on action came from competition by other jurisdictions and the demands of major investors.

The role of institutional shareholders again came under the spotlight:

The emphasis placed by institutional shareholders on duty towards them alone is restrictive. If our duty as directors is to be widened, that can only work if it is accompanied by a cultural change in the attitude of our own shareholders. As long as they are going to see that our only legitimate duty is towards them, creating towards shareholder value, they are likely to see anything else as being inconsistent with that. Duty towards suppliers? Of course you've got a duty towards suppliers, it's a duty to screw them into the ground. Duty towards customers? Of course a duty to our customers, give them the finest products, the best service, to enhance our profits. Why? Because it creates shareholder value ... I personally would welcome a widening of company law to require directors to have regard to those wider interests, because it's a personal view that we should anyhow, but I find it difficult at the moment to develop those wider interests because of the pressures from institutional investors. Unless new legislation eased the pressure from institutional shareholders and itself established the cultural change I've talked about, I don't think it would work, not in this country.

This was echoed by another company secretary:

At the moment it is pretty clear where the directors' responsibilities lie. I think most public companies will look at the wider picture anyway. I don't think any public company will only look at shareholders. I think if you say you have to take all these groups of people into account before you make a decision – at the end of the day, the shareholders own the company. How are we going to explain to them that, looking at everyone's interests as a whole, we did not wish to make 1,000 people redundant because we were concerned about that wider responsibility, therefore profits are affected and their dividends are being cut? I think that would be quite a difficult one to explain to shareholders, personally! I think that if the law is changed, there'll have to be a change in the mindset of shareholders. Otherwise the directors are going to be between a rock and a hard place.

It was yet another company secretary who voiced concerns about excessive regulation and bureaucracy:

I know Hampel said that we shouldn't just be box-tickers, shareholder value and performance is really what counts, all of which I agree with. I know the approach of institutional shareholder representatives who send out reports on AGM resolutions – their voting recommendations are based purely on corporate governance. Not one of them would say: 'The company's performed outstandingly for the past three years, so even though on the face of it they don't seem to comply with that particular provision, they are obviously a well-run business.' We tend to find that, being a family business, there are certain areas where we don't comply with best practice, and indeed we say so. We have a combined Chairman/Chief Executive, and we have some non-executives who are part of our larger controlling shareholder group, although distantly related to executive management, who are fiercely independent. We maintain that having a significant financial stake in the business aligns their interest more closely with the shareholders than someone who has no tie and, if things get difficult, is able to walk away. That is not accepted because on the face of it there's some relationship ... therefore you get a black mark. That seems to me to ignore the success or otherwise of the business ... I'm not sure that the level of disclosure we have to make helps. I'm not sure many people read it apart from people who commentate on it for a living and I'm not sure it actually helps to inform shareholders.

Other contributors also raised directors' responsibilities other than in 'core' company law:

Why do we need to do that [expressly extend directors' duties] when there is social policy and environmental legislation? If that's not enough, how does making directors say: 'I've thought about the environment' help? I might have thought about the environment and decided to ignore it! What is it that we're trying to encompass in company law that has teeth on it? If we just put obligations that require us to make statements in the Annual Report, what does that really do, does that really impact on the way we behave, unless those statements can be followed up to prove you have or haven't done something? Or is it saying there are not enough companies that think on this broader scale and it's trying to force more companies to do that? ... The second concern is with smaller companies which are publicly listed. Can they afford to spend the money on these wider obligations, or should they be operating within a general legislative framework rather than a specific corporate law framework which is in addition to that?

Further discussion along the same lines came in another meeting:

I think there's too much time being spent on the legislative side and not enough on the business needs. Nowhere in Cadbury and Greenbury has anyone said: 'Have you got enough new products coming on line to ensure the continuity of this business?' We're now into the world of internal controls and general financial controls. When you see a business the size of GEC with people spending weeks and weeks on this compliance and a business our size, there's an imbalance. I would like to see different rules and regulations for plcs our size compared with others ... I just do not believe embodying all of this in the Companies Act would change the way directors behave. If you're saying some directors ignore these other issues, I don't think the Companies Act helps you or would force directors to consider them, because I think those other issues are the directors' responsibility already. If they fail to abide by them now, they're going to fail to abide by them under the Companies Act.

A concern was expressed in two separate interviews that the increasing volume of legislation was designed to trap a small number of determined miscreants, who would disregard the rules in any event:

A director can't treat employees in a way that's outside the law. There's regulation about how you treat customers, sale of merchantable goods, how to treat creditors – there's a whole range of legislation that constrains how directors can run a business. In a sense, we are almost too constrained. We have to be answerable to the shareholders, but we have to run a business according to all these rules ... Most legislation is concerned to prevent the 5% or 4% or 3% of unscrupulous people in any walk of life, whether it be employers, trade unionists or whoever. 95%, 96%, 97% of people will behave in a reasonable manner according to the lights of the times that they live in ... The trouble is that all these laws are passed to try to trap the 5%. They don't trap the 5% because they still evade the law – I bet there are still plenty of employers paying less than the minimum wage in certain industries, though most of us are obeying the minimum wage law.

Expressing a similar view was this comment from another interview:

At the end of the day there are companies that behave very responsibly and companies that don't. I take the view that in all matters, including remuneration, 98% of directors and the companies try to do their job as well as they can, as efficiently as they can and with integrity and proper concern for all the groups of people involved. There's a very small percentage of boards that don't. One thing that's worried me over the years is that the press takes it the other way, that 98% are crooks and only 2% are decent human beings! ... Drawing up a tighter legal framework is not going to make a big difference, there's always going to be somebody who finds a way around everything. If you take directors' responsibilities, I don't know how many hundreds of pages they are, and I'd add that I take the view, which many others hold, that corporate governance has gone far too far. Company reports have reached the stage where most shareholders don't want 80 pages, we have to send out a condensed version ... I think it's just gone out of control and we should let things settle down.

More 'paperwork' that did not change the way people behaved in practice was, understandably, not wanted. There are, however, different ways of drafting rules and standards.

Four participants did feel that a recasting of directors' duties would be useful in various ways, so as more closely to reflect the reality of the way they carried on business and to make the board's obligations more transparent. As one director said:

> The issue really is whether one wants to have a restatement of the position to say that it is permissible, in exercising their functions, for directors to have regard, among other matters but not exclusively, to all these things. Employees, customers, suppliers, creditors ... the question is whether you need a statement that encapsulates that permissiveness, and I think the fear of many people is that if you do that it will lead to there becoming a duty to have regard to and commercial decisions will end up being the subject of constant attack and judicial review ... But it cannot be beyond the wit of man to develop a coherent statement of what the various factors that can be considered are and without imposing further duties on directors and without their commercial decisions being open to attack ... I think it's quite difficult logically to argue against this encapsulation in the Act if one accepts this is what happens, as long as you ensure this doesn't give rise to a whole series of enforceable duties. For example, if in reaching a decision the board had considered the interests of various stakeholders, would it be open at the current time for one of those groups too bring an action on the grounds that the directors were in breach of duty because they had given insufficient weight to one of those stakeholder groups? The answer must be: 'No'. So even if you put a statement in the law, it cannot be beyond the wit of man to create a statement that doesn't give rise to any litigation by those groups ... It wouldn't change the way things are done here ... You can only decide what's in the best interests of the company by having regard to the interests of all these different groups anyway.

It is far from easy to frame such responsibilities in primary legislation, as Chapter 5 discussed. The responsibility to the company as an institution is again emphasised in the following remarks from another interview:

> I don't want directors to be tied down to a checklist, but they need to have a framework, they need to understand their responsibilities. They need to realise that executives and non-executives are a team and they need to understand they have social and business responsibilities and I think that's the way they should be judged ... I think we want to see better management of our companies and then shareholder value will come naturally, rather than shareholder value by rape and pillage, which has often happened in the past when people have done the most cut throat things in order to achieve the most dazzling revenues ... There's a mortgaging of the future and a kind of fashion parade to sell it off at an inflated figure, which of course the company can't sustain. There are a lot of things like that which we should make sure can't happen ... The important thing about the social implications is that it should be – I won't say a legislated measure, but people should be aware they can expect to be judged on it. If your statement of account does not make any statement

relating to risk, which can relate to sexual harassment, unfair dismissal, environmental issues and so on – if you've not done that, I do think it's right that you should say: 'How have we allowed for this? These are the elements of new legislation which I do think are important.'

The view was reiterated in another interview that there need not be a conflict between directors' duties to the company and delivering value to the shareholders:

If you follow the model I was describing, doing the best for the company and taking into account the different stakeholders, whatever the law says, you'll still be arriving at the same decision. If you're looking at shareholder value, the best way to increase your shareholder value is to follow that process of doing what's best for the company. If you've got a stakeholder, say the employee, who doesn't like what you're doing to increase shareholder value, if you don't take that stakeholder view into account, at the extreme you're going to have a strike and that will affect your value. You've got to manage that stakeholder and that's the best way to maximise your shareholder value. It's for the Chairman and the Chief Executive to persuade the stakeholders that their decisions are for the benefit of the company and if it's for the benefit of the company it will also be for the benefit of shareholder value.

Another participant broadly agreed with this:

The directors' duties are owed to the company, but they're answerable to the shareholders in law. That's a subtle difference, but it's very important. The duties of directors are towards the future of the company, to keep it and make it prosper. Their duties are not owed to a particular body of shareholders who happen to be there today. They have to be accountable, but what they're accountable for is their stewardship of the company. I think you could define more closely what directors' duties are in the Act. I don't think there's any problem about that and I'm inclined to think that they should be defined. The Germans have no difficulty under their law in defining the duties of supervisory and management boards. I don't see any reason why we should have any difficulty in defining the duties of executive and non-executive directors. In practice there should be different duties of care. I would like to see duties of directors more clearly spelt out.

Striking an appropriate balance between helpful clarity and over-restrictive detail will not be easy. Most officers naturally wanted guidance rather than penalties.

A line was drawn by another director between assembling and 'streamlining' existing rules and adding new provisions to impose 'best practice':

If what it's doing is trying to assemble the range of publications there are in various other bits of law, then I think it's a good thing because it's important for everybody to understand where they are, not least directors themselves, because at times they're not clear as to what their responsibilities are ... In terms of additional legislation, ie additional burdens ... if they aim to reduce bad practice that's a very useful thing. I think the bulk of directors, while they would be nervous, would ultimately welcome that because directors have high standards and ideally don't want to suffer from those who feel they can abuse the system. On the other hand, if legislation means the opposite, which is encouraging high standards, then I think there is more of a problem ... You can legislate against bad practice more easily, but if you try to enforce high standards this is more problematic. I don't think any legislator is clever enough to be able to think of all the ways that a director can be good!

A similar distinction was made by another interviewee:

The problem you come up against in expressing responsibility to those groups is that you actually try to define it too carefully ... If you don't have good products, if you don't have customers, if you don't have good suppliers, never mind what the financial rules say, you have no business. The danger of having company law legislating these things is that I fear they might go down the financial route ... What I can see could be of some advantage, though it may make the whole thing more cumbersome, is if within company law you're able to pull together more of the legislation, but it has become so complex. Employment law alone is so complex, you need full time expertise on that. But the danger there is that company law is for companies, employment law is for sole traders, partnerships, companies, everyone. If you are actually going to pull all that together, you're going to end up with an unworkable solution. If you start looking at suppliers, you start talking about the legislation on payment of creditors. Shareholders' rights are encompassed within company law already. If you pull all that together, I just can't see how it's going to be a workable document.

Of changes to directors' duties in law, one director said:

In principle, no. I think it's in danger of its becoming a load of third way rubbish! I think there's a danger of fluffy thinking. I think one has to use shareholder priority as an effective way of focusing.

There are clear issues of practicality:

Can you imagine trying to write a statutory duty relative to customers? You do for customers what you have to do to win the business and keep the business. How would you legislate for that? It's the same for employees, you need to keep employees, you can't keep hiring new ones. Attrition, employee turnover, is one of the biggest costs companies have. Other than what you've already got on Health and Safety etc, how would you define a further contractual relationship?

It was somewhat predictable that officers of companies would be nervous about possible extension of their legal responsibilities. The fundamental division between the (relatively small) group who perceived themselves as agents of shareholders who in turn 'own' the company and those who took a more 'corporatist' view was again evident here. The logical outcome of pursuing the former position would be a reconsideration of cases that appear to have given priority to the company as an entity (rather than individual shareholders) and repeal (without replacement) of s 309 of the Companies Act 1985. Given that this course of action seems politically unacceptable in any event,[14] a pursuit of the more expressly stakeholder-inclusive statement of duties is seen by some company directors to be desirable, though the directors interviewed would resist any move to empower stakeholders to challenge board decisions in court. The current proposed Trial Draft Statutory Statement of Directors' Duties is something of a hybrid, encompassing an 'inclusive' statement of matters 'to which (a director) is to have regard' within a framework of shareholder primacy.[15] It is difficult to imagine such a compromise satisfying many of the parties concerned.

8.9 CHANGES TO BOARD STRUCTURE

Many of the directors and company secretaries interviewed were sceptical about any change and felt that the present (UK) board system was effective. For example:

> I think English company law works pretty well. It depends on the person, but it can be quite dangerous to have particular representation of groups on a board. Take worker representatives – are they representing their members or are they representing what's best for the company? I think it's difficult for employee representatives as they have in France and Germany to think: 'What is the best for the company?' because they're not there for the company, they're there to represent their particular stakeholder. I don't favour that ... In this country big companies operate on that dual level anyway. It's more structured on the continent, they would have levels of what can be decided by each board. In practice we have delegated financial authority ... Formalising it to comply with German law, for instance, which says: 'You must comply with this structure' doesn't make much difference.

Appropriate board size has been an issue for some public companies, as one interviewee noted:

> When we had the main board reduced in size we then set up a managing directorate which consists of the directors of all the trading operations with the managing directors of all the local companies. The group is not a board of directors as such, it's an operating group, and the Chief Executive of that group is on the main board. As it happens it's the Chairman, which is not necessarily an ideal situation, but that's how we have dealt with it. I am not a great believer in working on the basis of having such-and-such representation. Here we have meetings, we explain to people what's going on, we're perfectly open with them, and that is much better communication ... As soon as employees go on the board, they're not really employee representatives at all, they're directors, unless they're just sitting there as observers and I can't see any benefit in that at all. So no, I don't support that idea.

Some expressed their opposition to change more strongly:

I would firmly state that the longer we can avoid having supervisory boards the better. I think what we've got works well. You need to be able to work quickly and efficiently. I'm not convinced certainly from our experiences in Europe dealing with supervisory boards. The longer we can keep away from it the better! I have to be perfectly honest, I don't think (employee representation) is something I would relish. There are also questions of confidentiality.

Another example of such views came from a company secretary:

We've got direct experience of the split level board because we did have a large Dutch subsidiary until earlier this year and a German subsidiary before that, so we're quite used to dealing with supervisory boards and Works Councils. Having had that experience, we would all be unanimous in saying the UK system is considerably better. It's much easier for decisions to be made. Unfortunately the split-level system can really prolong timetables when in today's world, frankly, you often don't have a lot of time to make decisions. If an acquisition comes your way, you've got to get on with it ... We would be against introducing two-tier boards. The US structure, which is weighted towards non-executive directors, I suppose we almost reflect in the way we run this group at the moment, because we only have three executive directors and three non-executives. The three executive directors are the Chief Executive, the Finance Director and myself as Legal Director, so we're not typical.

Very uncompromisingly a director gave his view that:

Stakeholder representation at the board level would be an absolute catastrophe, because very few people who stakeholders would put in there would have the skills necessary to drive the business forward in the terms we've talked about. We talked about a small board of competent, knowledgeable, relevant people. Would you put in some kind of union representative and leave out the scientist or would you have 20 people on the board – what would you do? I know what Germany does and it's a farce, in as much as one board and the other board are hardly linked.

Two main concerns, then, appeared to be that representative directors would lack the necessary managerial skills and insofar as they were effective, this would be divisive. Neither of these necessarily follows from introducing a two-tier system, but obviously impressions were coloured by actual experience.

The issue of delay and time was raised again in another interview:

I have seen the two-tier board at work because our main German subsidiary is an AG listed on the Stock Exchange ... I think what happens is you get supervisory boards representing external interests, the banks and employees. They look at major financial matters like the annual budgeting process and statutory review and on the whole I think those matters are dealt with superficially ... You may have the Chief Executive there, but apart from that you've got nobody there who knows the business in detail, so when a budget comes up to them ... the chances are they will pass it through on the nod because they don't understand it ... Now under our system, with a unitary board meeting regularly, more often than supervisory boards, even our non-executive directors, who are selected for what they can bring to the company rather than because they work for a particular bank, have much more detailed knowledge of us as a company. Their backgrounds enable them to look sensibly at, for example, the budget and say: 'Do you really think you're going to achieve that sales growth? Are things as bad as your budgeting suggests? – in other words sensibly and actively and involvedly to raise questions on it ... I think it leads to quicker and more effective decision making to have that unitary structure. I have seen when we have been buying businesses on the continent that management can, maybe on occasion must, shelter behind their supervisory board. They say: Yes we have done a deal with you, but we'll have to refer it to the supervisory board and they next meet in ten weeks' time – sorry. ... I've seen that lead to some very lengthy negotiating procedures, transactions falling away.

A participant whose experience of the two-tier system in Germany and France had generally been more positive made the same point:

I found having those supervisory boards with employee participation did not stop us from doing what was right in the long-term for the business ... The way you manage those boards is critical. Openness of communication and the creation of trust facilitate those boards behaving in a constructive way. If you create an adversarial relationship, a union versus anti-union culture those boards aren't going to work so well, are they? In both France and Germany, there is a social context within which those boards operate. You can't just impose that kind of system without understanding the wider issues ... I think the role of the non-execs is ultimately to ensure that executive directors are acting in the interests of shareholders and, given what we were saying about safety and the environment, the non-execs ought to be the conscience of the management on those issues. It comes back to how you create shareholder value in the long term. Non-execs can ask those sorts of questions – 'Have you thought about your safety plans? Have you thought through the implications of what you're doing? How are you treating your employees? '– because that's good for the shareholder ... I don't think you need to impose the formality of a supervisory board with different representatives on it. One of the issues is that the more people you have to consult on decisions, the slower the decisions. It's almost axiomatic that it takes longer ... because if people represent their constituencies, they have to go back to their constituencies.

Looking from the outside, an interviewee commented that:

The German system sounds incredibly convoluted. Smart people I know from Germany say that you just have to go through the system in the right way and in the end you get what you want, it just takes longer. A lot of it is charade anyway, but it's got to be done. But if you look at the performance of German industry over the past five to six years, it's been pretty pedestrian.

The issue of board unity exercised two interviewees in particular. One commented:

> The way we work now is that employee representation on the board is through the Managing Director, customer representation is through the Marketing Director, and we have people who are responsible for the environment and suppliers ... By their very nature, people who get on the board are like-minded enough, or they wouldn't get on. There's a lot of criticism of 'old boy networks', that if you're a woman you won't get on the board, if you're a foreigner or if you've worked your way up from the factory floor you won't get on the board, and that's valid. I think we do need to have a debate on the board because I know people do say: 'That's terrible', but at the same time, when you look at the people who do get on the board they've already been pre-screened. This person, they might come up with ideas, they won't agree with everything that's there, but they're not going to drive us up the wall, they're not going to cause a great amount of disharmony or confrontation, because if you did that, you wouldn't get on the board.

The other participant who had similar views said:

> I personally think it's quite important that there must be an ultimate decision making entity that has the final 'yea' or 'nay'. I can see why some people will say that worker representation at board level is important, but I'm not sure I'm convinced by it. Your workforce is probably your most important asset and therefore a constructive relationship with them is essential to the business, but I think ultimately there has to be a board which is controlling and implementing the policies it deems to be appropriate for the business. In our own case, we're too small to have a two-tier board in any event. I can understand, if you have a thirty-thousand-man workforce, unionised, that some form of senior representation is important, but I still am not sure. I've not had practical experience of how they work, but I think my personal preference would be to see a single, responsible entity, a unitary board where ultimately the buck stops.

Criticism of the close-knit oligarchy featured in another analysis based on experience:

> As to different representation, I think there is some merit and a case to examine in Britain as to whether we should move to a two-tier board, a supervisory board which is responsible to shareholders and an operational board which has representation of stakeholders but must execute the policy of the supervisory board. There might well be a lot of logic in that ... It's interesting that these structures tend to come from the political system, so in America you have a President who executes and a supervisory board which plays the role of Congress. In fact, they often get hi jacked and you'll find that you have a Chief Executive who's President of the company and Chairman of the board, so what you really have is a dictator. I've seen many cases in many major American companies and I don't think it's very helpful! ... The real schism that exists currently among public company directors is between executives and non-executives, and we might eventually see a split. You might find that the executive board then brings in more of the stakeholder elements. One of the

problems with companies is that directors in effect elect themselves. You get the oligarchy back again, the old boy network.

One contributor expressed further concern about potential conflicts if different groups had board representation:

There's no question that an organisation constituted in that way would lead to an even more powerful board which was less accountable to anybody than the Chairman and the board currently are. We do have the problem of making the group accountable, as they currently in law are accountable, but making them accountable fully to the very large group outside which cannot act very easily to hold the board of directors to account. If you divide that group itself into these factions who are going to argue about how things are done, or you go for the Dutch style where the board is not responsible to any group, then you have conferred enormous authority on a group that is unaccountable ... One reason that's often given in favour of representation of additional groups on the board is that all additional information helps to make better decisions but that information comes anyway and you can draw in by whatever means are necessary. If the board is doing its job in a way which is as thorough and comprehensive as possible, it will want to consider information about the effects of its operation, insofar as the board itself is making those decisions that affect those constituencies. Another thing you need to bear in mind is that the kinds of decisions the board tends to make are the large-scale decisions, so very general decisions, and not the specifics. The board may make very general statements about how employees should be treated – those are statements of ethics, of fair practice and ethical principle. It's not ever going to get involved in setting the remuneration or the rewards, except for the CEO.

Another director was more relaxed about employee representation in principle but still had reservations about its practical effect:

Non-executives should just be independent, they should not be representatives of any particular group. I have no problem with the idea of worker-elected directors. I'm an advocate of a system of Works Councils. That's operated in the group for a long time, it's been very successful ... Anyone who takes the position of a worker director has to take on all the responsibilities of the other directors and take into account all the other aspects of the business, and I think some people find it quite difficult. When you do examine all the other business factors, it may not be easy to sell that to your electorate.

The issue of the role of non-executive directors is a crucial one, as the following response clearly shows:

The principle of having people from outside the company with other, wider experience and abilities is a good one. I personally think the British system is as good as or better than the supervisory board. America has a different system again. I think every system works in one degree or another, there are examples in every system where it works extremely well and examples where it has failed. I don't have a strong view as to whether the supervisory board is better than the unitary board, but certainly outside experience and involvement in discussion and debate is sound. I can't say I'm terribly impressed with the

German system and the idea that you should have a director who represents the workers' interests, because it seems to me that every member of the board should be seriously interested and involved in the workers' wellbeing because a satisfied, well-motivated staff is good for the board and the company. So I'm not at all convinced that you should have one person doing it. In fact I could make the argument that it would be to the detriment of the staff, because that single person would be isolated and seen as having only one point of view, the workers' point of view ... That type of board structure, I'm not in favour of, I'm against it.

A different perspective on this question was the following:

The advantage of our approach, of having executives and non-executives is that, albeit that company law has the illusion that we all have the same duties and responsibilities, in reality you have a bunch of, by definition, amateurs who come up to meetings six times a year while the rest of us work here every day of our lives and it's an illusion to pretend we're all doing the same thing. However that model which, albeit occasionally, has the two groups coming together as peers does optimise the engagement of the non-executives – I believe that if they're sitting as some abstract board, perhaps with the Chief Executive and people coming in to make presentations, they can't be as closely in touch with the reality and the complexities of the business and therefore can't add value to the business. I agree that you could say, they're different animals, some non-executives are clearly members of the great and good from outside, and they're really just representing external interests, whether that equates to shareholders or whoever, surely you should acknowledge that differentiation? I say 'No' to that, because all that does is to exacerbate the inherent difference between the two groups and after all, we're all trying to do the same thing. I think having execs and non-execs as an integrated board, albeit that it will only meet x times a year, increases the chances of a common understanding, by them of the business we run, and by us of where they're coming from and their perspective.

Whatever the legal structure, the implication of many of the discussions on this area seemed to be that directors who are not involved in day-to-day management will only influence the executives if the non-executives are perceived as having 'heavyweight' commercial experience (very often from a similar background). This may have consequences not only for 'stakeholders' but also for diversity policies generally.

Two directors, on the other hand, felt that supervisory board structures could or should be permitted, but ought not to be imposed, on UK public companies, and one went on:

I think the question of worker representation on boards is a quite different issue and one shouldn't muddle up the two. The reason it works reasonably in Germany is because it's part of a system where there are Works Councils and a whole atmosphere of what they call *Mitbestimmung* pervades the way in which it operates. I don't think that would suit the Anglo Saxons, but I can see that it is an alternative ... I can't see any reason why if a company wanted to run things that way it shouldn't do it. I certainly wouldn't impose it. If people hated it, they'd find a way round it ... The Germans manage to do a hell of a lot better in industrial terms than we do! You can't put that entirely down to the business structure ... but you can't say they've been held back by it! Non-executives if they're a decent bunch improve the whole process of decision making simply by being there. The executives have to analyse and explain what it is they propose to do and that in itself is beneficial. It makes people do their homework, it stops people shooting from the hip too much and occasionally their contribution is to get rid of the Chief Executive and replace him. Part of the time their job is to encourage the Chief Executive and the other executives who have a lonely task battling against their competitors and to back them up and inspire them ... Encouraging management in their entrepreneurial efforts, driving the business forward, is a very important function.

Arguing more forcefully in favour of allowing, not compelling, different structures, another director said of introducing supervisory boards:

If one company feels it's in their interests to do that, fine, but don't make everybody do it. If you lay down certain ways things should be done, you might well miss something someone's doing that's very successful, that works for them. I think it would be much better if you put duties on boards and let them sort out the best way to accommodate those duties. I would be in favour of ruling out nothing, but not compelling a particular framework. Large companies may have a board with a majority of non-executive directors, which in a way is like having a supervisory board, and then there's day to day management that goes on underneath that. Smaller companies probably do it all in one. We for example have two non-executive directors. They do the job with informal consultation and formal board meetings on a regular basis in which the non-execs provide a balance to us ... I would be sorry to see legislation which forced us to run our business in a particular way.

The effectiveness and efficiency of the process were the key point for many contributors, as this extract from an experienced executive who now holds non-executive director posts shows:

My view is that I want a mechanism that works, that allows the greatest interaction so we actually know what's going on. Our system is quite good provided you've got the right representation and the right mechanism. One of the dangers is that you can have a group management board and the plc board, which involves the non-executives, doesn't really have any involvement with that – it may be management by seeing the bits of paper ... I don't mind what the structure is. A team should be open, it should have well-defined roles and responsibilities, it should have well-defined review procedures and the interactions should involve customers, shareholders as well as employees. All of these things are important.

There was, then, generally strong resistance to any imposition of a representative or two-tier board structure for UK public companies. This came both from those who are strongly of the view that shareholders 'own' (and hence should control) public companies and those who believe that directors should aim to balance the interests of different groups and come to conclusions in the interests of the business as a whole. Direct board representation is one way of dealing with involvement from stakeholders, as an alternative to either informal channels or legal rights to challenge decisions *ex post facto*. Of these options, however, stakeholder board membership raised the most objections from current public company officers. Concerns about speed and efficiency were raised as described above. It was acknowledged that supervisory boards or non-executive director majorities might work well in other jurisdictions and might even be worth trying in UK organisations,[16] but the consensus was very firmly against any compulsory change to UK board structure.

8.10 CONCLUSION

One senior manager from a major accountancy firm expressed scepticism when the project was mentioned that one could obtain 'sensible' answers regarding governance questions 'except at the very top' (that is, the very largest companies). Happily, this proved not to be the case. Most people, particularly further down the public company 'pecking order' were, as he put it, 'too busy worrying about whether they'll have a business next year'. Yet, as Hampel says, good governance is as important for smaller companies as for the largest. Legislation which helps to promulgate the most effective practice is surely to be welcomed, rather than feared. It would assist directors in their dealings with investors and with employees to highlight board responsibility for the corporation as an entity.

The task of those in senior positions in business is to articulate a clear vision of the organisation's goals and ethos. The modern so-called 'triple bottom line' of social and environmental value and financial performance will concern ever-increasing numbers of employees, customers and shareholders.[17] If the law does not reflect this reality, it will be out of line with real boardroom life.[18] As many of the interviewees acknowledged, corporate reputation provides the direct link between treatment of stakeholders and profitability. Information is more open and accessible today than ever before. This means that consistency of approach and ethics are also more important than ever. Whether operating globally, nationally or locally, a favourable

---

14 Company Law Review Steering Group, *Modern Company Law for a Competitive Economy – The Strategic Framework*, February 1999, pp 41–42.

15 Company Law Review Steering Group, n 13 above, paras 3.37–3.82.

image with the public who are potential consumers and employees and investors is a valuable, if fragile, asset. Directors are responsible for protecting it.

There are pressures from consumers and employees – and perhaps more importantly potential consumers and employees of particular companies – towards 'corporate social responsibility.' Such 'responsibility' embraces not only donations and 'peripheral' corporate activity, but also the manner in which core business is actually carried out. As Ridderstrale and Nordstrom, authors of the popular *Funky Business*, put it (in typically colourful language):

> All things being equal, the caring capitalist will always beat the evil enterprise. The Body Shop's Anita Roddick created a temporary monopoly from the simple idea that there was a market for cosmetics that had not been tested on animals and which only contained natural ingredients. Companies increasingly want to appear caring. For example, the automotive company Toyota is currently developing trees that absorb toxic gases.[19]

There were some differences between directors working in different sectors, in that, for example, those involved in retailing were more customer-centred and high-technology industries depend on skilled staff. Any new legal regime would therefore need to be sufficiently flexible to take variations of approach into account. Difficulties in pinning down responsibilities to multiple stakeholders in legislation were also pointed out by many of the interview subjects. At the same time, almost all claimed to be aware of the needs and demands of shareholders, employees and customers and the wider community in their own organisations. Negotiation with stakeholder groups in the context of reviewing existing businesses and new opportunities can fit with the UK culture. Even if they appear to impose greater regulation, UK legal rules might enhance competitiveness if they did further this approach.

It was notable that views expressed in interview did not always accord with those set out in the corporate literature. The participants were speaking in a personal capacity and giving their own opinions frankly. Where large public companies have Codes of Practice, this highlights the fact that they have sometimes been written by public relations departments. Voluntary action is inadequate to produce consistent results from all major companies. Existing legislation on employment issues and the environment have, however, changed attitudes and enforced new practice. There is no reason to doubt that broader-ranging new duties with an enforcement mechanisms (discussed in Chapters 5 and 6) would change the conduct and focus of boards.

The question then arises as to the role of the nation state in the modern world. Many companies, like individuals, feel under intense pressure as competition speeds up. The state can act as a mediator and an enabler, rather

---

16 Company Law Review Steering Group, *Modern Company Law for a Competitive Economy*

than a 'threat' to business. Noting these stresses, David Howell, a former Conservative Minister, comments:

Something is missing between the two new trends [of globalization and localization], both of them fraught with enormous dangers. A restraining middle way, a moderating concept between the excesses of localization, with its potential for anarchic fragmentation and extremism and the excesses of globalization, with its potential for the over-centralization of remote and unaccountable power, is clearly required ... So if not our old friend the sovereign nation state, for all its faults and weaknesses, then what? Could it be that the old scale – larger than the tribe or region, smaller than the world – still fits, but that the state has come to mean something different from the traditional hierarchical image of central authority?[20]

Clearly no definitive conclusions can be drawn from meeting with such a small sample of public company officers. Strong impressions were, however, formed in the course of the first two meetings and reinforced by later interviews. Many of the directors felt that the dichotomy posited in the DTI's *Company Law Strategic Framework* document between shareholder value (no one objected to 'enlightenment'!) and 'pluralism' was false, as the only way to deliver strong and sustainable returns to shareholders was to pay attention to all stakeholders, particularly customers, employees and suppliers but also the natural and social environment. This was so even though many (about half, in the writer's impression) of the participants would have been mildly or very sceptical about the use of 'stakeholding' language. They nevertheless were **personally committed to employees and customers and business relationships.** Several of them also made the point that the demands of the market, and particularly institutional shareholders, constrained the board's freedom of action. It was said that new rules to give other stakeholders more attention would have to be accompanied by a cultural change on the part of major shareholders. If new statements and duties in company law helped to achieve this, many of the public company directors and secretaries who were interviewed would approve of them.

Public company directors, on the evidence collected in these meetings, well understand that their primary responsibility is to develop and maintain the business for the long-term. The extent to which they feel able, in practice, to do this depends on the demands of finance providers. In the real public company boardroom, no director can operate without reference to customers, employees and suppliers and the world outside the company. Institutional investors are beginning to appreciate that their interests as providers of

– *The Strategic Framework*, February 1999, pp 45–46.

17 Elkington, J and Fennell, S, 'Can Business Leaders Satisfy the Triple Bottom Line?' (1998) 1 Visions of Ethical Business 34.

18 Chandler, G, 'Annual General Meeting of X plc, May 2005: The Chairman's Speech – A Vision' (1998) 1 Visions of Ethical Business 18.

pension payments and insurance cover, often 30 and sometimes up to 50 years hence, coincide with those of the companies in which they invest.[21] John Monks, general secretary of the TUC, has called for a new approach of industrial partnership to recognise stakeholder interests and align the interests of employees as employees with those of employees as consumers and investors.[22] It seems that many leaders of major businesses would not fundamentally disagree with this, while many of them would emphasise commitment to their customers and the community where they operate, as well as the vital importance of meeting shareholder expectations.

19   Ridderstrale, J and Nordstrom, K, *Funky Business*, 1999, p 236.

CHAPTER 9

CONCLUSION: THE FUTURE
OF UK COMPANY LAW

9.1 'THE BUSINESS OF BUSINESS'

There is widespread acknowledgment, noted in Chapters 4 and 8, that if it is to become and remain a thriving business enterprise, a public company needs to do three (possibly four) closely interrelated things: to produce competitive returns for shareholders, to satisfy its customers in order to produce those profits and to recruit and motivate excellent employees (and, where appropriate, build successful relationships with suppliers) so as to achieve those goals. Several of the public company directors and secretaries interviewed for this study also commented that they needed to operate, and to be seen to be operating, in a way that was acceptable to society, not least because otherwise, there was the threat of yet more legislation. Many of them regarded attention to these issues as simply matters of 'common sense' or suggested that consideration of primary stakeholders was implicitly required by current company law and regulation. However, there was some recognition that a change in company law might help to alleviate misunderstandings of what was required and foster good practice on the part of corporate leaders who might otherwise conduct business in a less desirable manner. Corporate reputation in this way provided the link between ethics and profitability. This concluding chapter will explore the economic implications of potential new legislation and the form any new rules might take.

Another driver for change in management has been the concept of the 'balanced scorecard' as a measure of a company's overall performance, which has been taken up by several major organisations in one form or another.[1] Some have begun producing separate environmental and social reports in addition to their statutory financial reports. Others choose to include information as to social and environmental activity and impacts within their mainstream annual reports.[2] This development is evidently seen as important for optimum corporate performance in the new economy and recognises that many stakeholders may use the information published by public companies.

---

1 Kaplan, R and Norton, D, 'The Balanced Scorecard: Measures that Drive Performance' (1992) Harvard Business Review 280.
2 Major international organisations such as BP, Shell, BT and Cable & Wireless have produced separate documents while British household names such as Tesco and Marks & Spencer use their annual reports; organisations such as the Co-operative Bank and Traidcraft have been pathfinders in 'Partnership' or 'Stakeholder' reporting.

As long as publication of such social and environmental information remains voluntary, both the form and content of reporting will continue to vary widely. In the interests of 'levelling the playing field', the DTI Company Law Review Steering Group sets out a possible form of Operating and Financial Review for public companies.[3]

As the private sector continues to participate in an increasing number of activities that were once the domain of government, the 'partnership' approach between public agencies and corporations[4] is likely to grow in importance. The rigid separation between the domain of 'business people' who are interested only in profit and that of 'public servants' who are concerned solely with service provision is dissolving. Continental Europe and to some extent the United States have long had cultures that encourage the brightest and best individuals to move between industry and government service. There are indications of a similar trend in the UK,[5] which should begin to dispel some misunderstandings between the two sectors. Where formerly public functions have been transferred to private companies, the consequence for directors in practice has been heavier regulation and a higher public profile than the previous management. By widening the UK shareholder base, privatisations have brought about greater scrutiny of the public company sector, with consequences the architects of government privatisation policies may not have foreseen.[6]

Where major companies choose to be socially and environmentally active, they are increasingly looking to tie their efforts to key areas of their commercial operations and to gain public approval, and sometimes political capital, by their discretionary expenditure. As central and local government seeks to manage, rather than to supply, key services, those organisations that are seen to have contributed positively to the wider community will have an advantage in demonstrating that they can deliver all-round 'Best Value'.[7] Governmental bodies, in turn, can attract and maintain major investment by managing the provision of infrastructure and an attractive environment. More generally, better education, improved health of the workforce and regeneration of deprived urban and rural areas help to improve both productivity and markets. Profit over the long term for shareholders, many of

3   Company Law Review Steering Group, *Modern Company Law for a Competitive Economy – Final Report*, July 2001, Chapter 8.

4   See for example the Consultation Paper *Modernising Social Services* (1998) and plans for the public-private partnership to fund modernisation of the London Underground system.

5   The Cabinet Office, for example, has established a senior-level secondment exchange scheme between business and the Civil Service.

6   Geddes, R, 'Ownership, Regulation and Managerial Monitoring in the Electric Utility Industry' (1997) 40 Journal of Law and Economics 261.

7   As local authorities are required by Part I of the Local Government Act 1999 (which came into force on 1 April 2000) to provide.

whom will be institutions representing individual savers, is compatible with tackling these issues. Indeed investors themselves are increasingly looking to optimise the long-term benefit of their investments.[8]

What has recently become known as 'brand value' (aptly defined by Stephen Bayley, former Creative Director of the Millennium Dome, as: 'that intangible, but valuable mixture of associations and expectations that all successful products carry')[9] is a key component in public company success or failure. The main point for contemporary business is that products that match their advertising and deliver good value can only meet these expectations. At much the same time as Bayley's words appeared, Unilever, one of the largest multinational organisations, announced plans to focus its efforts on 400 of its 1,600 global brands.[10] Another Anglo-Dutch behemoth, Royal Dutch-Shell, has taken some time (and considerable attention to matters of corporate governance) to recover from damage to its reputation and 'brand value'.[11] Journalist Naomi Klein's best-selling book *No Logo* criticises holders of some of the best-known global brands, including Nike and McDonalds, for exploiting workers, consumers, the environment and the communities in which they operate.[12] More positively, in *The Future of Brands*, Clifton and Maughan comment: 'The term 'stakeholder brands' ... suggests a 'third way' for brand futures that reflects political trends: capitalism with a strong social agenda.'[13]

On the global scale, Castells gives a reminder that between 1995 and 1999, the top five growth stocks in the Standard and Poor's index were Dell Computer, Cisco Systems, Sun Microsystems, Qualcomm and Charles Schwabb, all companies that are building their business around the internet. He comments: 'Internet stock frenzy is in fact an indicator of the decisive shift of the economy to the new sources of value and growth.'[14] The so-called 'new economy' makes finance, employment, products and supplies more unpredictable. Adaptability demands quick responsiveness to changes in the demands of stakeholders, customers, employees and others. Many will choose to list on stock exchanges in the United States, in London and in Tokyo, so

---

8   This concern with the 'long-term' and an inclusive approach is reflected in the Company Law Review Steering Group's draft statement of directors' duties above fn 3, Annex C, but without sanctions to back the exhortations.

9   Bayley, S, 'Hallelujah! Praise the Brand' (2000) 169 Blueprint 40, 41.

10 Roddick, A and Roddick, G, 'Shell Still has Much to Do', *The Guardian*, 18 September 2000; Gow, D, 'Fuel Gauge: Shell Profits Back on Track', *The Guardian*, 11 February 2000.

11 Finch, J, 'Unilever Washes Hands of 1,200 Brands', *The Guardian*, 22 September 1999; Doward, J and Islam, F, 'Household Names Face Axe as Unilever Slims Down', *The Guardian*, 26 September 1999.

12 Klein, N, *No Logo: Taking Aim at the Brand Bullies*, 2000.

13 Clifton, R and Maughan, E, *The Future of Brands*, 2000, p 106.

14 Castells, M, 'Information Technology and Global Capitalism' in Hutton, W and Giddens, A, *On the Edge: Living with Global Capitalism*, 2000, pp 52, 63.

that their shares can be traded for 24 hours a day around the globe. High standards of information and administration are required to serve the needs of new and growing 'high-tech' companies.

As far as setting board structures for UK public companies in the light of these challenges is concerned, when the Hampel Report stated that: 'there is no support (among UK business leaders) for the unitary board', it conflated two issues that can better be considered separately. There is indeed little evidence of support for 'constituency' representation in UK public companies. In practice, executive and non-executive functions are separated into different board committees, with the executive often having to 'sell' ideas to the non-executives and expecting to account to them for the execution of plans. It is also regarded as important by many directors that the board, while taking responsibility for the future and development of the whole business, should have among its members individuals with good knowledge of the key stakeholders who can alert all directors to their concerns. The European Works Council model of employee representation will gradually become familiar in Britain and consumers' organisations continue to develop their brand of activism. Awareness of the importance of those specific groups, in particular, can be expected to spread even to public companies that have so far resisted 'stakeholder' or 'inclusive' approaches.

A new statement of directors' duties (as part of a new Companies Act in due course) is recommended, as explained in Chapter 5 above, in order to spell out the internal and external zones of responsibility of public company directors in this changing environment. This would help to shift the balance of power in the relationship between public company executives and major institutional investors. It would be ineffectual, particularly in organisations where it might have most impact on managerial viewpoints, if there were not sanctions as a last resort to require public company directors to take proper account of the requirements of their main participants. It is therefore recommended, in Chapter 6 above, that the primary stakeholders in public companies should have a legal right of action (by analogy with the statutory right of action for shareholders under s 459 of the Companies Act 1985) if they can show that they have suffered unfair prejudice as a result of directorial decisions. In addition, it needs to be clear in company law that directors do have the right to consider such matters as the natural environment and the wider community. That would make it all the more important to have a diverse range of people of appropriate calibre and experience on public company boards.

9.2 ECONOMIC EFFECTS OF LEGISLATION

While governments have increasingly used cost–benefit analysis to assess proposed legislation in recent years, Ogus argues that their techniques have been unsophisticated and insensitive to many important issues.[15] The 'Law and Economics' approach and body of scholarship, he adds, has much to contribute to the debate. Regulators aim to govern the prices charged by firms that are natural monopolies, so as to secure the maximum 'social surplus' from the organisation's activities and distribute it between consumers and shareholders as they see fit.[16] The motivation and control of managers who may have their own agenda in running a company, distinct from that of the shareholders or other interested parties, is another problem that economic analysis has addressed.[17]

Several major sectors of the economy are not correctly or appropriately valued by the free market, including healthcare and education, basic research and public infrastructure projects, as political economist Robert Kuttner points out. In addition, airlines, railways, power companies and telecommunications are prone to monopoly pricing in the absence of substantial regulation.[18] National governments therefore still have an important role to play in balancing reasonable profit with social value. There will also be an important place for international regulations to entrench environmental, employment and social standards, firstly, across Europe, secondly throughout the industrialised world, and as an ultimate goal, for all nations.[19]

English commercial law as a discipline arose out of the common law contractual tradition which, unlike civil law, does not recognise the duty of 'bargaining in good faith', nor indeed the enforceability of promises not secured by consideration. Nevertheless, equity and statute law have increasingly sought to protect the expectations of contracting parties and those whose bargaining position was perceived to be relatively weak. In the employment context, UK law has long ago left behind the notion that freedom of contract between employees and workers is sufficient and that government therefore should not intervene.[20] In the consumer area, too, there is

---

15 Ogus, AI, 'Regulatory Appraisal: A Neglected Opportunity for Law and Economics' (1998) 6 European Journal of Law and Economics 53.

16 Salanie, B, *The Economics of Contracts*, 1997, pp 41–42 discusses the problem in theoretical terms.

17 *Ibid*, pp 138–39.

18 Kuttner, R, 'The Role of Governments in the New Economy' in Hutton and Giddens, n 14 above, pp 147, 154.

19 Ball, R, 'Making Accounting More International: Why, How and How Far Will It Go?' in Rutterford, J, *Financial Strategy: Adding Stakeholder Value*, 1998; FT.com site, 'Big Win Hangs in the Balance for Accountants', 6 June 2000.

20 The latest scheme of regulation is set out in the Employment Relations Act 1999.

substantial legal regulation.[21] As the market has inexorably extended its reach, especially throughout the 1980s, there has also been a demand for more 'active government', more particularly in the late 1990s. This extends to regulation and governance of the largest businesses including public limited companies. A common justification for its introduction is so-called 'market failure' as a result of lack of perfect information or barriers to entry. Benington aptly observes that: 'In the 1990s thinking has tended to move beyond ... polarisation and demarcation between public and private sectors, market and state, to recognise both the interdependencies and the blurring of the boundaries between the two.'[22]

Considerations of 'economic efficiency' in law are increasingly influential in debates about legal reform. If the law provides a framework to structure enforcement of bargains and to reduce transaction costs, it is seen as economically beneficial. The idea of efficient resource allocation according to utilitarian goals is prioritised.[23] Such definitions of efficiency are not, however, value-free.[24] Many of the changes in the Employment Relations Act 1999, for example, were introduced despite initial opposition from business leaders. The UK government has declared that, particularly where privatised utilities are concerned, but also in regulation of businesses such as banks and supermarkets, it wishes to end what the Chancellor of the Exchequer and the Secretary of State for Trade and Industry called 'rip-off Britain'.[25] A balance of public services and regulated markets 'serving the common good' is a declared political objective of the Labour Party, stated in its constitution. That there should be some connection between access to funds by public offerings and corporate accountability and responsibility seems a proposition that is difficult to refute in principle.

Much regulation of business is of course separate from company law, being found, for example, in specific employment and environmental rules that apply not only to companies, but also to partnerships and sole traders. Pressures for more extensive and specific regulation are likely to increase in the absence of renewed trust in business and business leaders. It would be more congenial to many such leaders to examine these matters in the context of the long-term success of the business. A requirement to create a balance of interests makes running a corporation complex but beneficial to society at large. The Turnbull Committee's recent accounting guidelines were concerned

---

21 See eg the Sale of Goods Act 1979, the Supply of Goods and Services Act 1984 and the Consumer Protection Act 1987.

22 Benington, J, 'Risk and Reciprocity: Local Governance Rooted in Civil Society' in Coulson, A, *Trust and Contracts*, 1998, p 227 at p 231.

23 Maughan, CW and Copp, SF, 'Company Law Reform and Economic Methodology Revisited' (2000) 21 Co Law 14, 18.

24 *Ibid*, 20.

25 See eg speeches by Gordon Brown and Stephen Byers in September 1999 at the Labour Party Annual Conference.

with the management of risk and recommended that directors should confirm in their Annual Reports that their companies had a sound system for 'identifying, evaluating and managing the company's key risks'.[26] This will encompass full acknowledgment and awareness of the connections between environmental and social issues and 'bottom line' business performance.

The Combined Code, which in turn encompasses the recommendations of the Hampel and Greenbury Committees, is now part of the Listing Rules.[27] This does not go as far as many of the most radical commentators on corporate governance issues would have wished. For example, it does not make institutional shareholder voting compulsory, nor does it do more than urging 'progress towards' one-year service contracts for directors. It gives no right for shareholders to vote on the board's remuneration report or on reward packages for individual directors. It does, however, consolidate the position of non-executive directors and standardise the arrangement whereby different people must occupy the positions of chairman and chief executive unless some good reason to the contrary is adduced. The importance of independence of non-executives is reinforced by their role as set out in the Combined Code.

The major public companies (in the FTSE 100 and FTSE 250 indexes) are best able to absorb the costs of additional regulation, since they can afford to employ the people to deal with it, as officers from both ends of the public company spectrum pointed out. Establishing sound managerial principles and systems of governance is, however, just as important for smaller public companies as for the largest. If choice and competition are regarded as good in most business decisions, facilitating different board structures so that their results can be assessed would seem to be a logical step, and it is one the Company Law Review's Strategic Framework mentions as a possible option. A fair and open stock market for trading also demands full and equitable disclosure of relevant factors affecting business success. There seems to be a general consensus emerging, albeit with important differences of tone, that relationships with primary stakeholders fall in to this category. The Company Law Review Steering Group reflects this in its comments about reporting standards and the proposals for the new Operating and Financial Review.

Shocking incidents that have caused critics to call the corporate form itself 'potentially criminogenic' (even when the individuals involved thought of themselves as law-abiding) include the P&O *Herald of Free Enterprise* disaster[28] and the rail crashes at Clapham and Paddington, as well as cost–benefit analysis of car and drug safety effectively balancing profits against the lives of

---

26 All UK listed companies have been required by the Stock Exchange to comply with these general standards since 1999.

27 It is published as an Appendix to the Listing Rules.

28 Slapper, G and Tombs, S, *Corporate Crime*, 1999, p 149.

consumers.[29] Those at the centre of such large organisations need to take responsibility for the establishment of systems to ensure that fiscal, social, environmental, health and safety and consumer regulations are properly respected. Cultural change within such bodies is perhaps the single most powerful preventative agent against serious wrongdoing. Company law can send out important signals about managerial responsibilities to those who would not consider themselves as subjects of criminal law.[30] More active and vigilant customers and suppliers and empowered employees are a line of defence against criminality that arises from systemic failure rather than deliberate acts of individuals. If they were given sufficient influence to challenge the financial priorities of the board, they could have a salutary effect on the conduct of public companies.

9.3 THE UK COMPANY LAW REVIEW PROCESS

It appears to have been recognised early in the Labour government's term of office (from 1997) that there would not be time during that term to pilot complex companies legislation through Parliament. It was decided to make a virtue of the necessity of a wait of several years for new legislation and to instigate a thorough process of review. During that process, the government's relationships with business and with prominent businesspeople – from Bernie Ecclestone of Formula One motor racing and the controversy over tobacco advertising, via Richard Branson who in the public's perception failed to make his Virgin Trains run on time and lost his National Lottery gamble, to the Hinduja brothers and the passport application that toppled Peter Mandelson – has been responsible for many of its most dangerous media storms. It will be interesting to see whether the second-term Labour administration, will want to change the terms of its relationship with the private sector or distance itself from those links.

The input of highly respected Non-Governmental Organisations (NGOs) such as Oxfam, Traidcraft Exchange, Amnesty International and War on Want demonstrates that the Review has to some extent succeeded in its aim of extending the debate beyond the confines of 'City' institutions and corporations. It is recognised that the operation of business has a direct impact beyond the executives and investment managers, and even beyond employees and customers of corporations. NGOs and others are highlighting the broader issues in a constructive manner. The fundamental tension is between those

---

29   *Ibid*, p 141.
30   Ferrarese, MR, 'An Entrepreneurial Conception of the Law? The American Model through Italian Eyes' in Nelken, D, *Comparing Legal Cultures*, 1997, p 157, provides an interesting perspective.

who see the company as a means for economic ends alone and those who view public companies as social actors. With a UK government that is keen to engage with business but also wishes to address the concerns of the trade unions and has highlighted consumer interests and difficulties faced by small suppliers, any simple 'profit maximisation' *dictum* will not suffice. Attempting to move towards a consensus has been a slow process[31] and the overall result must be examined for its coherence and workability.

The response from the DTI has been cautious. As far as the international standing of UK company law is concerned, the DTI have had some concern that other common law jurisdictions had 'left the UK behind' in their modernisation and streamlining of company codes, Canada and New Zealand being regarded with particular favour. Less familiar traditions such as those of continental Europe are regarded with greater scepticism, if not outright distrust. Institutional frameworks and ideology are important in defining regulatory restraints.[32] For example in the discussion of 'The Scope of Company Law', the Steering Group contrasted 'Enlightened Shareholder Value' with 'Pluralism' (essentially the 'stakeholding' or 'inclusive' approach). Ferran remarks: 'responses in the media to the publication of the first consultation document (in February 1999) tended to favour the view that discussion of the Pluralist approach was probably included precisely in order for it to be shot down',[33] though she acknowledges that enhanced reporting obligations may go some way to deal with 'Pluralist' objections.

There is a danger that the quality of the final legislative product could be adversely affected by the fact that the Company Law Review adopted a narrow, traditional 'core company law' focus. The whole debate about the parties to whom directors should owe their responsibilities was excluded from the Review's original statement of its objectives. This was despite the acknowledgment that the current s 309 needed to be retained or replaced if the impression of retrograde motion was to be avoided. The further step which was surely quite logical – namely questioning whether employees and shareholders alone should have a privileged position in this respect and why employees should not be allowed to bring actions on their own account – was ignored (or side-stepped). The desirability in principle of employees and the major customers and suppliers having a place in board decisions fits with management priorities in real public companies. There are, however, many possible methods of achieving this effect in law.

The principle for the new Companies Act of 'think small first' (that is, concentrating on material which will be suitable for 'close' private companies

---

31 The Steering Group submitted a final report to the Secretary of State for Trade and Industry in July 2001.

32 Haag, G, 'Theories on the Economics of Regulation: A Survey of the Literature from a European Perspective,' (1997) 4 European Journal of Law and Economics 337.

33 Ferran, E, *Company Law and Corporate Finance*, 1999, p 642.

as the default option and adding the provisions for public companies separately) means that additional matters applicable only to public companies should be clearly identifiable. 'Core' company law is never likely to encompass more than a broad-brush outline of accounting and reporting responsibilities. Accounting standards are sophisticated and change with developing business priorities and technologies. Nor is it foreseeable that the influence over composition and membership of listed company boards would be removed from the listing authority (the Financial Services Authority). The expertise required within the top management of a publicly held corporation could usefully be broadened so as to affirm that, to give two examples, employee relations in a 'people' business and supplier links in manufacturing are an essential part of the corporation. The law needs to reflect this commercial reality.

The quality and quantity of representations and comments made to the DTI have an impact on the prospects for reform. After a sluggish start to the public dialogue, there are some encouraging signs in this regard and the latest major consultation document shows the influence of some of the submissions. The political task is to ensure that the opinions of all relevant groups are taken into account and integrated into a coherent whole. The style of any new legislation may be more purposive and accessible than previously, nor could it be expected that purely technical and specific regulation would last the necessary period of time.[34] The majority of the responses received to the Consultation Document published by the Company Law Review Steering Group dealt in some manner with the issue of the scope of company law. Not surprisingly, those who are not usually engaged in dealing with the technicalities of company law, such as the social and environmental NGOs, are most inclined to express their views on the principles that should underlie corporate reform (the so-called 'scope' question).[35]

Dr Cento Veljanovski, a leading commentator on law and economics, points out: 'In practice, it is astounding how rarely lawyers and civil servants are prepared to state clearly the goal of a law or to assess the extent to which specific laws have achieved their intended results.'[36] The law is regarded by economists, as Veljanovski puts it, as a 'giant pricing machine' that imposes 'constraints and penalties that alter the net benefits of different courses of action' and thus influences behaviour.[37] It seems intuitively much more plausible that people acting in a business capacity would be guided by a rational cost-benefit analysis than that individuals about to embark on a

---

34 DTI Consultation Paper, *Modern Company Law for a Competitive Economy*, March 1998, para 1.5.

35 DTI, *Summary of Responses to the Consultation Document*, published by the Company Law Review Steering Group, December 1999.

36 Veljanovski, C, *The Economics of Law*, 1990, p 36.

37 *Ibid*, p 87.

criminal act of violence, for example, would be deterred by possible penalties. It is, however, for Parliament as a democratic political body to set the results it wishes to attain by using these tools. The DTI commissioned empirical research focusing on the needs and views of entrepreneurs and finance providers (both shareholders and to a lesser extent lenders, particularly banks).[38] The fact that others, including employees and customers but also representatives of the environment and society, may have different interests in and concerns about corporations is not expressly acknowledged within the research programme or by the DTI.

9.4 THE COMPANY LAW REVIEW – POSSIBLE OUTCOMES

One danger of a review over a long period of time, carried out by disparate groups of people, is that the results may end up as a melange of ideas included to accommodate a range of interest groups, with no one taking responsibility for the coherence of the product. Furthermore, as the European Union's experience has amply demonstrated, where there is no agreement on the fundamental principles underlying law reform, it is extremely difficult to reach any consensus on the details. The DTI's concepts of 'modernising' the law and ensuring that the UK is 'competitive' remain helpful in a general sense but somewhat vague. As any awareness of the German, Japanese and US corporate systems indicates, many different 'modern' structures have succeeded in producing successful businesses. The UK has always been in the position of needing to decide where its own loyalties and priorities lie, given its strong links to Europe, the Commonwealth and North America. If it can harness the economic dynamism that comes from relatively light regulation to deliver the avowed political ends of greater fairness and sustainability, it will have achieved some of the best of all worlds.

As Deakin and Michie note, game theory in economics predicts that: 'unfettered competition may not be welfare-maximising' and 'regulatory intervention may increase economic welfare'.[39] More generally, they acknowledge the strong argument that: 'a contract which is optimal from the point of view of the immediate parties to the transaction may have sub-optimal effects for society as a whole'.[40] The authors also point out that nexus-of-contract theory is unrealistic in some key respects: '[T]he theory acknowledges that constraints on information exist at the level of the principal's capacity to observe the agent's characteristics and behaviour, but takes little account of the transaction costs of designing and implementing the

---

38 Company Law Review Steering Group, *Modern Company Law for a Competitive Economy – Developing the Framework*, March 2000, Chapter 11.

39 Deakin, S and Michie, J, *Contracts, Co-operation and Competition*, 1997, p 9.

40 *Ibid*, p 7.

incentive structures which contracts are understood to embody.'[41] This is written in the context of a discussion on the trade-off between formal contracts, co-operation and competition, but could equally well apply to those who argue that the company is simply a 'nexus of contracts' and that directors are solely agents of shareholders. Deakin, Lane and Wilkinson assert that institutional structures are fundamentally important, given the significant failures of market contracting. Such legal frameworks are not a substitute for, but should be a support for, trust and specific long-term relationships, which are also economically important.[42]

Several of the public company officers in interviews conducted for this study adverted to the fact that they were faced with a plethora of specific 'constituency' legislation. Environmental protection, for example, was subjected to a comprehensive regime of rules by comprehensive UK legislation in 1990. Employment law was developing under the Employment Relations Act 1999 in a direction more favourable to workers than had been seen since the 1970s, while consumers enjoyed legal protection of a high order. Perhaps the missing piece of the puzzle was stronger legal enforcement in the UK of the agreements and relationships between suppliers and purchasers. There was general agreement that it was impossible to legislate for and enforce corporate responsibility to the wider community.[43] Given that consideration of all of these groups was essential to sound directorial thinking, to legislate for an appropriate balance so as to locate the other major pieces of legislation in a comprehensible structure was regarded by many as a laudable aim.

Greater flexibility and lack of prescriptiveness have been cited as the advantages of 'best practice' and 'codes', as opposed to legislation. Where a company competes with another enterprise that is not adhering to the same standards of accountability and governance, it faces unequal, arguably 'unfair', competition. In order to enjoy the advantages of limited liability and public status, a company needs to be prepared to undertake corresponding obligations. These should be debated and their parameters set in the political arena, rather than inside the Stock Exchange or the Financial Services Authority. The 'professionalization' of the directorial task will involve: 'the need for an agreed and publicly accountable director assessment and registration process' and 'an agreed and policeable code of conduct to determine the ethical relationships between directors, shareholders and stakeholders'.[44] This will, in turn, feed in to the corporate policy and strategy, internal supervision of management and external accounting rules.

---

41 *Ibid*, p 7.

42 *Ibid*, Chapter 5: Deakin, S, Lane, C and Wilkinson, F, 'Contract Law, Trust Relations and Incentives for Co-operation: A Comparative Study.'

43 Nobel, P, 'Social Responsibility of Corporations' (1999) 84 Cornell Law Review 1255.

44 Garratt, B, *The Fish Rots from the Head*, 1997, p 207.

Other bodies such as the Stock Exchange and the Financial Service Authority are concerned with corporate governance, while public company directors and their advisers have to deal with several different systems, the most significant demands being the requirements for the application for and maintenance of their listings. There is at present little co-ordination of the different regimes that affect such companies. For example, the Companies Act 1985 as regards takeovers allows compulsory purchase of the remaining shares once the offer has been accepted by 90% of the 'target' shareholders. At the same time, the City Code on Takeovers on Mergers provides (Rule 9) that once a holding has reached 30%, a bid for the remaining shares is mandatory (save in exceptional circumstances). Some progress had been made in the European Union towards harmonisation of takeovers with a view to facilitating the growth of major enterprises across markets which on their own would not be large enough to sustain corporations that could compete with those of North America and Asia. The Mandatory Bid Rule has not yet been introduced in continental Europe, where long-standing shareholding arrangements are common, though the draft European Union Takeovers Directive proposed such a change along the lines of the UK City Code.[45]

Here again one sees evidence of the UK being torn between its European Union obligations and the gradually increasing influence of European Law, on the one hand, and on the other, a continuing attraction to the ideas of common law jurisdictions that have already modernised their company law. Both traditions in fact would suggest shorter, clearer codes with somewhat less attempt than in past Companies Acts to set out all the details in the primary legislation. Nevertheless a coherent and modern philosophy would entail the recognition that the financial system is operated to serve the investment needs of the business community, which in turn is in place to meet the demands for goods and services from the wider community. The United States of America, with its federal competition in corporate law and Japan, with its cross-shareholdings and employee power, have different priorities. Both also present problems of their own.[46] Worthwhile ideas that can be fitted in to the existing corporate governance system are to be welcomed whatever their provenance.

Comments from the Company Law Review Steering Group's Final Report, though warm towards other particpants generally, are not favourable to ousting shareholders from the position of superiority. However, the question of how duties to other stakeholders might be enforced, quite rightly a major concern, has not been addressed in the way this book has sought to do. The final recommendations emanating from the DTI will, of course, need to go

---

45 Draft 13th Company Law Directive, first proposal COM/1995/655 (7.2.1996), last amended COM/1997/565 (10.11.1997).

46 Cunningham, LA, 'Commonalities and Prescriptions in the Vertical Dimension of Global Corporate Governance' (1999) 84 Cornell Law Review 1133.

through a full political process in which the interests of employees and consumers may be accorded greater prominence. Internationally, too, the issue of 'taming' large corporations to work in the widest possible social interest is fast becoming a, perhaps the, crucial task for politicians.

9.5 EUROPEAN AND GLOBAL INFLUENCES

As the greater co-ordination of social and commercial law across the European Union gathers pace, one may expect political pressure for 'levelling up' of regulation to ensure high standards of consumer and environmental protection. The increased volume of intra-Single Market trade is necessitating greater co-operation on control of corporate mergers, which in turn is almost bound to influence corporate structures, as noted in Chapter 7 above. Continental Europe has traditionally been more ready than the English-speaking word to recognise the corporation as a distinct social entity. Further afield, even though it has usually been argued that deregulation is the norm across the Atlantic, measures such as the increased minimum wage and action against pollution have shown a different trend in the 1990s. In the Pacific region, there is still somewhat greater reluctance to accept legal measures that would set limits to competitive practices. However, this has been in the context of traditional cultures which set clear rules of conduct and if those break down under the increasing pressure of globalisation, there may be greater acceptance of a need for new legislation in future.

Given the trend towards greater decentralisation of large organisations, including multinational companies, the challenge of compliance with national law in their various countries of operation should not prove to be insurmountable. Agreements as to basic minimum standards between the major countries will help to prevent 'capital flight' from more regulated economies. Where laws are found to conduce to good economic performance, they can become a source of competitive advantage. The use of new technology and efficient administration so that government departments and agencies match the performance standards that international business sets for itself is important. Taxation rates are also more significant than core company law in the major location decisions of multinational companies. The European Union will need to decide how far it is prepared to allow competition on tax between Member States, but for the time being the UK government is prepared to undercut its continental neighbours in this respect.

It is submitted that trade is not in practice as 'globalised' as some commentators have suggested and that it remains feasible to set and enforce standards at the national level.[47] In primary production and simple

---

47   Hirst, P and Thompson, G, *Globalization in Question*, 1999.

manufactures, there is little doubt that environmental and labour standards need to be agreed internationally and this is slowly being achieved. An increasing part of the economy, however, consists of service activities and more technologically advanced manufacturers that are not, in fact, internationally mobile to any significant extent. The UK government thus has considerable 'regulatory space' within which to govern the activities of corporate business registered in Britain. Capital is the most internationally mobile factor of production and major investors have an incentive to choose jurisdictions with high regulatory standards. If social protections are to be maintained for unskilled workers in the face of new global competitive pressures, Europe will need to act collectively and to foster innovation and quality in production.

Deakin, Lane and Wilkinson conducted a comparative study on contracts, co-operation and competition in Britain, Germany and Italy respectively and sought to identify the key features of national systems. They found distinct differences in that: '[N]early all of the German firms replied that they normally used continuous contracts (agreement to take a particular quantity of supplies over an indefinite duration or, more usually, for a fixed period of one year or more), compared to around a quarter of the British firms, and less than a fifth of the German firms.' Framework contracts (for delivery on demand) were normal in over half of the Italian firms, around a quarter of the British firms and less than a fifth of the German firms. *Ad hoc* repeat contracts were used by none of the German firms but the remainder (approximately half) of British and Italian firms.[48] The researchers acknowledge that there is a trade-off between flexibility and responsiveness to changing economic circumstances, on the one hand, and stability and predictability of institutions and relationships, on the other. Each legal system and business culture finds a different way of managing this particular balancing act.

As far as the role of business people in society is concerned, entrepreneurs in the USA, from Ford and Rockerfeller to Gates and Dell, may be considered ruthless about the pursuit of their objectives, but once they have achieved their commercial aims, they have often give away a large proportion of their wealth in philanthropy.[49] By contrast, in general European business is subject to higher costs and more stringent regulation but contributes less of its profits to charitable and social activity. In the UK, politically, there is a perceived need for greater investment in many public services, yet a reluctance to will the means to pay for them by general taxation. There is every sign that

---

48 Deakin, S, Lane, C and Wilkinson, F, in Deakin and Michie, n 39 above, p 119.

49 Cf British publications such as *Directory of Social Change, A Guide to Company Giving* (published annually) and Hollis, *Sponsorship and Donations Yearbook* (annual), which show a more restrictive approach with many UK companies stating that they will only give to projects 'local' to their area of operation or do not consider unsolicited appeals.

business will continue to be engaged by government to help meet economic and social aims. Very recently, great controversy has surrounded the decision of BMW to sell its Rover cars production facility at Longbridge.[50] That of Barclays Bank to close rural branches at the same time as proposing large bonuses for some directors has also caused considerable public debate and disquiet.[51]

Shareholder activism and the role of non-executive directors have in some high-profile cases crossed the Atlantic to Britain, with investors challenging, for example, bonuses and payoffs to executives.[52] Works Councils and manufacturer's liability have come to the UK mainly through European Union directives. At a global level, the OECD Principles of Corporate Governance represent an inter-governmental effort to map out a set of criteria to deal with the issues that arise from the separation of ownership and control. These include a principle that directors should consider stakeholder issues as well as provision for the protection of shareholder interests.[53] The model has been greatly influenced by the Anglo-American style of corporation (Dignam even refers to the OECD as 'a free market think tank').[54] It will be of great interest to see how the Principles are applied in other cultures unaccustomed to negotiated regulation (which Dignam said was 'becoming increasingly discredited' in the UK[55] especially as they are 'non-binding and do not aim at detailed prescriptions' but 'can be used by policy makers as they examine and develop their legal and regulatory frameworks for corporate governance that reflect their own economic, legal social and cultural circumstances'.[56]

As Chapter 7 demonstrated, there is much that UK legislators could learn from the legal systems of continental Europe, as well as the former commonwealth and the global economic giants, the USA and Japan. 'Deregulation' is not the only message to be heard from their successes.

---

50 FT.com site, 'BMW Sells Rover for GBP 10' (10 May 2000) and 'BMW Directors Under Fire' (16 May 2000).

51 FT.com site, 'Barclays Postpones ATM Decision' (23 April 2000) and 'Barclays Says Sorry for Closures' (27 April 2000).

52 Following a barrage of questioning at its AGM in July 2000, British Airways agreed to review the payoff, worth £2,000,000, given to its former Chief Executive Bob Ayling (Odell, M, 'Shareholders disrupt BA Annual Meeting over Ayling Pay-off', *Financial Times*, 12th July 2000, front page). Vodafone faced shareholder pressure for pledges that a £10,000,000 payment to Chris Gent following the takeover of Mannesmann (Odell, M, 'Vodafone to Bow to Pressure over Bonuses', 12 July 2000, business section front page).

53 OECD, *Principles of Corporate Governance* (OECD, 1998, at www.oecd.org) Principle V and *passim*.

54 Dignam, A, 'Exporting Corporate Governance: UK Regulatory Systems in a Global Economy' (2000) 21 Co Law 70, 74.

55 *Ibid*, 76.

56 OECD, n 53 above, Preamble.

Systems that foster workplace partnership and customer focus appear, on the evidence of the past two generations, literally to pay dividends. While there are certainly arguments about adapting specific methodologies to national cultures, with the increasing speed of change and cultural globalisation, those arguments are perhaps not as strong as they were, enabling ideas which have been seen to succeed to be transplanted across national boundaries. All states hope to attract major corporations and thus lucrative jobs and tax revenues. Governments in the major industrialised nations can only hope to put mechanisms in place in their own corporate regulation so that such developments in business benefit all stakeholders and the wider community.

Tackling unemployment also remains a European Union priority. As *The Economist* magazine has noted, France has responded to the pressures of 'Anglo-American' deregulation while reducing working hours and largely maintaining benefits for individuals.

> In recent years, the government has relaxed regulations on part-time work, fixed-term contracts and temporary work agencies... Contrary to widespread fears, the 35-hour week does not seem to have destroyed jobs: if anything, it seems to have increased flexibility in working hours.[57]

German confidence in a shareholder-driven economy, meanwhile, has taken something of a battering from collapses in the prices of 'new technology' shares recently (in late 2000 and early 2001). This may lead to a change in approach, according to *The Economist*:

> Investors are planning to leave money in for several years, rather than hoping to make a killing in a few months. Most have also twigged that they will sleep more soundly by putting their money in a diversified fund.[58]

There is international pressure to make company accounts and reports more transparent and comparable across boundaries. Use of the internet and the falling costs of communication should mean a greater volume of cross-border investment in future. Indeed many of the European Union's directives in relation to companies deal with accounting and auditing rules. Companies listing on several stock markets have sometimes found that their stock was valued quite differently in different jurisdictions. This is not sustainable in the long run given the level of product and labour competition across boundaries. More relevant and reliable figures and facts are needed from public companies in order to permit fair comparisons by investors, employees, customers and suppliers.

---

57 *The Economist*, 'France 1 Germany 0', 17 March 2001, p 108.
58 *The Economist*, 'Germans take to Shares', 10 March 2001, p 110.

9.6 DIRECTORS' DUTIES

The public company officers who were interviewed for this study (as set out in Chapter 8) could be divided into two groups – those who saw themselves as agents of shareholders and those who perceived their responsibilities as being to the company as an institution. The former are arguably closer to 19th century notions of directorial responsibility than to current judicial and managerial understandings of the role of the board. As institutional investors assert their power, for example, in determining the outcome of hostile takeover bids, it is unsurprising that directors feel under pressure in a commercial sense to prioritise shareholder concerns. The picture is, however, more complex than that. There is no large surplus pool of labour in the UK or the US in 2001, a fact that clearly increases the bargaining power of workers.[59] At the same time, consumers remain price-conscious and in Britain buyers are increasingly aware of goods being sold more cheaply in continental Europe and North America.[60]

Leadbeater offers business leaders six reasons: 'Why it pays to be good (eventually)'. He lists, first, the need to attract 'bright, young, intelligent, mobile staff' who are concerned about the company's reputation; secondly, that trust is 'vital to the exploitation of knowledge'; thirdly, that 'large, regulated companies in quasi-public markets, risk the loss of their licence to operate if people think they are acting to operate'; fourthly, companies 'find themselves facing angry, affluent consumers in their domestic markets, unhappy with their labour practices'; fifthly, as economic value shifts to intangible assets, 'corporate brands that can be trusted will become ever more important' and finally, 'social engagement can help to spur innovation within a company'.[61] All corporate boards will have to deal with these issues. Failure to do so would indeed be a factor impacting on corporate performance. This is particularly the case for retail companies, which rely on their brand images. With internet companies attracting major investment, despite most having made no profit as yet, the power of ideas and brand recognition is also strong in the new economy.

Among non-executive directors, there is a similar dichotomy between those who take the view that they should keep returns to shareholders 'honest' and those who see the non-executives as potentially providing a wider perspective for the board's discussions. Even among public companies, there is a range of sizes, and while some are adopting a *de facto* two-tier board by the use of executive committees and non-executive monitoring, smaller

---

59 See Hutton, W, *The Ethics of Good Business* (Report of a Young Fabian Conference held on 17 July 1999) p 18.

60 See Hughes, B, *ibid*, p 15.

61 Leadbeater, C, 'Why it Pays to be Good (Eventually)', *New Statesman*, 6 March 2000, 26.

public companies express concern that they have difficulty in finding directors who are willing to serve in a non-executive capacity. The benchmarks under the Combined Code that the board should contain at least one-third non-executive directors and that non-executive audit and compensation committees be established appear to be effective in terms of structure. Increasingly detailed reporting of directors' remuneration and recommendations that executive service contracts be granted for only one year have had rather less practical effect.

If directors are given broader responsibilities to stakeholders, they can obtain their information as to stakeholder views in a number of creative ways. Partnerships with trade unions are being entered into by increasing numbers of large organisations, even ahead of the introduction of statutory trade union recognition rights in the UK. Consumers are being encouraged to assert their rights and preferences as they do in the US. Many of the largest public companies have dedicated 'public affairs' teams whose task it is to deal with opinion formers and pressure groups and to discuss their concerns, using such methods as surveys and 'focus groups'.

One of the UK's largest investing institutions with investments exceeding 4% of the UK stock market, the Prudential Assurance Company, announced in 1999 that it was 'mainstreaming' the environmental and ethical assessment of businesses throughout its portfolio by instructing the respected analysts EIRIS to review all companies in which it invests. The Prudential's ethical investment policy states: 'We expect those companies in which we invest to be able to demonstrate and report on appropriate environmental and social policies.'[62] If this form of proactive investment management is taken up widely (beyond the ethical funds *per se*), it will have a large impact on the London stock market as a whole. All UK pension funds are now obliged to publish their policies as far as ethical investment criteria are concerned (though not to pursue a particular ethical agenda) and on exercising their shareholder rights (including voting).[63] Eventually this could help to bridge the gap between the interests and demands of shareholders and the responsibility of business to serve the wider community and enhance the environment.

There is already a large volume of legislation constraining directors, for example in the environmental and employment areas. This strives with difficulty to keep up with the latest business standards. It is often not effectively enforced in practice (it will be interesting to see what the impact of the new Environment Agency and increasing trade union membership will

---

62 Available at www.prudential.co.uk.

63 Occupational Pension Schemes Amendment Regulations 1999 (SI 1999 No 1849) reg 2(4), adding new reg 11A to Occupational Pension Schemes (Investment) Regulations 1996.

be). Bringing together the requirements at the decision making stage would be less costly than trying to remedy the situation later.

The suggestion that on first becoming company directors, individuals should be required to sign a form which contains a statement of their duties or at least acknowledges that they have read such a statement would undoubtedly be helpful. At the public company level, however, a more sophisticated regime of training and analysis is required. Klein[64] observes that, while there is a positive linkage between executive input in finance committees and corporate performance, overall non-executive input into business strategy is essential. This presumably underlies the idea, now encapsulated in the Listing Rules, that a public company whose shares are to be quoted should have sufficient depth and breadth of expertise on its main board to meet the demands of investors and analysts. Other stakeholders need to be informed and included.

The principal actors in setting corporate agendas are inevitably the board members, though other senior employees often have important responsibilities. While there is a single dominant individual, the organisation can come to be identified with him or her. This is a situation that presents increasing risks of abuse as the corporation grows. There needs to be sense of collective responsibility between all board members. Legal responsibilities to all key stakeholders and the prospect in the last resort of legal action by stakeholders would enable directors to put demands by shareholders in an appropriate context. Non-executives can play a key role in contributing to assessment of all of the relevant factors.

9.7 STAKEHOLDER REMEDIES

The notion that stakeholders other than shareholders should have the right to impugn board decisions is understandably one that provokes concern, and indeed outright resistance, among some public company officers. Since current legal remedies for shareholders are not easily accessible (s 459, the main statutory provision, has been interpreted in a manner unhelpful to shareholders in public companies,[65] while institutional and other investors with small holdings have effectively been discouraged from taking derivative actions on behalf of large companies against the wishes of the general meeting[66]) and incentives for shareholders to monitor board performance are

---

64 Klein, A, 'Firm Performance and Board Committee Structure' (1998) 41 Journal of Law and Economics 275.

65 *Re Blue Arrow plc* [1987] BCLC 383; *Re Astec (BSR) plc* [1998] 2 BCLC 556.

66 *Prudential Assurance Co Ltd v Newman Industries Ltd* [1982] Ch 204; *Smith v Croft (No 2)* [1988] Ch 114.

still relatively weak, more and broader accountability is, nevertheless, surely to be welcomed. It is something of a truism that shareholders in UK public companies have little prospect of making any impact on executive decisions. Some powerful financial institutions are changing this situation, but are somewhat hampered by the lack of any effective sanction except the sale of their shareholdings. In the light of great uncertainty about whether takeovers really deliver value for the premiums paid to the shareholders of bidding companies, this is surely regrettable.

If it is accepted that employee loyalty, customer relationships and public trust will be crucial to business success in future and are underpinned by moral convictions,[67] then introducing legal mechanisms that will ensure greater concentration upon those matters is doing no more than spreading best practice. Some commentators have objected that without a single overriding objective, directors will be unable to make effective decisions or will be freed from any genuine accountability.[68] To this, the response must be that the long-term benefit of the company as an institution provides an intelligible and clear guideline for managerial conduct. Provision of the products or services, rather than short term profits, is the motivation for lasting success. Innovation is vital in the information technology and communications sectors, and also in manufacturing and retail.

It is too early to say with confidence that the decision of *O'Neill v Phillips* in the House of Lords will be restrictive on shareholders. Judges have experience in difficult cases such as *Re Welfab Engineering* of balancing social interests in companies. A clearer and broader definition of stakeholder remedies would provide a more open and firmer basis for such balancing acts. Without this, the takeover market will continue to be the only effective control on UK directors.

There are strong arguments to the effect that a requirement to report on a wider range of issues than the immediately financial would be beneficial to business as well as to its stakeholders and would be entirely practicable. Any astute investor seeking long-term rewards will be concerned to assess the quality of a company's relationships with its key stakeholders and its broader social and environmental policies as well as its financial structure.[69] Economic development has advanced at a great pace in Western Europe and North America, at the expense of the environment and of social cohesion. Some balance is now being restored as the governments of major industrialised

---

67 Gibson, K, 'The Moral Basis of Stakeholder Theory' (2000) 26 Journal of Business Ethics 245.

68 Sternberg, E, *Just Business*, 2nd edn 2000, is a well-known example. See also Wood, J, 'Undermining the Case for Capitalism' in Treasure, J, *Business Responsibilities*, 1997, p 101 (and reply given by Michael Ivens – n 86 below).

69 Ball, R, 'Making Accounting More International: Why, How and How Far Will It Go?' in Rutterford, J, *Financial Strategy: Adding Stakeholder Value*, 1998.

countries acknowledge that collective and individual action is necessary as a safeguard against environmental degradation and abuses of human rights. Basic indicators of performance and impacts are required both in business and in government.

Organisations of and for shareholders, such as PIRC, the National Association of Pension Funds and the Association of British Insurers, are putting in place their own codes and standards on corporate governance matters which build on, and in some cases go beyond, the demands of the Model Code. By recommending voting on resolutions at company Annual General Meetings, they are forcing public company directors to explain and justify measures that do not accord with best practice. They are greatly exercised by matters such as directors' remuneration and performance. In addition, many such 'active shareholders' also have explicit concerns with environmental and human rights issues. In practice, these bodies take the attention of company directors and sometimes claim publicity in the print and broadcast media.

Stakeholders in other jurisdictions are at present much more accustomed to the idea of asserting their legal rights through access to law. Consumers in the United States are an obvious example, as are environmental pressure groups in Scandinavia. The culture that there is little or nothing that can be done to prevent the financial dominance of a few corporations harming the interests of these stakeholders is largely a British one. If the benefits of doing business in Britain are perceived to be sufficiently great, inward investment need not be affected. This will require significant public investment to ensure that human resources and basic infrastructure reach the required standards, to upkeep of which profitable businesses, in turn, should contribute through taxation.

The perspective of trade unions and consumer groups in Britain has been much less co-operative with management than is the case in continental Europe. This is unsurprising when the primary objective of the public company system has traditionally been to secure rewards for shareholders, an orientation that has led to disaffection among both workers and consumers.[70] A culture of secrecy and impenetrable corporate plans has added to the general impression that directors and senior managers are 'not to be trusted'. This does nothing to facilitate new accommodations with stakeholders when market demands change or technological developments demand speedy responses. Takeovers in the British system of liquid capital markets have arguably reduced consumer choice and affected the earning capacities of many workers.

---

70 Bauman, Z, *Work, Consumerism and the New Poor*, 1998, Chapter 2; Franks, S, *Having None of It: Women, Men, and the Future of Work*, 1999, Chapter 3.

As high-technology industries grow in size and importance, increasing flexibility to pursue fresh ideas without the impediments of slow bureaucracy or control from a conservative, out-of-touch group at the apex of the organisation are at a premium in world markets. In many respects the UK system looks likely to serve this new commercial world well. Unitary boards, distinct divisions of liability between companies within groups and relative shareholder aquiescence (at least as long as the rate of return meets their demands) are all conducive to 'strong leadership' and adaptability. On the other hand, a workforce that lacks the education new industries demand and infrastructure that will not enable it to operate to its full capacity are potentially limiting factors. As public–private partnerships and Private Finance Initiative contracts require the private sector to take the risks of delivering public infrastructure, from hospitals to rail, on time and of maintaining them, the concept of public provision is being transformed. Such activities are secure business opportunities but may not yield the rates of return that UK institutional investors have come to expect.

9.8 ENTITLEMENT AND EMPOWERMENT IN COMPANY LAW

There is a trade-off between flexibility and inclusiveness in corporate governance systems. Macey points out that all arrangements must to some extent be a compromise between extreme positions:

> Taken literally, no corporation could sustain either the abstract goal of shareholder wealth maximisation or the broad stakeholder model. Sustained application of the generalized shareholder-primacy norm is unachievable given management's control, power and relationship to other constituents. Similarly, the fact that shareholders supply the capital necessary to fuel the corporate engine precludes the sustained application of the generalized stakeholder model.[71]

Public companies in reality have considerable scope to distribute the profits from their activities in many different ways. Who benefits most from corporate profitability depends to a considerable extent on the legal system under which the company operates.

The discussion so far has made clear that companies in practice have to deal with new challenges as technology progresses. One is the changing nature of work in a post-modern, post-industrial society. Another is globalisation, or at least the internationalisation of many product markets. The effect of these phenomena on corporate legal structures will be considered

---

71 Macey, JR, 'Convergence in Corporate Governance' (1999) 84 Cornell Law Review 1166, 1171.

below. As O'Neill says: 'companies operating solely within one jurisdiction with limited international business do not appear to be about to be subjected to further radical change by way of European corporate directive'.[72] Many companies are essentially domestic and national laws need to work within and with particular national cultures.

Commercial dependence on knowledge workers is continually increasing. Co-determination by way of the German corporate structure has, however, produced supervisory boards that tend to be unwieldy, meet infrequently and receive less information than smaller unitary boards. The belief that employee representatives could misuse information may have led to the weakening of the supervisory board.[73] Employee ownership is growing in Anglo-American corporations as another means of enhancing employee identification with the corporation. If it means that workers are investing their savings as well as their labour without gaining overall control, it may not ultimately be beneficial to them. Respect for and consideration of the time investment of employees need to be balanced with the rights of other constituencies.

While some employment lawyers have focused on company law as a vehicle for enhanced labour rights, there has been less structural analysis of companies concerning customers and suppliers. Nevertheless a producer focus is *prima facie* no more efficient commercially than short-term financial focus. All parties in long-term relationships can suffer when takeovers or sales of businesses occur. Sharing of business risks among stakeholders is reasonable and equitable. Information and consultation are the keys to developing sound relationships that facilitate this flexibility. Litigation should be reserved for use as a weapon of last resort, seldom needed if channels of communication are sound.

Cross-border mergers and strategic alliances are changing the shape of business in many sectors. An important, unresolved, debate is whether one corporate governance system will become dominant or whether different methods of monitoring can co-exist as being equally effective ways of dealing with the same issues. In alliances of companies: 'it is difficult to know where the boundary of one firm ends and another begins.'[74] This may mean changes to the law on groups of companies in the UK, for example. As difficulties with the Daimler–Chrysler merger showed, bringing together different cultures in terms of ownership and remuneration can be problematic. Moves to unify

---

72 O'Neill, M, 'When European Integration meets Corporate Harmonisation' (2000) 21 Co Law 173, 178.

73 Gordon, J, 'Pathways to Corporate Governance? Two Steps on the Road to Shareholder Capitalism in Germany' (1999) 5 Columbia Journal of European Law 219, 232.

74 Bradley, M, Schipani, CA, Sundaram, AK and Walsh, JP, 'The Purpose and Accountability of the Corporation in Contemporary Society' (1999) 62 Law and Contemporary Problems 9, 31.

European Stock Exchanges are in train but are also likely to bring problems of cultural difference.[75]

Each corporate governance system needs to be understood as an integrated whole. Kohl points out that: 'The principal monitoring mechanisms [over management] are market competition (in capital and product markets), takeovers, a good board of directors and/or a concentrated shareholder.'[76] At least two of these mechanisms need to be strong in a given system to ensure that the vast majority of companies do have effective monitoring, though different jurisdictions may have different balances between the various methods. Bratton and McCahery state following a review of literature and performance that: 'Germany and Japan held out no institutional practices suited to fill America's monitoring gap.'[77] Executive compensation and short term planning horizons show that the Anglo-American system has its own faults. The law is, however, commonly interpreted to give directors more discretion than the 'shareholder primacy' rhetoric would suggest.

Accenture, formerly Anderson Consulting, in its report *The Connected Corporation* (published 2001) identifies new imperatives for corporate success in a networked (and networking) world. None of them are about short-term gains to shareholders by exploitation of other stakeholders. On the contrary, Accenture's ideas demand attention to all the key stakeholders. They are as follows:

(1) Take a new approach to strategy development involving a wide range of participants;

(2) Establish a common purpose and values that transcend change to win and retain both customers and employees;

(3) Focus on distinctive capabilities and assets;

(4) Unleash the energy and talent of the workforce;

(5) Benefit from corporate social responsibility engaging in partnerships that enhance the brand.[78]

This brings one back to consideration of the fundamental questions posed by Chapters 2 and 3. What is the true nature of the corporation? It is inconsistent (as economic liberals tend to do) both to say that the corporation is simply a nexus of contracts and to say that the shareholders 'own' it. It is better to

---

75 London Stock Exchange Press Release, 'London Stock Exchange and Deutsche Borse to Merge to Create iX. Agreement with Nasdaq to Create a High Growth Market', 3 May 2000; J Mackintosh, 'UK Regulator Stands Firm on Exchange Merger', *Financial Times*, 20 July 2000.

76 Kohl, H, 'Path Dependence and German Corporate Law' (1999) 5 Columbia Journal of European Law 189, 209.

77 Bratton, WW and McCahery, JA, 'Comparative Corporate Governance and the Theory of the Firm: The Case against Global Cross Reference' (1999) 38 Columbia Journal of Transnational Law 213, 265.

78 Accenture, *The Connected Corporation*, 2001, pp 13–21.

recognise the identity of the corporation. What is the proper task of the board? They must be in charge of co-ordinating all the inputs and taking care of corporate reputation. A system that delivers anything less will not produce the conditions for lasting business success.

Focus on the corporation as an institution is a starting point for broadening of directorial focus, but it does need 'teeth' in the form of legal remedies. Sarra asserts:

> Although the recasting of the purpose of the company to a goal of enterprise wealth maximisation is the first step in taking account of the stakeholders such as workers, it may be inadequate as a singular strategy ... Any extension of fiduciary duty must be accompanied by enforcement mechanisms ... Just as the courts have enforced the reasonable expectations of shareholders in determining the scope of the fiduciary obligation, judicial guidance regarding the obligation to workers could be based on the same notions of reasonable expectations.[79]

This part of Sarra's argument accords with the views advanced in Chapters 5 and 6. Re-formulated directors' duties and judicial enforcement of stakeholder rights are both necessary for further progress.

9.9 CONCLUSION

Prime Minister Tony Blair has stated:

> Just as joined-up thinking is now vital to the way we must do government, so it is with business. That means focusing on all aspects of business – on flexibility and family-friendly employment policies, on learning and qualifications, on products and markets, on partnership and working together, on environmental standards and customer satisfaction, on bottom-line finances and long-term thinking, on responsibility and prosperity.[80]

The DTI, as a government department, is presumably expected to share in advancing this vision when formulating the new Companies Act. The main difficulties are that competition is still often not open and fair and that prosperity is unevenly distributed. If UK company law is to be truly 'modern', all stakeholders will need to have rights and responsibilities under it.

Even if it were desirable, it is impractical when drafting company law to be prescriptive as to the results to be attained by businesses or the distribution of profits. That public company status should be matched by greater accountability seems a difficult proposition to refute in principle. The current

---

79   Sarra, J, 'Corporate Governance Reform: Recognition of Workers' Equitable Investments in the Firm' (1999) 32 Canadian Business Law Journal 384.

80   In a foreword to the Report of the Committee of Inquiry, *A New Vision for Business* (1999).

Draft Statutory Statement of Directors' Duties promulgated by the Company Law Review Steering Group speaks of a duty to: 'promote the success of the company *for the benefit of its members as a whole*'[81] (emphasis added), which does not adequately recognise the social role of corporations. Reference is also made, importantly, to both: 'the company's need to foster its business relationships, including those with its employees and suppliers and the customers for its products and services' and: 'the impact of its operations on the communities affected and on the environment', but without introducing remedies for the parties mentioned.

In the field of reporting requirements, there is some readiness on the part of the DTI to impose appropriate requirements specifically on public companies.[82] There seems no good reason why broader duties in this respect should not be imposed on the directors of such companies. With ever more communication available via the internet and email anywhere in the world, the information demands of customers, investors and employees are likely to intensify even further.[83] Public company directors have become accustomed to the fact that their remuneration is published[84] and they are subject to restrictions on the extent to which they can deal in their shareholdings.[85] They also have to face Annual General Meetings and handle public announcements of major developments in corporate life. Greater openness is part of the answer to corporate misfeasance, but not the whole of it since prevention is better than remedy.

Structural changes to the public company board have also been discussed in detail above. The point that representation of stakeholders would be alien to British industrial relations culture has some salience at present. Progress such as European Works Councils and trade union partnerships may gradually change this, but that may take a generation. Non-executive directors are generally seen to have performed a useful function, but the way is not yet clear for them to become a majority on public company boards in the UK as they are in the USA. The place of executives who both know their particular industry and are committed to the work of their company is assured. If executives and non-executives are to collaborate successfully, they need to share a vision of what their company is trying to achieve over the long term.

---

81 See n 8 above.

82 See n 3 above.

83 The controversy surrounding the Government's Regulation of Investigatory Powers Act 2000 demonstrate that it has not yet fully worked out a legal response to the issues raised by e-commerce.

84 In the company's Annual Report as the Listing Rules require.

85 Most listed public companies follow the Model Code on Sharedealing in their own constitutions.

Turning to enforcement of the new 'inclusive' duties, courts have already been called upon to deal with interpretation of wording such as 'unfair prejudice' and 'just and equitable' considerations. In so doing, they have paid due attention to the circumstances of each case including the expectations of the various parties. There is no reason to believe that they would not be equipped to deal with the requirement that public company boards should give due consideration to stakeholders. Courts have also shown a willingness to adapt their judgments of company directors' duties to changing business expectations and would be able to do so if deciding petitions within a new framework of stakeholder rights. Distinctions between the levels of different stakeholders and their representation (direct or indirect) which make for a complex commercial 'balancing act' on public company boards. Renewed corporate governance arrangements leading to long-term profitability and social cohesion would have benefits within and beyond the commercial sphere.

Most public companies have accepted their business and social responsibilities, even if it was: 'as Moliere's Monsieur Jourdan spoke prose without being aware of doing so.'[86] A new Companies Act can give greater force and clarity to the whole debate about the proper role of business. Koslowski writes in his examination of the ethics of capitalism:

> Against the critique of interest groups of the allocation and distribution effects of a capitalist economy, one must recall one of the oldest views of justice in the European tradition, the idea of balance and measure. The theory of market failure as well as that of governmental failure indicates that a balance must be found between society and state, between markets and votes.[87]

This book has attempted to reach just such a balance.

---

86 Ivens, M, 'The Case for Business Responsibilities' in Treasure, n 68 above, 107, 111 (responding to John Wood – n 68 above).

87 Koslowski, PF, 'The Ethics of Capitalism' in Harvey B, *Business Ethics: A European Approach*, 1994, p 236, at p 245.

APPENDIX 1

LETTER SENT TO PUBLIC COMPANY DIRECTORS AND SECRETARIES

[Brunel University]

Dear

I am conducting doctoral research in the Department of Law at Brunel University and examining company law and more specifically directors' duties and stakeholding. I am writing to ask if you would be willing to assist in this work by giving your own views on key topics in this field.

In the light of Cadbury, Greenbury, Hampel and most recently the Company Law Green Paper, you will be aware of the ongoing debate as to whether directors should owe duties to shareholders alone, or also to employees and customers, or to wider constituencies (for example, the community, the environment) as well. In order to discuss current and possible future law on the subject, it is vitally important to gather the opinions of experienced public company directors themselves as to how they see their role and how they might respond to any new legislation. I would be very grateful if you could spare a little of your time at your convenience to meet me to discuss some of these matters and so make the thesis representative and practically grounded.

If you are willing to participate, I would like to assure you of several important points:

1   All views expressed will be treated in the strictest confidence and used only for the purposes of this research. Individual responses (for example, interview records) will be seen only by myself and my supervising tutor at Brunel and not by anyone else.

2   No individual director will be identified in or identifiable from the thesis. Responses will be used as a basis for general discussion of the opinions of plc directors overall.

3   The research project is entirely independent academic work, designed to provide a greater understanding of public company directors' perspectives and the implications for the law; it is funded by a studentship of the Department of Law at Brunel.

In order to gain a true picture of the views of public company directors on these important matters, I will need the help of many people as possible. This will involve a discussion lasting up to one hour and covering the issues mentioned above with ample opportunity for you to express your opinions.

If you would be willing in principle to help in this work, the location and time for interviews will of course be at your convenience. Perhaps you would confirm by post or email if you would be willing to spare up to an hour for me to visit and I will contact you to arrange an appointment.

Thank you for your attention to this letter. I look forward to hearing from you in due course.

Yours sincerely

Janice L Dean

Janice L Dean
MA (Oxon), LLM (Manchester), Solicitor

APPENDIX 2

COMPANY DIRECTORS AND SECRETARIES: QUESTIONS ASKED OF PUBLIC COMPANY OFFICERS

Ai Executive Directors

1 What is your role in the company/on the board?

(for example, departmental responsibility, technical expertise)

2 How does the task of a director differ from general management work?

How much time is spent on board responsibilities as such in a typical month?

(Do your feel that the board enables and encourages you to take a long-termist view of planning?)

3 Have you ever experienced conflict between your responsibilities as a director and the demands of your executive position?

(How can the independence and objectivity of all Board members be preserved?)

Aii Non-executive directors

1 What is your role on the board/in other companies?

(for example, committee membership, executive positions)

2 What can a part-time 'outsider' director contribute to a board?

How much time is spent on board responsibilities in a typical month?

(Do you feel that the board enables and encourages you to provide critical scrutiny?)

3 By what means do you obtain your information on the operation of the company and on the performance of executives?

(How can the independence and objectivity of all board members be preserved?)

B Board decisions

1 In making decisions as a director, whose interests do you regularly consider? (Possible responses listed below)

Shareholders and investors

Employees and managers

Customers

Suppliers

Local communities

Other groups

2   At what stage in the decision making process are these relevant interests examined?

How (for example, presentations at/reports to board meetings, consultation exercises)?

Why (for example, long-term gain from good public relations, on principle)?

3   Does one particular group take precedence over all others when decisions are made?

If so, why is this?

4   What is the 'ranking order' of the various relevant groups in decision making?

Why is this?

5   How is conflict between the interests of the relevant groups usually resolved?

Do you see it as part of the role of directors to balance these interests?

6   Do public companies have additional roles in society (for example, environmental protection, supporting charity?)

In practice how are these responsibilities kept under review and balanced against accountability to the relevant interest groups?

C   Changes to the law

1   Would you favour a change in the law on directors' duties to include other 'stakeholding' groups?

Why or why not?

2   If yes, which groups would you wish to see included?

Should these groups have the right to take legal action if their interests are not considered?

3   What practical differences might such a change make to you and to your board

– if the legal statement of directors' duties were to change

– if the included groups had a legal right of action?

4   If there were to be a change in the law, might your board need to alter its decision making process to be more inclusive of the relevant groups, which might include employees and customers, the community and environment?

If so, how might its decision making change?

D   Board structure

1   Should interest groups other than shareholders be directly represented on the board? Why or why not?

If so, which groups (for example, employees, community, major customers or suppliers) should be represented?

2   Should executive managers and non-executive monitors be separated in the board structure? Why or why not?

If so, how should members of the supervisory level be selected?

BIBLIOGRAPHY

BOOKS

Alkhafaji, AF, *A Stakeholder Approach to Corporate Governance* (New York, Quorum Books, 1989)

Archibald, GC, *The Theory of the Firm* (Harmondsworth: Penguin, 1971)

Ayres, I and Braithwaite, J, *Responsive Regulation* (Oxford: OUP, 1992)

Barber, B, *Jihad versus McWorld* (New York: Ballantine, 1997)

Bauman, Z, *Work, Consumerism and the New Poor* (Buckingham: Open University Press, 1998)

Bauman, Z, *Globalization: The Human Consequences* (Cambridge: Polity, 1998)

Beatson, J and Freeman, D, *Good Faith and Fault in Contract Law* (Oxford: Clarendon, 1995)

Beesley, ME, *Privatisation, Regulation and Deregulation*, (London: Routledge, 2nd edn 1997)

Belanger, J, Edwards, P and Haiven, L, *Workplace Industrial Relations and the Global Challenge* (New York: ILR, 1994)

Berle, AA and Means, GC, *The Modern Corporation and Private Property* (New York: Macmillan, 1932, rev edn 1968; London: Transaction, new edn 1997)

Bidault, F, Gomez, P-Y and Marion, G, *Trust: Firm and Society* (Basingstoke: Macmillan, 1997)

Bieber, R, Dehousse, R, Pinder, J and Weiler, JHH, *One European Market* (Baden-Baden: Nomos, 1992)

Bishop, M, Kay, J and Mayer, C, *The Regulatory Challenge* (Oxford: OUP, 1995)

Blair, M, *Ownership and Control: Rethinking Corporate Governance for the Twenty-First Century* (Washington, DC: Brookings Institution, 1995)

Blair, M, *Wealth Creation and Wealth Sharing: A Colloquium on Corporate Governance and Investment in Human Capital* (Washington, DC: Brookings Institution, 1996)

Blair, T, *New Britain* (London: Fourth Estate, 1996)

Blair, T, *The Third Way* (London: Fabian Society, 1998)

Boisot, M, *East-West Business Collaboration* (London: Routledge, 1994)

Bowen, WG, *Inside the Boardroom: Governance by Directors and Trustees* (Chichester: John Wiley, 1994)

Braes, D, *Corporate governance: company responses to Cadbury and a review of the issue* (Master's thesis, Kingston University, 1996)

Brown, AD, *Organisational Culture* (London: Pitman, 1995)

Buchanan, D and Huczynski, A, *Organizational Behaviour*, 3rd edn (Hemel Hempstead: Prentice Hall, 1997)

Buckley, V and Michie, J, *Firms, Organisations and Contracts* (Oxford: OUP, 1996)

Bulow, J and Klemperer, P, *Rational Frenzies and Crashes* (London: CEPR, 1991)

Cadbury, Adrian (Sir), *The Company Chairman* (Hemel Hempstead: Director, 2nd edn 1995)

Campbell, J, *Media, Mania and the Markets* (London: Fleet Street, 1994)

Cannon, T, *Corporate Responsibility* (London: Pitman, 1994)

Carnall, C and Maxwell, S, *Management: Principles and Policy* (Cambridge: ICSA, 1988)

Carroll, AB, *Business and Society – Ethics and Stakeholder Management* (Cincinnati: South-Western, 2nd edn 1993)

Cassis, Y, Crouzet, F and Gourvish, T, *Management and Business in Britain and France* (Oxford: Clarendon, 1995)

Casson, M, *Enterprise and Competitiveness: A Systems View of International Business* (Oxford: Clarendon, 1990)

Casson, M, *The Economics of Business Culture* (Oxford: Clarendon, 1991)

Castro, B, *Business and Society* (Oxford: OUP, 1996)

Charkham, J, *Corporate Governance and the Market for Companies: Aspects of the Shareholder's Role* (London: Bank of England, 1989)

Charkham, J, *Keeping Good Company: A Study of Corporate Governance in Five Countries* (Oxford: OUP, 1994)

Cheffins, BR, *Company Law: Theory, Structure and Operation* (Oxford: Clarendon, 1997)

Chew, D, *Studies in International Corporate Finance and Governance Systems* (Oxford: OUP, 1997)

Clifton, R and Maughan, E, *The Future of Brands* (Basingstoke: Macmillan, 2000)

Collins, JC and Porras, JI, *Built to Last* (London: Century Business, 1994)

Corbridge, M and Pilbeam, S, *Employment Resourcing* (London: Financial Times Management, 1998)

Cosh, A, *Takeovers and Short-Termism in the UK* (London: IPPR, 1990)

Cotterrell, R, *The Sociology of Law: An Introduction* (London: Butterworths, 1984)

Coulson, A, *Trust and Contracts* (London: Polity, 1998)

Coulson-Thomas, C, *Creating Excellence in the Boardroom* (Maidenhead: McGraw-Hill, 1993)

Coulson-Thomas, C, *The Future of the Organisation* (London: Kogan Page, 1997)

Cyert, J and March, J, *A Behavioral Theory of the Firm* (Oxford: Blackwell, 1992)

Davies, PL, *Gower's Principles of Modern Company Law* (London: Sweet & Maxwell, 6th edn 1997)

Dawkins, R, *The Selfish Gene* (Oxford: OUP, rev edn 1989)

Davies, PWF, *Current Issues in Business Ethics* (London: Routledge, 1997)

Deakin, S and Michie, J, *Contracts, Co-operation and Competition* (Oxford: OUP, 1997)

Denison, DR, *Corporate Culture and Organisational Effectiveness* (Chichester: John Wiley, 1990)

Directory of Social Change, *A Guide to Company Giving* (London: Directory of Social Change, published annually)

Dowling, GR, *Corporate Reputation: Strategies for Developing the Corporate Brand* (London: Kogan Page, 1994)

Drucker, PF, *Management: Tasks, Responsibilities, Practices* (London: William Heinemann, 1974)

Drury, RR and Xuereb, PG *European Company Laws* (Aldershot: Dartmouth, 1991)

Dworkin, R, *A Matter of Principle* (Cambridge, Mass: Harvard UP, 1985)

Easterbrook, F and Fischel, D, *The Economic Structure of Corporate Law* (Cambridge, Mass: Harvard UP, 1991)

Farrar, J and Hannigan, B, *Farrar's Company Law* (London: Butterworth, 4th edn 1998)

Ferran, E, *Company Law and Corporate Finance* (Oxford: OUP, 1999)

Fincham, R and Rhodes, PS, *The Individual, Work and Organisation*, (London: Weidenfeld & Nicolson, 2nd edn 1992)

Fogarty, M and Christie, I, *Companies and Communities: Promoting Business Involvement in the Community* (London: PSI, 1990)

Franks, S, *Having None of It: Women, Men, and the Future of Work* (London: Granta, 1999)

Frederick, W, Post, J and Davis, K, *Business and Society*, (Singapore: McGraw-Hill, 7th edn 1992)

Freeman, RE, *Strategic Management: A Stakeholder Approach* (London: Pitman, 1984)

Fruin, WM, *The Japanese Enterprise System* (Oxford: Clarendon, 1992)

Fukuyama, F, *The End of History and the Last Man* (London: Hamish Hamilton, 1992)

Fukuyama, F, *The Great Disruption: Human Nature and the Reconstitution of Social Order* (London: Profile, 1999)

Fukuyama, F, *Trust: The Social Virtues and the Creation of Prosperity* (London: Hamish Hamilton, 1995

Gabor, A, *The Capitalist Philosophers* (Chichester: John Wiley, 2000)

Galbraith, JK, *The Good Society* (London: Sinclair Stevenson, 1996)

Garratt, B, *The Fish Rots from the Head* (London: HarperCollins, 1997)

Gates, J, *The Ownership Solution* (Harmondsworth: Penguin, 1998)

Giddens, A, *The Third Way and its Critics* (Cambridge: Polity, 2000)

Goyder, G, *The Just Enterprise* (London: Free Press, 1993)

Goyder, M, *Living Tomorrow's Company* (Aldershot: Gower, 1998)

Gray, J, *False Dawn* (London: Granta, 1998)

Grier, N, *UK Company Law* (Chichester: John Wiley, 1998)

Griffiths, A, *Corporate Governance and the Uses of the Company* (Manchester: University of Manchester Faculty of Law Working Paper No 18, 1993)

Hambro Company Guide (London: Hemmington Scott, quarterly)

Handy, C, *Beyond Certainty* (London: Arrow, 1996)

Handy, C, *The Hungry Spirit* (London: Random House, 1997)

Harlow, C and Rawlings, R, *Law and Administration* (London: Butterworth, 1997)

Harris, D, *Remedies in Contract and Tort* (London: Weidenfeld & Nicolson, 1988)

Harvey, B, *Business Ethics: A European Approach* (Hemel Hempstead: Prentice Hall, 1994)

Herman, ES, *Corporate Control, Corporate Power* (Cambridge: CUP, 1981)

Hertz, N, *The Silent Takeover: Global Capitalism and the Death of Democracy* (London: Heinemann, 2001)

Hill, P, *Towards a New Philosophy of Management: The Corporate Development Programme of Shell UK Ltd,* (London: Gower, 2nd edn 1976)

Hirst, P and Thompson, G, *Globalization in Question* (Oxford: OUP, 1999)

Hollis Sponsorship and Donations Yearbook (Teddington: Hollis, annual)

Hutton, W and Giddens, A, *On the Edge: Living with Global Capitalism* (London: Jonathan Cape, 2000)

Hutton, W, *The Stakeholding Society* (London: Polity, 1999)

Hutton, W, *The State to Come* (London: Vintage, 1997)

Hutton, W, *The State We're In* (London: Jonathan Cape, 1995)

Institute of Directors, *Guidelines for Directors,* (London: Director, 6th edn 1995)

Jacobs, J, *Systems of Survival: A Dialogue on the Moral Foundations of Commerce and Politics* (London: Hodder & Stoughton, 1993)

Kay, J, *Foundations of Corporate Success* (Oxford: OUP, 1993)

Keasey, K, Thompson, S and Wright, MJ, *Corporate Governance: Economic and Financial Issues* (Oxford: OUP, 1997)

Keasey, K and Wright, MJ, *Corporate Governance: Responsibilities, Risks and Remuneration* (Chichester: John Wiley, 1997)

Kelly, G, Kelly, D and Gamble,A, *Stakeholder Capitalism* (Basingstoke: Macmillan, 1997)

Kitson, A and Campbell, R, *The Ethical Organisation: Ethical Theory and Corporate Behaviour* (Basingstoke: Macmillan, 1996)

Klein, N, *No Logo: Taking Aim at the Brand Bullies* (London: Flamingo, 2000)

Kompass Company Information Register (East Grinstead: Reed Business Information, annual)

Kotter, JP and Heskett, JL, *Corporate Culture and Performance* (New York: Free Press, 1992)

Kuhn, JW and Shriver, DW (Jr), *Beyond Success: Corporations and Their Critics in the 1990s* (Oxford: OUP, 1991)

Levine, D, *Working in the Twenty-First Century* (New York: ME Sharpe, 1998)

Lorange, P and Roos, J, *Strategic Alliances* (Oxford: Blackwell, 1992)

Maclagan, P, *Management and Morality* (London: Sage, 1998)

Maitland-Walker, J, *Guide to European Company Laws* (London: Sweet & Maxwell, 1993)

Marquand, D and Seldon, A, *The Ideas that Shaped Post-War Britain* (London: Fontana, 1996)

Mayer, C, *Corporate Governance, Competition and Performance*, Economics Department Working Paper No 164 (Paris: OECD)

McGregor, D, *The Human Side of Enterprise* (New York: McGraw-Hill, 1960)

Michie, J and Grieve Smith, J, *Globalization, Growth and Governance* (Oxford: OUP, 1998)

Mills, Sir Geoffrey, *Controlling Companies* (London: Unwin Hyman, 1988)

Minford, P, *Markets Not Stakes* (London: Orion Business, 1998)

Mitchell, NJ, *The Generous Corporation: A Political Analysis of Economic Power* (New Haven: Yale UP, 1989)

Monks, RAG and Minow, N, *Corporate Governance* (Oxford: Blackwell, 1995)

Monks, RAG and Minow, N, *Watching the Watchers: Corporate Governance for the Twenty-First Century* (Oxford: Blackwell, 1996)

Mueller, RK, *Anchoring Points for Corporate Directors: Obeying the Unenforceable* (London: Quorum, 1996)

Nader, R, *No Access to Law: Alternatives to the American Judicial System* (New York: Academic Press, 1980)

Nasi, J, *Understanding Stakeholder Thinking* (Helsinki: LSR, 1995)

Nelken, D, *Comparing Legal Cultures* (Aldershot: Dartmouth, 1997)

Oakland, JS, *Total Quality Management: Text with Cases* (Oxford: Butterworth-Heinemann, 1995)

Ogus, AI, Regulation (Oxford: Clarendon, 1994)

Parker, H, *Letters to a New Chairman* (London: Director, 1979)

Parkinson, JE, *Corporate Power and Responsibility* (Oxford: Clarendon, 1993)

Parkinson, JE, Kelly, G and Gamble, A, *The Political Economy of the Company* (Oxford: Hart, 2000)

Macmillan Patfield, F, *Perspectives on Company Law 1* (Deventer, Netherlands: Kluwer, 1995)

Macmillan Patfield, F, *Perspectives on Company Law 2* (London: Kluwer, 1997)

Paxman, J, *Friends in High Places* (London: Michael Joseph, 1990)

Peters, TJ and Waterman, RH, *In Search of Excellence* (London: Harper and Row, 1982)

Phelps, N, *Multinationals and European Integration* (London: Jessica Kingsley, 1997)

Picciotto, S, *International Business Taxation* (London: Weidenfeld & Nicholson, 1992)

Plender, J, *The Stakeholding Solution* (London: Nicholas Brealey, 1997)

Porter, M, Takeuchi, H and Skokibara, M *et al, Can Japan Compete?* (New York: Macmillan, 2000)

Prentice, DD and Holland, PRJ, *Contemporary Issues in Corporate Governance* (Oxford: Clarendon, 1993)

Puckey, Walter (Sir), *The Board Room* (London: Hutchinson, 1969)

Randlesome, C, *Business Cultures in Europe* (Oxford: Heinemann, 1990)

Robertson, Sir Lewis, *Corporate Governance*, Hume Papers on Public Policy, Vol 3, No 4 (Edinburgh: Edinburgh UP, 1995)

Rock, S and Kennedy, C, *Power, Performance and Ethics* (London: Butterworth-Heinemann, 1992)

Romano, R, *Foundations of Corporate Law* (Oxford: OUP, 1993)

Rutterford, J, *Financial Strategy: Adding Stakeholder Value* (Chichester: John Wiley, 1998)

Salanie, B, *The Economics of Contracts* (Cambridge, Mass: MIT, 1997)

Samuel, G, *Sourcebook on Obligations and Legal Remedies* (London: Cavendish Publishing, 1995)

Schwartz, DE, *Commentaries on Corporate Structure and Governance: the ALI-ABA Symposiums 1977–78* (Philadelphia: ALI-ABA, 1979)

Schwartz, HS, *Narcissistic Process and Corporate Decay* (New York: New York UP, 1990)

Seybold, P, *Customers.com* (London: Century, 1998)

Sheikh, S and Rees, W *Corporate Governance and Corporate Control* (London: Cavendish Publishing, 1995)

Sheikh, S, *Corporate Social Responsibilities: Law and Practice* (London: Cavendish Publishing, 1996)

Sifonis, JG and Goldberg, B, *Corporation on a Tightrope* (Oxford: OUP, 1996)

Slapper, G and Tombs, S, *Corporate Crime* (London: Pearson, 1999)

Smith, A, *The Wealth of Nations* (1776; Everyman's Library edn, 1910)

Smith, NC, *Morality and the Market* (London: Routledge, 1990)

Smyth, JC, Dorward, C and Reback, J, *Corporate Reputation: Managing the New Strategic Asset* (London: Century Business, 1992)

Solomon, RC, *Ethics and Excellence: Cooperation and Integrity in Business* (Oxford: OUP, 1993)

Stapledon, GP, *Institutional Shareholders and Corporate Governance* (Oxford: Clarendon, 1996)

Sternberg, E, *Just Business* (London: Warner, 1994)

Stewart, R, *Managing Today and Tomorrow* (Basingstoke: Macmillan, paperback edn, 1994)

Stone, CD, *Where the Law Ends: The Social Control of Corporate Behaviour* (New York: Harper & Row, 1975)

Streeck, W, *Social Institutions and Economic Performance* (London: Sage, 1992)

Sutton, B, *The Legitimate Corporation* (Oxford: Blackwell, 1993)

Treasure, J, *Business Responsibilities*, Issues Paper No 2 (London: Foundation for Business Responsibilities, 1997)

Tricker, RI, *Corporate Governance: Practices, Procedures and Powers in British Companies and Their Boards of Directors* (Aldershot: Gower, 1984)

Twining, W, *Legal Theory and Common Law* (Oxford: Blackwell, 1986)

Varallo, GA and Dreisbach, DA, *Fundamentals of Corporate Governance* (Chicago: American Bar Association, 1996)

Veljanovski, C, *The Economics of Law*, Hobart Papers 114 (London: IEA, 1990)

Wade, Sir William and Forsyth, CF, *Administrative Law* (Oxford: Clarendon, 7th edn, 1994)

Ward, R, *Twenty-First Century Corporate Board* (New York: John Wiley, 1997)

Warner, M, *International Encyclopedia of Business and Management* (London: Routledge, 1996)

Wheeler, D and Sillanpaa, M, *The Stakeholder Corporation: A Blueprint for Maximising Stakeholder Value* (London: Pitman, 1997)

White, TI, *Business Ethics: A Philosophical Reader* (Englewood Cliffs: Prentice Hall, 1993)

Zander, M, *The Law-Making Process*, (London: Butterworths, 4th edn, 1994)

Zingales, L, *Corporate Governance* (London: Centre for Economic Policy Research, 1998)

ARTICLES

Addison, JT, Siebert, WS, Wagner, J and Wei, X, 'Worker Participation and Firm Performance' (2000) 38 British Journal of Industrial Relations 7

Albert, M and Gonenc, R, 'The Future of Rheinish Capitalism' (1996) 67 Political Quarterly 184

Allen, WT, 'Contracts and Communities in Corporation Law' (1993) 50 Washington and Lee Law Review 1395

Andenas, M, 'European Company Law Reform and the United Kingdom' (2000) 21 Co Law 36

Barnard, J, 'Hampel: A Transatlantic Critique' (1998) 19 Co Law 110

Bayley, S, 'Hallelujah! Praise the Brand' (2000) 169 Blueprint 40

Belcher, A, 'Codes of Conduct and Accountability for NHS Boards' [1995] Public Law 288

Benoit, B, Dombey, D, O'Connor, A and Targett, S, 'EMI set for Clash on Virgin's Future', *Financial Times*, 1 May 2001

Black, BS and Coffee, JC, 'Hail Britannia? Institutional Investor Behavior Under Limited Regulation' (1994) 92 Michigan Law Review 1997

Blair, M, 'For Whom Should Corporations Be Run: An Economic Rationale for Stakeholder Management' (1998) 31 Long Range Planning 195

Bowe, C, Heckel, M, Peel, M and Shrimsley, R, 'Motorola Faces the Sacks 3100 Workers', *Financial Times*, 25 April 2001

Bradley, M, Schipani, CA, Sundaram, AK and Walsh, JP, 'The Purpose and Accountability of the Corporation in Contemporary Society' (1999) 62 Law and Contemporary Problems 9

Bratton WW and McCahery, JA, 'Comparative Corporate Governance and the Theory of the Firm: The Case Against Global Cross Reference' (1999) 38 Columbia Journal of Transnational Law 213

Brooks, R, 'Why Loyal Employees and Customers Improve the Bottom Line' (2000) 23 Journal for Quality and Participation 40

Brown, K, 'Byers to Calm Fears on Company Law Review', *Financial Times*, 7 June 2000, p 2

Brudney, V, 'Corporate Governance, Agency Costs and the Rhetoric of Contract' (1985) 85 Columbia Law Review 1403

Buckby, S, 'Ethical Codes of Practice Not Being Implemented', *Financial Times*, 1 December 1998, p 10

Bushrod, L, 'Private Equity – Continental Buyouts Surge as Small UK Deals Face Squeeze', European Venture Capital Journal, 1 May 2000, 1

Business Europe Editorial, 'Germany's Tax Reform', *Business Europe*, 30 June 1999, p 6

Business Week Editorial, 'Shareholders Are Grabbing the Reins in Europe', *Business Week*, 29 November 1999, p 30

Cadbury, Adrian (Sir), 'What are the Trends in Corporate Governance? How Will They Impact Your Business?' (1999) 32 Long Range Planning 12

Chandler, G, 'Annual General Meeting of X plc, May 2005: The Chairman's Speech – A Vision' (1998) 1 Visions of Ethical Business 18

Charny, D, 'Competition Among Jurisdictions in Formulating Corporate Law Rules' (1991) 32 Harvard International Law Journal 423

Clarke, J, 'Shareholders and Corporate Community Involvement in Britain' (1997) 6 Business Ethics: A European Review 201

Clarke, T, 'The Stakeholder Corporation: A Business Philosophy for the Information Age' (1998) 31 Long Range Planning 182

Clarkson, MBE, 'A Stakeholder Framework for Analysing and Evaluating Corporate Social Performance' (1995) 20 Academy of Management Review 92

Coase, RH, 'The Nature of the Firm' (1937) 4 Economica 386

Coffee, JC, 'Shareholders versus Managers: The Strain in the Corporate Web' (1986) 85 Michigan Law Review 1

Company Lawyer editiorial, 'Only Mad Cows and Englishmen' (1997) 18 Co Law 65

Cook, J and Deakin, S, 'Regulation and the Boundaries of the Law', research paper at www.dti.gov.uk

Cook, J and Deakin, S, 'Stakeholding and Corporate Governance: Theory and Evidence on Economic Performance', research paper at www.dti.gov.uk

Copp S, and Goddard, R, 'Corporate Governance Principles on Trial' (1998) 19 Co Law 277

Corporate Finance supplement, 'Germany Meets the Challenge', *Corporate Finance*, May 2000

Cunningham, LA, 'Commonalities and Prescriptions in the Vertical Dimension of Global Corporate Governance' (1999) 84 Cornell Law Review 1133

Currie, D, 'Does EMU Need Political Union?' (June 1998) Prospect 60

Dahrendorf, R, 'On the Dahrendorf Report' (text of a speech delivered to the House of Lords on 21 February 1996) (1996) 67 Political Quarterly 195

David, P, 'Britain: A Power in the World', *The Economist*, 6 November 1999, S15

Davis, JH, Schoorman, FD and Donaldson, L, 'Towards a Stewardship Theory of Management' (1997) 22 Academy of Management Review 47

Deakin, S, Lane, C and Wilkinson, F, '"Trust" or Law? Towards an Integrated Theory of Contractual Relations Between Firms' (1994) 21 Journal of Law and Society 329

Dignam, A, 'Exporting Corporate Governance: UK Regulatory Systems in a Global Economy' (2000) 21 Co Law 70

Dombey, D and Voyle, S 'Marks and Spencer Claims Clearance on Belgian Jobs', *Financial Times*, 25 April 2001

Donaldson, T and Preston, LE, 'The Stakeholder Theory of the Firm: Concepts, Evidence and Implications' (1995) 20 Academy of Management Review 65

Doward, J and Islam, F, 'Household Names Face Axe as Unilever Slims Down', *The Guardian*, 26 September 1999

Dowling, A, 'Revolt Over Reuters Chief's Pay Deal', *Financial Times*, 25 April 2001

du Plessis, JJ and Dine, J, 'The Fate of the Draft Fifth Directive on Company Law' [1997] JBL 45–46

Drucker, P, 'Knowledge Work' (2000) 17 Executive Excellence 11

Drury, R, 'A Review of the European Community's Company Law Harmonisation Programme' (1992) 24 Bracton Law Journal 45

Eaglesham, J, 'Directors Face Prospect of Greater Duty of Care', *Financial Times*, 31 March 2000, p 8

Easterbrook FH and Fischel, DR, 'The Corporate Contract' (1989) 89 Columbia Law Review 1416

The Economist, 'Business: Germany Unlocked' *The Economist*, 8 January 2000, p 62

The Economist, 'The Global Gambles of General Motors' and 'Car Making in Asia – Politics of Scale' *The Economist*, 24 June 2000

Eisenberg, MA, 'Symposium on Corporate Governance: An Overview' (1992) 48 The Business Lawyer 1271

Eisenberg, MA, 'The Structure of Corporation Law' (1989) 89 Columbia Law Review 1461

Elkington, J and Fennell, S, 'Can Business Leaders Satisfy the Triple Bottom Line?' (1998) 1 Visions of Ethical Business 34

Emmett, A, Levine, S and Slepicka, M, 'Shareholders Strike Back', America's Network, June 2000, Telecom Investor supplement 14

Fabian, C, 'Answering Hard Questions in the Stakeholder Age', Marketing, 17 February 2000, p 24

Fama, EF and Jensen, MC, 'Separation of Ownership and Control' (1983) XXVI Journal of Law and Economics 312

Feldman, A, 'Shareholders of the World, Unite!' (2000) 29 Money 1333

Fieser, J, 'Do Businesses have Moral Obligations Beyond What the Law Requires?' (1996) 15 Journal of Business Ethics 457

Financial Times Editorial, 'All at Sea Over Disposal of Oil Rigs; Industry and Environmentalists Remain as Far Apart as ever Despite Solution for Brent Spar', *Financial Times*, 29 January 1998

Finch, J, 'Unilever Washes Hands of 1,200 Brands', *The Guardian*, 22 September 1999

Fischel, DR, 'The Corporate Governance Movement' (1985) 35 Vanderbilt Law Review 1259

Franks, J and Meyer, C, 'Governance as a Source of Managerial Discipline', report at www.dti.gov.uk

Garratt, B, 'Developing Effective Directors and Building Dynamic Boards' (1999) 32 Long Range Planning 28

Geddes, R, 'Ownership, Regulation and Managerial Monitoring in the Electric Utility Industry' (1997) 40 Journal of Law and Economics 261

Gibson, K, 'The Moral Basis of Stakeholder Theory' (2000) 26 Journal of Business Ethics 245

Giddens, A, 'After the Left's Paralysis', *New Statesman*, 1 May 1998, p 18

Glasbeek, H, 'The Corporate Social Responsibility Movement' (1988) 11 Dalhousie Law Journal 363

Gobert, J, 'Corporate Criminality: Four Models of Fault' (1994) 14 Legal Studies 393

Goddard, R, 'Closing the Categories of Unfair Prejudice' (1999) 20 Co Law 333

Goldenberg, P, 'Shareholders v Stakeholders: the Bogus Argument' (1998) 19 Co Law 34

Goodpaster, KE and Matthews, JB (Jr), 'Can a Corporation have a Conscience?' (1982) Harvard Business Review 132

Gordon, J, 'Pathways to Corporate Governance? Two Steps on the Road to Shareholder Capitalism in Germany' (1999) 5 Columbia Journal of European Law 219

Gow, D, 'Fuel Gauge: Shell Profits Back on Track', *The Guardian*, 11 February 2000

Graham, B and Hart, M, 'Cohesion and Diversity in the European Union: Irreconcilable Forces? (1999) 33 Regional Studies 259

Guehenno, J-M, 'The French Resistance' (June 1998) Prospect 31

Haag, G, 'Theories on the Economics of Regulation: A Survey of the Literature from a European Perspective' (1997) 4 European Journal of Law and Economics 337

Hain, P, 'Regulating for the Common Good' (1994) Utilities Law Review 88

Handy, C, 'Subsidiarity is the Word for It' (1999) 36 Across the Board 7

Harrington, LK, 'Ethics and Public Policy Analysis: Stakeholders' Interests and Regulatory Policy' (1996) 15 Journal of Business Ethics 375

Henley, J, 'Vive La Belle France', *The Observer*, 25 June 2000, p 19

Hill, CWL and Jones, TM, 'Stakeholder-Agency Theory' (1992) 29 Journal of Management Studies 131

Hosmer, LT, 'Trust: the Connecting Link Between Organizational Theory and Philosophial Ethics' (1995) 20 Academy of Management Review 379

The Independent Editorial, 'Greens Claim Victory as Shell Recycles Brent Spar', *The Independent*, 29 January 1998, Environment section

Jones, TM, 'Instrumental Stakeholder Theory: A Synthesis of Ethics and Economics' (1995) 20 Academy of Management Review 404

Kaltenheuser, S, 'The Best Place to Do Business' (2000) 13 World Trade 28

Kaplan, R and Norton, D, 'The Balanced Scorecard: Measures that Drive Performance' (1992) Harvard Business Review 280

Kaplan, R and Norton, D, 'Using the Balanced Scorecard as a Strategic Management System' (January 1996) Harvard Business Review 75

Karmel, RS, 'Implications of the Stakeholder Model' (1996) 61 George Washington Law Review 1156

Kay, J and Silberston, A, 'Corporate Governance' (1995) National Institute Economic Review 87

Klein, A, 'Firm Performance and Board Committee Structure' (1998) 41 Journal of Law and Economics 275

Kohl, H, 'Path Dependence and German Corporate Law' (1999) 5 Columbia Journal of European Law 189

LaBerge, M and Svendsen, A, 'New Growth: Fostering Collaborative Business Relationships' (2000) 23 Journal for Quality and Participation 48

Leadbeater, C, 'Why It Pays to Be Good (Eventually)', New Statesman, 6 March 2000, p 26

Legrand, P, 'Structuring EC Law: Tacit Knowledge Matters' (1998) 21 Hastings International and Comparative Law Review 871

Leonard, M, 'Why the Annual Report Might Just Restore Faith in Politics', New Statesman, 7 August 1998, p 18

Letza, S, Hardwick, P and Ashton, J, 'Who Disciplines Management in Poorly Performing Companies? An Updated Study', report at www.dti.gov.uk

Levine, R and Ahmed, S, 'The Legal Environment, Banks and Economic Growth' (1998) 30 Journal of Money, Credit and Banking 596

Lewis, X, 'A Common Law Fortress under Attack: is English Law being Europeanized?' (1995) 2 Columbia Journal of European Law 1

Logsdon, JM and Yuthas, K, 'Corporate Social Performance, Stakeholder Orientation, and Organizational Moral Development' (1997) 16 Journal of Business Ethics 1213

Loredo, E and Suarez, E, 'Corporate Governance in Europe: is Convergence Desirable?' (1998) 15 International Journal of Management 525

Luoma, P and Goodstein, J, 'Stakeholders and Corporate Boards: Institutional Influences on Board Composition' in (1999) 42 Academy of Management Journal 553

Macey, JR and Miller, GP, 'Corporate Stakeholders: A Contractual Perspective' (1993) 43 University of Toronto Law Journal 423

Macey, JR, 'Convergence in Corporate Governance' (1999) 84 Cornell Law Review 1166

MacIntosh, J, 'Designing an Efficient Fiduciary Law', 43 University of Toronto Law Journal 425

MacShane, D 'The Great Supermarket Rip-off', *New Statesman*, 4 September 1998, p 14

Maitland, A, 'Displaying the Ability to Make a Measurable Difference', *Financial Times*, 13 December 2000

Martinson, J, 'Half of Top Companies Fail to Comply with Hampel', *Financial Times*, 1 December 1998, p 10

Matheson, JH and Olson, B, 'Relationship Management and the Trialogical Imperative for Corporate Law' (1994) 78 Minnesota Law Review 1443

Maughan, CW and Copp, SF, 'Company Law Reform and Economic Methodology Revisited (2000) 21 Co Law 14

McCallin, J, 'The Engagement Ring: How Shareholders Are Starting to Put Pressure on Management', *The Guardian*, 6 May 2000, Money section

Millstein, IM, 'The Professional Board' (1995) 50 Business Lawyer 1427

Millstein, IM, 'The Responsible Board' (1997) 52 Business Lawyer 407

Ming-Hong Lai, G, 'Knowing Who You are Doing Business with in Japan: A Managerial View of Keiretsu and Keiretsu Business Groups' (1999) 34 Journal of World Business 423

Mitchell, LE, 'A Critical Look at Corporate Governance' (1992) 45 Vanderbilt Law Review 1313

Mitchell, LE, 'Groundwork of the Metaphysics of Corporate Law' (1993) 50 Washington & Lee Law Review 1479

Mitchell, LE, 'Private Law, Public Interest? The ALI Principles of Corporate Governance' (1992) 61 George Washington Law Review 871

Mitchell, RK, Agle BR, and Wood, DJ, 'Toward a Theory of Stakeholder Identification and Salience: Defining the Principle of Who and What Really Counts' (1997) 22 Academy of Management Review 853

Monaghan, P, 'Warts and All Reporting' (1999) 124 Accountancy 61

Moore, G, 'Corporate Community Involvement in the UK – Investment or Atonement?' (1995) 4 Business Ethics: A European Review 171

Moss Kanter, R, 'Are You Ready to Lead the E-Culture Revolution?' (2000) 22 Inc 43

New Statesman Special Supplement, The Bare Necessities (utilities regulation), *New Statesman*, 24 July 1998

Nicolle, L, 'UK.com Leads Europe' (2000) 125 Accountancy 70

Nobel, P, 'Social Responsibility of Corporations' (1999) 84 Cornell Law Review 1255

O'Connor, A, 'ON Digital's Give-away Suffers Poor Reception', *Financial Times*, 14 April 2001

Odell, M, 'Shareholders disrupt BA Annual Meeting over Ayling Pay-off', *Financial Times*, 12 July 2000, front page

Odell, M, 'Vodafone to Bow to Pressure over Bonuses', *Financial Times*, 12 July 2000, business section, front page

Ogus, A, 'Regulatory Appraisal: A Neglected Opportunity for Law and Economics' (1998) 6 European Journal of Law and Economics 53

Oliver, RW, 'Killer Keiretsu' (1999) 88 Management Review 10

O'Neill, M, 'When European Integration Meets Corporate Harmonisation' (2000) 21 Co Law 173

Papworth, J, 'Ethical Investment Keeping Pensions Free from Pollution: Moves to Bring in Socially Responsible Investment', *The Guardian*, 6 May 2000, Money section

Pettet, B, 'The Stirrings of Corporate Social Conscience' (1997) 50 Current Legal Problems 289

Preston, LE and Sapienza, HJ, 'Stakeholder Management and Corporate Performance' (1990) 19 Journal of Behavioral Economics 361

Reed, S and Matlack, C, 'The Big Grab', *Business Week*, 24 January 2000, p 130

Roddick, A, 'A Third Way for Business, too?', *New Statesman*, 3 April 1998, p 24

Roddick, A and Roddick, G, 'Shell Still Has Much to Do', *The Guardian*, 18 September 2000

Romano, 'R, The State Competition Debate in Corporate Law' (1987) 8 Cardozo Law Review 709

Rossant, J, 'En garde, French shareholders', *Business Week*, 8 May 2000, p 18

Rothnie, D, 'M&A Commentary: From One High to Another', European Venture Capital Journal, 1 February 2000, 1

Rowley, TJ, 'Moving Beyond Dyadic Ties: A Network Theory of Stakeholder Influences' (1997) 22 Academy of Management Review 887

Sappideen, R, 'Ownership of the Large Corporation: Why Clothe the Emperor?' (1996) 7 King's College Law Journal 53

Sarra, J, 'Corporate Governance Reform: Recognition of Workers' Equitable Investments in the Firm' (1999) 32 Canadian Business Law Journal 384

Scholes, E and Clutterbuck, D, 'Communication with Stakeholders; an Integrated Approach' (1998) 31 Long Range Planning 227

Schwab, C, 'What's Best for Your Customers? ' (2000) 17 Executive Excellence 20

Secretan, L, 'Customer Connections' (2000) 10 Industry Week 25

Skapinker, M, 'Diverse Qualities Vie for Attention', *Financial Times*, 13 December 2000

Stone, CD, 'Corporate Social Responsibility: What It Might Mean if It Were Really to Matter' (1986) 71 Iowa Law Review 557

Stratton, IC, 'Non-Executive Directors – Are They Superfluous?' (1996) 17 Co Law 162

Targett, S, 'Boards Get the Message on Bonus Culture', *Financial Times*, 21 April 2001

Taverne, D, 'Europe and the Tax Question' (July 2000) Prospect 54

Teubner, G, 'Enterprise Corporatism: New Industrial Policy and the "Essence" of the Legal Person' (1988) 36 American Journal of Comparative Law 130

Tylecote, A, Doo Cho, Y and Zhang, W, 'National Technological Styles Explained in Terms of Stakeholding Patterns, Enfranchisements and Cultural Differences: Britain and Japan' (1998) 10 Technology Analysis and Strategic Management 423

Useem, M, 'Shareholders as a Strategic Asset' (1996) 39 California Management Review 8

Utset, MA, 'Towards a Bargaining Theory of the Firm' (1995) 80 Cornell Law Review 540

Van der Weide, M, 'Against Fiduciary Duties to Corporate Stakeholders' (1996) 21 Delaware Journal of Corporate Law 27

Wallace, W and Zielonka, J, 'Misunderstanding Europe' (1998) 77 Foreign Affairs 65

Walters, A, 'Directors' Duties: The Impact of the Company Directors Disqualification Act 1986' (2000) 21 Co Law 110

Wheeler, D and Sillanpaa, M, 'Including the Stakeholders: the Business Case' (1998) 31 Long Range Planning 201

White, JB, 'How Should We Talk About Corporations? The Languages of Economics and of Citizenship' (1983) 94 Yale Law Journal 1416

Whysall, P, 'Stakeholder Mismanagement in Retailing: A British Perspective' (2000) 23 Journal of Business Ethics 19

Williamson, J, 'The Road to Stakeholding' (1996) 67 Political Quarterly 209

Williamson, OE, 'The Logic of Economic Organisation' (1988) 4 Journal of Law Economics and Organisation 65

Wolfe, A, 'The Modern Corporation: Private Agent or Public Actor?' (1993) 50 Washington and Lee Law Review 1673

Wong, A, 'Integrating Supplier Satisfaction with Customer Satisfaction' (2000) 11 Total Quality Management S427

Wright, MJ, 'Corporate Governance and Directors' Social Responsibilities: Responsible Inefficiency or Irresponsible Efficiency?' (1996) 17 Business Law Review 178

Zadek, S, 'Balancing Performance, Ethics and Accountability' (1998) 17 Journal of Business Ethics 1421

REPORTS

American Law Institute, *Principles of Corporate Governance: Analysis and Recommendations* (Philadelphia: ALI, 1992)

Audit Commission, *Taken on Board – Corporate Governance in the NHS: Developing the Role of Non-Executive Directors* (London: Audit Commission, 1995)

CBI, *Fraud: Risk and Practice* (London: CBI, 2000)

Channel 4 Commission on *Poverty in Britain, Report* (London: Channel 4 Publications, 1996)

Centre for Tomorrow's Company, *The Inclusive Approach and Business Success: The Research Evidence* (Aldershot: Gower, 1998)

Committee on Corporate Governance (Chair: Sir Ronald Hampel), *Final Report* (January 1998)

Commission on Public Policy and British Business, *Promoting Prosperity: A Business Agenda for Britain* (London: Vintage, 1997)

Committee on the Financial Aspects of Corporate Governance (Chair: Sir Adrian Cadbury), *Final Report* together with Code of Best Practice (December 1992)

Company Law Review Steering Group, *Modern Company Law for a Competitive Economy – The Strategic Framework* (London: DTI, February 1999)

Company Law Review Steering Group, *Modern Company Law for a Competitive Economy – Developing the Framework* (London: DTI, March 2000)

Company Law Review Steering Group, *Modern Company Law for a Competitive Economy – Completing the Structure* (London: DTI, November 2000)

Company Law Review Steering Group, *Modern Company Law for a Competitive Economy – Final Report* (London: DTI, July 2001)

DTI Consultation Paper, *Modern Company Law for a Competitive Economy* (London: DTI, March 1998)

DTI Consultation Paper, *A Fair Deal for Consumers: Modernising the Framework for Utilities Regulation* (London: DTI, March 1998)

Gilson, RJ and Kraakman, R, 'Reinventing the Outside Director: An Agenda for Institutional Investors', paper presented on 14–15 June 1990 at the Saloman Brothers Center and Rutgers Centers *Conference on the Fiduciary Responsibilities of Institutional Investors*

Institute of Directors, *The Government's Company Law Review Modern Company Law for a Competitive Economy – The IOD's Initial Response* (London: IOD, 1998)

Law Commission Consultation Paper, *Company Directors: Regulating Conflicts of Interests and Formulating a Statement of Duties* (Consultation Paper No 153, September 1998)

Law Commission Report, *Company Directors: Regulating Conflicts of Interests and Formulating a Statement of Duties* (Report No 261, September 1999)

Law Commission Report, *Fiduciary Duties and Regulatory Rules* (Report No 236, December 1995)

Law Society: Company Law Committee, *The Reform of Company Law* (Law Society Memorandum No 394, February 2000)

Maitland, R, *Employee Morale in the High Performance Organisation* (London: ISRL, 1994

OFTEL, *Annual Report 1996* (London: OFTEL, 1996)

Prodhan, B, *Corporate Governance and Long Term Performance* (Oxford: Templeton College Management Paper 13, 1993)

RSA Inquiry: *Tomorrow's Company* (London: RSA, 1995)

Study Group on *Directors' Remuneration* (Chair: Sir Richard Greenbury), Final Report together with Code of Best Practice (July 1995)

INDEX